68000 Assembly Language

Techniques for
Building Programs

68000 Assembly Language

Techniques for Building Programs

Donald Krantz
James Stanley

Addison-Wesley Publishing Company, Inc.

Reading, Massachusetts   Menlo Park, California
Don Mills, Ontario   Wokingham, England   Amsterdam   Bonn
Sydney   Singapore   Tokyo   Madrid   Bogotá   Santiago   San Juan

Appendices C and D reprinted with permission of Motorola, Inc.

Library of Congress Cataloging-in-Publication Data

Krantz, Donald.
  68000 Assembly Language.

  Includes index.
  1. Motorola 68000 (Microprocessor)—Programming.
2. Assembler language (Computer program language).
I. Stanley, James. II. Title. III. Title: Sixty-eight
thousand assembly language.
QA76.8.M6895K73   1986   005.265   86-17503
ISBN 0-201-11659-6

Cover design by Doliber Skeffington
Set in 10 pt Garamond by Ampersand Publisher Services, Inc., Rutland, VT

BCDEFGHIJ—AL—8987
Second Printing, April 1987

Table of Contents

Acknowledgments   *vi*
Introduction   *vii*

1   68000 Architecture   *1*
2   Addressing Modes   *9*
3   Data Transfer Instructions   *19*
4   Arithmetic Instructions   *35*
5   Logical, Shift, and Rotate Instructions   *65*
6   Jump, Branch, and Trap Instructions   *85*
7   Bit Instructions   *95*
8   Miscellaneous Instructions   *101*
9   The Nitty-Gritty Details   *105*
10   Parameter Passing Techniques   *119*
11   Exceptions   *127*
12   Text Editor Overview   *137*
13   Input/Output Interfaces   *149*
14   Data Management   *177*
15   The User Interface   *199*
16   The Hard Stuff That the Computer Usually Takes Care Of   *225*
17   Bit-Mapped Graphics   *241*
18   On the Bare Metal   *275*
19   The 68010 and 68020 Processors   *297*
20   The Last Step   *309*

Appendix A   The Rest of YASE   *317*
Appendix B   Math Routines   *355*
Appendix C   Instruction Format Summary (from Motorola)   *363*
Appendix D   MC68000 Instruction Execution Times (from Motorola)   *385*
Appendix E   ASCII Table   *395*

Index   *397*

Acknowledgements

The authors would like to express their thanks to the people and organizations who helped with this book.

Motorola Corporation provided background information about the development of the MC68000 microprocessor and gave us permission to reproduce the instruction formats and timing tables from *MC68000 8-/16-/32-Bit Microprocessors Programmer's Reference Manual,* Fourth Edition.

Dick Hallock and Hallock Systems Corporation provided an HSC PRO-68K board for our PC.

Hunter & Ready, Inc. let us work with their great realtime, multitasking operating system VRTX/68000, even though we could not in the end include a chapter on it in this book.

Tim Field and Tim Zappia critiqued the manuscript from a technical point of view.

Bill Kraetz unknowingly served as the prototype for the hardware engineers lampooned (he's not really like that at all).

Janice Byer copy-edited a complicated manuscript intelligently.

Steve Stansel, Si Goodwin, and Deb Warren at Addison-Wesley saw the project through with their usual expertise.

Introduction

In the middle to late 1970's, 8-bit microprocessors such as the Intel's 8080, Zilog's Z80, Motorola's 6800, and MOS Technology's 6502 began turning up in small computers that could do word processing, spreadsheets, and other useful things—the first true microcomputers. No sooner did this happen than everyone began talking about how nice it would be to have a 16-bit processor that would work like a minicomputer—the PDP-11, for example.

In 1978 Intel unveiled the 8086, the first 16-bit processor. The 8086 has four 8/16-bit general-purpose registers, and several more special-purpose registers. It can address 1 megabyte of memory, in 64K segments, limitations consistent with chip fabrication techniques of the time and also with a desire for compatibility with earlier Intel chips. The 8086 was an extension of the 8080 architecture. It certainly didn't look much like a minicomputer.

About a year later Motorola introduced a much more powerful 16-bit processor with true minicomputerlike architecture. It features eight general-purpose data registers and eight address pointer registers, all 32 bits long, and can directly address 16 megabytes of memory. Its nearly symmetrical (or orthogonal) instruction set uses relatively few op codes with multiple address modes and (for the most part) uniform function across all sixteen registers, memory, stack, and I/O.

A Clean Break with 8-Bit Design

Motorola called this new processor the 68000, making it sound like a more powerful version of the 8-bit 6800. The 68000 is much more than that. Unlike the 8086, with its concessions to earlier processors, the 68000 represents a clean break with the past. About the only concession it makes to 8-bit designs is a feature allowing it to address 8-bit 6800-series synchronous peripheral chips when necessary.

Numerous registers, capacity for linear addressing of large memory space, and auto increment/decrement instruction modes mean that, unlike the 8086, the 68000 is suitable in the same way the PDP-11 is for UNIX. It was certainly the most serious microprocessor that had appeared by the end of the 1970's.

The 1979 68000 ran at a clock speed of 4 MHz. By 1984, a version was available that ran at 12.5 MHz and executed a normal instruction mix at about one MIP (million instructions per second), a respectable speed indeed.

The 68000 has a number of technical features that add to its efficiency: for example, a prefetch queue speeds processing by making extremely efficient use of the bus (over 85 percent bus utilization). Another feature enables setting up ahead of time the two possible actions for a conditional branch.

From the point of view of design implementation, the 68000 was complicated enough so that it made sense to use microcoded rather than random or hybrid logic; for one thing, this has allowed greater flexibility in last-minute changes in the 68K and also in the development of more advanced 68000 family processors such as the 68010 and the 68020.

Finally, the 68000 has plenty of room for an upgrade into a true 32-bit microprocessor: the program counter is 32 bits long even though only 24 bits are brought out to pins; and the 68000's instructions are a subset of the instructions for the 32-bit processor Motorola introduced in 1985—the 68020.

Widely Adopted

The 68000 was adopted in many computer systems in the early 1980's: Fortune, Alpha-Micro, Altos, Sage (now the Stride), Apple Macintosh, Sun, Apollo, a number of Japanese machines such as Sord, and some AT&T desktops. When the Defense Department began looking for Ada compilers, some of the first were developed for 68000-based computers. Though Intel's 8086/8088 family of processors running MS- and PC-DOS captured the market for business microcomputers by riding on IBM's coattails, the 68000 has remained the professional programmer's choice for any sort of special application, particularly those involving bit-mapped graphics.

Many computer systems based on the 68000 are now offering upgraded versions featuring the 68020; the instruction set is almost the same. The 32-bit 68020 and the 16-bit 68010, both of which offer virtual memory management, will be covered in Chapter 19. Both of these processors use an instruction set that is compatible with, and in fact almost identical to, the 68000 instruction set laid out in this book.

The 68020 incorporates HCMOS fabrication and some fancy features such as an on-board instruction cache that lets it run at a solid 1.5 MIPS, about three times the speed of the original 68000. It has support chips providing virtual memory management and floating-point operations, and it has an interface so that it can be ganged with coprocessors; but, like the 68010, its design and instruction set are extensions rather than revisions of those on the classic 68000.

A Programmer's Processor

The 68000 family are programmer's processors. Writing large-scale assembly language programs for them is not a ridiculously difficult task. Moreover, excellent C compilers are available for all 68000-based machines, both for UNIX and for other operating systems such as CP/M-68K.

The symmetry of the instruction set make it a pleasure to use. Linear addressing makes segments an unpleasant memory. Plenty of data registers that all work the same makes constant shifting of values between accumulators and index registers unnecessary. The consistent and well-thought-out actions of the flag register make the foolish flag-related error almost nonexistent. Last, but by no means least, the powerful addressing modes make translation of pseudocode or high order language designs fast, easy, and reliable.

About This Book

This book is meant as a guide for programmers with some assembly language experience who want to move to systems using the 68000 and its more advanced relatives. Though the technical information presented here encompasses nearly everything found in Motorola's *16-Bit Microprocessor User's Manual*, we recommend that you buy that book, because the information in it is organized in a different way than it is presented here. For example, we group instructions by function groups, whereas Motorola presents them in the more traditional way— alphabetically. Anyway, it's a good idea to have the perspective of two points of view on a subject.

In the first two chapters of this book, we describe the architecture of the 68000, its instruction formats (generalized), and its fairly complex addressing modes. Chapters 3 through 8 describe the instruction set, instruction-by-instruction, but grouped into six classes:

- Data transfer
- Arithmetic
- Logical, shift, and rotate
- Jump, branch, and trap
- Bit manipulation
- Machine control

Short examples are given for each instruction.

Chapter 9 covers instruction bit formats for reference when writing assemblers, disassemblers, code generators, and the like. Chapter 10 treats parameter passing techniques used by assembly language programmers, including register and stack parameters passing. Chapter 11 deals with the 68K way of handling exceptions, including interrupts and system errors.

The technical features of the 68000 are presented in the first half of the book (through Chapter 11)—and these chapters, along with the appendices, will serve as a useful reference. The second half of the book is a tutorial showing how to build programs in 68K assembly language. Our philosophy is to present extensive examples—actual code from working programs. We concentrate on systems programming applications and assume that you've worked with assembly language before (you will notice that nowhere in this book can be found an explanation of how hexadecimal works), although not necessarily the 68K.

The main example program is a fairly long and fairly full-featured windowing screen editor called YASE (pronounced "Yeow-Sah"; for Yet Another Screen Editor), though at the time of writing there weren't all that many 68K editors floating around, and we ended up using this one in something of a bootstrap manner. YASE runs to 3500 lines.

Short examples are easy to write and are cohesive in that they can be counted on to do one thing well; but they tend not to do anything practical, and they never have to get down to dealing with special cases. We find that any reasonably complex piece of software ends up being mostly a handler of special cases. Long programs are just not put together like short ones, and long programs are usually the name of the game.

The main reasons we chose a screen editor for an example, though, is because its modules give a pretty good cross-section of design solutions and programming techniques. We get to take a look at I/O, a complicated user interface, data structures, memory management, tons of control structures, string operations—all kinds of good stuff.

Chapter 12 provides an overview of YASE. Appendix A gives a more formal "roadmap" of its structure and breakdown into modules.

Most of the individual sections of YASE are used in Chapters 13, 14, 15, and 16 in reference to I/O interfaces, data management, user interfaces (including windowing), and formatted output.

Chapter 17 deals with bit-mapped graphics, with a stand-alone example; Chapter 18 covers device interrupt servicing; Chapter 19 presents the additional instructions and other relevant features of the advanced 68K family processors—the 68010 and 68020; and Chapter 20 concludes the main text with some pointers on debugging and on some idiosyncrasies you'll run across on the 68K.

Appendices include the "roadmap" of YASE, the example modules that have not appeared in the main text, bit formats for the entire instruction set, timing charts, and, last and perhaps least, an ASCII table (it may be mundane, but we can never find one when we need one).

The code of the example programs is presented in two ways: short segments referenced in the text usually appear as inline code following the reference. They consist of assembly code and comments, with line numbers (the object code has been stripped for brevity). The line numbers refer to complete listings of the program modules involved. These can be found in a figure somewhere near the point of introduction. They are printed sideways across the page in 101 columns by 40 lines and include object code. The code is all tested output from an assembler, printed from the listing file on a daisy wheel printer, and photographed directly for the plates for this book. We hope this will eliminate any typesetting errors—but if errors do creep in, we'll blame the keyliner's Exacto knife. The first thing a successful systems programmer must learn is always to fix the blame on someone else.

68000 Assembly Language

Techniques for Building Programs

1

68000 Architecture

This chapter gives an overview of the programmer interface to the Motorola 68000 microprocessor hardware. We'll start by looking at the register set, the hardware-defined memory map, operating modes, and other details essential to programming. We won't look at any hardware details that aren't needed for the programmer interface.

Because the 68000 has a simple and consistent programming model, this chapter is fairly short. In fact, we don't present a lot of information not available in the manufacturer's manual until we actually start developing programs in the second half of the book. There just aren't all that many exceptions to rules and special cases to cover.

General Overview

The 68000 with its 16-bit data bus and 32-bit internal architecture is the first in a family of 16/32 bit processors from Motorola. The 68000 represents an order of magnitude increase in processing power over its predecessor, the 6800. Some of its hallmarks are its 16-megabyte linear addressing space (no segment registers!), simple, regular yet extremely powerful instruction set, wide variety of addressing modes, two state (user/supervisor mode) processing, and its support for high level language constructs. The 68000 also contains hardware and software support to enable multiple processors and devices to share resources.

The 68000 was designed to be easily programmed, rather than to be easy to implement in hardware. At the time it was designed, this was a radical break in design methodology. As you read through the rest of this chapter, note how the hardware design simplifies the programmer interface.

The Register Set

At any given time, the 68000 has eight data registers, eight address registers, a program counter and a status register. We say "any given time" because one address register is used for a hardware stack pointer and has a dual identity we'll explain later. All registers excepting the status register but including the program counter are 32 bits wide.

Data Registers

The data registers are referred to as D0 through D7. All eight of them operate identically. For example, any one of them can act as an accumulator. Most instructions affecting data registers allow you to specify byte (8-bit), word (16-bit), or longword (32-bit) operations. Two-digit BCD operations and bit operations are also supported for the data registers.

Operations on bytes and words within the 32-bit length of the data registers are self-contained. For example, if you rotate the lower 8 bits of a data register, only the lower 8 bits are affected. If an 8-bit add causes an overflow out of 8 bits, the carry flag is set, but only 8 bits of the data register are affected.

Generally, any operation, including a simple move, that can change the value of a data register affects the condition flags, although in certain cases where affecting the flags doesn't make sense, such as popping multiple registers off the stack, the flags aren't affected.

Byte operands occupy the least significant 8 bits of a data register, and word operands occupy the least significant 16 bits. Bits are numbered from 31 to 0, with the least significant bit being bit 0.

Address Registers

Eight address registers are labeled A0 through A7. They all operate identically, except for A7. A7 is used for the hardware stack pointer, and is therefore treated differently in some cases, as we will explain shortly.

Fewer operations are allowed for address registers than for data registers, and some operations act differently. Address registers are optimized for address-type operations. For example, storing a 16-bit value into an address register results in the value being sign-extended to 32 bits. Byte size (8-bit) operations are not allowed for address registers. But perhaps the most important distinction between the address registers and the data registers is that operations on the address registers almost never affect the status flags, meaning that we can fool with multiple-precision data operations using pointers without worrying about pointer manipulations affecting the condition flags.

The Stack

The 68000 uses the eighth address register (A7) as the hardware stack pointer. There are no instructions specifically intended for stack operations, like the PUSH and POP operations found in other processors' instruction sets, so any address register can be used for software stacks. Instructions that imply stack operations, such as subroutine calls, use the hardware stack. The 68000 stack grows from high memory towards low memory.

Objects are pushed and popped from the stack by using MOVE instructions and either the predecrement (for pushing) or postincrement (for popping) address register indirect addressing modes:

```
MOVE.L     D0,-(A7)      * A "push" operation
MOVE.L     (A7)+,D0      * A "pop" operation
```

(Note: 68000 assembler syntax always shows data moving from the left-hand operand as the source to the right-hand operand as the destination—this is exactly the opposite of Intel standard syntax.)

A7, unlike the other address registers, is adjusted when pushing or popping a byte value, in order to keep aligned on a word address. When implementing stacks with any of the other registers, care must be taken that byte values are pushed and popped in pairs to keep the stack aligned on an even boundary if you plan on pushing and popping word and longword values on the same stack (this is due to a requirement of the 68000 discussed later).

A7 has two identities, depending on the system privilege state. A different physical register is used for the 68000 user privilege state than is used for the 68000 supervisor privilege state, with the alternate register locked out. The correct A7 is selected automatically by the processor, the programmer doesn't need to make any distinction. This allows common reentrant code to be used by both an operating system module operating in supervisor mode and a user task operating in user mode. A special instruction allows access to the user stack pointer while operating in supervisor mode.

Most assemblers allow the mnemonic SP to be used in place of A7. The user stack pointer is called USP, and the supervisor stack is called SSP. We will be using "A7" for the stack pointer in all of our code examples throughout this book. Because the privilege state of the processor determines which A7 is in use at a given time, the mnemonics SSP and USP are not used in assembler source to indicate stack operations.

The Status/Condition Code Register

The 68000 has a 16-bit status register, as shown in Figure 1.1. Not all bits are used; some are reserved for future expansion of the 68000 family (and are actually used by the 68020: take care not to fool with the reserved bits if you plan on porting your code upwards). Note the

```
  15  14  13  12  11  10  9   8   7   6   5   4   3   2   1   0
+---+---+---+---+---+---+---+---+---+---+---+---+---+---+---+---+
| T |   | S |   |   |   | I2| I1| I0|   |   |   | X | N | Z | V | C |
+---+---+---+---+---+---+---+---+---+---+---+---+---+---+---+---+

   ^------- System Byte -------^    ^-------- User Byte --------^
                                       (Condition Code Register)

              T:              1 = Trace Mode
              S:              1 = Supervisor State
              I2, I1, I0:     Interrupt Mask
              X:              eXtend flag
              N:              Negative flag
              Z:              Zero flag
              V:              oVerflow flag
              C:              Carry flag
```

FIGURE 1-1:   Status/Condition Code Register

four different names used to refer to the status register and portions thereof. "Status Register" refers to all 16 bits; the mnemonic is SR. "Condition Code Register" refers to the lower 8 bits; the mnemonic is CCR. "User Byte" is a synonym for CCR. "System Byte" refers to the upper 8 bits of the status register.

The system byte is protected and can only be accessed while in supervisor mode, while the CCR is available to code operating in both user and supervisor mode.

The negative flag reflects the most significant bit of the last operation, and indicates the sign presuming a 2's complement operation. The flag is set, or considered "true," if the result of the last operation is negative. This bit is obviously meaningless if you're representing your data as unsigned values.

The zero flag indicates that the last operation produced a zero result. It's set to "1," or true, if the last operation produced a zero result.

The overflow flag indicates an overflow when operating on 2's complement integers, and is also affected by certain shift operations. Basically, this bit is affected when a carry into or a borrow out of the most significant bit has occurred, although certain other operations, such as shifts, will also affect this flag.

The carry flag indicates an overflow when operating on unsigned numbers, and is also affected by all of the shift operations. This flag is not used in multiple precision arithmetic as it is in many other processors; the extend flag is used for that. The carry flag is primarily intended to be used in control-flow applications, such as branch-if-carry-clear.

The extend flag becomes an operand in multiple precision arithmetic. Unlike the carry flag, which is stepped on even by simple data moves, the extend flag can be counted on to retain its value long enough to be useful for arithmetic. This distinction between the carry flag for program control and the extend flag for arithmetic is a special feature of the 68000.

The interrupt mask indicates which of the eight current interrupt levels is in effect (more on this later, in the interrupt section). The interrupt level can only be affected while operating in supervisor mode.

The supervisor bit, when true, indicates that the CPU is in supervisor mode, and can execute certain instructions not allowed in user mode.

The trace bit indicates that the CPU is in trace mode. The trace mode allows a master program to single-step through another program, even if that program is in ROM. More information on trace mode can be found in Chapter 11, where we discuss exceptions.

The Program Counter

The program counter (PC) is a 32-bit register; however, only 24 bits are brought out of the chip (actually, only 23 bits are, address bit 0 is treated specially, but the effect is the same because of certain hardware considerations we won't go into). Nevertheless, all 32 bits of the PC work and are affected by operations that affect the PC. Currently, any values present in the upper 8 bits of the PC are ignored. However, these bits are used by the 68020, so to keep code portable you may want to ensure that all 32 bits of the PC remain meaningful. No direct data value movement into or out of the PC are supported by 68000 instructions. Of course, a jump instruction moves a value into the PC, and a Load Effective Address (LEA) instruction can be used to read the PC, if you really have to for some reason.

That's about it for the register set. The register set is simple and operates predictably across the instruction set.

Memory Data Formats

The predefined integer data types for the 68000 are byte (8 bits), word (16 bits), longword (32 bits), and Binary-Coded-Decimal (BCD, 8 bits). Addresses are considered a distinct data type but are identical to longwords. Bits are also considered a data type.

No hardware distinction exists between signed and unsigned integers stored in memory. BCD numbers don't have an intrinsic sign associated with them, although BCD operations are carried out in 10's complement (just like 2's complement, only for base 10). With the same restriction as for binary numbers, namely a fixed number of digits, signed arithmetic is possible using BCD numbers.

The byte is the smallest unit of memory addressable by the 68000. Data types larger than 1 byte are always stored with the most significant byte at the lowest memory address and the least significant byte at the highest memory address. This is exactly the opposite of most Intel processors, and makes some operations, such as multiple precision arithmetic, more difficult. Something else that will eventually bite you old Intel programmers is that the 68000 requires all word or longword data types to be stored on an even (word) address boundary. Arrays are also stored low-to-high, with element zero having a lower memory address than element one. Figure 1-2 graphically shows data organization in memory.

```
                        Byte data  -    1 byte = 8 bits
         15   14   13   12   11   10   9    8    7    6    5    4    3    2    1    0
        +---+---+---+---+---+---+---+---+---+---+---+---+---+---+---+---+
        |msb         byte 0          lsb|            byte 1            |
        +---+---+---+---+---+---+---+---+---+---+---+---+---+---+---+---+
        |           byte 2             |            byte 3            |
        +---+---+---+---+---+---+---+---+---+---+---+---+---+---+---+---+


                        Word data  -   1 word = 16 bits
         15   14   13   12   11   10   9    8    7    6    5    4    3    2    1    0
        +---+---+---+---+---+---+---+---+---+---+---+---+---+---+---+---+
        |msb                         word 0                        lsb|
        +---+---+---+---+---+---+---+---+---+---+---+---+---+---+---+---+
        |                            word 1                           |
        +---+---+---+---+---+---+---+---+---+---+---+---+---+---+---+---+
        |                            word 2                           |
        +---+---+---+---+---+---+---+---+---+---+---+---+---+---+---+---+


                   Longword data  -  1 longword = 32 bits
         15   14   13   12   11   10   9    8    7    6    5    4    3    2    1    0
        +---+---+---+---+---+---+---+---+---+---+---+---+---+---+---+---+
        |msb  high order word                                         |
        + - + - + - + - + - + - + -Longword 0 - + - + - + - + - + - +
        |                                       low order word    lsb|
        +---+---+---+---+---+---+---+---+---+---+---+---+---+---+---+---+
        |                                                             |
        + - + - + - + - + - + - + -Longword 1 - + - + - + - + - + - +
        |                                                             |
        +---+---+---+---+---+---+---+---+---+---+---+---+---+---+---+---+
        |                                                             |
        + - + - + - + - + - + - + -Longword 2 - + - + - + - + - + - +
        |                                                             |
        +---+---+---+---+---+---+---+---+---+---+---+---+---+---+---+---+


                   BCD data   -   2 BCD digits = 1 byte
         15   14   13   12   11   10   9    8    7    6    5    4    3    2    1    0
        +---+---+---+---+---+---+---+---+---+---+---+---+---+---+---+---+
        |msd  BCD 0       |     BCD 1   lsd|     BCD 2       |    BCD 3     |
        +---+---+---+---+---+---+---+---+---+---+---+---+---+---+---+---+
        |     BCD 4       |     BCD 5      |     BCD 6       |    BCD 7     |
        +---+---+---+---+---+---+---+---+---+---+---+---+---+---+---+---+
```

FIGURE 1-2:   Data Organization in Memory

The Memory Map

The only hardware-constrained memory map is the exception vector table. This is called the interrupt vector table in some other processors. The exception vector table begins at address 0 and extends for 1024 bytes. It includes 256 vectors; each is one longword (4 bytes) long. The vectors are numbered from 0 to 255. To calculate the address of a vector table entry, simply multiply the vector number by four. An exception vector contains the address of a routine that handles an exception.

Vector zero is a special case. It is two longwords long, and contains an initial supervisor stack pointer value and program counter value for power-on reset. These vectors are automatically loaded into the stack pointer and program counter when the processor comes out of a hardware reset. There is technically no vector one, because the special-case vector zero extends over the space where you would expect to find it.

Some of the other vectors are reserved, and some are available for user definition. Figure 1-3 shows their individual assignments. Their uses will be explained in Chapter 11.

Vector	Address	Assignment
0	000	Reset initial supervisor stack pointer
	004	Reset initial program counter
2	008	Bus error
3	00C	Address error
4	010	Illegal Instruction
5	014	Divide-by-zero
6	018	CHK instruction
7	01C	TRAPV instruction
8	020	Privilege violation
9	024	Trace
10	028	Op Code 1010
11	02C	Op Code 1111
12	030	Reserved
13	034	Reserved
14	038	Reserved
15	03C	Uninitialized Interrupt Vector
16-23	040-05C	Reserved
24	060	Spurious Interrupt
25	068	Level 1 interrupt autovector
26	068	Level 2 interrupt autovector
27	06C	Level 3 interrupt autovector
28	070	Level 4 interrupt autovector
29	074	Level 5 interrupt autovector
30	078	Level 6 interrupt autovector
31	07C	Level 7 interrupt autovector
32-47	080-0BC	TRAP instruction vectors
48-63	0C0-0FC	Reserved
64-255	100-3FC	User definable interrupt vectors

FIGURE 1-3: Exception Vector Table

Privilege States

The 68000 operates in one of two privilege states: user or supervisor. The privilege state determines whether certain instructions are legal, which of the two stack pointers is active, and with the aid of optional external hardware, controls memory access.

Many 68000 systems include a memory management unit (MMU), a device that can be programmed to protect areas of memory in a variety of ways. An MMU is a complex device, far too complex to detail here. In fact, for an experienced assembly language programmer, it is much easier to learn to program the 68000 than it is to learn an MMU.

Suffice it to say that an MMU knows if the 68000 is in user or supervisor state, and can be instructed to make portions of memory read-only, supervisor-access only, or several combinations thereof. For example, it is possible to say "This area of memory is reserved for user code, this section is user data, this is supervisor data . . . " etc. This makes a secure system fairly easy to implement, because if a violation of the memory map is attempted, an exception, or software interrupt, is generated and control is taken away from the offending process.

The 68000 comes out of reset in the supervisor mode. There are several ways to enter user mode from supervisor mode, but the only way to go from user mode to supervisor mode is by processing an exception, which is an internally or externally generated interrupt. If the system is equipped with an MMU, a supervisor mode program can protect the exception vector table from user mode programs. Then, there's no way for a user process to get into supervisor state without the supervisor program allowing it, period.

In general, most programs execute in user mode, with only the operating system in supervisor mode. Instructions that may not be used in user mode ("privileged instructions") are STOP, RESET, MOVE to and from USP, and any instruction that modifies the system byte of the status register. When a user program attempts to execute one of these privileged instructions an exception is generated and control is passed to the routine that processes privilege violation exceptions.

This is a very general overview of the 68000. As we get into later chapters, we'll become more specific about most of these topics. An important topic not covered yet is the addressing modes allowed for 68000 instructions. Just by coincidence, addressing modes are the topic of our next chapter.

2
Addressing Modes

In this chapter we look at the operation, uses, and assembler syntax of the 68000 addressing modes.

The 68000 has fourteen addressing modes available. Not all modes work in all instances, but there is a definite pattern and logic to the use of the addressing modes in different instructions. There is also a strong influence from modern software engineering practices in the restrictions placed on the use of addressing modes—it's obvious that the design team placed a strong emphasis on support of structured techniques.

The wide array of addressing modes gives the 68000 much of its power. It will be to your advantage to spend a little extra time on this chapter and really understand the different addressing modes and how they work.

The Effective Address

Most instructions allow the use of an effective address to specify one operand of the instruction. An effective address is:

- A register
- An immediate operand
- The address of a memory operand generated by some combination of register contents and/or immediate data.

The effective address specifies where the operand for an instruction can be found.

We'll look at the addressing modes one at a time, using the MOVE instruction for examples. The MOVE instruction transfers data from one effective address to another, and is the only instruction that allows two effective addresses to be specified for one instruction. (The reason for this restriction is that it takes 6 bits to specify an effective address in an instruction. Two effective address fields in one instruction leaves only 4 bits for an op code, given the 68000's 16-bit instruction length. In fact, since the MOVE instruction can be specified to transfer either byte, word, or longword data, almost 20 percent of the 65,536 possible combinations of a 16-bit instruction format are reserved for the different MOVE instructions.)

An effective address is usually indicated in syntax diagrams as ⟨EA⟩. For example:

```
MOVE. W    ⟨EA⟩, ⟨EA⟩
```

The above indicates that for the instruction MOVE. W (Move Word) both the source and the destination may be an effective address.

The fourteen addressing modes are classed by Motorola into three groups: register direct; memory address; and special. We'll look at them in that order.

Register Direct Address Modes

The register direct address modes are so called because they specify that the operand to an instruction is contained in one of the sixteen registers.

Data Register Direct

Data register direct addressing specifies that the operand can be found in one of the data registers. Data register direct is indicated to the assembler by naming one of the data registers directly as an operand. For example, to move the contents of data register 1 (D1) to data register 2 (D2), we write:

```
MOVE. L    D1, D2
```

This particular instruction moves a longword. Note that the source is specified to the left of the destination. Nearly any instruction can use a data register as a source or a destination. When used as a destination, all condition codes excepting the extend flag are affected. The notation "Dn", where "n" is a register number from 0 to 7, is often used in syntax diagrams as a shorthand notation for data register direct addressing:

```
MOVE. L    Dn, Dn
```

Address Register Direct

Address register direct addressing specifies that the operand is in one of the address registers. Address register direct addressing is indicated by naming an address register directly as an operand. For example, to move the contents of address register 1 (A1) to data register 2 (D2), we write:

```
MOVE. L    A1, D2
```

The use of address register direct is somewhat restricted. It is illegal to specify an address register as the source or destination of an instruction expecting an 8-bit operand. Certain arithmetic instructions can't specify an address register as an operand. When an address register is used as a destination, and this includes the arithmetic instructions targeting address registers, the condition codes are not affected (the only exception being the "compare address register" instruction). The shorthand notation for address register direct addressing is "An":

```
MOVE. L    An, Dn
```

Memory Addressing Modes

Most of the 68000 addressing modes are different ways of pointing to memory locations. There's quite a variety. Unfortunately, there's no such thing as a free lunch, and as the memory addressing modes become more complicated and powerful, the size and the execution time of instructions taking advantage of the more powerful modes increase.

As we present each addressing mode, we'll indicate the instruction size penalty for using that addressing mode in terms of "extension words." Extension words are additional words of instruction. In the 68000 instruction format, extension words (if present) are always part of an effective address specification. The number of extension words ranges from zero for the register direct and indirect modes to a maximum of four extension words for certain combinations of operands to MOVE instructions. Nothing other than effective address extensions cause an instruction to exceed 16 bits.

Instruction extension words are always multiples of 16 bits, to preserve even address alignment of the code. Execution time penalties for using addressing modes with extension words are roughly proportional to the number of extension words needed.

The data and address register direct addressing modes don't use extension words to compute their effective address.

Address Register Indirect

The simplest memory addressing mode is address register indirect. If you're weak on your parlance, register indirect addressing means that the register holds the *address* of the operand, not the *operand* itself. In the case of address register indirect, an address register holds the address of the memory location that contains the operand. In C terms, the address register is a pointer to the operand.

Address register indirect is indicated to the assembler by enclosing the name of the register that holds the address in parentheses:

```
MOVE. B    (A1), (A2)
```

This instruction moves the byte at the memory location whose address is contained in register A1 to the memory location whose address is contained in register A2. If register A1 holds the value $1000 (the leading dollar sign indicates hexadecimal) and register A2 holds the value $2000, and memory location $1000 contains the byte value $12, after executing the above instruction memory location $2000 will contain the byte value $12.

The shorthand notation for address register indirect is "(An)," where "n" is '0' to '7':

```
MOVE. s    (An), (An)
```

This addressing mode is used for basic pointer operations, and uses no extension words.

Address Register Indirect with Postincrement

This addressing mode works just like address register indirect, except that after the data is accessed, the specified address register is incremented by the size of the data transferred. The postincrement mode is specified to the assembler by placing a plus sign ("+") after the parentheses enclosing the name of an address register. If A1 = $1000, A2 = $2000, and memory location $1000 = $55, after executing the instruction.

```
MOVE. B    (A1) +, (A2) +
```

memory location $2000 will contain the value $55, A1 = $1001, and A2 = $2001. If the instruction was MOVE. W (Move Word) instead of MOVE. B, A1 would equal $1002 and A2 would equal $2002. If the instruction had been MOVE. L (Move Longword), A1 would equal $1004 and A2 would equal $2004. The shorthand for this mode is "(An)+". This mode doesn't need an extension word.

This addressing mode is used to POP operands off stacks, or to maintain circular buffers, or in a loop to move blocks of memory, etc, and is an analog to the C language postfix operator "++". The C fragment

```
char *a1;

    while ( *a1++ );
```

which searches a character string until it finds the terminating null character, can be implemented in 68000 assembler as

```
LOOP    TST. B    (A1) +      * the TST sets the condition flags
        BNZ       LOOP        * branch-if-not-zero
```

Address Register Indirect with Predecrement

This mode works like address register indirect, except that before the transfer takes place, the named address register is decremented by the size of the data transferred. The predecrement mode is indicated to the assembler by placing a minus sign ("—") before the parenthesis enclosing the register name. If A1 contains $1000, A2 contains $2000, and memory location $0FFF contains $66, after the instruction

```
MOVE. B    −(A1),−(A2)
```

A1 will equal $0FFF, A2 will equal $1FFF, and memory location $1FFF will contain $66. The shorthand for this mode is "−(An)".

This mode is used to PUSH operands on stacks, etc., just like the postincrement addressing mode, and is an analog to the C prefix operator "−−". This mode doesn't need extension words.

Address Register Indirect with Displacement

This addressing mode works like address register indirect, except that a 16-bit displacement constant is sign-extended and added to the named register to compute the address of the operand. This mode is indicated to the assembler by placing a constant before the parenthesis enclosing the register name. If A1 contains $1000, A2 contains $2000, and memory location $1010 contains $32, after the instruction

```
MOVE. B    $10(A1), $20(A2)
```

memory location $2020 will contain $32. The shorthand notation for this mode is "d(An)". This mode uses one extension word, to hold the displacement.

It is primarily intended to offset into a data structure of some sort pointed to by the named address register. This includes record types, lookup tables, and parameters passed on the stack, to name some important examples.

Most assemblers allow the use of expressions and equated labels for the displacement constant:

```
MOVE. B    ALPHA(A1), BETA−2(A2)
```

Address Register Indirect with Index

This mode is similar to the preceding mode. An address is computed by starting with a base address contained in an address register. An 8—bit sign–extended displacement is then added to the base address. Finally, the contents of another register, either an address register or a data register (called the "index" register), is added to the sum of the base address and the displacement. This final value is the operand address. The index register may be specified as either a longword or a word portion of the register. If the index register is specified as a word portion, it is sign-extended before being added to the accumulated address. For example, if address $1050 contains the value $45, address register A1 contains the value $1000 (in this example, A1 is the "base" register), data register D1 contains the value $30 (D1 would be the "index" register), after the instruction

```
MOVE.B    $20(A1,D1.L), D2
```

data register D2 will contain the value $45 in the lower 8 bits.

The shorthand notation for this addressing mode is "d(An,Xn.s)". The "X" indicates either a data or address register is legal, and the ".s" may be replaced with either ".L" for longword or ".W" for word, indicating the size of the operand contributed by the index register. This addressing mode requires one extension word.

This mode is useful for implementing arrays. By using a zero displacement, arrays of scalars can be accessed, and by using non—zero displacements, arrays of data structures can be as easily accommodated. If the array component is more than 1 byte in size, the data register will need to hold the array index times the size of the component in bytes—the index is added in bytes, regardless of the final operand size.

Special Address Modes

The following address modes are called "special" by Motorola because of the way the bit packing is done in the assembled instruction.

Absolute Short Address

In this addressing mode, a 16—bit constant is sign-extended to form the address of the operand. This mode is called "direct addressing" in Intel terminology. The short address can only access addresses from $0000 thru $7FFF and $FF8000 thru $FFFFF. This mode is indicated to the assembler with a constant followed by ".W". If memory location $FFE000 contains the value $55, after the instruction

```
MOVE.B    $E000.W, D1
```

the lower 8 bits of register D1 will contain $55. The shorthand notation for absolute short address is "xxx.W", where "xxx" stands for the address constant. This addressing mode requires one extension word.

Absolute Long Address

This mode is just like absolute short except that a longword constant is used, allowing operand access anywhere in the 16-megabyte address space of the 68000. This mode is indicated to the assembler by postfixing a constant with ".L". Many assemblers automatically use the absolute short addressing mode if possible and if you leave off the postfix. Using the numbers from the last example, the instruction

    MOVE. B $FFE000. L, D1

will have the same effect as the example for absolute short addressing, but will require one more extension word (for a total of two extension words) of instruction. The shorthand for this addressing mode is "xxx. L", where "xxx" stands for the address constant.

Because the instruction set and addressing modes are so regular, it is perfectly legal to move data from memory to memory. If you use absolute long addressing for both the source and destination operand of a MOVE instruction, however, you'll end up with a 10—byte instruction (2 bytes for instruction and 4 bytes of extension for each operand). If more than one unit of data is to be moved, it's usually more efficient to set up address registers and use post-increment or predecrement addressing.

The absolute addressing modes do not allow for relocatable data sections—it is usually better to set up a data section and point one of the address registers at it, and use indexed or "with displacement" addressing if relocation after link—time is desired.

Program Counter with Displacement

This mode is exactly like the address register indirect with displacement d(An), except that here the program counter (PC) is used as the base register instead of an address register. The shorthand form for this mode is "d(PC)". Example:

    MOVE. B $10(PC), D1

This moves the byte located at the PC + 16 to D1. This mode requires one extension word.

Program Counter with Index

This mode is exactly like the address register indirect with index "d(An, Xn.s)", except that here the PC is used as the base register instead of an address register. The shorthand form for this mode is "d(PC, Xn.s)", Example:

MOVE. B $10(PC, A2.W), D1

This moves the byte at the PC + 16 + the sign-extended word in the lower half of A2 to register D1.

Both of the preceding PC-relative address modes must be used as source operands. This mode is never legal as a destination operand, probably due to the software engineering stigma associated with self-modifying code. Also, many operating systems on machines with the proper hardware support will write-protect the program's code area, making this mode useless for destination addressing anyhow. In the case where you just gotta use this mode to generate a destination address, you can use the LEA instruction to load the PC-relative address into an address register, and then use address register indirect to perform the transfer.

If you plan on using tricks to self-modify the code, be aware that newer 68K processors, such as the 68020, have instruction caches and may not fetch the modified code.

The PC addressing modes facilitate the development of relocatable code. Constants, strings, tables, etc., can be located in the code segment of the program and referenced by the PC and a constant offset.

This addressing mode requires one word of extension.

Immediate Data

This addressing mode includes the operand (which must be a source operand, never a destination operand) as part of the instruction. Immediate data is indicated to the assembler by prefixing a constant with a pound sign (#). Example:

MOVE. L   #$123456, A1

This example loads address register A1 with the value $123456.

The shorthand notation for immediate addressing is "#xxx" or sometimes "#n". Immediate mode addressing requires one extension word for either byte or word data, and two extension words for longword data.

It grates on an old Z80 hack to use up 16 bits of code space just for a measly byte operand, even though we know memory is cheap. Motorola has provided a special group of instructions, called the "quick" instructions, that can add, subtract, or move immediate data with values in the range 0 to 8 or 0 to 255 without *any* extension words. This is obviously a sop to us old-timers, but we'll take it any way we can get it.

Status Register and Condition Code Register Addressing

The last two addressing modes are status register direct and condition code register direct. These modes are allowed only as destinations in the logical immediate operations ANDI (AND immediate) EORI (Exclusive Or immediate) and ORI (OR immediate), and are used in some special MOVE instructions. The instruction

```
ANDI    $FE, CCR
```

clears the carry bit in the condition code register.

These two modes are used almost exclusively for setting or clearing flags in the status register. These modes don't use any extension words. Status register direct addressing is indicated to the assembler by using the "SR" reserved word as a destination operand, and condition register direct addressing is indicated to the assembler by using the "CCR" reserved word as a destination operand:

```
ORI     $01, CCR * condition code register direct

ORI     $2700, SR *status register direct
```

That covers all of the addressing modes. Remember, the extensive use of these addressing modes contributes to the small number of distinct instructions for the 68000. If you can't find an instruction you know ought to exist (like a PUSH, for example), recheck these addressing modes and see if the clever application of one or more of the addressing modes to one of the simpler instructions doesn't accomplish the same effect. Of course, we'll try to point out common instances as we cover the instruction set. If that fails, look through the comments in the example code in this book and see if we do something similar to what you want to do.

3
Data Transfer Instructions

In this chapter we look at the 68000 data transfer instruction group, which includes the MOVEs, LEA, PEA, EXG, and SWAP, LINK, and UNLK instructions. These instructions are the workhorses of the instruction set.

The MOVE Instruction

The MOVE instruction transfers data from a source operand to a destination operand. The operand size may be byte (.B), word (.W), or longword (.L). This operation affects the flags. Note that address register direct is not allowed as a destination effective address. The MOVEA instruction is used when an address register is desired as the destination, although almost all assemblers will generate a MOVEA instruction if you code a MOVE with an address register direct destination. Remember that in standard Motorola notation the source operand is to the left of the destination operand. This is backwards from standard Intel notation, and can be a source of sneaky errors if you are switching over.

Assembler Syntax:

```
MOVE. B    ⟨EA⟩, ⟨EA⟩
MOVE. W    ⟨EA⟩, ⟨EA⟩
MOVE. L    ⟨EA⟩, ⟨EA⟩
```

Examples of MOVE:

3008	move. w a0, d0
1010	move. b (a0), d0
23FC000010000000FF00	move. l #$1000, $FF00
2F08	move. l a0, -(a7)

Condition Flags Affected:

N Set if the data transferred is negative, otherwise cleared.

Z Set if the data transferred is zero, reset otherwise.

V Always cleared.

C Always cleared.

X Not affected.

Addressing Modes Allowed:

Source:

Dn	An	(An)	(An)+
−(An)	d(An)	d(An, Xi)	xxx. W
xxx. L	d(PC)	d(PC, Xi)	# xxx

Destination:

Dn		(An)	(An)+
−(An)	d(An)	d(An, Xi)	xxx. W
xxx. L			

The MOVE to CCR Instruction

The MOVE to CCR (Move to Condition Code Register) instruction moves a word source operand to the condition code register. The condition code register is the low byte of the status register. The upper byte of the source operand is ignored, but it's important to remember that the source operand is a word, because if you use a memory effective address the byte to be moved must be located at an odd address (with the effective address resolved to the preceding even address, the byte on the even address is ignored). Normally this instruction is used with immediate and stack operands, in which case the assembler or the hardware will take care of alignment for you.

Assembler Syntax:

MOVE. W   ⟨EA⟩, CCR

Example of MOVE to CCR:

44FC0000	move. w	#0, ccr
44DF	move. w	(a7)+, ccr

Condition Flags Affected:

N   Set to bit 3 of the source operand.

Z   Set to bit 2 of the source operand.

V   Set to bit 1 of the source operand.

C   Set to bit 0 of the source operand.

X   Set to bit 4 of the source operand.

Addressing Modes Allowed:

Source:

Dn   (An)   (An)+

−(An)   d(An)   d(An, Xi)   xxx. W

xxx. L   d(PC)   d(PC, Xi)   # xxx

The MOVE to SR Instruction

The MOVE to SR (Move to Status Register) instruction moves a word to the status register, affecting all 16 bits of the status register. The source operand is a word. This is a privileged instruction and may only be executed while in supervisor mode. If executed in user mode a privilege violation exception is generated.

This instruction is used for such system-level jobs as setting the interrupt mask level and changing from supervisor to user mode.

Assembler Syntax:

MOVE. W   ⟨EA⟩, SR

Example of MOVE to SR:

46FC2700   move. w #$2700, sr

46DF   move. w (a7) + , sr

Condition Flags Affected:

Set to the source operand low byte.

Addressing Modes Allowed:

Source:

Dn   (An)   (An)+

−(An)   d(An)   d(An, Xi)   xxx. W

xxx. L   d(PC)   d(PC, Xi)   # xxx

The MOVE from SR Instruction

The MOVE from SR (Move from Status Register) instruction moves the content of the status register to a destination effective address. The data size is word. An anomaly of this instruction is that a memory destination is read before it is written to, which could cause problems, for example, if you are writing to a memory-mapped LED latch for a gee-whizza-blinkin lights display, and the hardware doesn't provide the proper acknowledgement for reads to a write-only address. The primary uses of this instruction are to push flags onto the stack or to examine the status register to see if the machine is in supervisor or user mode before executing privileged instructions.

Assembler Syntax:

```
MOVE. W    SR, ⟨EA⟩
```

Example of MOVE from SR:

```
40F90000FF00    move. w  sr, $FF00
40E7            move. w  sr, −(a7)
```

Condition Flags Affected:

None.

Addressing Modes Allowed:

Destination:

Dn	(An)	(An)+
−(An) d(An)	d(An, Xi)	xxx. W
xxx. L		

The MOVE USP Instruction

The MOVE USP (Move to/from User Stack Pointer) instruction moves the contents of the user stack pointer (USP) to or from the specified address register. The size of the data transferred is longword. MOVE USP is a privileged instruction and may only be executed while the machine is in the supervisor mode. Executing this instruction while the machine is in user mode will cause a privilege violation exception.

This instruction is used by supervisor programs to set up user programs, and when switching tasks in multiprocessing environments.

Assembler Syntax:

```
MOVE. L    USP, An
MOVE. L    An, USP
```

Example of MOVE USP:

```
4E68     move. l   usp, a0
4E60     move. l   a0, usp
```

Condition Flags Affected:

None.

Addressing Modes Allowed:

An

The MOVEA Instruction

The MOVEA (Move Address) instruction moves a sign-extended word or a longword to an address register. Most assemblers will figure you mean MOVEA if you just use MOVE and specify an address register as the destination effective address. This is classed as a separate instruction because word data is sign-extended, byte size operands are not allowed, and the condition codes are not affected.

Assembler Syntax:

```
MOVE. W    ⟨EA⟩, An
MOVE. L    ⟨EA⟩, An
```

Example of MOVEA:

```
307CFFFF           movea. w   #$FFFF, a0
207C0000FFFF       movea. l   #$FFFF, a0
```

Condition Flags Affected:

None.

Addressing Modes Allowed:

Source:

Dn	An	(An)	(An)+
−(An)	d(An)	d(An, Xi)	xxx. W
xxx. L	d(PC)	d(PC, Xi)	# xxx

The MOVEM Instruction

The MOVEM (Move Multiple) instruction moves the contents of selected registers to or from memory. The intent of this instruction is to push or pop selected registers to or from the stack, or to save the complete machine state during task context switches in a multiprocessing environment. Either longword transfers or sign-extended word transfers are allowed. In memory, the data is always represented in 4 bytes, while the registers may be either affected as words or longwords. Remember, even if you specify loading registers with word data, when word data is specified for address registers the word is sign-extended and all 32 bits of address registers are always affected.

Three classes of address modes for the memory effective address are used, and each acts differently.

If the effective address is one of the memory reference modes (An), d(An), d(An, Xi), xxx. W or xx. L, the listed registers are transferred starting at the specified address and continue up through the higher address. Register order is data registers low through high, then address registers low through high. These modes are most useful for storing a task context during a task switch, although MOVEM can also be used in a loop to effect high-speed data transfers.

If the effective address is the address register indirect with predecrement, as in pushing onto the stack, only register to memory operations are allowed. In this case the registers are pushed starting with the high address register specified and ending with the low data register specified. This results in a memory organization just like that for the memory reference modes indicated in the previous paragraph. This mode works well for pushing selected registers used in subroutines.

If the effective address is the address register indirect with postincrement, as in popping off the stack, only memory to register operations are allowed. The registers are loaded from memory starting at the specified address and continuing towards higher memory. Data registers are loaded first, low to high, and then the address registers.

This instruction is specially optimized to use the instruction prefetch queue, and so when loading the registers from memory, an extra memory read occurs one address higher than you'd expect. The effect of this is that you need to be sure that real memory exists at this extra read address to avoid getting a bus error exception.

The register list is specified by listing the register names delimited by slashes, and/or register ranges. A register range is specified by naming two registers separated by a dash. To specify register D0, D1, D2, D3, D4, D5, A0, A1, A2, A5 to be pushed onto the stack, you can write either of the following:

```
MOVEM     D0/D1/D2/D3/D4/D5/A0/A1/A2/A5,-(A7)
MOVEM     D0-D5/A0-A2/A5,-(A7)
```

Obviously, when using the predecrement or postincrement modes, we want to avoid specifying the register used as the pointer.

Assembler Syntax:

```
MOVEM. W      ⟨EA⟩, ⟨register list⟩
MOVEM. W      ⟨register list⟩, ⟨EA⟩
MOVEM. L      ⟨EA⟩, ⟨register list⟩
MOVEM. L      ⟨register list⟩, ⟨EA⟩
```

Example of MOVEM:

```
48E7F000              movem. l   d0-d3,-(a7)
48F907010000FF00      movem. l   d0/a0-a2, $FF00
```

Condition Flags Affected:

None.

Addressing Modes Allowed:

Source:

		(An)	(An)+
	d(An)	d(An, Xi)	xxx. W
xxx. L	d(PC)	d(PC, Xi)	

Destination:

		(An)	
−(An)	d(An)	d(An, Xi)	xxx. W
xxx. L			

The MOVEP Instruction

The MOVEP (Move to/from Peripheral) instruction moves word or longword data between a data register and alternate bytes of memory. This instruction is intended to interface to 8-bit peripherals connected to either the high byte or the low byte of the data bus. The only time it will really save you much work is when you have a peripheral device, for example a math processor, with a multiple-byte internal register that's memory mapped externally. In other words, not too often.

The memory address is specified using address register indirect with displacement notation.

Assembler Syntax:

```
MOVEP    Dn, d(An)
MOVEP    d(An), Dn
```

Example of MOVEP:

```
01C80000    movep. l  d0, 0(a0)
01080000    movep. w  0 (a0), d0
```

Condition Flags Affected:

None.

The MOVEQ instruction

The MOVEQ (Move Quick) instruction provides a 16-bit instruction that includes 8 bits of immediate data to move into a data register. A value in the range 0 to 255 is sign-extended to 32 bits and loaded into the specified data register, affecting all 32 bits. Many assemblers will convert

```
MOVE. L    #xxx, Dn
```

to

```
MOVEQ      #xxx, Dn
```

if the immediate operand is in the proper range (-128 to $+127$).

Assembler Syntax:

```
MOVEQ    #xxx, Dn
```

Example of MOVEQ:

```
7002    moveq  #2, d0
```

Condition Flags Affected:

Set as for MOVE

The LEA Instruction

LEA (Load Effective Address) calculates an effective address and loads that address into the address register specified in the instruction. This works well for dereferencing pointers and that sort of thing. This is also a handy way to get to those PC relative addresses if you're so inclined.

Assembler Syntax:

LEA   ⟨EA⟩, An

Example of LEA:

```
41EE0006    lea  6(a6), a0
41F60008    lea  8(a6, d0. w), a0
```

Condition Flags Affected:

None.

Addressing Modes Allowed:

Source:

		(An)	
	d(An)	d(An, Xi)	xxx. W
xxx. L	d(PC)	d(PC, Xi)	

The PEA Instruction

PEA (Push Effective Address) calculates an effective address and pushes that address onto the stack. This is an efficient way to pass pointers to subroutines.

Assembler Syntax:

```
PEA    ⟨EA⟩
```

Example of PEA:

```
487A000A    pea  10(pc)
4850        pea  (a0)
```

Condition Flags Affected:

None.

Addressing Modes Allowed:

Source:

		(An)	
	d(An)	d(An, Xi)	xxx. W
xxx. L	d(PC)	d(PC, Xi)	

The EXG Instruction

The EXG (Exchange) instruction exchanges the contents of any two data or address registers. The exchange is always 32 bits.

Assembler Syntax:

```
EXG    Rn, Rn
```

Example of EXG:

```
C188    exg  a0, d0
C141    exg  d0, d1
```

Condition Flags Affected:

None.

The SWAP Instruction

The SWAP instruction exchanges the 16-bit halves of the specified data register. The high order word of the register takes the place of the low order word, and vice versa.

Assembler Syntax:

```
SWAP    Dn
```

Example of SWAP:

```
4840    swap  d0
```

Condition Flags Affected:

N   Set if bit 31 of the result is set; otherwise cleared.

Z   Set if the 32-bit result is zero; otherwise cleared.

V   Always cleared.

C   Always cleared.

X   Not affected.

The LINK Instruction

LINK establishes a stack frame reference and allocates temporary storage on the stack. The current content of a specified address register is pushed onto the stack. Then, the updated stack pointer is copied to the specified address register. Finally, a 16-bit sign-extended displacement is added to the stack pointer.

The intent is to pick an address register (let's say A6) to use as a frame pointer ("frame pointers" are discussed in Chapter 10) throughout your program. As you enter a subroutine, you link A6. The old A6 is pushed onto the stack. Presumably, this value is the frame pointer from the calling subroutine. Then, the stack pointer is copied to A6 to establish the stack frame. Whatever you do to the stack from now on, A6 will point to a spot 8 bytes away from any parameters pushed by the caller as parameters to this subroutine. Finally, a (usually negative) displacement is added to the stack pointer to allocate temporary storage for the current subroutine. A6, the frame pointer in this example, will also have a constant value relative to the temporary storage. The UNLK instruction (see the next section) is used to reverse the process at the end of the subroutine.

Assembler Syntax:

```
LINK    An, #xxx
```

Example of LINK:

```
4E560008    link  a6, #8
```

Condition Flags Affected:

None.

The UNLK Instruction

The UNLK (Unlink) instruction loads the stack pointer with the contents of the specified address register, which hopefully is the current stack frame pointer. Then, the longword at the top of the stack is popped into the specified address register. This instruction is intended to reverse the effect of the LINK instruction. Note that any data pushed onto the stack after the LINK instruction effectively vanishes when the UNLK instruction is executed, even if it was never removed from the stack.

Assembler Syntax:

```
UNLK    An
```

Example of UNLK:

```
4E5E    unlk  a6
```

Condition Flags Affected:

None.

4

Arithmetic Instructions

In this chapter we look at the 68000 arithmetic instruction group. This group includes the ADDs, CLRs, CMPs, DIVs, EXT, MULs, NEGs, SUBs, TAS, TST, and BCD instructions.

The ABCD Instruction

ABCD (Add BCD) adds two binary-coded-decimal (BCD) operands, along with the extend flag, and stores the result in the destination operand. Two operand addressing modes are allowed, data register direct and address register indirect with predecrement. The predecrement addressing mode allows the addition of multiple precision memory-based operands. Both operands must use the same addressing mode. This instruction acts only on byte operands.

Be sure to clear the extend bit and to set the zero flag before beginning a BCD addition sequence, and be sure that the flags are not affected by intermediate instructions. Note that the zero flag is designed to produce a valid value after multiple precision adds.

Binary-coded-decimal is a scheme for packing a decimal digit into 4 binary digits. Each byte has 8 bits, so 2 decimal digits fit into 1 byte. Four binary digits have 16 possible states, so 6 states are undefined as BCD digits. If one digit in a byte pair is undefined, all 16 states of the other digits can also be considered bad. The bottom line is that 100 states of a possible 256 in a byte are valid BCD numbers, and the other 156 states are bad.

BCD is not an especially efficient storage format for numbers, but it makes it easy to convert the numbers for output, and it's also easy to maintain decimal fractions as BCD numbers.

Assembler Syntax:

```
ABCD    Dn, Dn
ABCD    -(An),-(An)
```

Example of ABCD:

```
C300    abcd  d0, d1
C308    abcd  -(a0),-(a1)
```

Condition Flags Affected:

N   Undefined.

Z   Cleared if the result is non-zero, otherwise unchanged.

V   Undefined

C   Set if a decimal carry is generated, otherwise cleared.

X   Set if a decimal carry is generated, otherwise cleared.

The ADD Instruction

ADD adds a source operand to a destination operand, and stores the result into the destination operand. This instruction will operate on byte, word, or longword data. A data register always serves as one of the operands, and an effective address is the other operand. The effective address may be the destination operand in many cases.

Assembler Syntax:

[NOTE: . s = { . B .W. L}]

```
ADD. s    ⟨EA⟩, Dn
ADD. s    Dn, ⟨EA⟩
```

Example of ADD:

D07C0100	add. w #$100, d0
D088	add. l a0, d0
D0390000FF00	add. b $FF00, d0

Condition Flags Affected:

N Set if the result is negative, otherwise cleared.

Z Set if the result is zero, otherwise cleared.

V Set if an overflow is generated, otherwise cleared.

C Set if a carry is generated, otherwise cleared.

X Set if a carry is generated, otherwise cleared.

Addressing Modes Allowed:

Source:

Dn	An	(An)	(An)+
−(An)	d(An)	d(An, Xi)	xxx. W
xxx. L	d(PC)	d(PC, Xi)	#xxx

Destination:

Dn*

		(An)	(An)+
−(An)	d(An)	d(An, Xi)	xxx. W
xxx. L			

*Dn addressing technically is not allowed for the ⟨EA⟩ field, but since ⟨EA⟩ may be a source and the other operand must be a data register, the effect is the same as if it is. See Chapter 9 for details.

The ADDA Instruction

ADDA is basically an ADD instruction that allows an address register to be the destination. The differences are: flags are not affected; operation size may be only word or longword; and all 32 bits of the destination address register are affected (word size operations are sign-extended to longword before the addition takes place).

Assembler Syntax:

ADD. W   ⟨EA⟩, An

ADD. L   ⟨EA⟩. An

Example of ADDA:

D0FC0001   adda. w #1, a0

D1C0   adda. l d0, a0

Condition Flags Affected:

None.

Addressing Modes Allowed:

Source:

Dn	An	(An)	(An)+
−(An)	d(An)	d(An, Xi)	xxx. W
xxx. L	d(PC)	d(PC, Xi)	#xxx

The ADDI Instruction

ADDI (ADD Immediate) adds an immediate value to a destination effective address and stores the result in the destination. Note that this is very similar to an ADD instruction, with an immediate value taking the place of the data register (source operand form). Note that this allows adding an immediate value to most of the non-data register effective address operand types. The operation may be byte, word, or longword size. Many times, if a data register is the destination, the ADDQ instruction (see next section) may be a more optimal choice, if the immediate value is in the correct range. The ADDI instruction may be automatically chosen by the assembler if the source for an ADD instruction is immediate.

Assembler Syntax:

[NOTE: . s = { . B .W. L}]

    ADDI. s   #xxx, ⟨EA⟩

Example of ADDI:

    52790000FF00   addi. w #1, $FF00

    06900000FFFE   addi. l #$FFFE, (a0)   t

Condition Flags Affected:

    N Set if the result is negative, otherwise cleared.

    Z Set if the result is zero, otherwise cleared.

    V Set if an overflow is generated, otherwise cleared.

    C Set if a carry is generated, otherwise cleared.

    X Set if a carry is generated, otherwise cleared.

Addressing Modes Allowed:

Destination:

Dn		(An)	(An)+
−(An)	d(An)	d(An, Xi)	xxx. W
xxx. L			

The ADDQ Instruction

ADDQ (ADD Quick) adds an immediate value (in the range 1..8) to the destination effective address operand. Because this instruction is only one word long, including the immediate value, it provides a fast and efficient way to add small amounts to registers and memory operands. This instruction replaces the increment instructions found on most other processors, and is more flexible.

Note: When an address register is the destination, operations are restricted to word and longword size (there is no effective difference between specifying word size or longword size), and the flags are not affected.

Assembler Syntax:

```
ADDQ. B    #xxx, ⟨EA⟩
ADDQ. W    #xxx, ⟨EA⟩
ADDQ. L    #xxx, ⟨EA⟩
```

Example of ADDQ:

```
5240     addq. w    #1, d0
548F     addq. l    #2, a7
```

Condition Flags Affected:

N   Set if the result is negative, otherwise cleared.

Z   Set if the result is zero, otherwise cleared.

V   Set if an overflow is generated, otherwise cleared.

C   Set if a carry is generated, otherwise cleared.

X   Set if a carry is generated, otherwise cleared.

Addressing Modes Allowed:

Destination:

Dn	An	(An)	(An)+
−(An)	d(An)	d(An, Xi)	xxx. W
xxx. L			

The ADDX Instruction

ADDX (ADD Extended), more familiarly *Add with Carry* in other processors, adds the source operand to the destination operand and then adds the value of the X (extend) flag. Only two addressing modes are allowed, data register direct and address register indirect with predecrement. The addressing mode must be the same for both operands. This instruction is used to implement multiple precision additions.

Assembler Syntax:

[NOTE: . s = { . B .W. L}]

```
ADDX.s      Dn, Dn
ADDX. s     −(An),−(An)
```

Example of ADDX:

```
D380      addx. l   d0, d1
D348      addx. w   −(a0),−(a1)
```

Condition Flags Affected:

N Set if the result is negative, otherwise cleared.
Z Set if the result is zero, otherwise unchanged.
V Set if an overflow is generated, otherwise cleared.
C Set if a carry is generated, otherwise cleared.
X Set if a carry is generated, otherwise cleared.

[handwritten annotation: Cleared if the result is non-zero. Unchanged otherwise.]

The CLR Instruction

The CLR (Clear) instruction clears the destination operand to zero.

Assembler Syntax:

```
CLR. B    ⟨EA⟩
CLR. W    ⟨EA⟩
CLR. L    ⟨EA⟩
```

Example of CLR:

```
4240              clr. w  d0
42790000FF00      clr. w  $FF00
42280002          clr. b  2(a0)
```

Condition Flags Affected:

N Always cleared.

Z Always set.

V Always cleared.

C Always cleared.

X Not affected.

Addressing Modes Allowed:

Source:

```
Dn              (An)      (An)+
-(An)   d(An)   d(An, Xi) xxx. W
xxx. L
```

The CMP Instruction

CMP (Compare) subtracts the source operand (the left-hand operand) from the destination operand (the right-hand operand) setting the condition flags but throwing away the result of the subtraction (neither operand is affected). Only a data register may be the destination operand for this instruction.

The CMPA instruction is used when an address register is desired to be the destination operand, CMPM is used when memory-to-memory compares are desired, and CMPI is used when the source is immediate data. Many assemblers will automatically make the correct choice of instruction if you just use "CMP" for all compares.

This is one of the few irregular instruction groups in the 68000 instruction family, so it pays to spend a little extra time looking at allowed addressing modes.

Also note that since the source operand is subtracted from the destination operand, the sense of the compare is backwards from what is intuitive. Example:

    CMP. L   D0, D1

If the above instruction is immediately followed by a "Branch If Greater Than" instruction, the branch takes place if D1 is greater than D0. This seemingly minor point is guaranteed to bite you on at least a weekly basis.

Assembler Syntax:

    CMP. B   ⟨EA⟩, Dn
    CMP. W   ⟨EA⟩, Dn
    CMP. L   ⟨EA⟩, Dn

Example of CMP:

    B07C000A   cmp. w   #10, d0
    B090   cmp. l   (a0), d0

Condition Flags Affected:

N   Set if the result is negative, otherwise cleared.

Z   Set if the result is zero, otherwise cleared.

V   Set if an overflow is generated, otherwise cleared.

C   Set if a borrow is generated, otherwise cleared.

X   Not affected.

Addressing Modes Allowed:

Source:

Dn	An	(An)	(An)+
−(An)	d(An)	d(An, Xi)	xxx. W
xxx. L	d(PC)	d(PC, Xi)	#xxx

The CMPA Instruction

CMPA (Compare Address) works just like CMP, except that an address register may be the destination. Only word and longword sizes are allowed, and word operands are sign-extended to longword before the compare operation. See CMP for other comments.

Assembler Syntax:

```
CMPA. W    〈EA〉, An
CMPA. L    〈EA〉, An
```

Example of CMPA:

```
B1FC0000FF00    cmpa. l   #$FF00, a0
B1F90000FF00    cmpa. l   $FF00, a0
```

Condition Flags Affected:

N   Set if the result is negative, otherwise cleared.

Z   Set if the result is zero, otherwise cleared.

V   Set if an overflow is generated, otherwise cleared.

C   Set if a borrow is generated, otherwise cleared.

X   Not affected.

Addressing Modes Allowed:

Source:

Dn	An	(An)	(An)+
−(An)	d(An)	d(An, xi)	xxx. W
xxx. L	d(PC)	d(PC, xi)	#xxx

The CMPI Instruction

CMPI (Compare Immediate) compares an immediate source operand to an effective address destination. This is the only compare instruction that allows an effective address as the destination operand. See CMP for additional comments.

Assembler Syntax:

```
CMPI. B   #xxx, ⟨EA⟩
CMPI. W   #xxx, ⟨EA⟩
CMPI. L   #xxx, ⟨EA⟩
```

Example of CMPI:

```
0C400001            cmpi. w  #1, d0
0C3900050000FF00    cmpi. b  #5, $FF00
```

Condition Flags Affected:

N   Set if the result is negative, otherwise cleared.

Z   Set if the result is zero, otherwise cleared.

V   Set if an overflow is generated, otherwise cleared.

C   Set if a borrow is generated, otherwise cleared.

X   Not affected.

Addressing Modes Allowed:

Destination:

Dn   (An)   (An)+

−(An)   d(An)   d(An, Xi)   xxx. W

xxx. L

The CMPM Instruction

CMPM (Compare Memory) compares two memory operands. Address register indirect with postincrement addressing is used to address both memory operands. This facilitates the comparison of strings and multiple precision numeric values. See CMP for additional comments.

Assembler Syntax:

    CMPM. B   (An)+, (An)+
    CMPM. W   (An)+, (An)+
    CMPM. L   (An)+, (An)+

Example of CMPM:

    B308   cmpm. b (a0)+, (a1)+
    B348   cmpm. w (a0)+, (a1)+

Condition Flags Affected:

N   Set if the result is negative, otherwise cleared.

Z   Set if the result is zero, otherwise cleared.

V   Set if an overflow is generated, otherwise cleared.

C   Set if a borrow is generated, otherwise cleared.

X   Not affected.

The DIVS Instruction

DIVS (Signed Divide) divides a 32-bit destination data register operand by a 16-bit source effective address operand, and stores the result in the data register destination operand. The division is carried out for 2's complement signed binary numbers.

The quotient is stored in the lower 16 bits of the destination. The remainder is stored in the upper 16 bits of the destination operand.

Two special cases can occur during a division: a divide by zero may be attempted, causing an exception to be generated; or an overflow may occur. If an overflow occurs the overflow flag is set but the destination operand is unaffected, and execution continues normally—no exception is generated.

Assembler Syntax:

DIVS   ⟨EA⟩, Dn

Example of DIVS:

```
81FC000A    divs  #10, d0
81D0        divs  (a0), d0
```

Condition Flags Affected:

N   Set if the quotient is negative, otherwise cleared.*

Z   Set if the quotient is zero, otherwise cleared.*

V   Set if an overflow is generated, otherwise cleared.

C   Always cleared.

X   Not affected.

*N and Z flags undefined if overflow.

Addressing Modes Allowed:

Source:

Dn	(An)	(An)+
−(An)	d(An)	d(An, Xi)	xxx. W
xxx. L	d(PC)	d(PC, Xi)	#xxx

The DIVU Instruction

DIVU (Unsigned Divided) works just like DIVS except that the operation is carried out for unsigned operands. See DIVS for additional comments.

Assembler Syntax:

DIVU   ⟨EA⟩, Dn

Example of DIVU:

| 80FC000A | divu | #10, d0 |
| 80D0 | divu | (a0), d0 |

Condition Flags Affected:

N   Set if bit 15 of the quotient is set, otherwise cleared.*

Z   Set if the quotient is zero, otherwise cleared.*

V   Set if an overflow is generated, otherwise cleared.

C   Always cleared.

X   Not affected.

*N and Z flags are undefined if overflow.

Addressing Modes Allowed:

Source:

Dn		(An)	(An)+
-(An)	d(An)	d(An, Xi)	xxx. W
xxx. L	d(PC)	d(PC, Xi)	#xxx

The EXT Instruction

EXT (Extend) performs sign extension on a data register. Signs may be extended from a byte to a word (EXT. W), or from a word to a longword (EXT. L). In sign extension, the most significant bit of an operand is duplicated to the left, "promoting" the operand to the next larger data size. Sign extension preserves the sign and the absolute value of a 2's complement positive or negative number.

Assembler Syntax:

```
EXT. W    Dn
EXT. L    Dn
```

Example of EXT:

```
4880    ext. w  d0
48C0    ext. l  d0
```

Condition Flags Affected:

N   Set if the result is negative, otherwise cleared.

Z   Set if the result is zero, otherwise cleared.

V   Always cleared.

C   Always cleared.

X   Not affected.

The MULS Instruction

MULS (Signed Multiply) multiplies two 16-bit 2's complement operands (an effective address source operand and a data register destination operand) and stores the 32-bit result in the destination register. The lower 16 bits of data register operand(s) are used.

Note that overflow is not possible with this instruction.

Assembler Syntax:

```
MULS    ⟨EA⟩, Dn
```

Example of MULS:

```
C1FC000A    muls  #10, d0
C1D0        muls  (a0), d0
```

Condition Flags Affected:

N   Set if the result is negative, otherwise cleared.

Z   Set if the result is zero, otherwise cleared.

V   Set if overflow, otherwise cleared.

C   Always cleared.

X   Not affected.

Addressing Modes Allowed:

Source:

Dn	(An)	(An)+
−(An) d(An)	d(An, Xi)	xxx. W
xxx. L d(PC)	d(PC, Xi)	#xxx

The MULU Instruction

MULU (Unsigned Multiply) works just like MULS, except that the operands are 16-bit unsigned values, and the result is unsigned.

Assembler Syntax:

MULU   ⟨EA⟩, Dn

Example of MULU:

```
COFCOOOA    mulu   #10, d0
CODO        mulu   (a0), d0
```

Condition Flags Affected:

N   Set if bit 31 of the result is set, otherwise cleared.

Z   Set if the result is zero, otherwise cleared.

V   Set if overflow, otherwise cleared.

C   Always cleared.

X   Not affected.

Addressing Modes Allowed:

Source:

Dn		(An)	(An)+
−(An)	d(An)	d(An, Xi)	xxx. W
xxx. L	d(PC)	d(PC, Xi)	#xxx

The NBCD Instruction

NBCD (Negate BCD with Extend) negates the effective address BCD operand. The extend bit is included to allow the negation of multiple precision numbers in 10's complement. 10's complement works the same way and is done for the same reason you do 2's complement, only it's decimal and not binary. Note the operation of the flags; they're optimized for multiple precision operations. This is a byte operation. See ABCD for more information.

Assembler Syntax:

```
NBCD    ⟨EA⟩
```

Example of NBCD:

```
4800    nbcd  d0
4810    nbcd  (a0)
```

Condition Flags Affected:

N   Undefined.

Z   Cleared if the result is not zero, otherwise not affected.

V   Undefined.

C   Set if a decimal borrow is generated, otherwise cleared.

X   Set if a decimal borrow is generated, otherwise cleared.

Addressing Modes Allowed:

Destination:

```
Dn              (An)      (An)+
−(An)    d(An)  d(An, Xi)  xxx. W
xxx. L
```

The NEG Instruction

The NEG (Negate) instruction negates the effective address operand (makes the 2's complement) and stores the result back into the operand.

Assembler Syntax:

    NEG. B   ⟨EA⟩
    NEG. W   ⟨EA⟩
    NEG. L   ⟨EA⟩

Example of NEG:

    4480   neg. l   d0
    4450   neg. w   (a0)

Condition Flags Affected:

N Set if the result is negative, otherwise cleared.

Z Set if the result is zero, otherwise cleared.

V Set if an overflow is generated, otherwise cleared.

C Cleared if the result is zero, otherwise set.

X Cleared if the result is zero, otherwise set.

Addressing Modes Allowed:

Destination:

    Dn   (An)   (An)+
    −(An)   d(An)   d(An, Xi)   xxx. W
    xxx. L

The NEGX Instruction

NEGX (Negate with Extend) works like NEG but also includes the extend flag in the negation. Note the operation of the flags to facilitate multiple precision operations.

Assembler Syntax:

```
NEGX. B    ⟨EA⟩
NEGX. W    ⟨EA⟩
NEGX. L    ⟨EA⟩
```

Example of NEGX:

```
4080    negx. l  d0
4058    negx. w  (a0)+
```

Condition Flags Affected:

N   Set if the result is negative, otherwise cleared.

Z   Cleared if the result is not zero, otherwise not affected.

V   Set if an overflow is generated, otherwise cleared.

C   Set if a borrow is generated, otherwise cleared.

X   Set if a borrow is generated, otherwise cleared.

Addressing Modes Allowed:

Destination:

```
Dn                    (An)      (An)+
-(An)     d(An)      d(An, Xi)   xxx. W
xxx. L
```

The SBCD Instruction

SBCD (Subtract BCD with extend) subtracts the source operand and the extend flag from the destination operand, leaving the result in the destination operand. Two addressing modes are allowed for the operands, data register direct and address register indirect with predecrement. Both operands must use the same addressing mode. This is a byte operation. Note the operation of the flags, facilitating multiple precision operations. See ABCD for more information.

Assembler Syntax:

```
SBCD    Dn, Dn
SBCD    -(An),-(An)
```

Example of SBCD:

```
8300    sbcd  d0, d1
8308    sbcd  -(a0),-(a1)
```

Condition Flags Affected:

N Undefined

Z Cleared if the result is not zero, otherwise not affected.

V Undefined.

C Set if a decimal borrow is generated, otherwise cleared.

X Set if a decimal borrow is generated, otherwise cleared.

The SUB Instruction

SUB (Subtract) subtracts a source operand from a destination operand and stores the result in the destination operand. One of the operands must be a data register, the other is an effective address. This instruction operates on byte, word, and longword operands, except when an address register is used as the source, in which case byte operations are not allowed.

When an address register is required as the destination of a subtract, the SUBA instruction is used. SUBI and SUBQ are used when immediate data is the source operand for a subtraction. Most assemblers will insert the proper instruction in place of a SUB, so the SUB mnemonic may be used universally.

Assembler Syntax:

[NOTE: . s = { . B .W. L}]

SUB. s   Dn, ⟨EA⟩

SUB. s   ⟨EA⟩, Dn

Example of SUB:

90B90000FF00   sub. l $FF00, d0

91390000FF00   sub. b   d0, $FF00

Condition Flags Affected:

N   Set if the result is negative, otherwise cleared.

Z   Set if the result is zero, otherwise cleared.

V   Set if an overflow is generated, otherwise cleared.

C   Set if a borrow is generated, otherwise cleared.

X   Set if a borrow is generated, otherwise cleared.

Addressing Modes Allowed:

Source:

Dn	An	(An)	(An)+
−(An)	d(An)	d(An, Xi)	xxx. W
xxx. L	d(PC)	d(PC, Xi)	#xxx

Destination:

*Dn

		(An)	(An)+
−(An)	d(An)	d(An, xi)	xxx. W
xxx. L			

*Dn addressing technically is not allowed for the ⟨EA⟩ field, but since ⟨EA⟩ may be a source and the other operand must be a data register, the effect is the same as if it is. See Chapter 9 for the gory details.

The SUBA Instruction

SUBA (Subtract Address) works just like SUB, and in fact uses the same bit coding in the machine instruction, only the operation is restricted to word and longword operations and the flags are not affected. Word operations are sign-extended to longword before the operation, and the entire 32-bit result is placed in the destination address register.

Assembler Syntax:

```
SUBA. W    ⟨EA⟩, An
SUBA. L    ⟨EA⟩, An
```

Example of SUBA:

```
90FCFFFF    suba. w  #$FFFF, a0
91C0        suba. l  d0, a0
```

Condition Flags Affected:

None.

Addressing Modes Allowed:

Source:

Dn	An	(An)	(An)+
−(An)	d(An)	d(An, Xi)	xxx. W
xxx. L	d(PC)	d(PC, Xi)	#xxx

The SUBI Instruction

SUBI (Subtract Immediate) subtracts an immediate operand from a destination effective address operand, and stores the result in the destination operand. The operation may be byte, word or longword.

Assembler Syntax:

```
SUBI. B    #xxx, ⟨EA⟩
SUBI. W    #xxx, ⟨EA⟩
SUBI. L    #xxx, ⟨EA⟩
```

Example of SUBI:

```
53390000FF00    subi. b  #1, $FF00
558F            subi. l  #2, a7
```

Condition Flags Affected:

N   Set if the result is negative, otherwise cleared.

Z   Set if the result is zero, otherwise cleared.

V   Set if an overflow is generated, otherwise cleared.

C   Set if a borrow is generated, otherwise cleared.

X   Set if a borrow is generated, otherwise cleared.

Addressing Modes Allowed:

Destination:

Dn   (An)   (An)+

-(An)   d(An)   d(An, Xi)   xxx. W

xxx. L

The SUBQ Instruction

SUBQ (Subtract Quick) subtracts an immediate value in the range 1..8 from a destination effective address operand. Because the assembled machine instruction, including the immediate data, is only one word long, this instruction provides an efficient way to subtract small quantities from an operand. This instruction takes the place of (and extends the capabilities of) the decrement instruction found in many micro instruction sets.

The operation size may be byte, word, or longword, except when the destination operand is an address register. In this case, only word and longword operations are allowed, the flags are not affected, and the entire address register is affected even if word size is specified.

This instruction may automatically be chosen by the assembler if the operands are correct and the SUB mnemonic is used.

Assembler Syntax:

```
SUBQ. B    #xxx, ⟨EA⟩
SUBQ. W    #xxx, ⟨EA⟩
SUBQ. L    #xxx, ⟨EA⟩
```

Example of SUBQ:

```
5940    subq. w  #4, d0
558F    subq. l  #2, a7
```

Condition Flags Affected:

N   Set if the result is negative, otherwise cleared.

Z   Set if the result is zero, otherwise cleared.

V   Set if an overflow is generated, otherwise cleared.

C   Set if a borrow is generated, otherwise cleared.

X   Set if a borrow is generated, otherwise cleared.

Addressing Modes Allowed:

Destination:

Dn   An   (An)   (An)+

−(An)   d(An)   d(An, Xi)   xxx. W

xxx. L

The SUBX Instruction

SUBX (Subtract Extend) subtracts the source operand from the destination operand, along with the extend flag, and stores the result into the destination operand. This process extends the SUB instruction for multiple precision subtractions. (Note the operation of the flags to produce results valid for an entire multiple precision operation.) Two addressing modes are allowed for the operands, data register direct and address register indirect with predecrement. Both operands must use the same addressing mode.

This instruction operates on byte, word, or longword operands.

Assembler Syntax:

[NOTE: . s = { . B .W. L}]

SUBX. s   Dn, Dn

SUBX. s   −(An),−(An)

Condition Flags Affected:

N   Set if the result is negative, otherwise cleared.

Z   Cleared if the result is not zero, otherwise not affected.

V   Set if an overflow is generated, otherwise cleared.

C   Set if a borrow is generated, otherwise cleared.

X   Set if a borrow is generated, otherwise cleared.

The TAS Instruction

TAS (Test and Set) loads the byte addressed by the effective address operand, sets the N and Z flags according to the value of the byte, and then sets the high bit of the byte and returns it to the effective address from whence it came. This process is carried out using a read-modify-write (RMW) memory cycle, which does not allow the bus to be surrendered to other processors or DMA devices during the entire RMW cycle.

The intent of this instruction is to allow multiple processors using shared memory to pass information to each other. The way the scheme works is this:

Say you have a peripheral device (such as a printer) shared between two or more processors. If two processors were to output to the device simultaneously, the result would be interleaved garbage. Instead, you can set up a byte in shared memory to serve as a resource flag. When the resource is free, a zero value is stored in the byte. A processor needing the resource executes a TAS instruction on the flag. After the TAS, the byte is set non-zero, and the requesting processor's Z flag is set true, indicating that the resource now belongs to the requesting processor. A second process can then execute a TAS instruction, after which the byte will still be non-zero but the second processor's Z flag is false, indicating that the resource is busy. When the first processor is finished, it sets the flag back to zero with a MOVE or CLR instruction, freeing the resource.

If a divisible sequence, such as a MOVE-JNZ-MOVE, were used, every now and then two processors could load a zero byte from the flag before either could mark the resource as busy. This sort of thing leads to subtle and mysterious bugs and glitches which take days to duplicate themselves and weeks to debug, and which are eliminated by using the TAS instruction.

Assembler Syntax:

TAS   〈EA〉

Example of TAS:

```
4AF90000FF00     tas  $FF00
4AD0             tas  (a0)
```

Condition Flags Affected:

N   Set if the high bit of the operand is set, otherwise cleared.

Z   Set if the operand was zero, otherwise cleared.

V   Always cleared.

C   Always cleared.

X   Not affected.

Addressing Modes Allowed:

Source:

```
Dn                    (An)      (An)+
−(An)     d(An)     d(An, Xi)   xxx. W
xxx. L
```

The TST Instruction

TST (Test) subtracts zero from the effective address operand and discards the result. The flags, however, are set according to the result. This operation may be on a byte, word, or longword.

Assembler Syntax:

```
TST. B   ⟨EA⟩
TST. W   ⟨EA⟩
TST. L   ⟨EA⟩
```

Example of TST:

    4A90   tst. l (a0)

    4A00   tst. b d0

Condition Flags Affected:

    N   Set if the result is negative, otherwise cleared.

    Z   Set if the result is zero, otherwise cleared.

    V   Always cleared.

    C   Always cleared.

    X   Not affected.

Addressing Modes Allowed:

Source:

    Dn   (An)   (An)+

    −(An)   d(An)   d(An, Xi)   xxx. W

    xxx. L

5

Logical, Shift, and Rotate Instructions

The instruction group discussed in this chapter includes the ANDs, ORs, EORs, ASL, ASR, LSL, LSR, NOT, ROL, ROR, ROXL, and ROXR instructions. This group is especially useful for machine control and for optimal speed code in certain circumstances. For example, very fast multiplications and divisions by powers of 2 are accomplished using the arithmetic shifts.

The AND Instruction

AND (AND Logical) performs a logical AND on the source and destination operands and stores the result in the destination operand. One operand may be an effective address operand, and the other must be a data register. The operation may be byte, word, or longword.

Your assembler may substitute an ANDI instruction if you use the AND mnemonic and the operands are correct.

Assembler Syntax:

[NOTE: . s = { . B .W. L}]

     AND. s   ⟨EA⟩, Dn
     AND. s   Dn, ⟨EA⟩

Example of AND:

```
C07CFFBF        and. w  #$FFBF,d0
C1B90000FF00    and. l  d0, $FF00
```

Condition Flags Affected:

N   Set if the high bit of the result is set, otherwise cleared.

Z   Set if the result is zero, otherwise cleared.

V   Always cleared.

C   Always cleared.

X   Not Affected.

Addressing Modes Allowed:

Source:

Dn		(An)	(An)+
−(An)	d(An)	d(An, Xi)	xxx. W
xxx. L	d(PC)	d(PC, Xi)	#xxx

Destination:

Dn*

		(An)	(An)+
−(An)	d(An)	d(An, Xi)	xxx. W
xxx. L			

*Dn addressing technically is not allowed for the ⟨EA⟩ field, but since ⟨EA⟩ may be a source and the other operand must be a data register, the effect is the same as if it is. See Chapter 9 for the gory details.

The ANDI Instruction

ANDI (AND Immediate) ANDs the source immediate operand with an effective address destination operand and stores the result in the destination operand. The operation size may be byte, word, or longword. The assembler may allow the use of the AND mnemonic in place of the ANDI mnemonic.

Assembler Syntax:

ANDI. B   #xxx, ⟨EA⟩

ANDI. W   #xxx, ⟨EA⟩

ANDI. L   #xxx, ⟨EA⟩

Condition Flags Affected:

N   Set if the high bit of the result is set, otherwise cleared.

Z   Set if the result is zero, otherwise cleared.

V   Always cleared.

C   Always cleared.

X   Not affected.

Addressing Modes Allowed:

Destination:

Dn   (An)   (An)+

−(An)   d(An)   d(An, Xi)   xxx. W

xxx. L

The ANDI to CCR Instruction

ANDI to CCR (AND Immediate to Condition Code Register) ANDs an immediate source operand with the condition code register and stores the result into the condition code register.

The source immediate data is an 8-bit value. This instruction is normally used to reset condition code flags prior to the extended arithmetic instructions.

Assembler Syntax:

ANDI   #xxx, CCR

Condition Flags Affected:

N   Cleared if bit 3 of the source is zero, otherwise unchanged.

Z   Cleared if bit 2 of the source is zero, otherwise unchanged.

V   Cleared if bit 1 of the source is zero, otherwise unchanged.

C   Cleared if bit 0 of the source is zero, otherwise unchanged.

X   Cleared if bit 4 of the source is zero, otherwise unchanged.

The ANDI to SR Instruction

ANDI to SR (AND Immediate to Status Register) ANDs an immediate source operand with the status register and stores the result into the status register. The source immediate data is 16 bits.

This is a privileged instruction and may only be successfully executed if the processor is in supervisor state. If the processor is in user state and this instruction is attempted, a privilege violation exception is generated.

This instruction is normally used to clear the trace and supervisor bits, or the interrupt mask, without affecting the rest of the processor status bits.

Assembler Syntax:

ANDI   #xxx, SR

Condition Flags Affected:

N   Cleared if bit 3 of the source is zero, otherwise unchanged.

Z   Cleared if bit 2 of the source is zero, otherwise unchanged.

V   Cleared if bit 1 of the source is zero, otherwise unchanged.

C   Cleared if bit 0 of the source is zero, otherwise unchanged.

X   Cleared if bit 4 of the source is zero, otherwise unchanged.

The ASL and ASR Instructions

ASL (Arithmetic Shift Left) and ASR (Arithmetic Shift Right) shift the destination operand by either 1 or by a count in the indicated direction. If a shift count is specified it takes the position of the source operand in the assembler source. The count may be an immediate value in the range 1..8 or it may be a value of any size contained in a data register. For memory based effective address operands the shift count is always one, and the operation size must be word.

When shifting Arithmetic Right, the sign bit of the operand is duplicated and shifted into the left end of the operand. The bit in the right end of the operand is shifted into the carry flag and extend flag. If the shift count is more than one, the operation is repeated, and the last bit shifted out of the right end of the destination operand is in the carry and extend flags.

When shifting Arithmetic Left, zeros are shifted into the right end of the operand, and the bit shifted out of the left end of the operand is duplicated in the carry and extend flags. If the shift count is more than one the last bit shifted out ends up in the extend and carry flags.

For either right or left shifts, if the shift count is zero the carry flag is cleared and the extend flag is not affected. Operation size may be specified to be byte, word, or longword for register operands.

This instruction is normally used in strength-reduction optimizations. ("Strength-reduction" is the replacement of a general-purpose instruction with a faster, less general instruction that does the same thing in a specific case.) For example, a divide by the constant 2 can be replaced with an arithmetic shift right. The right-shift operation preserves the sign of the operand. Note that there is no difference between a logical shift left and an arithmetic shift left except for the behavior of the V (overflow) flag.

Assembler Syntax:

[NOTE: . s = { . B .W. L}]

```
ASL. s     Dn, Dn
ASL. s     #xxx, Dn
ASL. W     ⟨EA⟩
```

Assembler Syntax:

ASR. s   Dn, Dn

ASR. s   #xxx, Dn

ASR. W   ⟨EA⟩

Condition Flags Affected:

N Set if the high bit of the result is set, otherwise cleared.

Z Set if the result is zero, otherwise cleared.

V Set if the high bit changes anytime during the operation, otherwise cleared.

C Set to the last bit shifted out of the operand. Cleared if the shift count was zero.

X Set to the last bit shifted out of the operand. Unaffected if the shift count was zero.

Addressing Modes Allowed:

Destination:

               (An)   (An)+

−(An)   d(An)   d(An, Xi) xxx. W

xxx. L

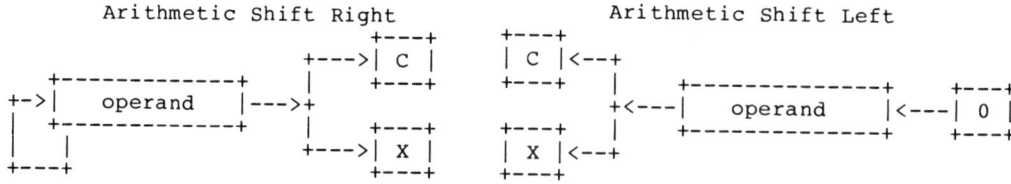

The EOR Instruction

EOR (Exclusive OR) exclusive-ORs the source operand with the destination operand and stores the result into the destination operand. The source operand must be a data register. Memory to data register exclusive OR operations are not allowed in the 68000. The assembler may use this instruction's mnemonic to generate an EORI instruction if immediate data is specified as the source operand. Byte, word, and longword sizes may be specified for this operation.

EORs are normally used to selectively invert bits in the destination operand.

Assembler Syntax:

EOR. B   Dn, ⟨EA⟩

EOR. W   Dn, ⟨EA⟩

EOR. L   Dn, ⟨EA⟩

Condition Flags Affected:

N   Set if the high bit of the result is set, otherwise cleared.

Z   Set if the result is zero, otherwise cleared.

V   Always cleared.

C   Always cleared.

X   Not affected.

Addressing Modes Allowed:

Destination:

Dn   (An)   (An)+

−(An)   d(An)   d(An, Xi)   xxx. W

xxx. L

The EORI Instruction

EORI (Exclusive OR Immediate) exclusive-ORs a source immediate operand with a destination effective address operand and stores the result in the effective address operand. Byte, word, and longword sizes may be specified. This instruction may be chosen by your assembler if an EOR mnemonic is used with the proper operands.

Assembler Syntax:

EORI. B   #xxx, ⟨EA⟩

EORI. W   #xxx, ⟨EA⟩

EORI. L   #xxx, ⟨EA⟩

Condition Flags Affected:

N   Set if the high bit of the result is set, otherwise cleared.

Z   Set if the result is zero, otherwise cleared.

V   Always cleared.

C   Always cleared.

X   Not affected.

Addressing Modes Allowed:

Destination:

Dn		(An)	(An)+
−(An)	d(An)	d(An, Xi)	xxx. W
xxx. L			

The EORI to CCR Instruction

EORI to CCR (Exclusive OR Immediate to Condition Code Register) exclusive-ORs a source immediate operand with the CCR and stores the result in the CCR. This is a byte operation.

Assembler Syntax:

```
EORI    #xxx, CCR
```

Condition Flags Affected:

N   Inverted if bit 3 of the source is 1, otherwise unchanged.

Z   Inverted if bit 2 of the source is 1, otherwise unchanged.

V   Inverted if bit 1 of the source is 1, otherwise unchanged.

C   Inverted if bit 0 of the source is 1, otherwise unchanged.

X   Inverted if bit 4 of the source is 1, otherwise unchanged.

The EORI to SR Instruction

EORI to SR (Exclusive OR Immediate to Status Register) exclusive-ORs a source immediate operand with the status register and stores the result in the status register. This is a word size operation.

This is a privileged instruction; the processor must be operating in supervisor state to successfully execute this instruction. If the processor is in user state and this instruction is executed, a privilege violation exception will be generated.

Assembler Syntax:

```
EORI    #xxx, CCR
```

Condition Flags Affected:

N   Inverted if bit 3 of the source is 1, otherwise unchanged.

Z   Inverted if bit 2 of the source is 1, otherwise unchanged.

V   Inverted if bit 1 of the source is 1, otherwise unchanged.

C   Inverted if bit 0 of the source is 1, otherwise unchanged.

X   Inverted if bit 4 of the source is 1, otherwise unchanged.

The LSL and LSR Instructions

LSL (Logic Shift Left) and LSR (Logic Shift Right) shift the destination operand by either 1 or by a count in the indicated direction. If a count is specified it takes the position of the source operand in the assembler syntax. The count may be an immediate value in the range 1..8 or it may be a value of any size contained in a data register. For memory based effective address operands the shift count is always 1 and the operation size must be word.

When shifting logic right, zeros are shifted into the left end of the operand, and the bit shifted out of the right end of the operand is duplicated in the carry and extend flags. If the shift count is more than one, the operation is repeated, and the last bit shifted out of the right end of the destination operand is in the carry and extend flags.

When shifting logic left, zeros are shifted into the right end of the operand, and the bit shifted out of the left end of the operand is duplicated in the carry and extend flags. If the shift count is more than one, the last bit shifted out ends up in the extend and carry flags.

For either right or left shifts, if the shift count is zero, the carry flag is cleared and the extend flag is not affected. Operation size may be specified to be byte, word, or longword if a data register is the destination operand.

This instruction is normally used for machine-control types of operations (such as graphics). For arithmetic strength-reduction, the arithmetic shifts are normally used.

Assembler Syntax:

[NOTE: . s = { . B .W. L}]

LSL. s   Dn, Dn

LSL. s   #xxx, Dn

LSL. W   ⟨EA⟩

Assembler Syntax:

LSR. s   Dn, Dn

LSR. s   #xxx, Dn

LSR. W   ⟨EA⟩

Condition Flags Affected:

N   Set if the high bit of the result is set, otherwise cleared.

Z   Set if the result is zero, otherwise cleared.

V   Always cleared.

C   Set to the last bit shifted out of the operand. Cleared if the shift count was zero.

X   Set to the last bit shifted out of the operand. Unaffected if the shift count was zero.

Addressing Modes Allowed:

Destination:

```
                    (An)        (An)+
  -(An)     d(An)    d(An, Xi)    xxx. W
  xxx. L
```

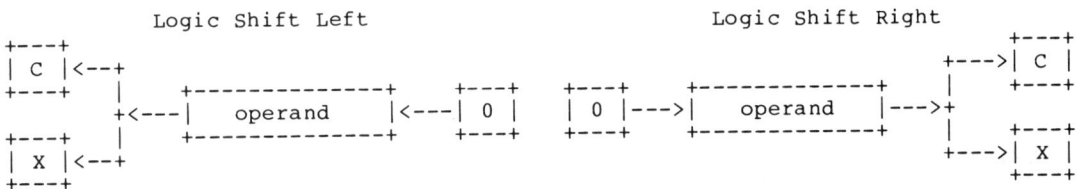

The NOT Instruction

NOT (Logical NOT) takes the 1's complement of the effective source operand and stores the result back in the effective address operand. This instruction is commonly used to invert masks. Two's complement operations are normally done with the NEG and NEGX instructions.

Assembler Syntax:

```
NOT. B    ⟨EA⟩
NOT. W    ⟨EA⟩
NOT. L    ⟨EA⟩
```

Condition Flags Affected:

N   Set if the result is negative, otherwise cleared.

Z   Set if the result is zero, otherwise cleared.

V   Always cleared.

C   Always cleared.

X   Not affected.

Addressing Modes Allowed:

Source:

Dn		(An)	(An)+
−(An)	d(An)	d(An, Xi)	xxx. W
xxx. L			

The OR Instruction

The OR instruction ORs a source operand with a destination operand and stores the result in the destination operand. One of the operands must be a data register, the other operand is an effective address operand. Byte, word, or longword operands may be specified. Your assembler may select the ORI instruction if you use the OR mnemonic and the operands are correct.

Assembler Syntax:

[NOTE: . s = { . B .W. L}]

OR. s   Dn, ⟨EA⟩

OR. s   ⟨EA⟩, Dn

Condition Flags Affected:

N   Set if the high bit of the result is set, otherwise cleared.

Z   Set if the result is zero, otherwise cleared.

V   Always cleared.

C   Always cleared.

X   Not affected.

Addressing Modes Allowed:

Source:

Dn		(An)	(An)+
−(An)	d(An)	d(An, Xi)	xxx. W
xxx. L	d(PC)	d(PC, Xi)	#xxx

Destination:

Dn*

		(An)	(An)+
−(An)	d(An)	d(An, Xi)	xxx. W
xxx. L			

*Dn addressing technically is not allowed for the ⟨EA⟩ field, but since ⟨EA⟩ may be a source and the other operand must be a data register, the effect is the same as if it is. See Chapter 9 for the gory details.

The ORI Instruction

ORI (Or Immediate) ORs an immediate source operand with an effective address destination operand and stores the result into the destination operand. The operation may be byte, word, or longword size. Your assembler may select this instruction if you use an OR mnemonic and the operands are correct.

Assembler Syntax:

ORI. B   #xxx, ⟨EA⟩

ORI. W   #xxx, ⟨EA⟩

ORI. L   #xxx, ⟨EA⟩

Condition Flags Affected:

N   Set if the high bit of the result is set, otherwise cleared.

Z   Set if the result is zero, otherwise cleared.

V   Always cleared.

C   Always cleared.

X   Not affected.

Addressing Modes Allowed:

Destination:

Dn   (An)   (An)+

−(An)   d(An)   d(An, Xi)   xxx. W

xxx. L

The ORI to CCR Instruction

ORI to CCR (OR Immediate to Condition Code Register) ORs an immediate source operand with the CCR and stores the result into the CCR. This is a byte operation. This instruction is normally used to set one or more of the condition flags without affecting the other flags.

Assembler Syntax:

ORI   #xxx, CCR

Condition Flags Affected:

N Set if bit 3 of the source operand is 1, otherwise unchanged.

Z Set if bit 2 of the source operand is 1, otherwise unchanged.

V Set if bit 1 of the source operand is 1, otherwise unchanged.

C Set if bit 0 of the source operand is 1, otherwise unchanged.

X Set if bit 4 of the source operand is 1, otherwise unchanged.

The ORI to SR Instruction

ORI to SR (OR Immediate to Status Register) ORs an immediate source operand with the status register and stores the result back into the status register. This is a word operation.

ORI to SR is a privileged instruction. The processor must be operating in supervisor mode to successfully execute this instruction. If the processor is in user mode and you attempt to execute this instruction, a privilege violation exception will be generated.

This instruction is normally used to modify the interrupt register without affecting the other privileged status bits.

Assembler Syntax:

ORI   #xxx, SR

Condition Flags Affected:

N Set if bit 3 of the source operand is 1, otherwise unchanged.

Z Set if bit 2 of the source operand is 1, otherwise unchanged.

V Set if bit 1 of the source operand is 1, otherwise unchanged.

C Set if bit 0 of the source operand is 1, otherwise unchanged.

X Set if bit 4 of the source operand is 1, otherwise unchanged.

The ROR and ROL Instructions

ROR (Rotate Right) and ROL (Rotate Left) rotate the bits of the destination operand in the specified direction. If the operand is in memory, a rotation of one is allowed, and the operand size must be word. If the destination operand is a data register, a rotate count may be specified in two ways: by an immediate count in the range 1..8, or by a count of any size contained in another data register. Data register destination operands may be specified to be byte, word, or longword.

For ROR, the bit shifted out of the low order position is fed back into the high order position and is also placed in the carry flag. If the shift count is more than one, the operation is repeated and the last bit shifted out of the low order position is left in the carry flag. If the shift count is zero, the carry flag is cleared.

For ROL, the bit shifted out off the high order position is fed back into the low order position and is also placed into the carry flag. If the shift count is more than one, the operation is repeated and the last bit shifted out of the high order position is left in the carry flag. If the shift count is zero, the carry flag is cleared.

Assembler Syntax:

[NOTE: . s = { . B .W. L}]

> ROL. s   Dn, Dn
>
> ROL. s   #xxx, Dn
>
> ROL. W   ⟨EA⟩

Assembler Syntax:

[NOTE: . s = { . B .W. L}]

> ROR. s   Dn, Dn
>
> ROR. s   #xxx, Dn
>
> ROR. W   ⟨EA⟩

Condition Flags Affected:

> N   Set if the high bit of the result is set, otherwise cleared.
>
> Z   Set if the result is zero, otherwise cleared.

V   Always cleared.

C   Set to the last bit shifted out of the operand. Cleared if the shift count was zero.

X   Not affected.

Addressing Modes Allowed:

Destination:

		(An)	(An)+
-(An)	d(An)	d(An, Xi)	xxx. W
xxx. L			

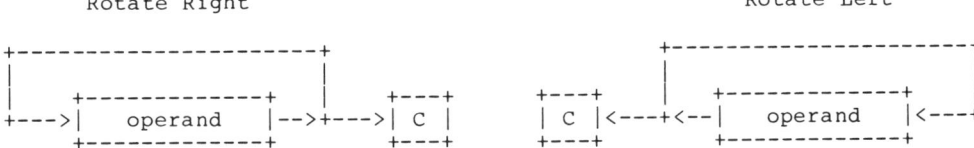

The ROXR and ROXL Instructions

ROXR (Rotate Right with extend) and ROXL (Rotate Left with extend) rotate the bits of the destination operand through the extend flag in the specified direction. If the operand is in memory, a rotation of one is allowed, and the operation size must be word. If the destination operand is a data register, a rotate count may be specified in two ways: by an immediate count in the range 1..8, or by a count of any size contained in another data register. Data register destination operands may be specified to be byte, word, or longword.

For ROXR, the bit shifted out of the low order position is fed into the extend flag and the carry flag and the previous extend flag is fed back into the high order position of the destination operand. If the shift count is more than one, the operation is repeated and the last bit shifted out of the low order position is left in the extend and carry flags. If the shift count is zero, the carry flag is cleared and the extend flag is unchanged.

For ROXL, the bit shifted out of the high order position is fed into the extend and carry flags and the previous contents of the extend flag is fed back into the low order position of the destination operand. If the shift count is more than one, the operation is repeated and the last bit shifted out of the high order position is left in the carry and extend flags. If the shift count is zero, the carry flag is cleared and the extend flag is unaffected.

Assembler Syntax:

[NOTE: . s = { . B .W. L}]

ROXL. s   Dn, Dn

ROXL. s   #xxx, Dn

ROXL. W   ⟨EA⟩

Assembler Syntax:

ROXR. s   Dn, Dn

ROXR. s   #xxx, Dn

ROXR. W   ⟨EA⟩

Condition Flags Affected:

N   Set if the high bit of the result is set, otherwise cleared.

Z   Set if the result is zero, otherwise cleared.

V   Always cleared.

C   Set to the last bit shifted out of the operand. Set to the previous value of the extend flag if the shift count was zero.

X   Set to the last bit shifted out of the operand. Not affected if the shift count was zero.

Addressing Modes Allowed:

Destination:

	(An)	(An)+
−(An) d(An)	d(An, Xi)	xxx. W

xxx. L

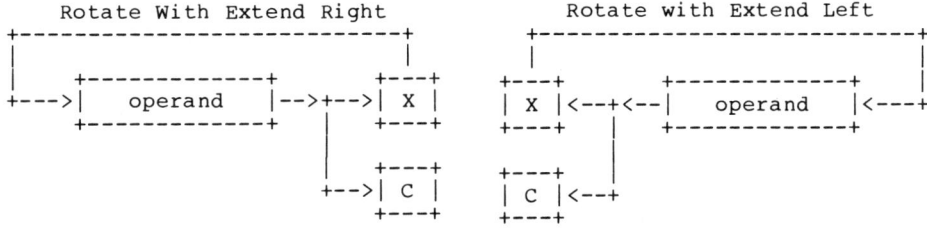

6

Conditional, Branch, and Trap Instructions

The instruction group discussed in this chapter includes the Bcc, BRA, DBcc, CHK, Scc, BSR, JSR, RTS, RTR, TRAP, TRAPV, and JMP instructions. This group provides the decision-making capability of the computer.

The Bcc Instruction

Bcc (Branch Conditionally) causes a branch if the condition specified is true. See Figure 6-2 for mnemonics and Boolean equations for the conditions. (Example: BCS = Branch Carry Set.) Bcc is a relative branch instruction, and the maximum range of the branch is +32767 to −32768, measured from the opcode + 2. A branch range of +127 to −128 can be optimized by the assembler into a one-word instruction instead of the normal two words. The implementation of this optimization in the 68000 makes it impossible to branch to the instruction immediately following the conditional branch. (Big deal.)

Assembler Syntax:

    Bcc   〈label〉

Example of Bcc

    6764   beq   label 1
    6E62   bgt   label 2

Condition Flags Affected:

None.

The BRA Instruction

BRA (Branch Always) causes program execution to continue at a specified location. This is a relative branch instruction, and the maximum range of the branch is +32767 to −32768, measured from the opcode + 2. A branch range of +127 to −128 can be optimized by the assembler into a one-word instruction instead of the normal two words. The implementation of this optimization in the 68000 makes it impossible to branch to the instruction following the BRA instruction.

Your assembler may allow the BT (Branch True) mnemonic to be used interchangeably with BRA.

Assembler Syntax:

```
BRA    ⟨label⟩
```


Example of BRA:

```
6060    bra   label 3
```


Condition Flags Affected:

None.

The BSR Instruction

BSR (Branch to Subroutine) causes a branch to the specified subroutine. A return address is pushed on the hardware stack. This is a relative branch instruction, and the maximum range of the branch is +32767 to −32768, measured from the opcode + 2. A branch range of +127 to −128 can be optimized by the assembler into a one-word instruction instead of the normal two words. The implementation of this optimization in the 68000 makes it impossible to branch to the following instruction.

Assembler Syntax:

```
BSR    ⟨label⟩
```

Example of BSR:

```
615E    bsr   label 4
```

Condition Flags Affected:

None.

The CHK Instruction

CHK (Check register against bounds) checks the value of the destination data register against an upper bound addressed by a source effective address operand. If the data register lower word (this is a word size operation only) is less than zero or greater than the source effective address operand, a CHK exception is generated. Note that the flags can get trashed either way.

This instruction is intended to facilitate error checking in high order languages. For example, some high order languages require bounds checking on array indices and on the values of numeric types. The upper bound is stored somewhere in memory and is referenced by a CHK instruction whenever an object of one of these types is modified, or the index of an array is checked just before each array access.

Assembler Syntax:

```
CHK    ⟨EA⟩, Dn
```

Example of CHK:

```
41BC000A        chk  #10, d0
41B90000FF00    chk  $FF00, d0
```

Condition Flags Affected:

N Set if Dn.W is less than O, cleared if Dn.W is greater than $\langle EA \rangle$, otherwise undefined.

Z Undefined.

V Undefined.

C Undefined.

X Not affected.

Addressing Modes Allowed:

Source:

Dn		(An)	(An)+
−(An)	d(An)	d(An, xi)	xxx. W
xxx. L	d(PC)	d(PC, xi)	#xxx

The DBcc Instruction

DBcc (Test, Decrement, and Branch) is a loop termination instruction. The condition specified as "cc" (see Figure 6-2 on page 92) is tested, and if true, the loop falls through to the next instruction. If not true, the lower 16 bits of a specified data register are decremented. If the result is −1, the loop also falls through. If neither termination condition is met, a branch is taken to the specified location. This is a relative branch; the range is +32767 to −32768, measured from the opcode +2. A simple decrement-and-branch is coded DBF. Your assembler may recognize the DBRA mnemonic as a synonym for DBF.

If the loop is entered by branching to the DBcc instruction, the data register count will equal the number of loop iterations. If a loop is entered by falling into the loop at the top, the data register count should be one less than the desired number of iterations. (See Figure 6-1.)

Assembler Syntax:

    DBcc   Dn, ⟨label⟩

Example of DBcc:

```
51C8005C    dbf    dO, label 5
57C80058    dbeq   dO, label 6
```

Condition Flags Affected:

None.

```
**********************************************************************
* Example of loop where D0 = number of desired iterations:
        <execution falls into loop from here>
        BRA         LOOP_TEST      * start by jumping to loop test
LOOP_TOP:
        <loop body goes here>
LOOP_TEST:
        DBRA        D0,LOOP_TOP    * loop test
**********************************************************************
* Example of loop where D0 = number of iterations minus one
        <execution falls into loop from here>
LOOP_TOP2:
        <loop body goes here>
        DBRA        D0,LOOP_TOP2   * loop test
**********************************************************************
```

FIGURE 6-1:   Loop Test

The JMP Instruction

JMP (Jump) causes execution to continue at an effective address operand. Most often you'll be using an absolute long effective address, but very effective use can be made of the other addressing modes allowed.

The BRA instruction is most often used for unconditional jumps, because the BRA instruction is a relative jump, as opposed to the absolute jump of JMP. It is much easier to relocate a BRA-addressed module than a JMP-addressed module.

Assembler Syntax

```
JMP    〈EA〉
```

Example of JMP:

```
4EF9000001E8    jmp   label 7
4ED0            jmp   (a0)
```

Condition Flags Affected:

None.

Addressing Modes Allowed:

		(An)	
	d(An)	d(An, Xi)	xxx. W
xxx. L	d(PC)	d(PC, Xi)	

The JSR Instruction

JSR (Jump to Subroutine) pushes a return address on the hardware stack and then jumps to the effective address operand. Most often you'll be using an absolute long effective address, but very effective use can be made of the other addressing modes allowed.

The BSR instruction is normally used instead of the JSR instruction because it is relative, as opposed to the absolute address of the JSR instruction.

Assembler Syntax:

```
JSR    ⟨EA⟩
```

Example of JSR:

```
6142    jsr  label 8
4E90    jsr  (a0)
```

Condition Flags Affected:

None.

Addressing Modes Allowed:

	(An)	
d(An)	d(An, xi)	xxx. W
xxx. L	d(PC)	d(PC, xi)

The RTR Instruction

RTR (Return and Restore CCR) pops the condition codes and a return address from the stack, in that order. The supervisor portion of the status register is unaffected.

Assembler Syntax:

```
RTR
```

Example of RTR:

```
4E77    rtr
```

Condition Flags Affected:

Set to the word pulled from the stack.

The Scc Instruction

Scc (Set According to Condition) checks the condition flags for the specified condition (see Figure 6-2), and if true, the byte specified by the effective address operand is set to all ones, otherwise the byte is set to all zeros. The effective address operand is byte size only.

Note: A memory destination operand is read before being written (RMW cycle), which in obscure cases could cause problems.

Assembler Syntax:

```
Scc    ⟨EA⟩
```

```
        Mnemonic              Equation
        --------              --------

CC    carry clear         $\overline{C}$

CS    carry set           C

EQ    equal               Z

GE    greater/equal       $N*V + \overline{N}*\overline{V}$

GT    greater than        $N*V*\overline{Z} + \overline{N}*\overline{V}*\overline{Z}$

HI    high                $\overline{C}*\overline{Z}$

LE    less/equal          $Z + N*\overline{V} + \overline{N}*V$

LS    low or same         C + Z

LT    less than           $N*\overline{V} + \overline{N}*V$

MI    minus               N

NE    not equal           $\overline{Z}$

PL    plus                $\overline{N}$

VC    overflow clear      $\overline{V}$

VS    overflow set        V

T     true                1

F*    false               0

V = Overflow Flag        C = Carry Flag
N = Negative Flag        Z = Zero Flag

*"F" not allowed for Bcc instruction.
```

FIGURE 6-2.   Condition Code Mnemonics and Equations

Example of Scc:

```
57D0              seq  (A0)
5DF90000F00       slt  $FF00
```

Condition Flags Affected:

None.

Addressing Modes Allowed:

Destination:

```
Dn              (An)        (An)+
-(An)   d(An)   d(An, Xi)   xxx. W
xxx. L
```

The RTS Instruction

RTS (Return from Subroutine) pops a return address from the stack. This instruction is used to return from a subroutine.

Assembler Syntax:

```
RTS
```

Example of RTS:

```
4E75    rts
```

Condition Flags Affected:

None.

The TRAP Instruction

TRAP causes an exception, which is vectored to one of the sixteen TRAP vectors. This instruction is normally used to initiate an operating system service call.

Assembler Syntax:

```
TRAP    #xxx
```

Example of TRAP:

```
4E41    TRAP  #1
```

Condition Flags Affected:

None.

The TRAPV Instruction

TRAPV causes the TRAPV exception to be generated if the overflow (V) flag is set. If the flag is not set, no action is taken. This instruction facilitates high level language runtime support.

Assembler Syntax:

TRAPV

Example of TRAPV:

```
4E76    trapv
```

Condition Flags Affected:

None.

7

Bit Instructions

The group of instructions discussed in this chapter includes BTST, BSET, BCLR, and BCHG. These provide the four basic bit manipulation operations. The term "source count," as used below, indicates a static or dynamic number that references a given bit within an operand. Bits are numbered with bit zero being the least significant bit. For example, a source count of "4" in a bit instruction indicates an operation to be performed in bit 4 of the operand.

The BCHG Instruction

BCHG (Test Bit and Change) tests the bit pointed to by the source operand in the destination effective address operand, setting the zero flag to the opposite state (if the bit is zero, the zero flag is set TRUE, or one). The addressed bit is then inverted and placed back into the destination operand.

The source count may be immediate data (a "static" count), or it may be taken from a data register (a "dynamic" count). If a data register is the destination operand, the source count is taken mod 32, allowing any of the 32 bits of the data register to be tested and modified. If the destination is a memory operand, only a byte may be addressed, and the source count is taken mod 8.

Assembler Syntax:

```
BCHG    Dn, ⟨EA⟩
BCHG    #xxx, ⟨EA⟩
```

Example of BCHG:

```
0141                    bchg   d0, d1
087900020000FF00        bchg   #2, $FF00
```

Condition Flags Affected:

N   Not affected.

Z   Set if the bit tested is zero, otherwise cleared.

V   Not affected.

C   Not affected.

X   Not affected.

Addressing Modes Allowed:

Destination:

Dn		(An)	(An)+
−(An)	d(An)	d(An, Xi)	xxx. W
xxx. L			

The BCLR Instruction

BCLR (Test Bit and Clear) tests the bit pointed to by the source operand in the destination effective address operand, setting the zero flag to the opposite state (if the bit is zero, the zero flag is set TRUE, or one). The addressed bit is then cleared and placed back into the destination operand.

The source count may be immediate data (a "static" count), or it may be taken from a data register (a "dynamic" count). If a data register is the destination operand, the source count is taken mod 32, allowing any of the 32 bits of the data register to be tested and modified. If the destination is a memory operand, only a byte may be addressed, and the source count is taken mod 8.

Assembler Syntax:

    BCLR   Dn, ⟨EA⟩
    BCLR   #xxx, ⟨EA⟩

Example of BCLR:

    0181   bclr   d0, d1
    08B900020000FF00   bclr   #2, $FF00

Condition Flags Affected:

N   Not affected.

Z   Set if the bit tested is zero, otherwise cleared.

V   Not affected.

C   Not affected.

X   Not affected.

Addressing Modes Allowed:

Destination:

    Dn   (An)   (An)+
    −(An)   d(An)   d(An, Xi)   xxx. W
    xxx. L

The BSET Instruction

BSET (Test Bit and Set) tests the bit pointed to by the source operand in the destination effective address operand, setting the zero flag to the opposite state (if the bit is zero, the zero flag is set TRUE, or one). The addressed bit is then set to one and placed back into the destination operand.

The source count may be immediate data (a "static" count), or it may be taken from a data register (a "dynamic" count). If a data register is the destination operand, the source count is taken mod 32, allowing any of the 32 bits of the data register to be tested and modified. If the destination is a memory operand, only a byte may be addressed, and the source count is taken mod 8.

Assembler Syntax:

```
BSET    Dn,⟨EA⟩
BSET    #xxx,⟨EA⟩
```

Example of BSET:

```
01C1                    bset  d0, d1
08F900020000FF00        bset  #2, $FF00
```

Condition Flags Affected:

N   Not affected.

Z   Set if the bit tested is zero, otherwise cleared.

V   Not affected.

C   Not affected.

X   Not affected.

Addressing Modes Allowed:

Destination:

```
Dn              (An)      (An)+
-(An)    d(An)  d(An, Xi)  xxx. W
xxx. L
```

The BTST Instruction

BTST (Test Bit) tests the bit pointed to by the source operand in the destination effective address operand, setting the zero flag to the opposite state (if the bit is zero, the zero flag is set TRUE, or one).

The source count may be immediate data (a "static" count), or it may be taken from a data register (a "dynamic" count). If a data register is the destination operand, the source count is taken mod 32, allowing any of the 32 bits of the data register to be tested and modified. If the destination is a memory operand, only a byte may be addressed, and the source count is taken mod 8.

Assembler Syntax:

```
BTST    Dn, ⟨EA⟩
BTST    #xxx, ⟨EA⟩
```

Example of BTST:

```
0101                    btst  d0, d1
083900020000FF00        btst  #2, $FF00
```

Condition Flags Affected:

N   Not affected.

Z   Set if the bit tested is zero, otherwise cleared.

V   Not affected.

C   Not affected.

X   Not affected.

Addressing Modes Allowed:

Destination:

Dn	(An)	(An)+
−(An) d(An)	d(An, Xi)	xxx. W
xxx. L d(PC)	d(PC, xi)	

8

Miscellaneous Instructions

The group of instructions discussed here includes the RESET, RTE, and STOP. These instruction are restricted to use in supervisor mode.

The RESET Instruction

RESET causes the external RESET hardware line to be asserted, resetting all the external devices (assuming the hardware designer hooked things up properly). The processor itself is not reset, and continues processing.

This is a privileged instruction.

Assembler Syntax:

    RESET

Example of RESET:

    4E70   reset

Condition Flags Affected:

None.

The RTE Instruction

RTE (Return from Exception) pops the status register and a return address from the supervisor stack, in that order. This instruction is a privileged instruction. Executing this instruction may place the machine into user state, depending on the value of the status word on the stack. This instruction is normally used when returning from an exception handler.

Assembler Syntax:

    RTE

Example of RTE:

    4E73   rte

Condition Flags Affected:

Set to the word popped from the stack.

The STOP Instruction

STOP loads its immediate operand into the status register, the PC is advanced to the next instruction, and the processor halts. Processing resumes if a trace, interrupt, or reset exception occurs.

A trace exception will be generated if the trace flag was set before the execution of the instruction. An interrupt exception will occur if an external interrupt is asserted with a priority higher than the priority loaded into the interrupt mask. An external reset will always get things cranking again.

This is a privileged instruction, and a privilege violation exception will occur if the processor was not in supervisor mode before the STOP is executed, or if the bit in the immediate data corresponding to the S flag is not set.

This instruction has a fairly limited number of uses. Because the processor stops fetching and executing instructions, this may lower system power consumption. It can also be used to await an interrupt with a very low tolerable latency.

Assembler Syntax:

```
STOP    #xxx
```

Example of STOP:

```
4E720000    stop  #0
```

Condition Flags Affected:

Set to the source immediate operand.

9
The Nitty-Gritty Details

In this chapter, we'll examine the details of how 68000 instructions are bit-coded. We'll also take a quick look at the execution timing of the instructions. This sort of stuff makes for dull reading for all but the hardest-core assembly language fanatic, unless you plan on writing a code generator or disassembler. Nobody will be offended if you skip this chapter, or just refer to the tables on an as-needed basis.

With that out of the way, let's dive in. The op code for all 68000 instructions is coded in the upper 4 bits of the operation word. This allows for sixteen op codes, two of which are not used and are reserved for future expansion (and actually are used in the 68020). The instruction set is distributed among the remaining fourteen op codes as shown in Figure 9.1.

As we've mentioned, the instruction set is very regular, and this is reflected in the general regularity of the bit-coding.

Some general comments:

- If an effective address is used, the mode and register bits are always in bits 5 through 0 of the instruction word.
- If a second register appears in an instruction, it is always coded in bits 11 through 9. If 3-bit immediate data (shift counts, bit numbers, quick data) appear in an instruction, they are also coded in bits 11 through 9.
- If an operation size that includes the three possibilities byte, word, and longword is encoded, it is always coded in bits 7 and 6, with the exception of MOVE.s, where the size is encoded in the op code. This size field is often coded with 11 to indicate an "escape" to another instruction type.
- Condition codes (Figure 9-2) are always coded in bits 11 through 8.

	15	14	13	12	11	10	9	8	7	6	5	4	3	2	1	0
ORI	0	0	0	0	0	0	0	0	size		EA-mode			EA-reg-		
ANDI	0	0	0	0	0	0	1	0	size		EA-mode			EA-reg-		
SUBI	0	0	0	0	0	1	0	0	size		EA-mode			EA-reg-		
ADDI	0	0	0	0	0	1	1	0	size		EA-mode			EA-reg-		
EORI	0	0	0	0	1	0	1	0	size		EA-mode			EA-reg-		
CMPI	0	0	0	0	1	1	0	0	size		EA-mode			EA-reg-		
BTST	0	0	0	0	-Dreg--			1	0	0	EA-mode			EA-reg-		
BTST	0	0	0	0	1	0	0	0	0	0	EA-mode			EA-reg-		
BCHG	0	0	0	0	-Dreg--			1	0	1	EA-mode			EA-reg-		
BCHG	0	0	0	0	1	0	0	0	0	1	EA-mode			EA-reg-		
BCLR	0	0	0	0	-Dreg--			1	1	0	EA-mode			EA-reg-		
BCLR	0	0	0	0	1	0	0	0	1	0	EA-mode			EA-reg-		
BSET	0	0	0	0	-Dreg--			1	1	1	EA-mode			EA-reg-		
BSET	0	0	0	0	1	0	0	0	1	1	EA-mode			EA-reg-		
MOVEP	0	0	0	0	-Dreg--			1	X	S	0	0	1	-Areg--		
MOVE.B	0	0	0	1	EA-reg-			EA-mode			EA-mode			EA-reg-		
MOVE.L	0	0	1	0	EA-reg-			EA-mode			EA-mode			EA-reg-		
MOVE.W	0	0	1	1	EA-reg-			EA-mode			EA-mode			EA-reg-		
NEGX	0	1	0	0	0	0	0	0	size		EA-mode			EA-reg-		
MOVE<SR	0	1	0	0	0	0	0	0	1	1	EA-mode			EA-reg-		
CLR	0	1	0	0	0	0	1	0	size		EA-mode			EA-reg-		
NEG	0	1	0	0	0	1	0	0	size		EA-mode			EA-reg-		
MOVECCR	0	1	0	0	0	1	0	0	1	1	EA-mode			EA-reg-		
NOT	0	1	0	0	0	1	1	0	size		EA-mode			EA-reg-		
MOVE>SR	0	1	0	0	0	1	1	0	1	1	EA-mode			EA-reg-		
NBCD	0	1	0	0	1	0	0	0	0	0	EA-mode			EA-reg-		
SWAP	0	1	0	0	1	0	0	0	0	1	0	0	0	-Dreg--		
PEA	0	1	0	0	1	0	0	0	0	1	EA-mode			EA-reg-		
EXT	0	1	0	0	1	0	0	0	1	S	0	0	0	-Dreg--		
MOVEM	0	1	0	0	1	A	0	0	1	S	EA-mode			EA-reg-		
TST	0	1	0	0	1	0	1	0	size		EA-mode			EA-reg-		
TAS	0	1	0	0	1	0	1	0	1	1	EA-mode			EA-reg-		
ILLEGAL	0	1	0	0	1	0	1	0	1	1	1	1	1	1	0	0
TRAP	0	1	0	0	1	1	1	0	0	1	0	0	--vector--			
LINK	0	1	0	0	1	1	1	0	0	1	0	1	0	-Areg--		
UNLK	0	1	0	0	1	1	1	0	0	1	0	1	1	-Areg--		
MOVEUSP	0	1	0	0	1	1	1	0	0	1	1	0	T	-Areg--		
RESET	0	1	0	0	1	1	1	0	0	1	1	1	0	0	0	0
NOP	0	1	0	0	1	1	1	0	0	1	1	1	0	0	0	1
STOP	0	1	0	0	1	1	1	0	0	1	1	1	0	0	1	0
RTE	0	1	0	0	1	1	1	0	0	1	1	1	0	0	1	1
RTS	0	1	0	0	1	1	1	0	0	1	1	1	0	1	0	1
TRAPV	0	1	0	0	1	1	1	0	0	1	1	1	0	1	1	0
RTR	0	1	0	0	1	1	1	0	0	1	1	1	0	1	1	1
JSR	0	1	0	0	1	1	1	0	1	0	EA-mode			EA-reg-		
JMP	0	1	0	0	1	1	1	0	1	1	EA-mode			EA-reg-		
CHK	0	1	0	0	-Dreg--			1	1	0	EA-mode			EA-reg-		
LEA	0	1	0	0	-Areg--			1	1	1	EA-mode			EA-reg-		
ADDQ	0	1	0	1	-qdata-			0	size		EA-mode			EA-reg-		
SUBQ	0	1	0	1	-qdata-			1	size		EA-mode			EA-reg-		

FIGURE 9-1. 68000 Instruction Formats.

Scc	0	1	0	1	condition-		1 1	EA-mode	EA-reg-
DBcc	0	1	0	1	condition-		1 1	0 0 1	-Dreg--
Bcc	0	1	1	0	condition-		--8-bit-displacement--		
BSR	0	1	1	0	0 0 0 1		--8-bit-displacement--		
MOVEQ	0	1	1	1	-Dreg--	0	---8-bit-quick-data---		
DIVS	1	0	0	0	-Dreg--	1	1 1	EA-mode	EA-reg-
DIVU	1	0	0	0	-Dreg--	0	1 1	EA-mode	EA-reg-
OR	1	0	0	0	-Dreg--	B	size	EA-mode	EA-reg-
SBCD	1	0	0	0	--reg--	1	0 0	0 0 C	--reg--
SUB	1	0	0	1	-Dreg--	B	size	EA-mode	EA-reg-
SUBA	1	0	0	1	-Areg--	S	1 1	EA-mode	EA-reg-
SUBX	1	0	0	1	--reg--	1	size	0 0 C	--reg--
CMP	1	0	1	1	-Dreg--	0	size	EA-mode	EA-reg-
CMPA	1	0	1	1	-Areg--	S	1 1	EA-mode	EA-reg-
CMPM	1	0	1	1	-Areg--	1	size	0 0 1	-Areg--
EOR	1	0	1	1	-Dreg--	1	size	EA-mode	EA-reg-
AND	1	1	0	0	-Dreg--	B	size	EA-mode	EA-reg-
EXG	1	1	0	0	--reg--	1	--exg-mode---		--reg--
MULS	1	1	0	0	-Dreg--	1	1 1	EA-mode	EA-reg-
MULU	1	1	0	0	-Dreg--	0	1 1	EA-mode	EA-reg-
ABCD	1	1	0	0	--reg--	1	0 0	0 0 C	--reg--
ADD	1	1	0	1	-Dreg--	B	size	EA-mode	EA-reg-
ADDA	1	1	0	1	-Areg--	S	1 1	EA-mode	EA-reg-
ADDX	1	1	0	1	--reg--	1	size	0 0 C	--reg--
ASR	1	1	1	0	--cnt--	0	size	R 0 0	-Dreg--
ASR	1	1	1	0	0 0 0	0	1 1	EA-mode	EA-reg-
ASL	1	1	1	0	--cnt--	1	size	R 0 0	-Dreg--
ASL	1	1	1	0	0 0 0	1	1 1	EA-mode	EA-reg-
LSR	1	1	1	0	--cnt--	0	size	R 0 1	-Dreg--
LSR	1	1	1	0	0 0 1	0	1 1	EA-mode	EA-reg-
LSL	1	1	1	0	--cnt--	1	size	R 0 1	-Dreg--
LSL	1	1	1	0	0 0 1	1	1 1	EA-mode	EA-reg-
ROXR	1	1	1	0	--cnt--	0	size	R 1 0	-Dreg--
ROXR	1	1	1	0	0 1 0	0	1 1	EA-mode	EA-reg-
ROXL	1	1	1	0	--cnt--	1	size	R 1 0	-Dreg--
ROXL	1	1	1	0	0 1 0	1	1 1	EA-mode	EA-reg-
ROR	1	1	1	0	--cnt--	0	size	R 1 1	-Dreg--
ROR	1	1	1	0	0 1 1	0	1 1	EA-mode	EA-reg-
ROL	1	1	1	0	--cnt--	1	size	R 1 1	-Dreg--
ROL	1	1	1	0	0 1 1	1	1 1	EA-mode	EA-reg-

FIGURE 9-1 *(Cont'd)*

A   Indicates direction of transfer: 0 = register-to-memory,
        1 = memory-to-register.

B   Indicates destination: 0 = result to data register, 1 =
        result to effective address.

C   Indicates mode: 0 = operands are contained in data
        registers, 1 = operands are in memory, addressed by
        predecrement addressing mode.

R   Selects mode of --cnt-- field: When 0, --cnt-- is
        immediate data; when 1, --cnt-- is a data register.

S   Indicates size of data transfer: 0 = word, 1 = longword.

T   Indicates direction of transfer: 0 = register-to-USP,
        1 = USP-to-register.

X   Direction of transfer: When 0, transfer is from memory to
        a data register. When 1, transfer is from a data register
        to memory.

EA-mode Effective address mode field.

EA-reg- Effective address register field

--cnt-- an immediate value in the range 1..8 (000b = 8), or a
        data register containing a count, depending on value of R
        field.

size   Indicates size of data transfer: 00 = byte, 01 = word,
        and 10 = longword.

--vector--
        Trap vector number in the range 0..15.

-Dreg-- Any data register.

-Areg-- Any address register.

-qdata- Immediate data in the range 1..8 (000b = 8).

condition-
        A condition as shown in [condition code table].

-8-bit-quick-data-
        Immediate data in the range -128..127, sign extended to
        32 bits.

-8-bit-displacement-
        Transfer address displacement from PC, in the range -
        128..127. If zero, displacement is in extension word of
        the instruction.

-exg-mode-

Mode of exchange: 01000b = data register - data register
exchange, 01001b = address register - address register
exchange, 10001b = address register - data register
exchange.

FIGURE 9-1   *(Cont'd)*

Mnemonic	Condition	Encoding	Test
T	true	0000	1
F	false	0001	0
HI	high	0010	$\overline{C * Z}$
LS	low or same	0011	$C + Z$
CC HS	carry clear	0100	$\overline{C}$
CS LO	carry set	0101	C
NE	not equal	0110	$\overline{Z}$
EQ	equal	0111	Z
VC	overflow clear	1000	$\overline{V}$
VS	overflow set	1001	V
PL	plus	1010	$\overline{N}$
MI	minus	1011	N
GE	greater or equal	1100	$N*V + \overline{N}*\overline{V}$
LT	less than	1101	$N*\overline{V} + \overline{N}*V$
GT	greater than	1110	$N*V*\overline{Z} + \overline{N}*\overline{V}*\overline{Z}$
LE	less or equal	1111	$Z + N*\overline{V} + \overline{N}*V$

N = Negative Flag
Z = Zero Flag
V = Overflow Flag
C = Carry Flag

FIGURE 9-2. Condition Code Field.

As indicated in Figure 9-3, an instruction can be anywhere from 2 to 10 bytes long, and is always an even number of bytes. The first word is the instruction word. If immediate data is required and is not encoded in the instruction word, it appears in the one or two words following the instruction word. Several of the addressing modes require an extension word or two, and these follow the instruction word with the source extension words, if required, preceding the destination extension words. If immediate data requires an extension, the immediate data is always the source operand, and therefore we never see an immediate data extension at the same time as a source effective address extension.

Formats of the effective address extensions can be seen in Figures 9-4, 9-5, 9-6,and 9-7. Not shown are the extension words for the addressing modes absolute short addressing, address register indirect with displacement, and program counter with displacement, all of which are single word values that are sign-extended before use.

```
+-----------------------------------------------------+
|                  Operation Word                     |
|                   (one word)                        |
+-----------------------------------------------------+
|                Immediate Operand                    |
|            (zero, one, or two words)                |
+-----------------------------------------------------+
|        Source Effective Address Extension           |
|            (zero, one, or two words)                |
+-----------------------------------------------------+
|      Destination Effective Address Extension        |
|            (zero, one, or two words)                |
+-----------------------------------------------------+
```

FIGURE 9-3   Instruction Stream Format.

```
 15  14  13  12  11  10   9   8   7   6   5   4   3   2   1   0
+---+-----------+---+-----------+------------------------------+
| R | register  | S | 0   0   0 |     displacement integer     |
+---+-----------+---+-----------+------------------------------+

   bit 15:     0 = data register is index
               1 = address reg is index

   bit 14..12: Index register number

   bit 11:     0 = index register holds word displacement
               1 = index register holds longword displacement

   bit 7..0    displacement, to be sign extended
```

FIGURE 9-4.   Effective Address Extension, Address Register Indirect with Index.

```
 15  14  13  12  11  10   9   8   7   6   5   4   3   2   1   0
+-------------------------------------------------------------+
|               high order byte of absolute address           |
+-------------------------------------------------------------+
|               low order byte of absolute address            |
+-------------------------------------------------------------+
```

FIGURE 9-5. Effective Address Extension, Absolute Long Addressing.


```
 15  14  13  12  11  10   9   8   7   6   5   4   3   2   1   0
+---+----------+---+----------+------------------------------+
| R |  register| S | 0   0   0|    displacement integer      |
+---+----------+---+----------+------------------------------+
```

        bit 15:   0 = data register is index
                    1 = address reg is index

        bit 14..12: Index register number

        bit 11:   0 = index register holds word displacement
                    1 = index register holds longword displacement

        bit 7..0   displacement, to be sign extended

FIGURE 9-6. Effective Address Extension, Program Counter with Displacement.

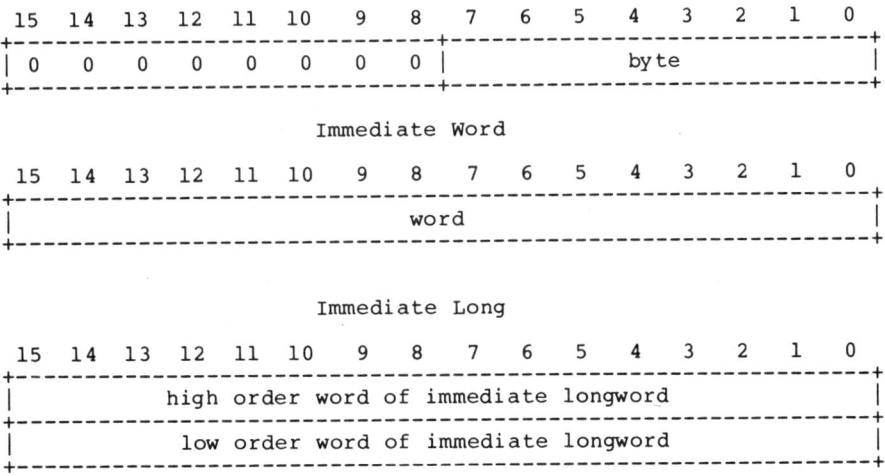

```
 15  14  13  12  11  10   9   8   7   6   5   4   3   2   1   0
+-----------------------------------+-------------------------+
| 0   0   0   0   0   0   0   0|             byte             |
+-----------------------------------+-------------------------+

                        Immediate Word

 15  14  13  12  11  10   9   8   7   6   5   4   3   2   1   0
+-------------------------------------------------------------+
|                           word                              |
+-------------------------------------------------------------+

                        Immediate Long

 15  14  13  12  11  10   9   8   7   6   5   4   3   2   1   0
+-------------------------------------------------------------+
|            high order word of immediate longword            |
+-------------------------------------------------------------+
|            low order word of immediate longword             |
+-------------------------------------------------------------+
```

FIGURE 9-7. Effective Address Extension, Immediate Byte.

Figure 9-8 shows the encoding for the effective address field of instructions that use an effective address. Only three instructions allow the use of two effective addresses, those being MOVE.B, MOVE.W, and MOVE.L. Note that in these three instructions, the mode and register field for the destination effective address field (bits 11 through 6) are reversed from the normal orientation.

Addressing Mode	Mode	Register	Syntax
Data Register Direct	000	(number)	Dn
Address Register Direct	001	(number)	An
Address Register Indirect	010	(number)	(An)
Address Register Indirect with Postincrement	011	(number)	(An)+
Address Register Indirect with Predecrement	100	(number)	-(An)
Address Register Indirect with Displacement	101	(number)	d(An)
Address Register Indirect with Index	110	(number)	d(An,Xi)
Absolute Short Address	111	000	xxx.W
Absolute Long Address	111	001	xxx.L
Program Counter with Displacement	111	010	d(PC)
Program Counter with Index	111	011	d(PC,Xi)
Immediate Data	111	*100	#xxx
Status Register	111	*100	SR or CCR

* Immediate data may only be used for a source operand, and the status register may only be used for a destination operand.

FIGURE 9-8. Effective Address Field.

With those preliminary comments, let's start through the instruction set in op code order. The commentary will be from a disassembly perspective. In other words, we'll be trying to tell you how to distinguish one operation word from another, similar operation word that does something else entirely. This is useful if you are trying to write a disassembler, of course, but it also highlights some peculiarities of the instruction set.

For example, refer to Figure 9-1. The instructions are laid out in pretty much ascending numeric order. At a glance, you'd think that disassembly would be trivial. Now, consider the AND instruction. Suppose we have the instruction:

AND.B   D1, D0

There are two possible ways to encode this, one possibilty being 1100 0011 0000 0000.

Now suppose we have the instruction:

ABCD   D0, D1

The only possibility for encoding this is 1100 0011 0000 0000. As all but the dullest Pascal programmer can see, the encoding is the same. This anomaly was the cause of a wasted Saturday afternoon spent flipping between reference works staring at bit pattern boxes and cursing typesetters, until a boldfaced note caught the eye of the author responsible for research. It seems that if a data register is the destination of the ADD instruction, it must be specified in the register field and not the effective address field. A little searching turned up additional instructions with this restriction: AND, OR, and SUB. Each of these has another instruction that can be confused with it. As it is the privilege (and yes, the duty) of writers to make up buzzwords, we shall call the AND, ADD, OR, and SUB instructions "shoehorned" instructions, as they have another instruction shoehorned into their bit map.

If we were writing a disassembler, we'd start an instruction disassembly by automatically translating bits 2 through 0 into a register number, bits 5 through 3 into an effective address mode, bits 7 and 6 into a "size" value, and bits 11 through 9 into a 3-bit integer. While not all of these values will be used for all instructions, they occur often enough that it pays not to duplicate calls to the decoding routines.

Then, we'd strip the op code in bits 15 through 12 and execute a case on this value. Following is a brief description of what each case limb would do to decode the instruction. Not described is extra operations such as decoding extension words.

Op Code 0000

This op code group includes the immediate operations, the bit test/set/clear/change group, and oddly enough, the MOVEP instruction. The EORI, ANDI, and ORI instructions in this group are allowed to use the status register and condition code register as a destination effective address.

MOVEP can be distinguished from the instructions in this group only because the effective address mode field of the instruction is 001—no instruction in this group can have an address register direct destination. Any immediate data for the instructions in this group are found in extension word(s). The immediate instructions always have at least one and possibly two extension words. MOVEP has one extension word for the displacement used in calculating the peripheral address.

The immediate instructions are distinguished from the bit instructions by the contents of bits 11 though 8. When bit 8 is zero, and bits 11, 10, and 9 are 100, a bit instruction with an extension word is selected. When bit 8 is one, a bit instruction is selected regardless of the values of bits 11 through 9.

Our decoding algorithm would first test for the MOVEP instruction by checking bits 5 through 3 for a 001 value.

Next, we'd test bit 8 for non-zero, indicating a dynamic bit instruction. Next, we'd look for a zero value in bits 10 through 8, indicating a static bit instruction. Bits 7 and 6 for both dynamic and static bit instructions tell us which bit instruction it is.

That leaves only the immediate instructions. These can be decoded by the value of bits 11 through 9. We would have already decoded these bits on general principles prior to the op code casing.

Op Codes 0001, 0010, 0011

These op codes are straightforward. We have the source effective address register and mode fields in bits 5 through 0 and the destination effective address register decoded in our general-purpose decoding. All we have to do is decode the destination mode field.

Op Code 0100

This op code is characterized by Motorola as "Miscellaneous." Four pairs of instructions in this group use the "size" field of the instruction word to distinguish between each other. They are: NEGX and MOVE from SR; NEGX and MOVE to CCR; NOT and MOVE to SR; TST and TAS. Two pairs of instructions use an absurd effective address mode field to distinguish between each other. They are: SWAP and PEA: and EXT and MOVEM. The rest of the instructions in this op code all have unique static bit patterns.

Bits 11 through 8 of the CHK instruction contain the number of the data register being checked. Bits 11 through 8 of the LEA instruction contain the number of the address register being loaded with the effective address.

The low order bit of the vector corresponds to the first register to be transferred. For all address modes except predecrement, the following register correspondence is used:

```
 15  14  13  12  11  10   9   8   7   6   5   4   3   2   1   0
+---------------------------------------------------------------+
| A7  A6  A5  A4  A3  A2  A1  A0  D7  D6  D5  D4  D3  D2  D1  D0 |
+---------------------------------------------------------------+
```

For the predecrement addressing mode, the following register correspondence is used:

```
 15  14  13  12  11  10   9   8   7   6   5   4   3   2   1   0
+---------------------------------------------------------------+
| D0  D1  D2  D3  D4  D5  D6  D7  A0  A1  A2  A3  A4  A5  A6  A7 |
+---------------------------------------------------------------+
```

FIGURE 9-9. MOVEM Register Vector.

The LINK instruction has an extension word containing a 16-bit displacement. MOVEM has an extension word with a register bit vector (see Figure 9-9). The STOP instruction has a one-word extension that is the value to be loaded into the status register.

Our disassembly algorithm would make a special check for CHK and LEA by looking for a non-zero bit 8. These can be further differentiated by bit 6.

Next, we'd make a "case" on bits 11 through 8. This breaks the op code into the following groups:

Subcode	Mnemonic
0000	NEGX, MOVE from SR
0010	CLR
0100	NEG, MOVE CCR
0110	NOT, MOVE to SR
1000	NBCD, SWAP, PEA, EXT, MOVEM (register → memory)
1010	TST, TAS, ILLEGAL
1100	MOVEM (memory → register)
1110	TRAP, LINK, ULNK, MOVE USP, RESET, NOP, STOP, RTE, RTS, TRAPV, RTR, JSR, JMP

Subcodes 0000, 0100, and 0110 can be finished off by looking at the "size" field, bits 7 and 6.

Subcode 1000 is crowded and cannot be intuitively decoded. The key is bits 7 and 6 plus the effective address mode field. We'd probably do a case on these bits, splitting into 00 for NBCD, 01 for SWAP and PEA, and 10/11 for EXT and MOVEM.

The pairs MOVEM/EXT and SWAP/PEA can be split apart by the effective address mode field. Note that this field is always 000 for SWAP and EXT (data register direct is not allowed for PEA and MOVEM).

Subcode 1010 can be divided by an explicit test for ILLEGAL, leaving TAS and TST to be distinguished by the size field, bits 7 and 6.

Subcode 1110 can use explicit tests for RESET, NOP, STOP, RTE, RTS, TRAPV, and RTR. JSR and JMP have bit 7 set, with bit 6 making the distinction between the two. Bits 7 through 4 can be cased to give TRAP for 0100, LINK and UNLK for 0101, and MOVE USP for 0110. Bit 3 distinguishes LINK and UNLK.

Op Code 0101

This group includes ADDQ, SUBQ, Scc, and DBcc. ADDQ and SUBQ are distinguished from Scc and DBcc by the "size" field.

DBcc always has an extension word that contains a 16-bit displacement.

We would use the "size" field to split ADDQ and SUBQ from Scc and DBcc. ADDQ and SUBQ are differentiated by bit 8. DBcc has a 001 value for the effective address mode field, an illegal mode for Scc.

Op Code 0110

This group includes only Bcc and BSR, plus one sneaky little gotcha. A BSR instruction codes exactly like a BF (Branch False) instruction. (If you ever do any hand patching while debugging and decide to turn a Bcc into a BF, you could be in for a surprise.) A BT (Branch True) is also called a BRA (Branch) and has the same bit pattern.

These instructions will have a one-word extension if the 8-bit displacement is zero.

We would test for the BSR and BRA conditions explicitly, and leave the rest of the conditions for Bcc.

Op Code 0111

This op code is straightforward.

Op Code 1000

This group includes DIVS, DIVU, OR, and SBCD. The divide instructions are distinguished by the 11 "size" field. SBCD is shoehorned into OR.

Bits 11 through 9 of the divide and SBCD instructions contain the number of the data register used as the destination operand.

We'd test for 00 in bits 5 and 4 to take care of SBCD, after which we'd test the "size" field to remove DIVS and DIVU from OR. DIVS and DIVU can then be distinguished by bit 8.

Op Code 1001

This group includes SUB, SUBA, and SUBX. SUBA has an 11 "size" field. SUBX is shoehorned into SUB.

Bits 11 through 9 of the SUBA and SUBX instructions specify the destination register.

When disassembling, we'd test for 00 in bits 5 and 4 to extract SUBX. The 11 "size" field then takes care of SUB and SUBA.

Op Code 1011

This group includes CMP, CMPA, CMPM, and EOR. CMPA is distinguished by the 11 "size" field. CMP has bit 8 reset to zero. CMPM and EOR can only be distinguished by the 001 mode field of the effective address field in CMPM. This would be an illegal destination for the EOR instruction.

Bits 11 through 9 of all four instructions contain the number of the destination register.

We'd first check for a 001 effective address mode field to pull out CMPM. Next, we'd check for a 11 "size" field and pull out CMPA. Last, we'd check bit 8 to differentiate between CMP and EOR.

Op Code 1100

This group includes AND, EXG, MULS, MULU, and ABCD, and is one of the harder to separate. MULS and MULU fall out because of the 11 "size" field. ABCD is shoehorned into AND, and the address register direct mode is also not allowed for the effective address field of AND. Since the ABCD and EXG instructions set the effective address to either 001 or 000, AND can be distinguished from ABCD and EXG by the mode field. Once narrowed down to ABCD and EXG, note that the "size" field of the ABCD instruction is always 00.

Bits 11 through 9 of the ABCD and multiply instructions specify the destination register.

Our algorithm would first check the "size" field for 11 and eliminate MULS and MULU. Use bit 8 to split MULS and MULU. Next, check bits 5 and 4 for not being 00 to decode AND. Next, check the "size" field for 00 to select ABCD over EXG.

Op Code 1101

This group includes ADD, ADDA, and ADDX. ADDA falls out because of the 11 "size" field. ADDX is shoehorned into ADD.

Bits 11 through 9 of the ADDA and ADDX instructions specify the destination register.

First, check for ADDA. Then check bits 5 and 4 for 00 to differentiate ADDX from ADD.

Op Code 1110

While this group looks complicated, it actually is pretty regular. Bit 8 specifies left or right operations. If the "size" field is 11, then a memory operand is specified by the effective address field, and the operation is specified by bits 10 and 9. If the "size" field is not 11, then the operation is specified by bits 4 and 3, and the operand is a data register.

The rest of the operations necessary for a disassembler are trivial and are left as an exercise for the reader. (In other words, we're too lazy to write them ourselves.)

A good disassembler can be a very useful systems programming tool, especially for a poorly documented operating system. For example, an interactive disassembler such as the public domain RESOURCE disassembler written by Ward Christensen for CP/M-80 beats the heck out of the DDT disassembler. Using a disassembler that can assign labels, insert comments, switch between code and data sections automatically, search for ASCII strings, etc., you can cut the time required to find why device drivers don't to one-tenth that needed when using a debugger.

Our favorite use for interactive dissassemblers is to rewrite the system disk formatting program for different disk formats when we have a microprogrammed disk controller with no published command specs, don't know what address the controller is at, and have no idea how the hardware designer jury-rigged the controller into the interrupt system and/or DMA controller(s). Believe it or not, we have done this dance more than once, and have a warm spot in our hearts for interactive disassemblers.

10

Parameter Passing Techniques

This chapter concentrates on the ways information is passed between code modules. We'll look at some of the techniques used in pure assembly language programming, as well as some of the methods used by high level compiled languages. The major points covered are:

- LINK and UNLK
- Standard Stack-based parameter passing
- Local storage
- Register passing
- Common memory passing
- General parameter conventions for C

LINK and UNLK

The 68000 LINK and UNLK instructions are designed to make stack frame parameter passing easy to use, especially when the code using these instructions is compiled from a high level language. We don't want to get too involved in high level language compilation and parameter passing techniques just yet, but as many of you are more familiar with high level languages than you are with assembler, we'll start at the top, with stack frames, and work down.

Stack frames are data structures contained in a stack. Usually, the stack referred to is the main stack, or hardware stack. To use a stack frame we need one thing in addition to a stack: a stack pointer. Stack pointers are address registers pointing at a specific location in memory, a location that can change as we add to and remove from the stack.

We can put data, such as parameters to subroutines and local variables, on the stack in addition to the normal stuff (return addresses, temporarily saved register values, etc.) we find there. Most modern structured languages make extensive use of the stack for parameters. Because the 68000 hardware stack starts in higher memory and builds towards lower memory as we add items to the stack, we can refer to data anywhere on the 68000 stack by using the stack pointer plus a positive displacement. Negative displacements point to undefined stack areas. Because of the possibility of interrupts using the stack at any time, areas with negative displacements from the stack pointer can never be trusted to contain useful information.

Since the stack pointer changes constantly as we use the stack, it becomes inconvenient to be constantly calculating the displacement to a given data item in the stack. To stabilize things a little, we can use a specialized stack pointer called a frame pointer. A frame pointer is a stack pointer that gets "frozen" at some point, so that it points at the same spot for some period of time. That way, we can set it and then calculate displacements only once. Usually, frame pointers are set at the beginning and end of blocks of code. A block can be a procedure, or a program, or anything your heart desires. In the case of high level languages, a block usually corresponds to a procedure or function.

The LINK instruction establishes one of the address registers as a frame pointer, and can at the same time move the hardware stack pointer some distance away from the frame pointer, so that a number of locations with negative displacements from the frame pointer are valid locations in the frame. These negatively displaced areas are normally used for local, or temporary, storage.

Compilers using the stack frame concept consistently use a single address register (quite often A6) for the frame pointer. Frame pointers are used in languages that allow nested procedure or function declarations, such as Pascal or Ada, but are less common in languages that don't allow nested declarations, such as C. By the clever copying of frame pointers from parent routines the parent's local variables and parameters are available to the children, even if the parents or children are recursive.

Because the frame pointer points to the stack location holding the previous contents of the frame pointer after the LINK, it is possible to retrace the thread of execution by following frame pointers back through the stack.

For example, the Ada language defines an exception mechanism (much different than the 68000 exception mechanism) that requires that procedure calls be retraced until an exception handler is found. Most Ada compilers will also provide a "walkback" if no handler is found. A walkback is a list of procedure and function calls tracing the thread of execution, starting with the routine where the error occurred and then back through the calling sequence, ending with the main procedure of the program.

Ada-type exceptions and walkbacks can be incorporated into assembly language programs by using the LINK instruction. This requires that as you enter any block that you wish to see in a walkback or have an exception handler you use the LINK instruction to establish a stack frame.

The frame pointer itself will not give enough information to generate a walkback or handle exceptions. You will also have to provide unique information in the frame to identify the routine. This can be as simple as a pointer to a data block containing a string with the name of the routine.

Let's look at a hypothetical routine "max" that incorporates two of the uses of a stack frame. This routine is passed two 16-bit integer values, and returns the larger of the two in register D0. If the two numbers are equal, we assume catastrophic failure elsewhere and call a routine walkback that will display the walkback sequence. The code calling "max" might look like this:

```
MOVE.W  D0,-(A7)        * Push parameter 1 on stack
MOVE.W  D1,-(A7)        * Push parameter 2 on stack
BSR     MAX             * Call "max"
```

The code for "max" could look like this:

```
MAX:    LINK    A6,-4        * LINK and make 4 byte extra space
        MOVE.L  #MX,-4(A6)   * Put address of name in frame
        MOVE.W  8(A6),D0     * Get parameter 1 to D0
        CMP.W   10(A6),D0    * Test against parameter 2
        BEQ     WALKBACK     * Do walkback if equal
        BLT     IS_P2        * Jump if P2 > P1
        BRA     EXIT         * P1 > P2
IS_P2:  MOVE.W  10(A6),D0    * Put parameter 2 into D0
EXIT:   UNLK    A6           * Unlink frame
        RTS                  * Get out of routine
MX:     DC.B    'MAX',0      * Name for walkback
```

As long as all the routines you want entered into the walkback use similar first two lines, a fairly simple scheme to print the walkback can be put together. For example, assuming that the program puts together a starting link with a zero name pointer, so that we know where the walkback ends, code similar to the following could print the walkback:

```
WALKBACK:
        MOVE.L  -4(A6),D0    * Get routine name address in D0
        BEQ     END_W        * If zero, end of walkback
        BSR     PRINT        * prints name from (D0)
        UNLK    A6           * Get caller's frame
        BRA     WALKBACK     * Repeat
END_W:  ...end the program
```

If Ada-style exception processing is added, things become slightly more complicated. Instead of storing a pointer to the name of the routine in the frame, a pointer to a data structure called an "activation record" is stored. This activation record will contain such items as the name of the routine, addresses for exception handlers, and other information as appropriate.

Standard Stack-Based Parameter Passing

The use of the LINK instruction for execution-thread tracing is not very common in assembly language, not because it isn't useful, but because many assembly language programmers are not aware of the possibilities, and because it takes extra discipline and effort to include this capability in a program. More commonly, the LINK is used in assembler to stabilize the stack frame to provide easy access to parameters and local variables. Reworking the "max" program a little, we can demonstrate local storage access:

```
MAX:      LINK    A6,-2            * LINK and make 2 byte extra space
          MOVE.W  8(A6),D0         * Get parameter 1 to D0
          CMP.W   10(A6),D0        * Test against parameter 2
          BLT     IS_P2            * Jump if P2 > P1
          BRA     SKIP             * P1 > P2
IS_P2:    MOVE.W  10(A6),D0        * Put parameter 2 into D0
SKIP:     MOVE.W  D0,-2(A6)        * Save max( P1, P2 ) in temp
          . . .
          . . . (any number of unbalanced pushes and pops)
          . . .
          MOVE.W  -2(A6),D0        * re-get value from temp storage
EXIT:     UNLK    A6               * Unlink frame
          RTS                      * Get out of routine
```

As was pointed out earlier, parameters to a routine use positive displacements from the frame pointer, and local storage uses negative displacements.

In simple assembly language routines, it doesn't pay to use the LINK technique. For one thing, most people write small enough modules that local storage isn't needed—all the values can be kept in registers. Let's take one more shot at "max," and write it like an experienced programmer would write it:

```
MAX:      MOVE.W  4(A7),D0         * Get parameter P1 to D0
          CMP.W   6(A7),D0         * Test against parameter 2
          BLT     IS_P2            * Jump if P2 < P1
          BRA     SKIP             * P1 > P2
IS_PS:    MOVE.W  6(A7),D0         * Put parameter 2 into D0
SKIP:     RTS                      * End of routine
```

As an exercise, you should probably take some paper and draw out the stack as the call to "max" is executed and as "max" executes, for all three examples of "max." This will help you to clearly visualize the stack formats and referencing that takes place with the different techniques.

Local and Variable Storage

We have been using local storage allocated by the LINK instruction, putting local storage on the stack. There are other schemes for local storage, but stack based storage is the most efficient given the 68000 architecture. Local storage referenced by any other method will take longer to get at. Another drawback to more traditional storage methods, such as a data section referenced by absolute (direct) addressing, is that most of them aren't very relocatable. Once assembled and linked, your program is constrained to loading and executing at a fixed location.

Even if you don't wish to use stack frames for variable storage, you can have storage assigned at run time and point another address register at it. This will give you a fixed reference to the data section. If the +32767..−32768 address range isn't big enough for you, you can always put pointers in the data section that reference other data sections, and so on.

The one important thing missing from almost any local storage scheme with the exception of stack-based is the ability to re-enter the code, either by recursion or by sharing common routines in a multitasking scheme. Any time you use a fixed location for local or temporary storage, you must take care that only one task can call the procedure at one time.

Register Passing

If your experience has been in the CP/M-80 world, you probably wrote most of your programs to pass data to and from subroutines in CPU registers. This is the most efficient method for passing parameters in the 68000 as well. With register passing, you stuff parameters into the registers that the subroutine you're calling expects them to be in, and make the call. This is very fast and doesn't grow the stack.

The problem is avoiding registers that contain data that you still need. If you have register conflicts, you have to push the old value before the call, and then pop it after the call to restore the old value. A second problem is remembering which register gets what value. Of course, with stack passing, you have to remember what order to push the stuff in. You have to be awake while you write code no matter what method you use.

Most of the "cheap" operating systems (by "cheap" we mean the operating systems affordable by individuals) for the 68000 use register passing when making operating system calls. This is because the stack pointers are switched when TRAP instructions are executed by user-mode code, and don't change when TRAPs are executed by supervisor-mode code. It doesn't pay for the operating system to spend time trying to figure which stack the parameters are on.

Common Memory Passing

Some of the more primitive ancestors of the 68000, such as the 6502 and 68xx families, have only a couple of registers and a very restricted stack. These ancient processors, suitable for use only as drill press controllers and the like, had very limited options as far as parameter passing techniques go. About the only thing you could do was dedicate memory locations to pass parameters in, or write procedures that took only one or two parameters.

While you can certainly use this technique with a 68000, it's a poor choice. Absolute memory references are slower than the register indirect modes, and are not relocatable or re-entrant. The design of the PC relative addressing modes, which could be useful for this type of parameter passing, makes these modes almost useless for data storage.

General C Parameter Passing Techniques

One of the really good reasons for learning how to code in 68000 assembler is to interface low level and often used assembly language routines to C and other high level language programs. Your UNIX buddies will tell you that there's no need to write assembly language programs if you have a C compiler, because C compilers for the 68000 output such good code.

There are several flaws to that line of thought. First, some people *like* to write assembly language code. When your UNIX buddies make nasty remarks about stone knives and bear skins, you can look scornful and tell them there's no accounting for taste.

Second, most of us can't afford the compilers that generate such good code, granting that they do indeed exist.

Third, a good assembly language programmer can write better code than the best C compiler. For one thing, the C language doesn't provide enough information about a program for a compiler to do a really fine job of optimizing. In fact, the only language that provides enough information about a program for the sort of optimizing that even an average (systems-level) assembly programmer can do is Ada. A good assembly language programmer can write code that runs much faster than that produced by an equivalent C program compiled on a cheap compiler.

In order to interface assembly language code to C programs, it's necessary to know what conventions are used when passing data back and forth between C functions. Since there are multitudes of C compilers for the 68000 from various vendors and for various operating systems, it's impossible to generalize about parameter passing conventions for all C compilers. However, in architecture the 68000 is similar to the machine that UNIX and C were designed on, and so certain C operations are most efficient when done a particular way. Because they are efficient, most compiler writers do them that way.

For example, consider the following C function call:

```
exmple ( a, b, c);
```

```
/* sample code to examine your C compiler's parameter passing
   conventions */

test( dummy )
   int dummy;
{
    test_call( (char)0x80, (short)0xF0, (int)0xABCD,
               (long)0xDCBA, (double)1.0 );
    return( 0 );
}
```

FIGURE 10-1.   C Checkout Program.

For the sake of this discussion, we will assume that the parameters a, b, and c are all 16-bit integers. Normally, these parameters will be pushed onto the system stack by the compiler from right to left. (Yes, we know the compiler doesn't push things, it emits code to push things.) In other words, the compiler will push the value for c, then the value for b, and last, the value for a. After parameter a is pushed, the compiler will insert a JSR or BSR to EXMPLE instruction.

The reason parameters are usually pushed right-to-left is that C does not require the number of parameters in a call to match the number of parameters in the function definition. The most common example is the printf() function. The first argument to printf() is a pointer to a control string. The control string specifies how many additional arguments will be found on the stack. If the arguments are pushed right-to-left, the first parameter can always be found right under the return address on the stack. If they were pushed left-to-right, we would have no way of knowing where to find the first argument. This problem could be solved by having the control string at the other end of the parameter string, but that wouldn't match the C standard.

The first step to finding how your compiler interfaces functions is to write a really simple function, compile, and then look at the assembly language code produced. Figure 10-1 illustrates a simple function which, when compiled, will tell you just about everything you need to know about how your compiler passes parameters. There're a bunch of things to look for.

- Does the compiler sign-extend characters when they're promoted to integers? Chances are good that it does, but check anyhow.
- How many bits are used by the different data types? You can bet the farm that pointers are 32 bits, but how about shorts, ints, and longs?
- In what order does the compiler push parameters?
- Does the compiler put extra stuff on the stack with the parameters? Some compilers will insert a byte count of the stack parameters, because it saves code space (though it increases time) if a library subroutine pulls parameters off the stack.
- Where does parameter removal occur, in the calling routine or in the called routine?
- How are values returned from functions? Many compilers will put scalar values in a register or a pair of registers, but other options include lifting the return address and sliding the return value in underneath, or maintaining a separate parameter stack for return values.
- What sort of pseudo-ops does the compiler put in?

These are most of the questions you need answered before you begin rewriting your C standard library to get a little more speed out of it. There are other items to look at before getting too fancy, however. For example, newer C compilers will pass structures and unions, rather than just pointers to these types, on the stack, and return them from functions. (The next thing you know, they'll be putting in strong type checking and parameter bounds checking, and adding Writeln() to the standard C library.) We'd advise you to check your compiler manual, but we haven't found a manual yet that was clear enough to write assembly language code without a little experimenting.

Summary

There are a variety of ways to pass parameters in any program, but no one "best" way, because the application may drive you to one method or another. All other things being equal, stack frame passing will give you the most general-purpose code, while register passing, if done correctly, will be the fastest.

11
Exceptions

This chapter presents the exception structure of the 68K, including software traps and exceptions, hardware interrupts and system errors, all of which share this method of requesting service. The major points covered are:

- Exception overview
- Exception processing
- Types of exceptions
- The two exception stack formats
- Exception handlers

Exception Overview

Exceptions (known as "interrupts" in some other processors) are the mechanism by which processing outside of the normal sequential execution of a program may occur.

In the 68000, exceptions are caused by the normal or abnormal action of instructions designed to cause exceptions, or by external stimuli. When an exception is taken, the processor pushes some of the processor context into the stack and then executes a special sequence of instructions called the exception handler. At the conclusion of the exception handler, some or all of the saved processor context is restored, and execution proceeds from the point at which it was interrupted by the exception.

A table of vectors, called the exception vector table, holds pointers to various exception handlers. The location of this table is fixed to a certain memory area by the properties of the 68000 chip. The exception vector table begins at address 0 and continues through address $0003FF. There are 255 vectors, numbered 0 and 2 through 255. Vector 0 contains the processor reset information and takes up 8 bytes. There is no vector 1. The address of each vector is calculated by multiplying the vector number times four.

Exception Processing

Although handlers vary from exception to exception, a specific sequence of events is common to all exceptions but RESET. The order of the following events is described in "black box" fashion. Internally, a slightly different order is taken, but since we can't see inside the CPU, who cares?

When an exception is *taken,* or accepted for processing, the CPU pushes first the PC and then the status register onto the *supervisor* stack. (A subsequent RTE instruction—usually executed at the end of the interrupt handler—will cause the processor to pop the return address and the status register and resume execution at the next instruction, with all the original flags, trace and supervisor/user flag included, restored.)

Next, the CPU is set into supervisor state with the trace flag turned off. This means that a TRAP or other exception cannot be traced. In a RESET or INTERRUPT exception the interrupt mask is also set, as detailed later.

Last, the exception number is determined, the vector address for that exception number is calculated, and the PC is loaded from the vector address. The next instruction is fetched from the address the PC is pointing at. What happens after that depends on the system software.

Types of Exceptions

There are a number of different exceptions that can occur, listed in Figure 11-1 in the order of their priority. An exception with a higher priority is processed before a simultaneous exception with a lower priority. What follows is a more detailed explanation of each exception.

```
Exception        Cause                                          Vector
---------        ------------------------------------------     ------
RESET            Asserting the hardware RESET pin               0
BUS ERROR        Asserting the hardware BUSERR pin              2
ADDRESS ERROR    Software problem, bad memory reference         3
TRACE            Trace bit in SR set                            9
INTERRUPT        External Hardware requests exception           *
ILLEGAL          A bad instruction was fetched                  4
PRIVILEGE        User program tries privileged instruction      8
TRAP             Normal Instruction processing                  32-47
TRAPV            Normal Instruction processing                  7
CHK              Normal Instruction processing                  6
Zero Divide      Division error in DIVS or DIVU                 5
```

   *depends on hardware configuration

FIGURE 11-1.   Exceptions and Priorities.

RESET

The RESET exception is the highest priority of all the exceptions. This is intended for power-up and failure recovery. When the external reset pin on the 68000 is asserted by hardware, either by a power-on delay scheme or a reset button, the 68000 drops whatever it's doing and reloads the supervisor stack pointer from location $000000. The PC is loaded from $000004. In addition, the CPU is set to supervisor mode, trace flag off, and the interrupt priority mask is set to 7, which disables all but non-maskable interrupts. Execution then begins at the address contained in the PC.

It is not possible to recover and resume execution from the point in a program where a RESET exception occurs. RESET is the only exception that does not save any of the processor context.

Note that a RESET exception is not the same as a RESET instruction. All that happens with a RESET instruction is that an external pin is asserted to reset peripheral devices. No exception is taken.

BUS ERROR

The BUS ERROR exception occurs when an external hardware arrangement asserts a pin on the 68000. What this normally means is that a memory reference was attempted where there is no memory. If your system has a memory management unit (MMU) attached, this exception may be taken if you attempt to access protected memory.

The PC pushed when this exception occurs may or may not point at the next instruction, but it will always point somewhere in the vicinity of the instruction that caused the error, even if that instruction is a jump or branch and the address error was because of the branch. Additional context information is pushed for this exception (see Figure 11-2).

The BUS ERROR exception is sometimes used to implement a virtual-memory machine. In combination with an MMU, it can cause a section of memory to be brought in from disk and the instruction that generated the bus error can be re-executed. The MMU translates a virtual address to a physical address once the missing memory is paged in. A virtual addressing

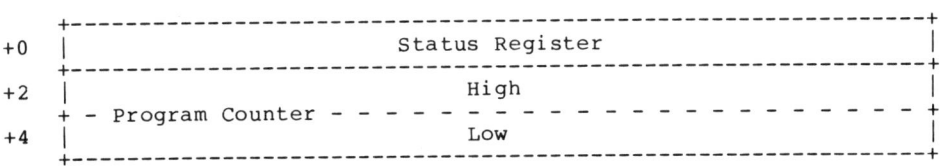

FIGURE 11-2. Standard Exception Stack.

scheme is not a Saturday afternoon project, by the way. The 68010 processor contains enhancements to the processing of ADDRESS ERROR and BUS ERROR exceptions that make it easier to write a virtual memory manager.

A BUS ERROR that occurs while processing another BUS ERROR, a RESET, or an AD-DRESS ERROR exception is called a "double bus error." If a double bus error occurs, the system locks up in a HALT state (which is different from a STOPped state) and does absolutely nothing until the hardware RESET pin is asserted. This lockup prevents a runaway exception loop that could cause the stack to overrun all of memory, making a postmortem dump useless.

A BUS ERROR taken while trying to get an external device to respond with an interrupt vector causes the SPURIOUS INTERRUPT vector to be taken. Some hardware designers will take advantage of this to implement external interrupts because their managers told them to make the system cheap. Consult the system specs or the schematics for details about your system.

ADDRESS ERROR

ADDRESS ERRORs occur when you attempt to access a word, longword, or an instruction at an odd address. Unlike the 8086, a 68000 word or longword access *must* be from an even address. This increases processing speed at the cost of wasted bytes here and there and some programmer inconvenience.

The PC pushed when this exception occurs may or may not point at the next instruction. It will be somewhere in the vicinity of the instruction that caused the error, even if that instruction is a jump or branch. Additional context information is pushed for this instruction (see Figure 11-3).

If an ADDRESS ERROR exception is taken while processing another ADDRESS ERROR, a BUS ERROR, or a RESET, a double bus error occurs. The RESET pin is the only guaranteed way to get the system going again, although in isolated instances threatening the CPU with a hammer may start it up, especially if it knows you've killed before.

TRACE

The TRACE exception is taken whenever an instruction is executed all the way through with the trace flag in the status register on. The exception is generated at the end of the instruction.

Certain other exceptions (RESET, BUS ERROR, ADDRESS ERROR, ILLEGAL, and PRIVILEGE) cause the instruction not to be executed all the way through, and a TRACE exception is not taken. An interrupt taken before the traced instruction will cause the TRACE exception to be delayed until after the interrupt returns (assuming it does). If an interrupt arrives while processing a traced instruction, the TRACE exception is taken first. Since the trace flag is turned off as part of the normal exception processing, tracing is disabled during the processing of a TRACE exception. Note that this same effect makes it impossible to trace

```
        15  14  13  12  11  10   9   8   7   6   5   4   3   2   1   0
      +---+---+---+---+---+---+---+---+---+---+---+---+---+---+-----------+
  +0  |   |   |   |   |   |   |   |   |   |   |   |   |R/W|I/N| Fnct. Cd  |
      +---+---+---+---+---+---+---+---+---+---+---+---+---+---+-----------+
  +2  |                             High                                 |
      + - Access Address  - - - - - - - - - - - - - - - - - - - - - - - -+
  +4  |                             Low                                  |
      +-----------------------------------------------------------------+
  +6  |                     Instruction Register                        |
      +-----------------------------------------------------------------+
  +8  |                      Status Register                            |
      +-----------------------------------------------------------------+
 +10  |                             High                                 |
      + - Program Counter - - - - - - - - - - - - - - - - - - - - - - - -+
 +12  |                             Low                                  |
      +-----------------------------------------------------------------+
```

```
R/W (Read/Write):
    1 = Read
    0 = Write

I/N (Instruction/Not):
    0 = Instruction
    1 = Not

Fnct. Cd (Function Code)
    0 0 0    (Unassigned)
    0 0 1    User mode, data reference
    0 1 0    User mode, program reference
    0 1 1    (Unassigned)
    1 1 0    (Unassigned)
    1 0 1    Supervisor mode, data reference
    1 1 0    Supervisor mode, program reference
    1 1 1    Interrupt Acknowledge
```

FIGURE 11-3.   Extended Exception Stack.

---

through a TRAP exception, as when making systems calls. Tracing will resume when the TRAP returns, because the RTE instruction reloads the status register.

The normal way to get into trace mode is to push a transfer address for the instruction to be traced, push a status word with the trace flag enabled, and then execute an RTE instruction. Other instructions that could be used to set the trace flag on or off are MOVE to SR, ORI to SR, ANDI to SR, and EORI to SR. Note that these are all privileged instructions; you must be in supervisor mode to enable tracing. It will also make your life difficult because tracing begins immediately after the instruction that sets the trace flag, while if you set the flag on the stack you can finish any other preparations (such as loading registers) without being bothered by extraneous trace exceptions.

INTERRUPT

There are seven levels of interrupt exception priorities, with three schemes for an external device to provide a vector number to the CPU. The hardware details are beyond the scope of this book (trust us, a miracle occurs and the processor goes somewhere predictable to service the interrupt), but there are a couple of details you need to know to set up software to handle interrupts.

First, get out the hardware manual for your computer (if available) and find out the vectors taken and the priority for each interrupt.

A hardware interrupt will only be recognized if it is priority seven (a non-maskable priority) or the priority of the interrupt is higher than the current setting of the interrupt mask in the status register.

Once you know the priority, you can determine when an interrupt will be taken. When an interrupt is taken, the interrupt mask in the status register is set to the priority of the interrupt being serviced. This ensures that the same interrupt won't be taken again without your doing something explicit to the status register, and that other interrupts of equal or lower priority will not be taken. The exception to the rule is that an interrupt of priority seven will *always* be recognized. There is no interrupt priority zero; if the interrupt mask in the SR is zero, all interrupts will be taken as they occur. (see Chapter 18 for a more detailed look at interrupt exceptions.)

ILLEGAL

The ILLEGAL exception is taken whenever the instruction fetched is either illegal or unimplemented. This includes legal op codes that have illegal addressing modes.

Three op codes are specially reserved as illegal. Two of them, $4AFA and $4AFB, are used by Motorola in systems products. The third, $4AFC, is guaranteed to always cause an illegal instruction exception, even in future 68K family products. Other currently illegal instructions, such as a MOVE to a PC-relative operand, cause exceptions in the 68000 but are not guaranteed to be illegal in future 68000-family processors.

There are two unimplemented op codes, where bits 15 through 12 are either 1010 or 1111 (op codes $Axxx or $Fxxx). Each has a separate vector. These op codes are sometimes used to software-emulate new instructions. For example, the 68020 uses op code $Fxxx for coprocessor instructions; these may be emulated in the 68K with an op code $Fxxx exception handler.

PRIVILEGE

The PRIVILEGE exception is taken whenever the processor is in user state and one of the privileged instructions STOP, RESET, RTE, MOVE to SR, ANDI to SR, ORI to SR, EORI to SR, or MOVE USP is fetched.

TRAP

TRAP is an exception taken in the normal course of program execution. The specified TRAP vector is taken. TRAPs are usually used to call system functions.

TRAPV

TRAPV is an exception taken in the normal course of program execution. The TRAPV vector is taken if the overflow flag is set and the TRAPV instruction is executed. TRAPV is often used by high level languages to abort a program when a math error occurs.

CHK

CHK is an exception taken in the normal course of program execution. The CHK vector is taken when the CHK instruction is executed and the proper conditions (for an explanation of CHK instruction, see Chapter 6) are fulfilled. The CHK instruction is often used by high level languages to perform bounds checking on array indices and subrange object assignments.

Zero Divide

Zero divide is an exception taken in the normal course of program execution. The zero divide vector is taken when a zero divisor is used in a DIVS or DIVU instruction.

Uninitialized

The uninitialized exception is generated by 68K family peripherals, such as the MC 68681 dual serial chip, if a hardware interrupt vector is requested from it before a vector is programmed into the chip. In other words, this is the default vector for 68K family chips, and is used to debug programming errors when writing device drivers.

The Two Exception Stack Formats

There are two stack formats generated by exception processing. The first, shown in Figure 11-2, is what most exceptions generate. The second, generated by ADDRESS ERROR and BUS ERROR, shown in Figure 11-3, has additional processor context information. After the PC and status are pushed, the first word (the op code) of the instruction being processed is pushed. Then, the address that caused the error is pushed. Finally, a data word is pushed that tells whether the access was a read or a write, whether or not the exception was taken while processing an instruction, and the function code displayed by the processor during the failed access. The function code indicates program code if the address is for an instruction fetch or a PC-relative addressing mode. All other references are data references.

Remember, the stack used for exception data is always the supervisor stack, no matter what mode the processor was in when the exception was taken.

Exception Handlers

OK, so you have an exception, it's taken, the CPU grabs a vector and off it goes. What's missing from this picture? Why, an exception handler, of course. Every exception needs to have some code to handle it—if nothing else, some code to print "UNHANDLED EXCEPTION" and return to the operating system.

If you're running under some sort of operating system, there are probably already vectors pointing to handlers for all the predefined exceptions that can happen by accident. Most microcomputer operating systems also allow you to install your own vectors in place of some or all of the predefined vectors. It's a good idea when installing vectors to use operating system calls, if possible, just on general principles. Among other things, this will make porting your code to the 68010 and 68020 easier.

If you're running on the bare metal (i.e., without the aid of an operating system), you can just store vectors at the appropriate addresses. It's a really good idea to put handler addresses in *all 255 vectors*. One of the authors spent thirty-six straight hours trying to debug some new hardware (not a 68000) that kept blowing up randomly. It turned out to be a high-active edge-triggered NMI (Non-Maskable-Interrupt) line, *tied to ground,* that was picking up spikes from surrounding traces. If he'd taken his own advice he would have found the problem in minutes. Don't you make the same mistake.

When writing exception handlers, there are some general principles that apply.

First, you need to decide if you're going to return control to the process that caused the exception. In most cases, the decision will be obvious, but in others it's not so easy to decide, expecially if you're trying to write a general-purpose code. The zero divide exception is one example.

A divide-by-zero is considered an error because anything divided by zero is infinity, and presumably has no representation. However, there is in fact such a thing as machine infinity. Machine infinity is the largest number that can be represented in the machine data type. Should you return machine infinity in an operating system divide by zero, or should you blow off the process? If you decide to return machine infinity, remember that there's also a negative machine infinity, and that positive machine infinity is different for signed and unsigned divides. And what's the proper remainder for divide by zero?

Once you decide whether or not to return, you know if you need to save the machine context. If processing an interrupt, you need to save and restore any registers you use while servicing the interrupt, because interrupts are asynchronous to the process interrupted, and you can't guarantee anything about the state of the processor when the interrupt occurs.

If you're writing operating system service traps, you'll probably be passing information to the operating system in registers, and returning information to the calling process in the same way. You'll most likely have to return the CPU in a somewhat altered state. If you're writing operating system calls, you get to make your own rules about side effects from system calls (one of the perks in writing operating systems), but the decent thing to do is to guarantee to the caller that the only registers changed are those that return values. This is, in fact, an almost universal convention.

If you decide not to return control to the process that caused a given exception, there are still some details to think about. For one thing, there's all this garp on the supervisor stack to think about. Also, it's nice to tell the operator that the process died, and give him a hint as to the reason. There are few things more frustrating than having the system prompt silently appear in the middle of a program. Many systems will spit out a register dump in these circumstances. It can be quite amusing to watch a Pascal programmer trying to figure out how the register dump relates to his program (unless, of course, it's you). Sometimes a load map from a linker will help, although load maps tend to have the symbols listed in alphabetical order, not by load address. A Real Programmer (i.e., an assembly language programmer) can just look up the instruction in the listing. Then all you have to do is figure out how you got there from here.

But we digress. If you're not returning control to the user, print a message telling what exception caused the failure, and maybe display the registers.

You may or may not have to clean up the supervisor stack in these cases. One thing you need to think about is closing open files in a disk environment. The CP/M series is famous for having a program write 31 Kbytes of output and then crash, leaving a zero byte file because the file was never closed and the debugging information from the file is in the twilight zone.

A nice touch is to allow a process to establish an error handling routine via a system call. If a fatal error occurs, you can call the error handler to give the process its last wishes. A technique like this puts the overhead into the operating system where it belongs, instead of each and every applications program. This is fairly easy to implement but is often overlooked.

12

Text Editor Overview

This chapter marks our transition from a reference mode to a tutorial mode. The preceding chapters give you the basic building blocks supplied with the 68000 processor. What they lack is a sense of context. Assuming that you were willing to wade through the hardware parts, you could get at least as much, and probably more, information from the Motorola data book. Now we would like to present code examples of how these building blocks are used.

We're going to use a full-screen text editor as one of our long examples. Text editors are wonderful vehicles for systems programming examples. A full screen editor has I/O, a complicated user interface, data structures, memory management, tons of control structures, string operations—all that good stuff. The next couple of chapters will have different parts of the text editor spread out as examples. Even if you already have a good editor on your system, you can profit by looking at what we did with ours: the first rule of systems programming is to steal all the ideas and all the code you can.

In this chapter we will provide a top-level view of the editor, and we'll look briefly at some of the design tradeoffs and some possible enhancements to the design. We're also going to look at some of the basic concepts common to 68K assemblers.

As with most programming jobs, the first thing to do when starting a design is to look at the intended use of the finished product. If the requirements can be defined before starting the design, it makes the design easier. You don't have to cobble stuff in later.

We have arbitrarily decided that our editor is to be a programmer's editor. Rather than having context-sensitive help and all that other stuff, we will concentrate on speed and utility. As a programmer's editor, we won't even consider making this a line editor—it has got to be full screen.

Having decided that, we can start adding features. If you've ever used an editor that can edit several files at once, cutting and pasting between files, you never want to go back to a one-file editor. We'll make this editor handle a variable number of files, depending on available memory.

Speaking of memory, we have to decide whether to make this a memory based editor, or if we want to spool large files to and from disk. As far as ease of coding is concerned, it's much easier to limit a file size to some unit of available memory. It saves great bunches of special cases in the code. However, no matter how large the limit you put on file size, sooner or later you have a file that exceeds the limit.

Memory is usually not a problem on a 68K system. In the early days of microcomputers, it was different, but with memory chips doubling in capacity and halving in price every year, we really don't need to worry that much about memory being available.

There are other considerations for memory limits, though. If you go back and look at the DBcc instruction, for example, you'll notice that it is limited to loops of 65,536 iterations or less. Although it really shouldn't be considered in a tradeoff study, it's much easier to manipulate data with the DBcc instruction than with a loop constructed with several other instructions. What should be considered in a tradeoff study is that a DBcc loop will execute significantly faster than other types of loops. The 64K limit on DBcc argues strongly for a 64K limit on file size, depending on the internal storage format used for text.

After considering these and some other factors, we decided to make our editor a memory-based editor with 64K file size limits. As it turns out, most programmers tend to write source code modules that run from 5 to 20K bytes, whether they be C, Pascal, Ada, assembly language, or whatever. It's much easier to manage small code modules, and compilers and assemblers being as slow as they are, it's easier on your nerves.

After making the big choice for a memory-based editor, we need to decide on the internal storage format for the text that we're editing. There's a huge variety of options available; we'll look at some of the more popular ones.

When screen editors started taking over from line editors, it was fairly common on mainframe systems to patch a full screen front-end onto the system line editor. In fact, if you have used a screen editor that has a "command" mode, where all of a sudden you can enter line editor–like commands, chances are real good that it's one of these hybrid editors. These hybrid editors, and some from-scratch full screen editors, keep text in memory in some sort of line orientation.

The simplest sort of line orientation is to chop the memory up into discrete intervals. You arbitrarily decide that lines shall be no longer than 80 or 132 characters (or whatever), and divide the memory up into 80- or 132-character "chunks." Each chunk stores one line, and each line has some sort of terminator character at its end, or a size-of-line counter at its beginning. This kind of scheme is easy to implement. You can insert lines by block-moving everything past the inserted line forward by one line increment. Editing is accomplished by pointing a simple line editor at a particular spot in memory. It's a trivial job to figure out line numbers and to jump to a given line. The chief disadvantages to this scheme are the need to move everything when you insert at the beginning of the file, the fixed limit on line length, and problems when searching for patterns that span lines. Another potential disadvantage is the wasted space at the end of each line. A blank line takes as much memory as a full line. (This is much less of a problem these days, for the reasons mentioned earlier.)

This simple line orientation can be enhanced by adding extra information to each line's chunk. For example, when re-editing an existing file, old lines can have their original line numbers encoded in the line's chunk, and new lines can be flagged on the screen as "new."

Stepping up in complexity, we can manage lines in a "heap." Space for each line is dynamically allocated as needed, and we keep track of the lines by holding an array of pointers to these lines, or by using a linked list approach. This allows us to use less memory than the simple "chunk" model. Lines can be added or removed without disturbing other lines. This model has fewer limits but still has its problems. For example, refreshing the display and searching for patterns are more complicated because of the indirect access to the text.

For our editor, we chose a memory model that has no line orientation at all. We maintain our text in one long string, with a line terminator separating each line in memory. This model has no overhead for line pointers, and no wasted space at the ends of the lines. The text can be maintained as an image of the disk file. The main problem with this model is that there's no way to calculate where lines begin and end; you have to look for the line terminator.

The major design problem here is how to go about inserting text. Most of the time you're using an editor you're inserting characters, or at least modifying characters around the cursor, so it makes sense to optimize the memory scheme accordingly.

If we keep the text as one long string, then each time we insert a character at the beginning we have to move the whole file down one character. A 68K can do this pretty quickly, but even so the process of repeatedly moving an entire file 1 byte at a time is bound to make the editor slow; and in our book, a sluggish editor is even more annoying than a slow compiler. To solve this problem we've chosen to use what we call a "gap" system.

With a gap system, we assign a fixed memory buffer for each file being edited. Everything in the file to the left of the cursor is packed up against the beginning of the buffer. Everything to the right of the cursor is packed up against the end of the buffer. A gap appears in the file at the cursor position. The advantage to this system is that nothing needs to be moved when inserting, because inserted characters go to the left of the cursor, at the start of the gap, and fill the gap in as more text is inserted.

The main disadvantage to the gap system is that every time you move the cursor you need to move characters across the gap. The other disadvantage, as we mentioned, is the problem of locating ends of lines. Except for these disadvantages, nearly every other operation in the editor is made easier by using this system.

Some of the other design tradeoffs involve the display device you're using. As a rule, 68K systems don't have memory-mapped display interfaces. Notable exceptions include some of the consumer computers, such as the Macintosh. To generalize the editor we're going to funnel all of our display ouput through a few very primitive I/O calls suitable either for memory-mapped displays or terminal output. To complicate the display interface, we also decided to make this a windowing editor. We can't count on advanced terminal features like window scrolling being available on your terminal, so we'll only assume a terminal able to move the cursor to a given spot on the screen and put a character there.

As for the input interface, we'll just assume that we can accept a character from the terminal without echo and without line buffering, and that we can look and see if a character is waiting from the input device. This may be a problem on some of the popular operating systems for the 68K, notably some versions of UNIX. There's always a way to do it; you just have to figure out how.

Some of the other support routines we'll need for this editor include numeric I/O, for displaying file sizes and line numbers, file I/O, for obvious reasons; some windowing stuff to keep track of our screen; and some control structures to make our life easier. That wraps up the top level requirements.

```
***********************************************************
* YASE Descriptor Definitions
link ┌─────────────────────────────────────┐ist window pointer
scr_ │.1    a0,-(a7)          * Push filename│urrent row in window
scr_ │.1    a1,-(a7)          * P┌───────────────────────────────────────────┐
ed_e │      open              * A│          move.w  w_ulcx(a5),d2   * d2 is screen
modi │w                        │                            * D5 is logica
c_co │  ┌─────────────────────────┐                                        │al
b_bu │.w│ *********************** │      move.1  b_buf(a5),a0    * a0 is │r
b_ga └──│ * Editor Dispatcher    │      move.1  b_gap(a5),d0    * compu │r
e_ga    │                        │      sub.1   a0,d0           * d0 is │or
e_buf  e│         xref    prtscr │      clr.w   d1              * d1 is │ck
blk_st e│         xref    _keyhi │      move.b  #10,d2          * do re─┘
blk_end e│        xref    prompt │      bra     sk0_nl          * loop
top_lef equ   38    * (long) │lp0_nl:
cur_lin equ   42    * (long) └─────────────────────────────────────────────┘
log_col equ   46    * (word) current logical column
```

FIGURE 12-1.   YASE Sample Screen.

The most important thing about any software project is, of course, choosing a name. We are calling our editor YASE (pronounced "Yeow-sah"), an acronym for Yet Another Screen Editor. Figure 12-1 shows a screen dump of YASE in action. The example shows five active windows. The window at the top of the display is a permanent window used for prompts and status information.

We will be discussing small pieces of the text editor routines to illustrate points. The specific fragment under discussion will be reproduced inline in the text, with line numbers. The entire module containing the fragment will be at the end of each chapter, because we feel it is important to see the code in context as well as examine it closely. We will be using this format for the rest of the book.

Module EXEC.PRN is a listing of the editor top level procedure. At line 78 we set the equate "BUFS" to the maximum number of windows we'll allow open at any one time:

```
78  BUFS     equ     5                * Max number of open windows
```

We're fixing this number at assembly rather than at runtime for two reasons. Number one, there's no standard way to determine maximum memory available on 68K systems. Number two, as far as possible we are going to make decisions at assemble time rather than at runtime. It reduces the code size and complexity and increases execution speed.

Entry to the program is at line 81, label "exec":

```
81    exec:
82            bsr     init            * Initialze local vars
83            bsr     cls             * Initialize virtual screen
84            move.l  #cmd_w,(a5)     * open command I/O window
85            bsr     border_w        *
86            bsr     get_buf         * open buffer
87    lpx:
88            bsr     edit            * do editing
```

Not much processing is needed to get going. We need to set up a few variables, open the command I/O window (the top window in Figure 12-2, and load in the first file. From there we begin editing via the call to "edit" at line 88. The "edit" procedure handles all text insertion and manipulations, but will return when a windowing command is issued, or when the user has indicated that the editing session is finished.

The procedure "edit" returns with D0 = 0 if the file is finished editing or non-zero if the user wants a window command (pop new window, shrink or stretch, rotate active window). The four lines following the call to "edit" figure out what action is required:

```
87    lpx:
88            bsr     edit            * do editing
89            tst.w   d0              * look at return code
90            beq     skx             * non-zero means window commands
91            bsr     g_3             * go do window commands
92            bra     lpx             * resume edit
```

If window commands are selected, we re-enter "edit" after any processing. Window commands are contained in another module that we'll see in a subsequent chapter.

Edit buffers are 64K data structures that contain the text being edited as well as all the editing state data and window parameters unique to a file. This data structure is described in Figure 12-2 as a set of offsets into the buffer. We'll see the uses of the fields in EDIT.H in this and other chapters. EDIT.H is included as a header file in most of YASE's modules.

If we determine that editing is complete on the current window, we recycle the edit buffer in lines 94 to 99:

```
94    skx:
95            move.l  free,a0         * save free list link
96            move.l  a5,free         * put current window in free list
97            move.l  (a5),a1         * get link to next item in chain
98            move.l  a1,used         * put used list back together
99            move.l  a0,(a5)         * link to free link
```

Edit buffers are maintained in two linked lists, a "free" list and a "used" list. When the editor is initialized, all of the buffers are in the free list, pointed to by the variable "free." On line 179 of Module EXEC "free" points to the first free buffer. This buffer's first 4 bytes are a pointer to the next free buffer, and so on to the last free buffer. The last free buffer has a pointer whose value is zero, to mark the end of the chain. The first in the chain of edit buffers currently in use is pointed to by the variable "used," line 180 of Module EXEC. As with the free list, the last used buffer has a null link pointer to mark the end of the free chain. If no buffer is in the free or used chain, the associated pointer variable ("free" or "used") is null.

```
*******************************************************************
* YASE Descriptor Definitions
linkage equ      0        * (long) Linked List window pointer
scr_row equ      4        * (word) Cursor current row in window
scr_col equ      6        * (word) Cursor current column in window
ed_err  equ      8        * (word) last editor error
modify  equ     10        * (word) file modified flag
c_col   equ     12        * (word) line virtual column
b_buf   equ     14        * (long) file buffer start address
b_gap   equ     18        * (long) file buffer gap start
e_gap   equ     22        * (long) file buffer gap end
e_buf   equ     26        * (long) file buffer end address
blk_st  equ     30        * (long) block start address
blk_end equ     34        * (long) block end address
top_lef equ     38        * (long) top-left char in window
cur_lin equ     42        * (long) current line start address
log_col equ     46        * (word) current logical column
log_lin equ     48        * (word) current logical line

w_ulbx  equ     50        * (word) left side window border
w_ulby  equ     52        * (word) top window border
w_lrbx  equ     54        * (word) right side window border
w_lrby  equ     56        * (word) bottom window border
w_ulcx  equ     58        * (word) window right character
w_ulcy  equ     60        * (word) window top character
w_lrcx  equ     62        * (word) window left character
w_lrcy  equ     64        * (word) window bottom character

w_rows  equ     66        * (word) window character rows
w_cols  equ     68        * (word) window character columns
w_off   equ     70        * (word) horizontal offset
insert  equ     72        * (word) insert toggle

fname   equ     74        * (string) associated filename
buffer  equ    126        * start of text buffer

DESC    equ   $10000      * end of available space
```

FIGURE 12-2.   Module EDIT.H

```
101           tst.l  used        * get top used window pointer
102           beq    ed_exit     * quit if no more windows
103           bsr    refresh     * redraw the screen
104           bra    lpx
105   ed_exit:
106           bsr    cls         * leave screen pretty
107           rts                * this is editor exit
```

If we determine that the user has not selected a window command, but has abandoned the last active window, the editor exits by executing a return after clearing the display.

The active buffer (the buffer currently being edited) is the first buffer in the used chain and is always pointed to by A5 as well. We have taken care that any reference to a buffer by the editing code is bound to the pointer in A5.

All we have to do to change the active window is to load a new value into A5 and bring to the foreground any portion of the new window that's been obscured. You'll find the code that does this with the window commands in a later chapter.

The code that obtains a buffer, opens a window, and loads a file is entered at label "get__buf", line 110:

```
110  get_buf:
111          tst.l    free              * check for buffer in free list
112          beq      no_buf            * jump on no buffer
```

"get__buf" exits silently if no buffer is available. Assuming you implement this editor on your system, you could add a warning message as an enhancement. This procedure is also referenced by the window commands module, so keep that in mind as you attack it with your editor.

Lines 113 to 115 take a buffer off the free chain, for use with the new editing window, and put the free chain back together:

```
113          move.l   free,a5           * get next free buffer
114          move.l   (a5),free         * replace free list link
115          move.l   used,(a5)         * link used link
```

Lines 117 to 126 are concerned with setting up the borders of the window being opened:

```
117          cmp.l    #end_d,defs       * see if we overran defaults
118          blt      sk0_gb            * jump if not
119          move.l   #s_def,defs       * reset defaults
120  sk0_gb:
121          move.l   defs,a3           * Get default size window address
122          addq.l   #8,defs           * move pointer for next time
123          move.w   (a3)+,d0          * Get default upper left X
124          move.w   (a3)+,d1          * Get default upper left Y
125          move.w   (a3)+,d2          * Get default lower right X
126          move.w   (a3)+,d3          * Get default lower right Y
```

Lines 164 to 171 are a table of windows of different sizes and positions:

```
164  defaults:
165          dc.w     lim_lx,lim_uy,lim_rx,lim_ly     * window 1
166  s_def:
167          dc.w     1,5,75,15         * Default size of window 2n
168          dc.w     2,7,76,17         * Default size of window 3n
169          dc.w     3,10,77,20        * Default size of window 4n
170          dc.w     4,12,78,22        * Default size of window 5n
171  end_d   equ      *
```

Each group of four words consists of two (X,Y) pairs, one defining the upper left corner of the window and one defining the lower right corner of the window. They're set now for the way we like them on our system. The first pattern is the maximum screen area and is used only for the first window opened. The next four rotate in a circular fashion as new windows are opened, which means that if you open and close a lot of files sooner or later you'll have windows directly on top of one another.

Note the way we test for the end of the default patterns—the equate "end__d" at line 171, which is set to the location counter at that point. The variable "defs" is a pointer to the next pattern to be used. When we need a new pattern, we test "defs" for being equal to "end__d," and if so, we reset "defs" to the first of the rotating patterns. This scheme is as easy as any other, but has one feature that many other schemes do not—it adjusts automatically to the number of patterns in the table. We can add or subtract patterns to either the ones used only once or the re-used patterns without having to hunt through the rest of the code for iteration counters or other hardcoded constants.

The call to "set__w" at line 127 does a little predigesting of the window sizing parameters to reduce computations later. The call to "set__edit" at line 128 does the same for the edit parameters as well as initializing other parameters. The call to "readfile" at line 129 asks the user for a filename and attempts to load the file. The rest of this procedure takes the filename from the global filename string and puts it into the edit buffer because the global filename gets overwritten. Note that lines 133 to 134 are the fastest byte-at-a-time string copy possible:

```
127             bsr     set_w           * Setup window parameters
128             bsr     set_edit        * Setup editor parameters
129             bsr     readfile        * Get filename and file
130             move.l  #filenm,a0      * Save name of file locally
131             lea     fname(a5),al    * Al is address where name goes
132     lp:
133             move.b  (a0)+,(al)+     * We just transfer bytes until
134             bne     lp              *  we find a null
```

Procedure "init," opens the command window, builds the free buffer list, and sets the universal editor variables to a known state. The universal variables are those like the paste buffer that are shared between all files:

```
142     init:
143             move.l  #cmd_w,a5       * Open command I/O window
144             move.w  #0,d0           * set command window limits
145             move.w  #0,dl
146             move.w  #79,d2
147             move.w  #3,d3
148             bsr     set_w           * init command window
149             clr.b   filenm          * zero out current filename
150             clr.l   used            * Zap the in-use buffer pointer
151             move.w  #BUFS-1,d0      * Buffer count
152             move.l  #win,al         * Start the linked list
153             move.l  al,free         * get the first pointer
154     lp0_li:
155             move.l  al,a0           * moves pointer up one node
156             add.l   #DESC,al        * calcs address of next buffer
157             move.l  al,(a0)         * loads address of next buffer
158             dbra    d0,lp0_li       * loop for BUFS times
159             clr.l   (a0)            * mark last buffer as end of list
160             move.l  #defaults,defs  * setup default window frame
161             rts
```

The executive module gives us a top level framework upon which we can start hanging the lower level routines. In the next chapters, we'll build the rest of the editor from the bottom up.

Module EXEC. PRN

```
  1                    ********************************************************
  2                    * EXEC - Editor Executive Routine & Globals
  3                    * Contains main editor loop and universal variables.
  4
  5                            xref    g_3,readfile,refresh,set_edit,open_w,cls,cmd_w
  6                            xref    filenm,edit,border_w,set_w
  7                            xdef    query,findpat,reppat,repflag,exec,p_buf,p_cnt
  8                            xdef    used,get_buf
  9
 10                    <<include EDIT.H>>
 47                    <<include CURSOR.H>>
 77
 78                    BUFS    equ     5               * Max number of open windows
 79                    ********************************************************
 80
 81                    exec:
 82  00000000 610000B6         bsr     init            * Initialze local vars
 83  00000004 61000000         bsr     cls             * Initialze virtual screen
 84  00000008 2ABC00000000     move.l  #cmd_w,(a5)     * open command I/O window
 85  0000000E 61000000         bsr     border_w
 86  00000012 6138             bsr     get_buf         * open buffer
 87                    lpx:
 88  00000014 61000000         bsr     edit            * do editing
 89  00000018 4A40             tst.w   d0              * look at return code
 90  0000001A 6706             beq     skx             * non-zero means window commands
 91  0000001C 61000000         bsr     g_3             * go do window commands
 92  00000020 60F2             bra     lpx             * resume edit
 93                    * Dump current window
 94                    skx:
 95  00000022 207900000F6      move.l  free,a0         * save free list link
 96  00000028 23CD000000F6     move.l  a5,free         * put current window in free list
 97  0000002E 2255             move.l  (a5),a1         * get link to next item in chain
 98  00000030 23C9000000FA     move.l  a1,used         * put used list back together
 99  00000036 2A88             move.l  a0,(a5)         * link to free link
100                    * Relink and Redraw
101  00000038 4AB9000000FA     tst.l   used            * get top used window pointer
102  0000003E 6706             beq     ed_exit         * quit if no more windows
103  00000040 61000000         bsr     refresh         * redraw the screen
104  00000044 60CE             bra     lpx
105                    ed_exit:
```

Module EXEC. PRN (continued)

```
106 00000046 61000000                  bsr     cls               * leave screen pretty
107 0000004A 4E75                       rts                       * this is editor exit
108 *************************************************************
109 * GET_BUF - finds and opens the next available window
110 get_buf:
111 0000004C 4AB9000000F6               tst.l   free              * check for buffer in free list
112 00000052 6762                       beq     no_buf            * jump on no buffer
113 00000054 2A79000000F6               move.l  free,a5           * get next free buffer
114 0000005A 23D5000000F6               move.l  (a5),free         * replace free list link
115 00000060 2AB9000000FA               move.l  used,(a5)         * link used link
116 00000066 23CD000000FA               move.l  a5,used           * replace used list link
117 0000006C 0CB90000013200 0000F2      cmp.l   #end_d,defs       * see if we overran defaults
118 00000076 6D0A                       blt     sk0_gb            * jump if not
119 00000078 23FC0000001200 0000F2      move.l  #s_def,defs       * reset defaults
120 sk0_gb:
121 00000082 2679000000F2               move.l  defs,a3           * Get default size window address
122 00000088 50B9000000F2               addq.l  #8,defs           * move pointer for next time
123 0000008E 301B                       move.w  (a3)+,d0          * Get default upper left X
124 00000090 321B                       move.w  (a3)+,d1          * Get default upper left Y
125 00000092 341B                       move.w  (a3)+,d2          * Get default lower right X
126 00000094 361B                       move.w  (a3)+,d3          * Get default lower right Y
127 00000096 61000000                   bsr     set_w             * Setup window parameters
128 0000009A 61000000                   bsr     set_edit          * Setup editor parameters
129 0000009E 61000000                   bsr     readfile          * Get filename and file
130 000000A2 207C00000000               move.l  #filenm,a0        * Save name of file locally
131 000000A8 43ED004A                   lea     fname(a5),a1      * A1 is address where name goes
132 lp:
133 000000AC 12D8                       move.b  (a0)+,(a1)+       * We just transfer bytes until
134 000000AE 66FC                       bne     lp                * we find a null
135 000000B0 61000000                   bsr     open_w            * Open the window
136 000000B4 4E75                       rts
137 no_buf:
138 * set correct edit error and return
139 000000B6 4E75                       rts
140 *************************************************************
141 * INIT - Initializes local variables
142 init:
143 000000B8 2A7C00000000               move.l  #cmd_w,a5         * Open command I/O window
144 000000BE 303C0000                   move.w  #0,d0             * set command window limits
145 000000C2 323C0000                   move.w  #0,d1
```

```
146  000000C6  343C004F              move.w  #79,d2
147  000000CA  363C0003              move.w  #3,d3
148  000000CE  61000000              bsr     set_w              * init command window
149  000000D2  423900000000          clr.b   filenm             * zero out current filename
150  000000D8  42B9000000FA          clr.l   used               * Zap the in-use buffer pointer
151  000000DE  303C0004              move.w  #BUFS-1,d0          * Buffer count
152  000000E2  227C000000FE          move.l  #win,a1            * Start the linked list
153  000000E8  23C9000000F6          move.l  a1,free            * get the first pointer
154                          lp0_li:
155  000000EE  2049                  move.l  a1,a0              * moves pointer up one node
156  000000F0  D3FC00010000          add.l   #DESC,a1           * calcs address of next buffer
157  000000F6  2089                  move.l  a1,(a0)            * loads address of next buffer
158  000000F8  51C8FFF4              dbra    d0,lp0_li          * loop for BUFS times
159  000000FC  4290                  clr.l   (a0)               * mark last buffer as end of list
160  000000FE  23FC0000010A000000F2  move.l  #defaults,defs     * setup default window frame
161  00000108  4E75                  rts

162  ****************************************************************
163  * Default window corners.
164                          defaults:
165  0000010A  00000004004F0016 s_def: dc.w  lim_lx,lim_uy,lim_rx,lim_ly   * window 1
166
167  00000112  00010005004B000F      dc.w    1,5,75,15          * Default size of window 2n
168  0000011A  00020007004C0011      dc.w    2,7,76,17          * Default size of window 3n
169  00000122  0003000A004D0014      dc.w    3,10,77,20         * Default size of window 4n
170  0000012A  0004000C004E0016      dc.w    4,12,78,22         * Default size of window 5n
171
172                          end_d   equ     *
     ****************************************************************
173  00000000                        bss
174  00000000                query:  ds.b    80                 * g.p. query buffer
175  00000050                findpat:ds.b    80                 * find string pattern
176  000000A0                reppat: ds.b    80                 * replace string buffer
177  000000F0                repflag:ds.w    1                  * "replace" request flag
178  000000F2                defs:   ds.l    1                  * current frame default
179  000000F6                free:   ds.l    1                  * free buffer linked list ptr
180  000000FA                used:   ds.l    1                  * in-use buffer link pointer
181  000000FE                win:    ds.b    DESC*BUFS          * editing buffers & pointers
182                          e_win   equ     *                  * end of windows
183  000500FE                p_cnt:  ds.w    1                  * Char count in paste buffer
184  00050100                p_buf:  ds.b    $10000             * 64K paste buffer
185
```

13

Input/Output Interfaces

In this chapter we discuss generalized I/O techniques, such as file and device streams. Our goal is to isolate and generalize I/O for the YASE editor to one small portion of the software system so that the end result will not only work for this editor but will be reusable in future programs. We will present an actual interface to the I/O calls of one operating system (CP/M-68K) and we will kludge the terminal I/O for our developmental system.

For our software development we're using a Hallock Systems (HSC) PRO-68 card, living in a Leading Edge model D PC clone, running OS9/68K or CP/M-68K Version 1.3 (HSC integration level 1.8). We chose this system because it was generic enough so that any software we wrote with the exception of the I/O could be ported easily. It also appeals to our twisted sense of humor to use the 8088 processor as a lowly I/O server for the 68000. Unfortunately, we have to interface through the CP/M-68K operating system for terminal I/O calls, putting yet another layer of overhead on the notoriously slow PC BIOS video support. Screen I/O speed is a real problem in our system. One of the routines we'll present here is a transparent and portable speedup module for slow CRTs.

It pays to spend some time on the design of fast full screen I/O. The trend for quite a while has been user-friendly software, even user-friendly systems software. It used to be (in the good old days) that systems software was nice small programs that took their parameters on the command line and executed silently unless a terse, one-line error message was required. UNIX is a perfect example of this philosophy.

As systems programmers, we have to rethink our user interfaces. On most programs it's no longer acceptable to use teletype-style output. This raises the spectre of cursor addressing on the zillions of different terminal devices in use. There is an ANSI standard for terminal escape sequences, but as far as we know only DEC and DEC clones have really gotten on the ANSI bandwagon.

There are several approaches to reconfiguring programs for different terminals. The UNIX systems quite often have a facility called "termcap" that knows about lots of terminals and can easily be configured for others. This represents the most generalized approach to configuration, but also the most expensive. You first need UNIX, which ain't cheap, and you also pay for the runtime overhead of termcap, which is written in C. You'll never be able to convince a UNIX hack, but it's a myth that UNIX C optimizes so well that it's foolish to write in assembler on a UNIX system. In addition, termcap adds to the overhead by making a lot of decisions at runtime while you're making terminal calls.

C is usually fast enough that you can use it for most of your work. However, some things are more appropriate in assembler, and we presume that's why you're reading this book. If you decide to write in assembly language, you have an implied obligation to make your code as fast as possible. To help you fulfill this obligation, we're going to show you some very fast terminal I/O routines.

While the terminal routines in this chapter were written to support YASE, we took some care to make them general enough to be useful for any project requiring terminal support. We chose an approach to reconfiguration that requires the program to be relinked if the terminal is changed. After we look at these, we'll look at a technique that lends itself to patching the finished object module, to reconfigure after linktime.

Module CRT.PRN shows the minimal terminal interface needed for menu driven software and, of course, text editors. We have three routines for output: a clear-screen procedure; a procedure to place the cursor at an arbitrary screen location; and a procedure to place a character on the screen and move the cursor to the next position on the screen. These three primitive procedures are all that are needed for windowing and menuing, and if required, clear-screen can be written in terms of the other two. You really can't count on other features, such as line delete and line insert, being present in a terminal device. For example, if your terminal device is actually memory-mapped, the three procedures listed are very suitable, while line delete/insert are more difficult to simulate. If you don't care about portability, of course, you should exploit every feature you can. Incidentally, this module can be linked to a C program under CP/M-68K and the routines called from C without any changes.

There are also two functions for terminal input. These are more difficult to implement, because they depend on operating system support that may not be there, or may be buried in the bowels of the BIOS. The first function, "__getkey," gets a character from the user. This seems simple except that it has to be unfiltered, unbuffered, and unechoed. Some operating systems trap control characters and buffer lines to enhance their multitasking. While this is useful in most applications, in editors it can be most unpleasant. We also don't want characters echoed on the screen because we want to control what goes on the screen and where.

The second function is even harder on some systems. "__keyhit" goes and looks to see if the user has struck a key and returns a Boolean result. This is not usually well supported on multitasking systems, because the operating system wants to put your task to sleep while it's waiting for an I/O service. If you bypass this by looping until a character is ready for input, you use the system resources to no good purpose. We'll see a use for this type of function later when we look at the editor screen refresh. For now, just remember to use this function sparingly and try not to hang in a loop waiting for character input. On a multitasking sytem, having to do this usually indicates a fundamental design flaw.

In the event that you want to write code for different terminals and don't want to distribute linkable code (although on some 68K systems, specifically CP/M-68K, this is very easy to do and reasonably secure), but still want to have the speed of code written for a specific terminal, you can fall back on the old idea of the jump table. This involves dedicating a section of code, usually at the very front of the program, large enough to hold the largest set of routines you'll ever use. The first entries are a series of jump vectors to the various routines in the module:

```
            xref    entry_point
            xdef    _crt_cls,_crt_cursor,_crt_put,_crt_get,_keyhit
            bra     entry_point    * branch to program start
    _crt_cls:
            bra     crt_cls
    _crt_cursor:
            bra     crt_cursor
    _crt_put:
            bra     crt_put
    _crt_get:
            bra     crt_get
    _keyhit:
            bra     keyhit
        << I/O code goes here >>
```

The first entry in the jump table is a branch to the program's main entry. The next five branches jump to the five routines. When new routines are needed, they are are just patched in over the old. The location of the five branches are fixed for all versions of the routines, so the substitution is transparent to the rest of the code. Assuming your operating system allows it and you're brave, you can even swap code in and out at run time.

With just the three output procedures and a slow terminal, the response of an editor or other full screen program tends to suffer. For example, in a windowing system, if we want to scroll the window, we essentially have to rewrite the whole window. Take the case in which we have a large window on the screen, with a single column of characters down the left edge of the window, and the rest of the window blank. A generalized scroll routine would rewrite the whole window, but actually change only a very small part of it. Now imagine this happening at 1200 baud over a phone modem. After about 10 minutes of this with a text editor, your user is either going to put his foot through the display or call up the system line editor.

Rewriting the Display

If you put some smarts into your application, you can avoid rewriting areas of the display that don't need it. This can get very involved in a program like a text editor, however, and you have to put this involved code into every full screen application you write.

Perhaps a better solution is a virtual screen interface, such as we have in Module VSCREEN.PRN. This is a layer of code that sits between the application and the CRT interface code we have in Module CRT.PRN. This code relies on the fact that the 68K is faster than anything but a memory-mapped display interface, and in fact, if you delete parts of the virtual screen, this code will work as an interface to a memory-mapped display, provided that the display stores characters in a compatible format. Except for the names of the routines, the calling sequence to the virtual interface is the same as for the routines in Figure 13-1 (page 156).

The idea works like this. Somewhere in memory, we keep a copy of what we think the screen looks like (line 103, label "v__scrn").

```
103  v_scrn: ds.b    (lines*cols)     * virtual screen memory
```

When the application issues a clear screen request (lines 27 to 47), we initialize both the virtual screen and the physical screen to blanks:

```
27   cls:
28           movem.l a0/d0/d1,-(a7)   * save user's registers
29           move.w  #(lines*cols),d0  Number of chars to blank
30           lsr.w   #1,d0            * Divide by to for word store
31           move.w  #' ',d1          * we'll use register for speed
32           move.l  #v_scrn,a0       * our memory copy
33           bra     loop_test        * Go do loop test
34   loop:
35           move.w  d1,(a0)+         * store two blanks at a crack
36   loop_test:
37           dbra    d0,loop          * loop thru all memory
38           bsr     _crt_cls         * clear physical screen
39           move.w  #1,sync          * set sync flag true
40           move.l  #v_scrn,my_curs  * sync my cursor
41           clr.l   -(a7)            * put two zero words on stack
42           bsr     _crt_cursor      * sync user's cursor
43           addq.l  #4,a7            * adjust stack
44           clr.w   his_lin          * clear user's line counter
45           clr.w   his_col          * clear user's column counter
46           movem.l (a7)+,a0/d0/d1   * restore user's registers
47           rts
```

Note in lines 29 to 31 that we set up blanks to store in our virtual screen, and that we're planning to store two blanks (one word) at a time. Our virtual screen is a byte array, but since we don't have some strongly typed compiler sniveling at us about type mismatches, we don't care. Storing a word at a pop cuts the loop iterations in half and speeds us up by a factor of two. We could just as well have stored a longword at a time, though the speedup is not another factor of two.

When the application code requests that we position the cursor (lines 50 to 62), we note the request and move the virtual cursor but do not move the physical cursor. We also set a flag "sync" signalling that the physical cursor is no longer matched to the virtual cursor:

```
50   cursor:
51           clr.w   sync             * set sync flag false
52           move.w  4(a7),his_col    * save crt screen X position
53           move.w  6(a7),his_lin    * save crt screen Y position
54           move.l  d0,-(a7)         * save D0 across calculation
55           clr.l   d0               * start with clean register
56           move.w  10(a7),d0        * get new line number
57           mulu    #cols,d0         * multiply by cols to get offset
58           add.w   8(a7),d0         * add in column offset
59           add.l   #v_scrn,d0       * add base to get address
60           move.l  d0,my_curs       * now we should be at same spot
61           move.l  (a7)+,d0         * restore d0
62           rts
```

When the application issues a character to be placed on the screen (lines 65 to 88), we compare it to the character in our virtual screen. If the character matches what ought to be on the screen (lines 69 to 71) we just return, resetting the sync flag to indicate that the cursors are not matched and updating the virtual cursor:

```
65   putc:
66           link    a6,#0          * freeze stack frame
67           movem.l d0/a0,-(a7)    * save user's stuff
68           move.w  8(a6),d0       * get char to output
69           move.l  my_curs,a0     * get my screen address
70           cmp.b   (a0),d0        * are they the same?
71           beq     no_put         * jump if yes
72           move.b  d0,(a0)        * Store char in virtual screen
73           tst.w   sync           * are we synced?
74           bne     synced         * jumps if synced
75           bsr     sync_curs      * sync cursors
76   synced:
77           move.w  8(a6),-(a7)    * push his character
78           bsr     _crt_put       * send to crt
79           addq.l  #2,a7          * adjust stack
80           bra     did_put        * set other vars
81   no_put:
82           clr.w   sync           * show out of sync
83   did_put:
84           addq.l  #1,my_curs     * increment my cursor
85           addq.w  #1,his_col     * and his column count
86           movem.l (a7)+,d0/a0    * restore user's stuff
87           unlk    a6
88           rts
```

If the characters don't match (lines 72 to 80), we update the virtual screen and look at the sync flag. If the cursors aren't synced, we sync them by updating the physical cursor. Then, in either case, we output the character to the physical screen.

Using this module, a typical display update can be sped up by a factor of 3, and a sparse display update can be sped up by a factor of 10 or more (measured on our system). These results make it well worth the effort of writing the code.

Words of Caution

There are some disadvantages and quirks to using this system, though. This interface is not at all suitable for a teletype-like output where the screen needs to scroll up as lines are added at the bottom, although it can be made to work that way—it just won't improve performance. Also, the physical cursor isn't usually where you think it ought to be. This is disconcerting when prompting the user for input, because the cursor can be blinking halfway across the screen from the prompt. While this is no problem for a Real Programmer, it drives end users crazy. That's why the "sync_curs" routine is declared global in this module. A call to this routine will match the cursors for you when prompting the user.

Another potential problem is the total absence of error checking. While most terminals will ignore requests to put the cursor at line 942, column 10144, the virtual interface will happily accept it. It's easy to get the virtual cursor off in the boonies somewhere, trashing the rest of your data area. For testing, you may want to stub these routines to use direct CRT calls until you get things working properly.

The routines in Modules CRT.PRN and VSCREEN.PRN are very device-specific. They are designed for terminal I/O, period. Even if your operating system could capture the transactions between the terminal and editor and redirect them to a pipe or disk file, what you would get out of the redirection would be pretty much useless. The CRT interfaces are suited only to realtime interaction with a user.

In general, though, it is better to have device independence and stream interfaces managed through the operating system for I/O. Disk files and one-way dumb devices like printers are suited to device-independent interfaces. We don't really care how long it takes to update these types of devices as long as they are eventually taken care of. Of course, somewhere, either in the operating system or the applications code, there's a separation into device drivers and a distinction between one type of device and another. Our goal is to bury these distinctions as low in the code as possible.

For example, in our text editor YASE, we will need to input and output files as we edit them. Since we don't know what operating systems you have available, we need to make the I/O system fairly flexible. There are two basic types of file I/O out there, block and stream.

Stream I/O is usually supported under the more modern operating systems with device independent interfaces. In stream I/O, we basically throw data (usually 1 byte at a time) into an output hole, or take data 1 byte at a time from an input dispenser. The stream manager takes care of details such as blocking and deblocking disk files, or redirecting the standard input and output streams. Stream I/O is easier on the applications level because data is most often handled sequentially, especially in text-oriented programs. However, stream I/O is usually slower than block I/O, because we're using the operating system, with all the associated overhead, every time we input or output a byte.

In block I/O, data is passed back and forth between the operating system and an application program in chunks of some size. For example, disk I/O is passed in "sectors," usually of some fixed size. Block I/O to files is usually faster than stream I/O, because we only have to use the operating system when blocks are ready or needed, but it imposes a bunch of overhead on the application, which must block and deblock data before calling the operating system. In addition, it's harder to switch between I/O to block devices like files and character devices like printers because the interfaces are much different. For example, in CP/M, files are blocked in sectors of 128 bytes, while printers and terminals are handled as stream interfaces.

We needed to make a choice as to which type of I/O to use for the examples in this book. As we've said, it's easier on the applications level to use stream I/O, so we decided to use a stream model for our file I/O. It is also easier to simulate stream I/O on a block I/O system than vice versa.

We wrote our YASE file interface for CP/M-68K. CP/M-68K is an upwards-compatible system from the original CP/M-80 operating system. When CP/M-80 was designed, it made sense to put as little functionality into the operating system as possible, so as not to penalize programs by hogging the restricted 8080 memory with unneeded services. However, to a programmer used to a modern operating system with all sorts of bells and whistles, not having these features is really inconvenient.

Module FILEPRIM.PRN is a listing of our stream interface to CP/M-68K. A quick look at the header will remind you C folks of the C Standard I/O Library character primitives. While the C I/O system is far from perfect, it has withstood the test of time, and lots of people are used to the way it operates. We tried to keep our interface pretty much the same.

If you have a stream-based operating system your interface routines will be much simpler. All you have to do is to find the *Advanced User Guide* to your system, turn past the chapters on "Unpacking Your New Computer," "Setting Up Your New Computer," "Operating the On/Off Switch on Your New Computer," "Determining the Top and Bottom Sides of Your New Computer's Floppy Disks," etc., and somewhere in the back will be a slim appendix with the I/O calls. Maybe. Otherwise you'll have to make 30 or 40 calls to the manufacturer's hotline.

CP/M deals with files through a File Control Block (FCB). This contains much of the same information the C FILE pointers point to, or the MS-DOS "handles" handle. The difference is that CP/M requires the application to keep set up and keep track of the storage for the FCB. Figure 13-1 is an include file that defines the offsets into a CP/M FCB, along with a few extensions of our own. For sequential files, the only fields we need to fool with are the first three, "drive," "name," and "ext." Our extensions include a character counter, a flag indicating that data has been modified, and a 128-byte buffer. An equate "file" is also defined to help us allocate the proper amount of memory when we create an FCB.

The usual procedure when using a CP/M file is to take a file name contained in a string (we use the C null-terminated string throughout this book) and parse it into the drive-name-ext fields of the FCB. The rest of the CP/M-defined FCB is then zeroed and a pointer to the FCB is passed to CP/M along with a request to open or create the file. Data is then transferred between CP/M and the application in the 128-byte buffer. What we'll do is try to make these operations transparent to our application, by designing calls similar to the C standard calls.

Refer to line 52 of Module FILEPRIM. This is the entry to the "open" procedure. We need to set up parameters to this routine before we call. In the comment header lines 30 to 35 we refer to parameters as "Px.s," where "x" is a number and "s" is a data size. The lower the number the closer it is to the top of the stack when we make the call. In the case of "open," P2.W is a word-sized parameter and is pushed first, and P0.L is a longword parameter and is pushed last.

The minimum amount of information needed to open a file in most systems is the file specification (the name and any path or drivespec) and whether or not to create the file if it doesn't exist—in other words, if we want to open the file for reading or writing. We are also including a pointer to a block of memory large enough to contain an FCB. In a C environment, this pointer would be returned to us as a FILE pointer by the fopen() function. We can't do this easily in CP/M because CP/M doesn't include memory managment. Later in the book we'll discuss dynamic memory allocation and deallocation, but we're going to leave the file

```
*********************************************************************
*   FCB Header File - CP/M-68K File Control Block information
*
drive      equ      0                      * Drive Byte offset
name       equ      1                      * First name char offset
type       equ      9                      * First type char offset
extent     equ      12                     * Extent byte offset
s2         equ      14                     * S2 byte offset
reccnt     equ      15                     * Record Count byte offset
currec     equ      32                     * Current record byte offset
r_zero     equ      33                     * R0 Random Record Number offset
r_one      equ      34                     * R1/R2 Random Record # offset

fcb_sz     equ      36                     * sizeof( file control block )
*
*********************************************************************
*   File Control Block Extensions for file utilities
curchr     equ      36                     * Offset to current char word
dirty      equ      38                     * Offset to dirty flag
dma_buf    equ      40                     * Offset to DMA buffer
file       equ      168                    * sizeof( extended FCB )
```

FIGURE 13-1.   Module FCB.H

routines as they are. Normally, it's not worth the overhead of including the memory manager just to simplify opening files.

Now, let's take a close look at the code for the "open" function, beginning on line 52:

```
52   open:
53              link     a6,#0              * Set stack frame
54              movem.l  d1/d2/a0/a1/a2,-(a7)
55              bsr      parse_name         * Parses filename to FCB
56              tst.w    d0                 * Check return from PARSE_NAME
57              bmi      exit_open          * Exit on error
58              bsr      fillfcb            * Set balance of FCB
59              move.l   8(a6),d1           * Get FCB addr for CP/M calls
60              tst.w    16(a6)             * Open new file or old?
61              bne      make_new           * Make new file, erase any old.
62   must_exist:
63              move.w   #$000f,d0          * CP/M OPEN FILE Function Code
64              trap     #2                 * Call CP/M - Open existing file
65              bra      exit_open          * Exit
66   make_new:
67              move.w   #$0013,d0          * CP/M DELETE FILE Function code
68              trap     #2                 * Call CP/M - delete any old file
69              move.w   #$0016,d0          * CP/M MAKE FILE Function code
70              trap     #2                 * Call CP/M - attempt create
71   exit_open:
72              ext.w    d0                 * Convert CP/M return to our type
73              movem.l  (a7)+,d1/d2/a0/a1/a2
74              unlk     a6                 * Restore caller's stack frame
75              rts
```

We start by freezing the stack frame using A6 as the stack frame pointer, because we have stack parameters being passed in. Next, we save all of the registers we'll use except for D0.

Saving all registers except D0 (and any other registers used to return values) is such a universal convention in 68K assembler that it's taken for granted by almost everyone. We are observing this convention with all of our general-purpose modules that have external interfaces. If you look at the rest of the body of "open," up to line 136, and compare registers referenced by the code to registers mentioned in the MOVEM instruction you'll notice that MOVEM mentions registers not used in the body of "open." Because we're writing this in assembler, we don't have to observe any conventions within the module, as long as the external interface conforms to whatever our standards are. As we keep going in the code, you'll see that we also use the stack frame established by "open" for all of the local procedures. Within the "open" procedure and its local procedures, we'll also make use of our knowledge of register allocation to avoid trashing register values needed elsewhere. The ability to bend coding standards is one of the things that make assembly language programs run faster and jump higher than machine generated code.

Let's take a top level view of the file open process for CP/M. We first parse our convenient C-style name string into the CP/M FCB format, checking for a malformed name. Then we fill the rest of the FCB with zeros, because CP/M likes it that way. A branch is taken at this point between two possible paths. If we're opening the file for reading, we try to open the file. If the file doesn't exist, we return an error. If we're opening the file for writing, we first make a blind attempt at deleting the file, and then try to create the file, returning CP/M's return code to the caller of "open."

The most complicated part of this operation is the parsing of the name. Figure 13-2 shows the format of the FCB name field, so that those of you without CP/M can follow along

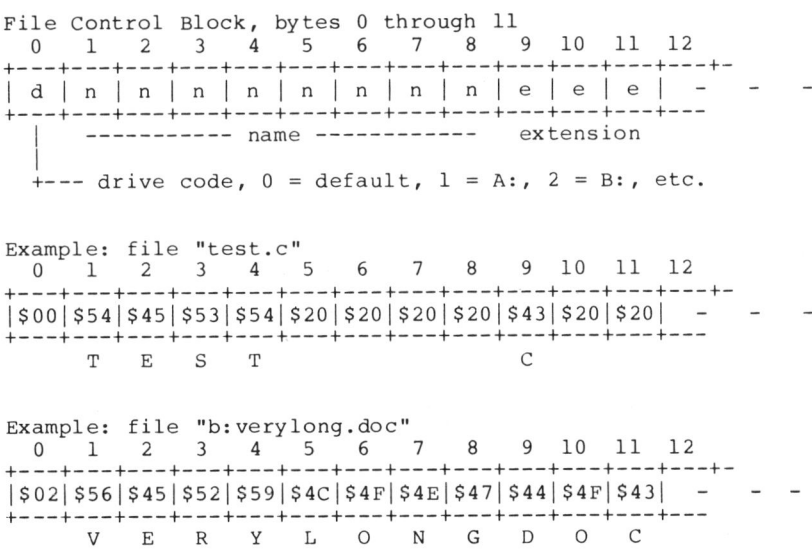

```
File Control Block, bytes 0 through 11
   0   1   2   3   4   5   6   7   8   9  10  11  12
 +---+---+---+---+---+---+---+---+---+---+---+---+---+-
 | d | n | n | n | n | n | n | n | n | e | e | e |  -    -    -
 +---+---+---+---+---+---+---+---+---+---+---+---+---+---
   |    ----------- name ------------   extension
   |
   +--- drive code, 0 = default, 1 = A:, 2 = B:, etc.


Example: file "test.c"
   0   1   2   3   4   5   6   7   8   9  10  11  12
 +---+---+---+---+---+---+---+---+---+---+---+---+---+-
 |$00|$54|$45|$53|$54|$20|$20|$20|$20|$43|$20|$20|  -    -    -
 +---+---+---+---+---+---+---+---+---+---+---+---+---+---
       T   E   S   T                   C


Example: file "b:verylong.doc"
   0   1   2   3   4   5   6   7   8   9  10  11  12
 +---+---+---+---+---+---+---+---+---+---+---+---+---+-
 |$02|$56|$45|$52|$59|$4C|$4F|$4E|$47|$44|$4F|$43|  -    -    -
 +---+---+---+---+---+---+---+---+---+---+---+---+---+---
       V   E   R   Y   L   O   N   G   D   O   C
```

FIGURE 13-2. CP/M Name Field

at home. The "drive" byte is either set to zero, to use the current default drive, or has a value in the range 1..16 for drives A through M. The name field is 8 characters long, and is padded with blanks at the end if the name is less than 8 characters. The extension field is 3 characters long, and is also blank padded at the end. Both the name and extension characters must be in upper case. A file created with lower-case letters or unprintable characters in it can't be deleted using standard operating system tools without more ingenuity than most end users are capable of.

The "parse__name" procedure begins at line 80:

```
80    parse_name:
81             move.l  8(a6),a0      * Pick up FCB address
82             move.l  12(a6),al     * Pick up name string
```

Notice at lines 81 to 82 how we pick off the parameters from the stack frame established by "open."

In lines 83 to 86 we fill the name portion of the FCB with blanks. We spent about twenty minutes on these four lines of code, making them as fast as we could. (This is an example of losing sight of the big picture. We maybe save five or ten microseconds over a less optimal solution, on a section of code executed only once, and just before we do a disk access that by comparison takes an eternity). We're filling from right to left, so that we can use our loop counter as an index into the FCB (line 85). Note that we also use a displacement of one to avoid overwriting the drive byte:

```
83             move.w  #10,d0        * Loop counter for blank filling
84    blank_loop:
85             move.b  #' ',1(a0,d0.w) * Blank fill name "backwards"
86             dbra    d0,blank_loop  * Continue for 11 bytes
```

Also notice the loop construction. At line 83 we load the loop counter D0 with the value 10. Since we're falling into the loop from the top, and executing the loop body before the loop test, the loop counter value must be one less than the desired number of iterations. This type of loop construction is only appropriate if you are certain that the loop body should be executed at least once.

Lines 88 to 95 decide if the file specification includes a drivespec:

```
88             cmp.b   #':',1(al)    * Check for drivespec
89             bne     no_drive      * No drivespec, jump over
90             move.b  (al),(a0)     * Transfer drivespec
91             and.b   #$0f,(a0)+    * Make into 0..16 drivecode
92             addq.l  #2,al         * Put pointer past drivespec
93             bra     name_xfr      * Go transfer name
94    no_drive:
95             clr.b   (a0)+         * Set default drivecode
```

In CP/M, we can be certain that, if a drivespec is included, the second character of the name string will be a colon.

Lines 98 to 127 pick up file specification string characters one at a time, checking each one for being a valid character and moving it into the FCB. We're doing a lot of checking here to be sure that the name has no more than 8 characters and the extension no more than 3. Something you may want to change is the requirement that the string be terminated immediately after the extension:

```
 98    name_loop:
 99            move.b   (al)+,d2          * Pickup name character
100            beq      parse_chk         * Found a terminal null...
101            cmp.b    #'.',d2           * Look for delimiter
102            beq      ext_xfr           * Parse extension
103            bsr      check             * Make uppercase & screen chars
104            tst.b    dl                * Dl = -l for illegal character
105            bmi      parse_err         * Exit if CHECK found error
106            move.b   d2,(a0)+          * Put char in FCB
107            dbra     d0,name_loop      * Try again
108    * If we're here, 8 filename chars were found. Skip period.
109            move.b   (al)+,d2          * Move pointer and check char
110            cmp.b    #'.',d2           * Double check for period
111            beq      ext_xfr           * OK, let's continue
112            bra      parse_err         * Badly formed name string.
113    ext_xfr:
114            move.l   8(a6),a0          * Re-sync FCB pointer
115            adda     #type,a0          * Point at TYPE field
116            move.w   #2,d0             * Three chars only for filetype
117    ext_loop:
118            move.b   (al)+,d2          * Pickup filetype char
119            beq      parse_chk         * Found terminal null...
120            bsr      check             * Make uppercase and screen chars
121            tst.b    dl                * Look for error return
122            bmi      parse_err         * Exit if CHECK found error.
123            move.b   d2,(a0)+          * Put filetype char into FCB
124            dbra     d0,ext_loop       * Go for next
125    * If we're here, 3 filetype chars were found. Check for null.
126            tst.b    (al)              * Is it null?
127            bne      parse_err         * No, return error
```

The last thing we do is look through the FCB to be sure that at least 1 character was specified for the name. CP/M will happily create file with a blank name if you're not careful.

```
128    parse_chk:
129            move.l   8(a6),a0          * Get FCB base addr again
130            cmp.b    #' ',name(a0)     * At least one name char?
131            beq      parse_err         * Nope, return error.
132            clr.w    d0                * "Good" return code
133            rts
```

The "fillfcb" routine at lines 140 to 152 simply zeros the rest of the FCB, including our extensions to manage the character buffer:

```
140  fillfcb:
141          move.l   8(a6),a0          * Load FCB base address
142          adda     #extent,a0        * Index past name portion
143          move.w   #dma_buf-extent-1,d0    * Loop count
144  fill_loop:
145          clr.b    (a0)+             * Load zeros in all FILE fields
146          dbra     d0,fill_loop      * Continue for all bytes in FILE
147          tst.w    16(a6)            * Is this a write?
148          bne      fill_exit         * Yes, CURCHR is ok as zero.
149          move.l   8(a6),a0          * Get FCB address again.
150          move.w   #128,curchr(a0)   * Mark as "Need to read"
151  fill_exit:
152          rts
```

Lines 149 to 150 are needed if we're opening the file for reading. When we load the current character ("curchr") field with 128, it triggers a buffer read the first time we ask for a character.

The procedure "check" has a couple of features very useful in all sorts of parsers. Lines 158 to 162 convert lower-case letters to upper-case:

```
158          cmp.b    #'a',d2           * Check for lowercase first.
159          blt      not_lower         * It's less than 'a'
160          cmp.b    #'z',d2           * Less than 'z'?
161          bgt      not_lower         * It's greater than 'z'
162          and.b    #$5f,d2           * Makes D2.B uppercase
163  not_lower:
```

If we were certain that the input character was a letter (and not, as in this case, possibly punctuation), line 162 would be the only one required. If you look at the ASCII set, the only difference between a lower-case letter and its upper-case equivalent is that bit 5 is set on lower-case letters.

Lines 164 to 169 compare the input character against an essentially random list of 19 illegal characters enumerated at line 176:

```
164          move.w   #18,d1            * 19 illegal name chars
165          lea      bad_chars,a2      * Get name array base
166  chk_loop:
167          cmp.b    (a2)+,d2          * Test for bad char
168          beq      chk_err           * Bad char, return error
169          dbra     d1,chk_loop       * Keep trying.
170          clr.w    d1                * "Good" error return
171          rts                        * "Good" exit
172  chk_err:
173          move.w   #-1,d1            * "Bad" error return
174          rts                        * "Bad" exit
175  bad_chars:
176          dc.b     '.:[]()<>=*&,!|?/;+-'
```

We've hardcoded the 19 iterations as a constant at line 164 (remember, the loop counter is one less than the number of iterations). If this illegal character set was subject to change, we could use a technique similar to that seen in Chapter 12 for window parameters, and have the assembler calculate the loop constant.

Line 177 contains the pseudo-op EVEN. In some assemblers, this is called ALIGN. This pseudo-op forces the instruction counter to an even address alignment after byte-size objects are coded inline. In some assemblers, forgetting this pseudo-op will cause a runtime address error exception because instructions are assembled on odd addresses.

The file close procedure begins on line 181 of Figure 13-20:

```
181   close:
182           link      a6,#0                     * Setup stack frame
183           movem.l   d1/a0/a1,-(a7)            * Save caller's registers
184           move.l    8(a6),a0                  * Pick up FCB base address
185           bsr       put_eof                   * Add ASCII EOF (^Z)
186           bmi       exit_close                * Branch if write failed
187           move.l    d1,a0                     * Setup CP/M parameter
188           move.w    #$0010,d0                 * CP/M CLOSE FILE function code
189           trap      #2                        * Close the file
190   exit_close:
191           ext.w     d0                        * Convert CP/M return to our type
192           movem.l   (a7)+,d1/a0/a1            * Restore caller's registers
193           unlk      a6                        * Restore caller's stack frame
194           rts
```

It's pretty simple. CP/M requires that files be multiples of 128 bytes, so we need to pad out the end of the current buffer with EOF characters, done by the call to "put__eof." Because many of the less robust tools, especially public domain tools, need to see that EOF character, we add another record completely full of EOF characters just in case the current record holds exactly 128 characters.

The routines are set up so that a file can be read up to a given point and then you can switch to writing. Given the way this "close" procedure works, a file will be truncated at the point where you finish writing. You can clean this up by adding more flags and logic (if you consider this a bug rather than a feature), but it's probably not worth it.

The procedure "fputc" at line 218 is a "write-behind" buffering scheme. This means that the buffer is not written out to disk until it is full, AND we have another character that needs to go into the buffer. In other words, while we write the buffer to disk we're hanging on to the character that would overflow the buffer:

```
217   fputc:
218           link      a6,#0                     * Freeze stack frame
219           movem.l   a0/d1,-(a7)               * Save caller's registers
220           move.l    8(a6),a0                  * Grab FCB
221           cmp.w     #128,curchr(a0)           * Check for record full
222           bne       just_put                  * Nope, we're OK.
223           bsr       write_buf                 * Flush current record
224   just_put:
225           move.w    curchr(a0),d0             * Get current char count
226           addq.w    #1,curchr(a0)             * Bump counter
227           move.w    #-1,dirty(a0)             * Make dirty
228           move.b    13(a6),dma_buf(a0,d0.w)   * Save character
229           movem.l   (a7)+,a0/d1               * Restore caller's registers
230           unlk      a6                        * Restore caller's stack frame
231           rts
```

This sort of design is usually more efficient than other designs, although in the case of a sequential file it doesn't make much difference. It does allow you to install an "unput" procedure later that can be guaranteed to remove the last character written into the buffer.

The procedure "fgetc" is similar. It refills the buffer only when it has to satisfy a character request. This allows an "unget" procedure to replace the last character read from a file if you overrun, because the last character read is always in the buffer except during a call to return another character. The "unget" procedure is helpful when writing lexical scanners that overrun when building a token. "fgetc" returns an end-of-file indication at the first EOF character or if no more records remain in the file:

```
251  fgetc:
252          link      a6,#0             * Establish stack frame
253          movem.l   d1/a0,-(a7)       * Save caller's registers
254          move.l    8(a6),a0          * Get FCB address
255          cmp.w     #128,curchr(a0)   * Do we need to read a record?
256          blt       no_read           * No, just get character
257          bsr       get_rec           * Read a record
258          tst.w     d0                * Was there an error?
259          bmi       fget_err          * Yes, return error to caller
260  no_read:
261          move.w    curchr(a0),d0     * Get current character counter
262          addq.w    #1,curchr(a0)     * Increment current char count
263          move.b    dma_buf(a0,d0.w),d0 * Load next character
264          cmp.b     #$1a,d0           * Is it EOF?
265          beq       fget_err          * Yes, return error.
266          ext.w     d0                * Make into type "int".
267          bra       fget_exit         * And return...
268  fget_err:
269          move.w    #-1,d0            * Indicate error
270  fget_exit:
271          movem.l   (a7)+,d1/a0       * Restore caller's registers
272          unlk      a6                * Restore caller's stack frame
273          rts
```

Module EDIT1.PRN shows the YASE interface to our file I/O primitives. These are two routines to manage editor files and blocks. "read__in" pulls the entire contents of a file into the editor buffer pointed to by A5, assuming it fits. "write__out" is more general, and writes an arbitrary number of bytes from an arbitrary location in memory.

Note the change in parameter passing technique as we switch from the general-purpose file primitives to the special-purpose YASE interface. The YASE interfaces won't be much use in other programs, mostly because they convert line ends between the CP/M return/newline and the YASE newline-only. We do this in YASE to save looking for a 2-character sequence as a line terminator. Because the YASE routines are specific to YASE, we can relax our interface control and use register parameters instead of the more universal stack parameters.

The CRT and file primitive modules presented in this chapter are fairly primitive, but they represent the nasty parts of machine interface. Once these are coded for your target machine, more general and more powerful procedures become almost trivial, and are very portable. In the next chapter, we'll look at data structures and data management, including a closer look at data structures used in this chapter.

Module CRT.PRN

```
*****************************************************
* CRT INTERFACE Routines - PRO68, CP/M68K, BIOS Rev 1.8,
* hosted on Leading Edge PC / PRO-68
* Count on all calls trashing D0.
*
* CRT_CURSOR
* This function sets the host cursor to an (X,Y) position.
* Calling sequence: Push Y offset, then X offset, then call.
* X and Y are binary numbers, offset zero, word length.
*
* CRT_CLS
* This function clears the host crt screen. No parameters.
*
* CRT_PUT
* This function dumps the next character typed directly to the
* CRT. Calling sequence: Push the character as the low byte of
* a word, then call.
*
* GET_KEY
* This function returns the next character typed at the console,
* without echo. Character is in low byte of D0.W
*
* KEYHIT
* This function returns non-zero in D0.W if a character is
* waiting for input from the console.
*
*****************************************************

        xdef    _crt_cls,_crt_cursor,_crt_put,_getkey,_keyhit


_crt_cls:
        move.w  d1,-(a7)        * Save caller's D1
        move.w  #$0006,d0       * CP/M Direct I/O call
        move.w  #$001A,d1       * Clear Screen
        trap    #2              * Call CP/M
        move.w  (a7)+,d1        * Restore caller's D1
        rts
*****************************************************

_crt_cursor:
        move.l  d1,-(a7)        * Save caller's D1
        move.w  #$0006,d0       * CP/M Direct I/O call
        move.w  #$001B,d1       * ESCape
        trap    #2              * Call CP/M
        move.w  #$0006,d0       * CP/M Direct I/O call
```

```
1
2
3
4
5
6
7
8
9
10
11
12
13
14
15
16
17
18
19
20
21
22
23
24
25
26
27
28
29
30
31
32  00000000  3F01
33  00000002  303C0006
34  00000006  323C001A
35  0000000A  4E42
36  0000000C  321F
37  0000000E  4E75
38
39
40  00000010  2F01
41  00000012  303C0006
42  00000016  323C001B
43  0000001A  4E42
44  0000001C  303C0006
```

Module CRT.PRN (continued)

```
45   00000020  323C003D              move.w  #$003D,d1        * Set Cursor
46   00000024  4E42                  trap    #2               * Call CP/M
47   00000026  303C0006              move.w  #$0006,d0        * CP/M Direct I/O call
48   0000002A  122F000B              move.b  ll(a7),d1        * Row Address
49   0000002E  4881                  ext.w   d1               * sign extend
50   00000030  D27C0020              add.w   #$20,d1          * offset by 32
51   00000034  4E42                  trap    #2               * Call CP/M
52   00000036  303C0006              move.w  #$0006,d0        * CP/M Direct I/O call
53   0000003A  122F0009              move.b  9(a7),d1         * Column Address
54   0000003E  4881                  ext.w   d1               * sign extend
55   00000040  D27C0020              add.w   #$20,d1          * offset by 32
56   00000044  4E42                  trap    #2               * Call CP/M
57   00000046  221F                  move.l  (a7)+,d1         * Restore caller's D1
58   00000048  4E75                  rts
59
*********************************************************************
60
_crt_put:
61   0000004A  2F01                  move.l  d1,-(a7)         * Save caller's D1
62   0000004C  303C0006              move.w  #$0006,d0        * CP/M direct I/O call
63   00000050  322F0008              move.w  8(a7),d1         * character to output
64   00000054  4E42                  trap    #2               * Call CP/M
65   00000056  221F                  move.l  (a7)+,d1         * Restore caller's D1
66   00000058  4E75                  rts
67
*********************************************************************
68
_getkey:
69   0000005A  3F01                  move.w  d1,-(a7)         * Save caller's D1
70   0000005C  303C0006              move.w  #$0006,d0        * CP/M direct I/O call
71   00000060  323C00FF              move.w  #$00FF,d1        * Console input flag
72   00000064  4E42                  trap    #2               * Call CP/M
73   00000066  321F                  move.w  (a7)+,d1         * Restore caller's D1
74   00000068  4E75                  rts
75
*********************************************************************
76
_keyhit:
77   0000006A  3F01                  move.w  d1,-(a7)         * Save caller's D1
78   0000006C  303C0006              move.w  #$0006,d0        * CP/M direct I/O call
79   00000070  323C00FE              move.w  #$00FE,d1        * Console status flag
80   00000074  4E42                  trap    #2               * Call CP/M
81   00000076  321F                  move.w  (a7)+,d1         * Restore caller's D1
82   00000078  4E75                  rts
83
84   0000007A                        end
```

Module VSCREEN.PRN

```
 1                          *********************************************************
 2                          * Virtual Screen - Maintains a virtual interface to a slow
 3                          * CRT output device. Scrolling not supported.
 4
 5                          lines   equ   24          * lines on actual screen
 6                          cols    equ   80          * columns on actual screen
 7
 8                                  xdef  cls,cursor,putc,sync_curs,v_scrn
 9                                  xref  _crt_cls,_crt_put,_crt_cursor
10
11                          * CLS
12                          * Clears the CRT. No parameters.
13                          *
14                          * CURSOR
15                          * Sets the cursor to an (X,Y) position. Calling sequence: push
16                          * Y, then X. X and Y are binary, zero-based, word length.
17                          *
18                          * PUTC
19                          * Outputs a character to the display. Calling sequence: push
20                          * the character to be output in the low byte os a word.
21                          *
22                          * SYNC_CURS
23                          * Syncs the actual CRT cursor with the virtual CRT cursor, as it
24                          * usually isn't where it ought to be, especially when doing
25                          * inputs. No parameters.
26                          *********************************************************
27                          cls:
28 00000000 48E7C080               movem.l a0/d0/d1,-(a7)      * save user's registers
29 00000004 303C0780               move.w  #(lines*cols),d0    * Number of chars to blank
30 00000008 E248                   lsr.w   #1,d0               * Divide by to for word store
31 0000000A 323C2020               move.w  #' ',d1             * we'll use register for speed
32 0000000E 207C00000002           move.l  #v_scrn,a0          * our memory copy
33 00000014 6002                   bra     loop_test           * Go do loop test
34                          loop:
35 00000016 30C1                   move.w  d1,(a0)+            * store two blanks at a crack
36                          loop_test:
37 00000018 51C8FFFC               dbra    d0,loop             * loop thru all memory
38 0000001C 61000000               bsr     crt_cls             * clear physical screen
39 00000020 33FC000100000000       move.w  #1,sync             * set sync flag true
40 00000028 23FC0000000200000782   move.l  #v_scrn,my_curs     * sync my cursor
```

Module VSCREEN.PRN (continued)

```
41  00000032  42A7                  clr.l    -(a7)              * put two zero words on stack
42  00000034  61000000              bsr      crt_cursor         * sync user's cursor
43  00000038  588F                  addq.l   #4,a7              * adjust stack
44  0000003A  42790000 0786         clr.w    his_lin            * clear user's line counter
45  00000040  42790000 0788         clr.w    his_col            * clear user's column counter
46  00000046  4CDF0103              movem.l  (a7)+,a0/d0/d1     * restore user's registers
47  0000004A  4E75                  rts

48
49  *************************************************************
50  * Sets cursor to arbitrary screen location
    cursor:
51  0000004C  42790000 0000         clr.w    sync               * set sync flag false
52  00000052  33EF0004 00000788     move.w   4(a7),his_col      * save crt screen X position
53  0000005A  33EF0006 00000786     move.w   6(a7),his_lin      * save crt screen Y position
54  00000062  2F00                  move.l   d0,-(a7)           * save D0 across calculation
55  00000064  4280                  clr.l    d0                 * start with clean register
56  00000066  302F000A              move.w   10(a7),d0          * get new line number
57  0000006A  C0FC0050              mulu     #cols,d0           * multiply by cols to get offset
58  0000006E  D06F0008              add.w    8(a7),d0           * add in column offset
59  00000072  D0BC0000 0002         add.l    #v_scrn,d0         * add base to get address
60  00000078  23C00000 0782         move.l   d0,my_curs         * now we should be at same spot
61  0000007E  201F                  move.l   (a7)+,d0           * restore d0
62  00000080  4E75                  rts

63
64  *************************************************************
65  * Output character to screen if necessary
    putc:
66  00000082  4E560000              link     a6,#0              * freeze stack frame
67  00000086  48E78080              movem.l  d0/a0,-(a7)        * save user's stuff
68  0000008A  302E0008              move.w   8(a6),d0           * get char to output
69  0000008E  20790000 0782         move.l   my_curs,a0         * get my screen address
70  00000094  B010                  cmp.b    (a0),d0            * are they the same?
71  00000096  6718                  beq      no_put             * jump if yes
72  00000098  1080                  move.b   d0,(a0)            * store char in virtual screen
73  0000009A  4A790000 0000         tst.w    sync               * are we synced?
74  000000A0  6602                  bne      synced             * jumps if synced
75  000000A2  6126                  bsr      sync_curs          * sync cursors
76                                  synced:
77  000000A4  3F2E0008              move.w   8(a6),-(a7)        * push his character
78  000000A8  61000000              bsr      crt_put            * send to crt
79  000000AC  548F                  addq.l   #2,a7              * adjust stack
80  000000AE  6006                  bra      did_put            * set other vars
```

```
 81
 82 000000B0 427900000000    no_put:
                             did_put:  clr.w    sync          * show out of sync
 83
 84 000000B6 52B900000782              addq.l   #1,my_curs     * increment my cursor
 85 000000BC 527900000788              addq.w   #1,his_col     * and his column count
 86 000000C2 4CDF0101                  movem.l  (a7)+,d0/a0    * restore user's stuff
 87 000000C6 4E5E                      unlk     a6
 88 000000C8 4E75                      rts
 89
 90                          ***********************************************
 91                          * SYNC_CURS - Syncs crt cursor to virtual cursor
                             sync_curs:
 92 000000CA 3F00                      move.w   d0,-(a7)       * Saving char across put call
 93 000000CC 3F3900000786              move.w   his_lin,-(a7)  * Push Y address
 94 000000D2 3F3900000788              move.w   his_col,-(a7)  * Push X address
 95 000000D8 61000000                  bsr      crt_cursor     * set actual cursor
 96 000000DC 588F                      addq.l   #4,a7          * adjust stack
 97 000000DE 33FC000100000000          move.w   #1,sync        * show synced
 98 000000E6 301F                      move.w   (a7)+,d0       * restore character
 99 000000E8 4E75                      rts
100                          ***********************************************
101 00000000                           bss
102 00000000                 sync:     ds.w     1              * actual display synced flag
103 00000002                 v_scrn:   ds.b     (lines*cols)   * virtual screen memory
104 00000782                 my_curs:  ds.l     1              * virtual screen cursor location
105 00000786                 his_lin:  ds.w     1              * actual screen line number
106 00000788                 his_col:  ds.w     1              * actual screen column number
107
108 0000078A                           end
```

Module FILEPRIM.PRN

```
 1     ****************************************************************
 2     * File Primitive Operations - CP/M-68K
 3     *
 4     * All routines interface to CP/M-68K files. FCB and FILE block
 5     * definitions are contained in FCB.H.
 6
 7           <<include FCB.H>>
 8
                 .xdef   open,close,fgetc,fputc

28     ****************************************************************
29
30     * Routines:   OPEN    Opens a file for input or output.
31     *                     Entry: P0.L points to FILE block. P1.L points to
32     *                            null-terminated name string. P2.W = 0
33     *                            for "File must Exist", nonzero
34     *                            for "Create new and erase old".
35     *                     Exit:  File opened or D0.W = -1
36     *
37     *             CLOSE   Closes a file. Flushes current buffer
38     *                     if dirty.
39     *                     Entry: P0.L points to FILE block.
40     *                     Exit:  File closed or D0.W = -1
41     *
42     *             FGETC   Returns next char from file.
43     *                     Entry: P0.L points to FILE block.
44     *                     Exit:  D0.W = char or -1 on error.
45     *
46     *             FPUTC   Writes next char to file.
47     *                     Entry: P0.L points to FILE block.
48     *                            P1.W is the char to write.
49     *                     Exit:  D0.W = 0 for success, -1 on failure.
50     *
51     ****************************************************************
52
53  00000000  4E560000   open:      link     a6,#0              * Set stack frame
54  00000004  48E760E0              movem.l  d1/d2/a0/a1/a2,-(a7)
55  00000008  6130                  bsr      parse_name         * Parses filename to FCB
56  0000000A  4A40                  tst.w    d0                 * Check return from PARSE_NAME
57  0000000C  6B22                  bmi      exit_open          * Exit on error
58  0000000E  610000B0              bsr      fillfcb            * Set balance of FCB
59  00000012  222E0008              move.l   8(a6),d1           * Get FCB addr for CP/M calls
60  00000016  4A6E0010              tst.w    16(a6)             * Open new file or old?
61  0000001A  6608                  bne      make_new           * Make new file, erase any old.
62
63  0000001C  303C000F   must_exist: move.w  #$000f,d0          * CP/M OPEN FILE Function Code
64  00000020  4E42                  trap     #2                 * Call CP/M - Open existing file
65  00000022  600C                  bra      exit_open          * Exit
```

```
make_new:
67  00000024  303C0013      move.w    #$0013,d0       * CP/M DELETE FILE Function code
68  00000028  4E42          trap      #2              * Call CP/M - delete any old file
69  0000002A  303C0016      move.w    #$0016,d0       * CP/M MAKE FILE Function code
70  0000002E  4E42          trap      #2              * Call CP/M - attempt create
71  exit_open:
72  00000030  4880          ext.w     d0              * Convert CP/M return to our type
73  00000032  4CDF0706      movem.l   (a7)+,d1/d2/a0/a1/a2
74  00000036  4E5E          unlk      a6              * Restore caller's stack frame
75  00000038  4E75          rts
76  *
77  ************************************************************
78  * PARSE_NAME parses a C name string into CP/M-68K FCB. Uses
79  * caller's stack frame. Consider this a local procedure to OPEN.
80  parse_name:
81  0000003A  206E0008      move.l    8(a6),a0        * Pick up FCB address
82  0000003E  226E000C      move.l    12(a6),a1       * Pick up name string
83  00000042  303C000A      move.w    #10,d0          * Loop counter for blank filling
84  blank_loop:
85  00000046  11BC00200001  move.b    #' ',1(a0,d0.w) * Blank fill name "backwards"
86  0000004C  51C8FFF8      dbra      d0,blank_loop   * Continue for 11 bytes
87  *
88  00000050  0C29003A0001  cmp.b     #':',1(a1)      * Check for drivespec
89  00000056  660A          bne       no_drive        * No drivespec, jump over
90  00000058  1091          move.b    (a1),(a0)       * Transfer drivespec
91  0000005A  0218000F      and.b     #$0f,(a0)+      * Make into 0..16 drivecode
92  0000005E  5489          addq.l    #2,a1           * Put pointer past drivespec
93  00000060  6002          bra       name_xfr        * Go transfer name
94  no_drive:
95  00000062  4218          clr.b     (a0)+           * Set default drivecode
96  name_xfr:
97  00000064  303C0007      move.w    #7,d0           * Start with filename part
98  name_loop:
99  00000068  1419          move.b    (a1)+,d2        * Pickup name character
100 0000006A  673E          beq       parse_chk       * Found a terminal null...
101 0000006C  B43C002E      cmp.b     #'.',d2         * Look for delimiter
102 00000070  6718          beq       ext_xfr         * Parse extension
103 00000072  61000070      bsr       check           * Make uppercase & screen chars
104 00000076  4A01          tst.b     d1              * D1 = -1 for illegal character
105 00000078  6B40          bmi       parse_err       * Exit if CHECK found error
106 0000007A  10C2          move.b    d2,(a0)+        * Put char in FCB
107 0000007C  51C8FFEA      dbra      d0,name_loop    * Try again
108 * If we're here, 8 filename chars were found. Skip period.
109 00000080  1419          move.b    (a1)+,d2        * Move pointer and check char
110 00000082  B43C002E      cmp.b     #'.',d2         * Double check for period
111 00000086  6702          beq       ext_xfr         * OK, let's continue
112 00000088  6030          bra       parse_err       * Badly formed name string.
```

Module FILEPRIM.PRN (continued)

```
113
114  0000008A  206E0008      ext_xfr:   move.l  8(a6),a0              * Re-sync FCB pointer
115  0000008E  D0FC0009                 adda    #type,a0             * Point at TYPE field
116  00000092  303C0002                 move.w  #2,d0                * Three chars only for filetype
117
118  00000096  1419          ext_loop:  move.b  (a1)+,d2             * Pickup filetype char
119  00000098  6710                     beq     parse_chk            * Found terminal null...
120  0000009A  6148                     bsr     check                * Make uppercase and screen chars
121  0000009C  4A01                     tst.b   d1                   * Look for error return
122  0000009E  6B1A                     bmi     parse_err            * Exit if CHECK found error.
123  000000A0  10C2                     move.b  d2,(a0)+             * Put filetype char into FCB
124  000000A2  51C8FFF2                 dbra    d0,ext_loop          * Go for next
125                          * If we're here, 3 filetype chars were found. Check for null.
126  000000A6  4A11          parse_chk: tst.b   (a1)                 * Is it null?
127  000000A8  6610                     bne     parse_err            * No, return error
128
129  000000AA  206E0008                 move.l  8(a6),a0             * Get FCB base addr again
130  000000AE  0C2800200001             cmp.b   #' ',name(a0)        * At least one name char?
131  000000B4  6704                     beq     parse_err            * Nope, return error.
132  000000B6  4240                     clr.w   d0                   * "Good" return code
133  000000B8  4E75                     rts
134
135  000000BA  303CFFFF      parse_err: move.w  #-1,d0               * "Bad" return code
136  000000BE  4E75                     rts
137                          *
138                          * **************************************************
139                          * FILLFCB zeros the non-name portion of the FCB. Local to OPEN.
140                          * **************************************************
141  000000C0  206E0008      fillfcb:   move.l  8(a6),a0             * Load FCB base address
142  000000C4  D0FC000C                 adda    #extent,a0           * Index past name portion
143  000000C8  303C001B                 move.w  #dma_buf-extent-1,d0 * Loop count
144
145  000000CC  4218          fill_loop: clr.b   (a0)+                * Load zeros in all FILE fields
146  000000CE  51C8FFFC                 dbra    d0,fill_loop         * Continue for all bytes in FILE
147  000000D2  4A6E0010                 tst.w   16(a6)               * Is this a write?
148  000000D6  660A                     bne     fill_exit            * Yes, CURCHR is ok as zero.
149  000000D8  206E0008                 move.l  8(a6),a0             * Get FCB address again.
150  000000DC  317C00800024             move.w  #128,curchr(a0)      * Mark as "Need to read"
151
152  000000E2  4E75          fill_exit: rts
153                          *
154                          * **************************************************
155                          * CHECK converts lowercase to uppercase and screens chars CP/M
156                          * considers illegal name characters.
157                          * **************************************************
158  000000E4  B43C0061      check:     cmp.b   #'a',d2              * Check for lowercase first.
159  000000E8  6D0A                     blt     not_lower            * It's less than 'a'
```

```
160  000000EA B43C007A         cmp.b   #'z',d2             * Less than 'z'?
161  000000EE 6E04             bgt     not_lower           * It's greater than 'z'
162  000000F0 C43C005F         and.b   #$5f,d2             * Makes D2.B uppercase
163
                      not_lower:
164  000000F4 323C0012         move.w  #18,d1              * 19 illegal name chars
165  000000F8 45F900000110     lea     bad_chars,a2        * Get name array base
166
                      chk_loop:
167  000000FE B41A             cmp.b   (a2)+,d2            * Test for bad char
168  00000100 6708             beq     chk_err             * Bad char, return error
169  00000102 51C9FFFA         dbra    d1,chk_loop         * Keep trying.
170  00000106 4241             clr.w   d1                  * "Good" error return
171  00000108 4E75             rts                         * "Good" exit
172
                      chk_err:
173  0000010A 323CFFFF         move.w  #-1,d1              * "Bad" error return
174  0000010E 4E75             rts                         * "Bad" exit
175
                      bad_chars:
176  00000110 2E3A5B5D28293C3E dc.b    '.:[]()<>=*&,!|?/;+-'
176  00000118 3D2A262C217C3F2F
176  00000120 3B2B2D
177  00000124
177  00000124                  even                        * Force alignment
178
179  *   ********************************************************
180  * CLOSE Closes a file. Flushes current buffer if dirty.
181                   close:
182  00000124 4E560000         link    a6,#0               * Setup stack frame
183  00000128 48E740C0         movem.l d1/a0/a1,-(a7)      * Save caller's registers
184  0000012C 206E0008         move.l  8(a6),a0            * Pick up FCB base address
185  00000130 6114             bsr     put_eof             * Add ASCII EOF (^Z)
186  00000132 6B08             bmi     exit_close          * Branch if write failed
187  00000134 2041             move.l  d1,a0               * Setup CP/M parameter
188  00000136 303C0010         move.w  #$0010,d0           * CP/M CLOSE FILE function code
189  0000013A 4E42             trap    #2                  * Close the file
190                   exit_close:
191  0000013C 4880             ext.w   d0                  * Convert CP/M return to our type
192  0000013E 4CDF0302         movem.l (a7)+,d1/a0/a1      * Restore caller's registers
193  00000142 4E5E             unlk    a6                  * Restore caller's stack frame
194  00000144 4E75             rts
195  *
196  * PUT EOF fills the end of the current DMA buffer with ^Z
197                   put_eof:
198
199  00000146 0C6808000024     cmp.w   #128,curchr(a0)     * Check if we need to add another
200  0000014C 6608             bne     do_rest             * record with EOFs. (jump on NO)
201  0000014E 4A680026         tst.w   dirty(a0)           * look for empty record
202  00000152 6702             beq     do_rest             * jump if this record empty
203  00000154 614E             bsr     write_buf           * Flush current record
```

```
204
205 00000156 303C007F         do_rest:
                                      move.w  #127,d0                  * Set up number of chars to fill
206 0000015A 90680024                 sub.w   curchr(a0),d0            * less current character count
207 0000015E D0E80024                 adda    curchr(a0),a0            * Get address of first fill char
208 00000162 D0FC0028                 adda    #dma_buf,a0              * Need this too.
209                            put_loop:
210 00000166 10FC001A                 move.b  #$1a,(a0)+               * Insert character
211 0000016A 51C8FFFA                 dbra    d0,put_loop              * Continue through buffer
212 0000016E 6134                     bsr     write_buf               * Flush filled record
213 00000170 4E75                     rts
214                            *
215                            ********************************************************************
216                            * FPUTC puts a character to a disk file.
217                            fputc:
218 00000172 4E560000                 link    a6,#0                   * Freeze stack frame
219 00000176 48E74080                 movem.l a0/d1,-(a7)             * Save caller's registers
220 0000017A 206E0008                 move.l  8(a6),a0                * Grab FCB
221 0000017E 0C6800800000024          cmp.w   #128,curchr(a0)         * Check for record full
222 00000184 6602                     bne     just_put                * Nope, we're OK.
223 00000186 611C                     bsr     write_buf               * Flush current record
224                            just_put:
225 00000188 30280024                 move.w  curchr(a0),d0           * Get current char count
226 0000018C 52680024                 addq.w  #1,curchr(a0)           * Bump counter
227 00000190 317CFFFF0026             move.w  #-1,dirty(a0)           * Make dirty
228 00000196 11AE000D0028             move.b  13(a6),dma_buf(a0,d0.w) * Save character
229 0000019C 4CDF0102                 movem.l (a7)+,a0/d1             * Restore caller's registers
230 000001A0 4E5E                     unlk    a6                      * Restore caller's stack frame
231 000001A2 4E75                     rts
232                            *
233                            ********************************************************************
234                            * WRITE_BUF writes the current record to disk and resets FILE buf
235                            write_buf:
236 000001A4 222E0008                 move.l  8(a6),d1                * Get FCB base address
237 000001A8 D2BC00000028             add.l   #dma_buf,d1             * Compute DMA buffer address
238 000001AE 303C001A                 move.w  #$001a,d0               * CP/M SET DMA ADDRESS Function
239 000001B2 4E42                     trap    #2                      * Setup DMA address
240 000001B4 206E0008                 move.l  8(a6),a0                * Get FCB base address
241 000001B8 42680026                 clr.w   dirty(a0)               * Mark dirty flag as "clean"
242 000001BC 42680024                 clr.w   curchr(a0)              * Set current char pointer to 0
243 000001C0 2208                     move.l  a0,d1                   * Get FCB address for CP/M
244 000001C4 303C0015                 move.w  #$0015,d0               * CP/M WRITE SEQUENTIAL Function
245 000001C6 4E42                     trap    #2                      * Write record
246 000001C8 4880                     ext.w   d0                      * Convert CP/M return to our type
247 000001CA 4E75                     rts
248                            *
249                            ********************************************************************
250                            * FGETC returns the next character from a file.
```

```
251
252  000001CC 4E560000      fgetc:    link     a6,#0              * Establish stack frame
253  000001D0 48E74080                movem.l  d1/a0,-(a7)        * Save caller's registers
254  000001D4 206E0008                move.l   8(a6),a0           * Get FCB address
255  000001D8 0C6800800024            cmp.w    #128,curchr(a0)    * Do we need to read a record?
256  000001DE 6D06                    blt      no_read            * No, just get character
257  000001E0 6126                    bsr      get_rec            * Read a record
258  000001E2 4A40                    tst.w    d0                 * Was there an error?
259  000001E4 6B16                    bmi      fget_err           * Yes, return error to caller
260          no_read:
261  000001E6 30280024                move.w   curchr(a0),d0      * Get current character counter
262  000001EA 52680024                addq.w   #1,curchr(a0)      * Increment current char count
263  000001EE 10300028                move.b   dma_buf(a0,d0.w),d0 * Load next character
264  000001F2 B03C001A                cmp.b    #$1a,d0            * Is it EOF?
265  000001F6 6704                    beq      fget_err           * Yes, return error.
266  000001F8 4880                    ext.w    d0                 * Make into type "int".
267  000001FA 6004                    bra      fget_exit          * And return...
268          fget_err:
269  000001FC 303CFFFF                move.w   #-1,d0             * Indicate error
270          fget_exit:
271  00000200 4CDF0102                movem.l  (a7)+,d1/a0        * Restore caller's registers
272  00000204 4E5E                    unlk     a6                 * Restore caller's stack frame
273  00000206 4E75                    rts
274          *
275  * *****************************************************************
276  * GET_REC - reads next record sequentially. Local to FGETx.
277  get_rec:
278  00000208 2208                    move.l   a0,d1              * Get FCB base address for CP/M
279  0000020A D2BC00000028            add.l    #dma_buf,d1        * Compute DMA buffer address
280  00000210 303C001A                move.w   #$001a,d0          * CP/M SET DMA ADDRESS Function
281  00000214 4E42                    trap     #2                 * Setup DMA address
282  00000216 2208                    move.l   a0,d1              * Get FCB base address for CP/M
283  00000218 303C0014                move.w   #$0014,d0          * CP/M READ SEQUENTIAL function
284  0000021C 4E42                    trap     #2                 * Get the record
285  0000021E 42680026                clr.w    dirty(a0)          * Mark record as "clean"
286  00000222 42680024                clr.w    curchr(a0)         * Reset character counter
287  00000226 4A00                    tst.b    d0                 * Look at return code
288  00000228 6602                    bne      grec_err           * Returned an error...
289  0000022A 4E75                    rts                         * Return success
290          grec_err:
291  0000022C 303CFFFF                move.w   #-1,d0             * Load error return
292  00000230 4E75                    rts                         * Return error
293  00000232                         end
```

Module EDIT1.PRN

```
                         ****************************************************
                         * EDIT1 - Editor file I/O routines.
                         *
                         * Routines:    READ_IN  Reads a file into an editing buffer.
                         *              Entry:   Register A5.L points to an initialized
                         *                       edit buffer descriptor block.
                         *                       Register A0.L points to filename string
                         *              Exit:    ed_err(a5) set if any problems.
                         *
                         *              WRITE_OUT writes a block of memory data to a
                         *                       file.
                         *              Entry:   Register A0.L points to filename string.
                         *                       Register A1.L points to the start of data
                         *                       area in memory. D1.W holds number of
                         *                       bytes to write into file.
                         *              Exit:    ed_err(a5) set if any problems.
                         *
                                        .xref  open,close,fgetc,fputc
                                        .xdef  read_in,write_out
                         <<include FCB.H>>
                         <<include EDIT.H>>
                         ****************************************************
                         * READ_IN - Reads a file into an editing buffer.
                         read_in:
 83 00000000 48E740C0             movem.l  dl/a0/al,-(a7)  * Save caller's registers.
 84 00000004 4E56FF58             link     a6,#-file       * Create an FCB on the stack
 85 00000008 224F                 move.l   a7,al           * get FCB address
 86 0000000A 3F3C0000             move.l   #0,-(a7)        * Push 0 for "File Must Exist"
 87 0000000E 2F08                 move.l   a0,-(a7)        * Push filename
 88 00000010 2F09                 move.l   al,-(a7)        * Push FCB address
 89 00000012 61000000             bsr      open            * Attempt open
 90 00000016 4A40                 tst.w    d0              * Did it work?
 91 00000018 6A06                 bpl      skl_read        * Yes.
 92 0000001A 303C0001             move.w   #1,d0           * Show "File-not-found" error
 93 0000001E 6030                 bra      read_exit       * Say goodbye.
                         skl_read:
 95 00000020 222D0016             move.l   e_gap(a5),dl    * Compute buffer length
 96 00000024 92AD0012             sub.l    b_gap(a5),dl
 97 00000028 226D0012             move.l   b_gap(a5),al    * Setup pointer to data area
 98 0000002C 6010                 bra      sk3_read        * Loop test done before read
                         lpl_read:
100 0000002E 61000000             bsr      fgetc           * Read character
101 00000032 4A40                 tst.w    d0              * Look for end of file
102 00000034 6B12                 bmi      sk2_read        * Yes, found end-of-file
103 00000036 B03C000D             cmp.b    #13,d0          * is this C/R?
```

```
104  0000003A  67F2                   beq      lpl_read       * yes, just skip it.
105  0000003C  12C0                   move.b   d0,(a1)+       * Store datum
106                        sk3_read:
107  0000003E  51C9FFEE               dbra     d1,lpl_read
108  00000042  303C0002               move.w   #2,d0          * Go for the next one.
109  00000046  6008                   bra      read_exit      * If we're here, file's too big.
110                                                           * So leave.
111  00000048  2B490012    sk2_read:  move.l   a1,b_gap(a5)   * save in descriptor structure
112  0000004C  303C0000               move.w   #0,d0          * Show successful read.
113                        read_exit:
114  00000050  4E5E                   unlk     a6             * Restore frame pointer
115  00000052  4CDF0302               movem.l  (a7)+,d1/a0/al * Restore caller's registers.
116  00000056  4E75                   rts
117                        ****************************************************
118                        * WRITE_OUT - writes a file to disk
119                        write_out:
120  00000058  48E740E0               movem.l  dl/a0-a2,-(a7) * Save caller's registers.
121  0000005C  4E56FF58               link     a6,#-file      * Create an FCB on the stack
122  00000060  244F                   move.l   a7,a2          * Get FCB address
123  00000062  3F3CFFFF               move.w   #$FFFF,-(a7)   * Push -1 for "Create File"
124  00000066  2F08                   move.l   a0,-(a7)       * Push filename
125  00000068  2F0A                   move.l   a2,-(a7)       * Push FCB address
126  0000006A  61000000               bsr      open           * Attempt open
127  0000006E  4A40                   tst.w    d0             * Did it work?
128  00000070  6A26                   bpl      sk4_write      * Yes, loop test before write.
129  00000072  303C0001               move.w   #1,d0          * Show "Can't make file" error
130  00000076  6036                   bra      write_exit     * Say goodbye.
131                        lpl_write:
132  00000078  0C11000A               cmp.b    #10,(a1)       * Is this a newline?
133  0000007C  660E                   bne      sk3_write      * No.
134  0000007E  1F7C000D0005           move.b   #13,5(a7)      * Store RETURN into stack
135  00000084  61000000               bsr      fputc          * write RETURN.
136  00000088  4A40                   tst.w    d0             * Look for error.
137  0000008A  6B1E                   bmi      sk2_write      * Yes, found error.
138                        sk3_write:
139  0000008C  1F590005               move.b   (a1)+,5(a7)    * Store parameter into stack
140  00000090  61000000               bsr      fputc          * write character
141  00000094  4A40                   tst.w    d0             * Look for error.
142  00000096  6B12                   bmi      sk2_write      * Yes, found error.
143                        sk4_write:
144  00000098  51C9FFDE               dbra     dl,lpl_write   * Go for the next one.
145  0000009C  2F0A                   move.l   a2,-(a7)       * push FCB address
146  0000009E  61000000               bsr      close          * close file
147  000000A2  4A40                   tst.w    d0             * smooth return code
148  000000A4  6B08                   bmi      write_exit     * error exit
149  000000A6  4240                   clr.w    d0             * show success
150  000000A8  6004                   bra      write_exit     * and get out of here.
```

Module EDIT1.PRN (continued)

```
                                  sk2_write:
151
152  000000AA  303C0001                 move.w   #1,d0            * Show error.
153                                write_exit:
154  000000AE  4E5E                       unlk     a6               * Restore frame pointer
155  000000B0  4CDF0702                   movem.l  (a7)+,d1/a0-a2   * Restore caller's registers.
156  000000B4  4E75                       rts
157
158  000000B6                            end
```

14

Data management

In this chapter, we look at the data structures used in assembly language programming. Many of these structures are used in the screen editor YASE, and we'll be showing YASE code fragments or pointing you towards the code in other chapters. Some of the more popular data structures are heaps, auxiliary stacks, linked lists, records, arrays, strings, and queues.

Before we take off into data types, we will briefly describe the memory model used by all 68K assemblers, and most high level languages. The standard memory model is composed of three logical segments: the text segment (TEXT), the data segment (DATA), and the block storage segment (BSS).

The text segment is reserved for program code. It's not clear why it's called "text" and not "code," but it is, and it's way too late to do anything about it. Anyhow, most assemblers default to assembling for the text segment. In other words, if you feed a source file to your assembler, and you don't tell it differently, it will place what it assembles into the text segment of the output object code.

It's important that you observe the distinction between data and object code if you want to maintain portability for your source files. On many "cheap" systems it doesn't really make much difference if you have writable data references into the text segment. On other systems, however, it can make a big difference. For example, if a system has a memory management unit (MMU) and a high test operating system, it's quite likely that the operating system will load your program text segment into a write-protected portion of memory, and the data and BSS segments into read-write memory. If you then try to write into text memory, or sometimes even read from the text segment without using a PC-relative addressing mode, the MMU generates an address error exception and your program bombs.

When programming ROM-able code, the distinction is just as important. If you forget and put a variable into the code segment by accident, you may not cause an exception to be generated, but your program won't work.

Most assemblers recognize the "TEXT" pseudo-op to indicate the start of a text segment. This pseudo-op can be used to switch back to text after assembling into the data or BSS segments.

The data segment contains variable data that needs to be initialized when the program starts execution. Operating systems will load initializing values into their proper places in the data segment if assembled in the data segment. The DC.s (Define Constant) pseudo-op is normally used to set the values of items in the data segment. The "DATA" pseudo-op is recognized by most assemblers to indicate the start of a data segment.

Note that when writing code for an embedded system (or any system without the benefit of an operating system to load your completed program) you can declare initialized data all day long and it will still be garbage when the program fires up. In these cases you must explicitly initialize items in the data segment before using them. Remember, initialized data is initialized by whatever loads your program—it isn't automatic. This is often a hard concept for people new to ROM code to grasp. If there isn't a loader (like an operating system), no data gets initialized.

The block storage segment (BSS) is used for uninitialized data storage. For example, if your program needs a 64K buffer, and you plan on filling it in yourself (it doesn't need to have an initial value of any sort), you would assemble a define space (DS) directive in the BSS. Many loaders will fill the BSS with zeros before kicking off a program (see ROM caution above). In an embedded or ROM application, the BSS and the data segment are equivalent. The advantage to using the BSS as opposed to the data segment is that items in the BSS don't need to be part of the load module (the executable file on your disk). Using our 64K buffer as an example: if assembled as part of the data segment, the load module will be 64K larger than if assembled as part of the BSS, and to no good purpose. Of course, users being what they are, if you're writing a program to sell you may want to include items normally placed in the BSS in the data segment—users feel better about paying $495 if they get a great big executable file. A small file makes them suspicious. Most assemblers accept the "BSS" pseudo-op to indicate the block storage segment.

Now that we've covered the basics, let's look at some of the data structures, and what we can do with them.

Heaps

Heaps have a really impressive formal definition in computer science textbooks, but we'll not repeat it here. A heap is essentially a pool of available memory managed by the operating system or your program. Memory is released from and returned to this pool as needed, usually in arbitrarily sized pieces. The heap normally extends from the end of a program to the start of the stack. The C functions malloc() and free() and the Pascal procedures New and Dispose usually operate on the program heap.

There are several popular schemes for implementing heap management systems. The most common, especially in the C environment, is called a "first fit" algorithm.

A first fit heap system starts with a block of contiguous memory of some fixed size. In a single user, single process system the heap normally consists of all memory left after the operating system and user program are loaded. The program is allowed to request chunks of memory in any random size. If enough memory is available, a block of memory is allocated and a pointer to the start of the block is returned to the program. If there isn't enough memory, an error indicator (usually a pointer to location $00000000, or NULL) is returned, and presumably the requesting process terminates or makes other arrangements. When previously requested memory blocks are no longer needed, the program can return blocks of memory to the heap. These returned blocks, which may have still-needed memory adjacent to them, are linked together into a chain of free memory blocks throughout the heap. As new requests for memory come in, the free chain is searched for a block large enough to fill the request, and the first block large enough to fit the specifications is removed from the free chain and returned to the caller. If no free block is large enough, the new block is taken from the end of the heap.

A variation on this scheme is to require the requesting process to release memory blocks in the reverse order of their allocation—the last block allocated must be the first block returned to the heap. This is easy to implement because the whole memory manager is just a pointer to the current end of the heap. As requests for memory are granted, the pointer is moved towards the end of memory. When a block is returned, the pointer to the end of the heap is just moved back towards the start of the heap. This scheme is called a "cheap screw" heap manager, and is essentially just a big stack.

The regular first fit technique (not the cheap screw) can be enhanced by checking on each side of a returned block for adjacent free blocks, and combining any adjacent free blocks into one larger free block. Another enhancement is to divide a block removed from the free list in response to an allocation request into the smallest block required to satisfy the request and a new small block to be added back to the free list. These enhancements complicate a memory manager, and add to the execution overhead; but they are usually worth building in, especially if you're designing a general-purpose memory manager.

Communication between the memory manager and the user process is usually done with a single pointer each way—the allocate routine returns a pointer to a block of memory, and the free routine wants to have the same pointer back when the memory is no longer needed. The big question is, how does the free routine know how much memory to put back into the heap?

The answer is that the memory manager needs to keep track of the size of each and every block of memory it hands out, and it needs to relate the size of the block to the pointer returned by the caller. A variety of methods to this can be dreamed up, ranging from the incredibly hard to the nearly impossible, but it turns out that there's also an easy way to do it. The code below can be used assuming that the address of a block large enough to satisfy the request (plus 4 bytes) is contained in A0, and the size of the block is in D0.L:

```
MOVE. L    DO, (AO)+
```

That's it! After executing this instruction, the value in A0 can be returned to the requesting process as the block pointer. When the block is freed, assuming that the address of the block is in A0, the free routine can load the size of the freed block into D0.L like this:

```
MOVE. L    −4(AO), DO
```

```
+-------+   +-------+   +-------+   +-------+   +-------+   +-------+
|       |   |       |   |       |   |///////|   |///////|   |///////|
| #1    |   | #1    |   | #1    |   |F R E E|   |F R E E|   |F R E E|
|       |   |       |   |       |   |///////|   |///////|   |///////|
+-------+   +-------+   +-------+   +-------+   +-------+   +-------+
|///////|   | #2    |   | #2    |   | #2    |   | #2    |   | #2    |
|///////|   +-------+   +-------+   +-------+   +-------+   +-------+
|///////|   |///////|   | #3    |   | #3    |   | #3    |   |F R E E|
|///////|   |///////|   +-------+   +-------+   +-------+   +-------+
|F R E E|   |F R E E|   |F R E E|   |F R E E|   |       |   |       |
|///////|   |///////|   |///////|   |///////|   | #4    |   | #4    |
|///////|   |///////|   |///////|   |///////|   |       |   |       |
|///////|   |///////|   |///////|   |///////|   +-------+   +-------+
|///////|   |///////|   |///////|   |///////|   |F R E E|   |F R E E|
+-------+   +-------+   +-------+   +-------+   +-------+   +-------+
   (a)         (b)         (c)         (d)         (e)         (f)
```

FIGURE 14-1. Heap Fragmentation

Storing the size of the block immediately before the block itself in memory is probably the easiest and most efficient method of recording the size of variable blocks. This does require that the memory manager trust the requesting process to return the same pointer it got from the allocator. If a "funny" pointer is passed to the free routine, ugly things can (and will) happen to your heap—the sort of strange bug that takes weeks of hunting to find.

The first fit class of memory manager has one big drawback. As memory is allocated and freed, the heap becomes fragmented. Figure 14-1 graphically illustrates this fragmentation (in a highly simplified way, of course).

In the section of Figure 14-1 labelled "(a)," a block of three units is allocated from a heap of ten units in size. In (b) and (c), two additional blocks of one unit apiece are allocated. In (d) block 1 is freed and returned to the heap, leaving eight units of free memory. In (e), a new block of four units is allocated, from the end of the heap because no free block is large enough. In (f), block 3 is freed, leaving five blocks allocated and five free. However, the largest request that can be filled at this point is three blocks, because the free blocks are fragmented through the heap. There's enough free memory, but it's not all in the same spot.

The heap fragmentation problem can be reduced somewhat by switching to a "best fit" algorithm. Best fit is similar to first fit, except that all free blocks are searched, and the smallest block that satisfies the request is allocated. This tends to prevent small requests from filling in holes left by large releases, but is more complicated to implement and takes longer to execute. Also, the problem of fragmentation is not eliminated, only reduced.

Embedded systems are the most susceptible to fragmenting problems. Embedded systems tend to run for a long time, days or weeks at a time—and they have different processes allocating and freeing different sized chunks of memory at different rates. You can't really predict if or when fragmentation will progress to the point where the system fails, but it's likely to happen at a point where the system is under maximum load. Embedded systems are also very likely to have custom memory managers written for them, rather than ones that are store-bought or are part of the operating system. So pay attention.

It's no big deal if an embedded processor in a microwave oven folds up and you have to cycle the power, but it could be very irritating if the processor controlling the brakes on a 747 buys the farm as you're coming in for the landing approach. Similarly, if you're writing an operating system and it keeps its own pool of memory, you don't want to have to reboot every couple of days because you can't get enough memory to start a file control block anymore.

The problem can be eliminated if memory requests are all the same size. If every request is exactly the same size, fragmenting can't occur, because a new request can always fit in a freed block's slot. You can still run out of memory, but you know exactly how many blocks will fit in the heap, and the heap will always hold that many blocks. In fact, given a reasonably large heap with a lot of traffic in and out, you'll run out of a heap a lot sooner by requesting exactly the right amount of memory needed than if you request a fixed amount each time. By requesting exactly the same amount of memory each time, you convert an nondeterministic memory manager into a deterministic memory manager.

If you make the decision to request fixed sized blocks, you can make a faster, safer, and more efficient memory manager than the first fit or best fit types described above. A typical approach to a fixed-size block (FSB) system is to set aside a section of memory for the heap. A portion of this is reserved for a bit vector allocation table. (This data structure technically is no longer called a "heap," but we're not going to quibble.) For example, if 128K bytes of memory is available for the heap, and you decide that the standard allocation size is 64 bytes, then you start with 2048 blocks in the free pool. An allocation table of 256 bytes is set up somewhere (maybe in the first four free blocks, maybe somewhere else) and set to zero. Each bit in the allocation table corresponds to one block of memory in the heap. As a block is removed from the free pool, the corresponding allocation bit is set. As the block is returned to the free pool the bit is first checked to be sure that it really was allocated, if you want a fairly foolproof system, and then the allocation bit is reset.

The algorithm for allocation is fairly simple. When a request for a block comes in, the allocation routine scans the allocation table for a byte that does not equal $FF, indicating at least one free block associated with the eight blocks represented by each byte. Then, each bit in the byte is tested for zero to find the first free block associated with the byte. Byte orientation of the allocation table is used so we can use the bit instructions to test, set, and reset bits.

A pointer to the free block can be generated directly from the offset of the allocation byte, the number of the first zero bit we find, and the base address of the table. If the block size is fixed at a power of 2, simple shifts and additions will get us the base address of the block. For example, given the example heap parameters, if the byte offset into the allocation table of a non-$FF byte is in D0.L, the bit number of a non-zero bit is in D1.L, and the base of the heap (and the base of the allocation as well, because we're using the first four blocks for the allocation table) is in A0.L, the following code will set the allocation bit in the table, and then place a pointer to the associated block in A0:

```
BLKSIZ  EQU     6                       * log2 of allocation block size
        BSET    D1,0(A0,D0.W)           * Sets the allocation bit
        LSL.L   #3,D0                   * Multiplies byte offset * 8
        ADD.L   D1,D0                   * Adds in bit offset - D0 is
                                        * now "block number" of block
        LSL.L   #BLKSIZ,D0              * Block number * 64 = block offset
        ADD.L   D0,A0                   * A0 is now pointer to block
```

Similarly, when a pointer is returned to free a block, the pointer can be easily regenerated. Assuming the example heap parameters, and that the pointer to be freed is in D0.L, and that the base address of the heap is in A0.L, the following code will decompose the pointer into the allocation byte offset and the number of the allocation bit, and will reset the allocation bit:

```
BLKSIZ  EQU     6                       * log2 of allocation block size
        SUB.L   A0,D0                   * Extract offset of block into heap
        LSR.L   #BLKSIZ,D0             * offset / 64 = block number
        MOVE.L  D0,D1                   * copy of block number to D1
        AND.L   #$00000007,D1          * D1 now = alloc bit number
        LSR.L   #3,D0                   * D0 now = alloc byte offset
        BCLR    D1,0(A0,D0.L)           * reset allocation bit
```

Remember, the code examples here are designed to work only with blocks of 64 bytes. Any power of two can be used for the block size by adjusting the value of the equate BLKSIZ to the log base 2 of the block size (the exponent of the power of 2 used for the block size). Blocks of sizes that are not powers of 2 can be used if you substitute multiplications for the LSL instructions and divides for the LSR instructions. This will add substantially to the execution time of the two code fragments.

The two code fragments shown can be easily generalized for different sized blocks if you wish to maintain heaps of different sizes. The base address of the allocation table can be added as parameters to the allocate and free routines.

One last word of caution. If you plan on sharing a memory manager in a multitasking environment (or in situations where interrupt-driven code needs the memory manager), be sure to disable task switching (normally by disabling interrupts) while in the memory manager. Because memory managers normally use static data structures (the data structures are in absolute memory locations) they aren't very re-entrant. Wonderfully nasty things can happen if a memory manager is interrupted and re-entered. The whole thing doesn't need to be protected, just the allocator, and just from the time a free block is first located to the point where the block is marked as allocated.

Auxiliary Stacks

Auxiliary stacks are another type of data structure. They're just like the regular hardware stack, but are managed entirely by you. You don't have to worry about interrupts or system calls piling stuff on (when you are operating in supervisor mode), and they don't get messed with when you switch from user mode to supervisor mode. Auxiliary stacks are good places to put things temporarily, especially when you don't know in advance how many things you have.

Perhaps the best use of auxiliary stacks is to maintain parameters used by several subprograms. For example, a recursive-descent parser usually needs a stack to put tokens while unraveling expressions. Error-walkback tables are another candidate for an auxiliary stack. An error walkback is a great debugging aid, and isn't hard to implement, but is almost never done with assembly language programs, primarily because assembly language programmers are cautious about making extra effort.

There's almost nothing to implementing an auxiliary stack. The most important thing is to remember to initialize the auxiliary stack pointer before you use the auxiliary stack, and of course to remember not to garbage the stack somewhere in your program. The easiest mistake to make is illustrated by the following code:

```
            MOVE.L    #aux_stack,A5 * We'll use A5 as aux stack ptr
            . . .
            . . .
            BSS                     * Block Storage Segment
aux_stack: DS.W $100                * stack of $100 words
            . . .
```

Can you see the bug? It bites us on a regular basis. The error is in setting the auxiliary stack pointer A5 to the low end of the space reserved for the auxiliary stack. The auxiliary stack never enters the reserved area. The correct code is this:

```
            MOVE.L    #aux_stack,A5 * We'll use A5 as aux stack ptr
            . . .
            . . .
            BSS                     * Block Storage Segment
            DS.W     $100           * Stack of $100 words
aux_stack: DS.W 1                   * a dummy
            . . .
```

The dummy define space directive is sometimes needed because some assemblers don't like labels in the BSS not associated with a defined space. There are, of course, other elegant ways to solve this problem.

Linked Lists

Linked lists are data structures that contain pointers to other data structures, usually of the same type. Linked lists work well when you need to maintain large objects in some sort of order, because the ordering of the list can be changed by rearranging the pointers, without having to move the data structures themselves. Some memory managers use linked lists to chain free blocks together. We use two linked list in our text editor to keep track of edit buffers, one for the free buffers and one for the buffers in use. The "exec" procedure in Module EXEC in Chapter 12 manages the linked lists. Module GROUP3.PRN in this chapter also deals somewhat with the YASE "used" link list. We'll expand on these routines a bit later.

Linked lists always have a "root" somewhere. A root is a pointer to the start of the linked list. If the root gets lost or changed by accident, we lose track of the whole linked list. Each data item in a linked list is called a "node," and contains at least one pointer and one true data item. The pointers within the node point to one or more other nodes, usually of the same data type. By following the pointers from one node to another, you can traverse the list in a fixed order.

A doubly-linked list has two pointers in each node, one pointing to the next node away from the root, and one pointing to the next node towards the root. A binary tree is a special case of a linked list, where each node points to two nodes that are farther away from the root.

A link pointer that doesn't point to anything (as at the end of a list) is traditionally set to zero, because in most processors, including the 68000, location zero is not available for general-purpose use; and so zero makes a good flag to indicate the end of the list.

Linked lists are characterized by easy design and hard debugging. A good, robust linked list can be designed and coded in a few minutes, but it always seems to take two or three days to get the bugs out of it. There's no good reason for it, it's just the way things are.

In YASE, as we mentioned, we keep a linked list of the active editing buffers. The buffer closest to the root is the buffer currently being edited. The first 4 bytes of each buffer are a link pointer to the next buffer. Lines 220 to 235 of Figure 14-6 are a procedure that rotates the buffer at the end of the list to the start of the list to become the currently edited buffer:

```
220    rotate:
221            move.l   a5,a0        * get active screen
222            move.l   a5,al        * prime "last good" pointer
223    lp0_rt:
224            tst.l    (a0)         * is there another window?
225            beq      sk0_rt       * no, jump out
226.           move.l   a0,al        * save this pointer
227            move.l   (a0),a0      * get next window
228            bra      lp0_rt       * keep looping
229    sk0_rt:
230            move.l   a5,(a0)      * link to former top window
231            move.l   a0,used      * move former bottom to root
232            move.l   a0,a5        * make former bottom active
233            clr.l    (al)         * mark last window
234            bsr      border_w     * re-establish correct frame
235            rts
```

This keeps the 64K editing buffers in order without having to actually move the buffers. On entry, register A5 contains the address of the currently active buffer. The first entry of this buffer is a pointer to the next buffer, and contains the same value contained in the root pointer "used," referenced on line 231.

We start at the first node and chase down the linked list until we find a null pointer, indicating the end of the active buffer list. The movement is done on line 227, where we get the pointer to the next window into A0. Register A1 keeps the "last good" pointer, because we want to mark the next to the last buffer as the end buffer when we find the last buffer on the list. When we find the last buffer (the new first buffer), we make it point at the former first buffer, and then point the root at the new first buffer.

The procedure "refresh" on lines 238 to 259 of Module GROUP3 illustrates the reason for keeping the buffers in an order:

```
238   refresh:
239           bsr      cls            * get rid of stuff on the screen
240           clr.w    dl             * count the windows to open
241           move.l   #cmd_w,a5      * we have to reopen cmd window
242           bsr      open_w         * so we do.
243           move.l   used,a5        * get first active window address
244   lp0_rf:
245           move.l   a5,-(a7)       * push a window address
246           beq      sk0_rf         * jump out if null
247           addq.w   #1,dl          * increment window count
248           move.l   (a5),a5        * get next window address
249           bra      lp0_rf         * and keep on doon it.
250   sk0_rf:
251           addq.l   #4,a7          * pop null on top of stack
252           bra      sk1_rf         * do loop test before loop
253   lp2_rf:
254           move.l   (a7)+,a5       * pop the window
255           bsr      open_w         * open the window
256           bsr      prtscr         * print the contents
257   sk1_rf:
258           dbra     dl,lp2_rf
259           rts
```

"refresh" refreshes the text display after some action (such as closing an edit buffer) makes it necessary to redraw the entire display. It's easiest to just clear the screen, and then draw the windows in reverse order—the bottom window first, then the next to the bottom, and so on, until we reach the active window. That way, we don't need to try and figure out if parts or all of windows are obscured by windows above them.

The method we use is to chase down the linked list, starting at the top buffer, and put buffer addresses on the stack as we go. When we get to the end, we pop the buffer addresses off the stack and redraw the windows in turn. As the top window is the first one on the stack, and the last one off, it gets drawn last.

Each edit buffer is a large record that defines the state of the editing process and holds the text. Records are the next data type we look at.

Records

Records are collections of related data items, usually of different types. Each data item is called a "member" of the record. Usually, but not always, records are collected into arrays or linked lists—it's not worth the effort of defining a record if only one copy of the record will be used.

Records are normally defined as a group of equates. The equates are offsets from the start of a record. For example, a record defining a complex number consisting of a long integer "real" part and a long integer "imaginary" part might be defined like this:

```
real    equ    0    * offset to real part of number
imag    equ    4    * offset to imaginary part
complex equ    8    * The size of this record, in bytes
```

A much more complicated record can be found back in Figure 12-6. The entire figure is a definition of the record that is a YASE editing buffer. Throughout the YASE program, all references to the editing buffer use this record definition to access any part of the editing buffer.

Generally, records are accessed by loading the base address into an address register, and then using a "with displacement" addressing mode. For example, if A0 holds the address of a complex number record as defined above, the following code will load the real part and the imaginary part into D0 and D1, respectively:

```
move.l  real(A0),D0    * get real part into D0
move.l  imag(A0),D1    * get imaginary part into Dl
```

Our YASE editor maintains the base address of the active editing buffer in register A5 throughout the code, so the edit buffer record is always available. Switching active buffers is a simple matter of loading a new edit buffer address into A5.

In other applications, this approach to accessing records is not always practical. For example, we mentioned that records are almost always in linked lists or arrays. There are two major methods used to reference a particular record in an array of records. The method you choose to use depends on several factors.

One way of accessing records is by using the "address register with index and displacement" addressing mode. When using this method, a data register holds the array index of the record, and an address register holds the base address of the array of records. At some point before accessing the record, the array index in the data register must be multiplied by the size (in bytes) of an individual record. For example, if A0.L contains the base address of an array of records of complex numbers as defined earlier, and D0.W contains an index into the array, the following code will adjust the index and load the "real" part of the selected record into D1, and the "imaginary" part of the record into D2:

```
mulu    #complex,D0       * index * sizeof( complex record )
move.l  real(A0,D0.L),Dl  * get real part
move.l  imag(A0,D0.L),D2  * get imaginary part
```

When using records whose sizes are powers of 2, shifts can be used instead of multiplies to speed things up. The above code could be modified like this:

```
lsl.w    #3,D0              * index * sizeof( complex record )
move.l   real(A0,D0.W),D1   * get real part
move.l   imag(A0,D0.W),D2   * get imaginary part
```

Note that we changed the index register D0's size in the last two lines to "word." A multiply is guaranteed to produce a longword result, while the shift is not (because we specified the index as being in D0.W).

This method of accessing record members restricts you to using records of about 128 bytes, because the displacement in the indexed-with-displacement addressing mode is an 8-bit sign-extended number. Of course, the limit is only to the start of the last member of the record—a very long member could extend way past the 128 byte limit, as long as it started inside the limit.

A second method of accessing records in an array is to modify the base address of the record in an address register before accessing the members. Given the same inputs as the example above (base address of the array of records in A0, index into the array in D0.W), the following code demonstrates this method:

```
mulu    #complex,D0     * index * sizeof( complex record )
adda.l  D0,A0           * set A0 to point to selected record
move.l  real(A0),D1     * get real part
move.l  imag(A0),D2     * get imaginary part
```

This method has the advantage that the displacement can be a sign-extended 16-bit number, with a limit on positive offsets of 32767.This can accommodate nearly any reasonable record size. A disadvantage is that we lose the base address of the array when computing the offset. An extra MOVE can eliminate that problem, of course.

The C "union" data type or the Pascal variant record can be easily simulated by defining overlapping equates. We use a standard (nonoverlapping) record in our queue record example in this chapter.

Arrays

An array is an ordered collection of identically-typed components. The 68K "address register indirect with index" addressing mode is well suited to array handling. A problem with this addressing mode is that the value of the data register used for the index is added directly to the base address in the address register. This means that an index into the array can only be used directly if the array base component is an 8-bit object. If the base component is larger than 8 bits, the index needs to be multiplied by the size of the component, as we did with arrays of records. An alternative is to maintain the index as a scaled value—for example, if the base component size is 4 bytes long, as in a longword, we can add four to the index each time we change it, instead of adding one and then multiplying by four when we need to access the array. This technique is especially suitable for a sequentially accessed array such as the one in the queue example in this chapter.

When designing records that contain arrays, place the arrays at the end of the record. The "address register indirect with index" addressing mode normally used to access arrays gives you a "free" displacement (the displacement doesn't cost you anything in code space or execution time) from the base address, so you can skip over the rest of the record to get to the array part. This means you don't have to add an offset to the index or base before accessing the array portion of the record.

Strings

Strings are a special case of arrays. The base component of a string is type "character," although in assembler you usually don't enforce this, and allow the component to have any 8-bit value.

There are two popular models used for strings, which we can call the "C" model and the "Pascal MT+" model. The C model is a character array of arbitrary length terminated with a null ($00) member. The MT+ model is a character array with a maximum size of either 255 or 65535 characters. The first byte (or word, depending on the maximum length chosen) is a count of how many characters are currently contained in the string. The characters themselves begin immediately after the first byte/word.

The C model is the most popular for 68K work, probably because most 68K programmers learned C somewhere along the way and are comfortable with the C model. There are two potential problems using the C model. First, the null character cannot be contained as part of the string, because it is always used as the string terminator. This is not normally a problem, as strings are used mainly for input and output. The null character has been reserved as a "don't care" character since the days of the Teletype, where nulls were sent after carriage returns to allow time for the print head to return to the start of the line. Even today, some terminals that used a software scroll will lose the first character or two on a new line after scrolling if nulls are not sent.

The second problem with the C string model is in calculating the size of a string. To find the number of characters in a string, each character must be counted until the terminal null is encountered. In the Pascal model, finding the length of a string is a trivial lookup.

The following illustrates a typical string copy routine for the C model string, with the address of the source string in A0, and the address of the destination string in A1:

```
STRCPY: MOVE.B  (A0)+,(A1)+
        BNE     STRCPY
        RTS
```

You can build protection into this loop by specifying a limit on the number of characters transferred, although this isn't suitable for general library use because it limits the flexibility of the routine:

```
STRNCPY: MOVE.W  #LIMIT-1,D0
LP:      MOVE.B  (A0)+,(A1)+
         DBEQ    D0,LP
```

The C model is generally preferred when fast and powerful string manipulations are required, as in language processors and the like.

The MT+ model is generally avoided by assembly language programmers because it reminds them of Pascal. The MT+ model does have the advantage that any possible 8-bit value may be contained within the string, and the maximum possible size of a string is known in advance. This model is harder to manipulate than the C model, however. Throughout this book, we will use the C model string.

Queues

Queues are another special form of array. A queue is a temporary storage mechanism for data, and is usually arranged so that the first data item placed into the queue is the first data out. This type of queue is known as a FIFO (First In, First Out).

Queues are quite often used to buffer data between unsynchronized processes. Probably the most familiar example of this is the keyboard FIFO that saves your keystrokes if you get ahead of your computer. Queues are also often used in less visible ways internally in multitasking operating systems. I/O is often handled via queues because I/O has different time constraints than the CPU itself, whether it's disk latency or a slow printer. I/O queues are often modified FIFO in more advanced operating systems. For example, a disk access request queue is often modified by applying a strategy routine to the queue as new entries are added, to put disk accesses that are physically close on the disk close together in the queue.

When queues are used to buffer data between asynchronous processes, special care must to be taken to protect the queue integrity during task switches, as with the heap managers we discussed earlier. Since the queues are shared resources, and share data structures, re-entering a queue manager at the wrong time will lead to unpleasant happenings. For example, if you implement a keyboard FIFO, you need to disable interrupts when reading or checking the keyboard queue, so that a keyboard interrupt won't corrupt the queue pointers.

For this reason, queues are often handled directly as system calls by multitasking operating systems. This also allows the operating system to reschedule tasks put to sleep while pending on a empty queue.

In Module QUEUE.PRN we have a general-purpose FIFO queue manager, with three entries, one to add an item to the queue ("enqueue" data), one to remove an item from the queue ("dequeue" data), and one to check the status of the queue. The code is designed to work with any number of queues, as long as they all hold objects of the same size. The size of the objects in the queues can be byte, word, or longword. The equate "object" on line 32 of Module QUEUE controls conditional assembly of the code to fix the size of the objects at assembly time.

Queues themselves are maintained as records, and the user program is responsible for setting up the record before using the queue. A template of the record is given in the comments on lines 8 to 12. The queues may be any size up to 64K bytes. The 64K limit is due to the algorithm we used—by using pointers instead of indexes you could implement a queue of any size.

Typically the items in a queue are never larger than a pointer. It doesn't make sense to move large chunks of data into and out of queues, so larger items are normally queued via pointers to the item. Often a process sending data into a queue will request memory from the heap for the data, and then enqueue the pointer to the memory block. The receiving process handles the data, and then returns the data memory block to the heap.

The queue code itself is fairly simple. The queue is just an array. There are two indexes into the array, a "head pointer" indicating where new data is to be stored, and a "tail pointer" indicating where data is to be removed from when dequeueing. When the queue is empty, the head pointer is the same as the tail pointer. When an item is added to the queue, the head pointer is incremented after storing the data ("postincremented"), leaving the tail pointer pointing at the data. When data is removed, the tail pointer is also postincremented.

In both cases, enqueueing and dequeueing, the pointers are checked for being past the end of the queue, and if so, are set back to the start of the queue. This type of wraparound action is called a "circular buffer."

We are also keeping a count of how many items are in the queue. The count can be determined by the difference between the head pointer and the tail pointer, so this "count" entry is not strictly necessary. However, the "count" is easy to understand and maintain, and the difference in execution speed between calculating the count and keeping it in the record is negligible.

An error can occur when the sending process overruns the receiving process and the queue becomes full. We are handling this by returning an error to the sending process. This type of response is appropriate for applications where all of the data, and the order of the data, is important, such as a keyboard FIFO. In other applications, such as a receive FIFO for a terminal program, it may be more important to have the freshest data possible. In these types of application, the data should be stored anyhow and the tail pointer moved up one slot.

Circular FIFOs are not the only way to implement queues. Another popular scheme is a linked list. The sending process links new data to one end of a list, and the receiving process removes data from the other end of the list. This scheme has the advantage that only the amount of memory required for queued data is tied up at any one time. The disadvantages are increased complexity, and the queue is competing for heap space with everyone else—there's no guaranteed minimum size for the queue.

The data types discussed in this chapter are by no means exhaustive, but they do represent the most popular data schemes. One of the great advantages of assembly language programming is the ability to optimize a data storage scheme to an application. Don't get bogged down trying to coerce an application into a predefined data mold. Remember, this isn't Pascal, this is Real Programming.

Module GROUP3.PRN

```
   1
   2
   3          *****************************************************************
              * GROUP 3 (WIndowing) Commands
   4                  xref    get_buf,prompt,prtscr,sync_cur,case,cursor
   5                  xref    getkey,cls,cmd_w,border_w,used,set_w,open_w
   6                  xdef    g_3,refresh
   7
   8          <<include EDIT.H>>
  45          <<include CURSOR.H>>
  76          *****************************************************************
  77          * G_3 - Group 3 (window) commands processor
  78          g_3:
  79 00000000 207C0000001E    move.l  #w_cmd,a0    * load prompt string address
  80 00000006 61000000        bsr     prompt       * output prompt
  81 0000000A 61000000        bsr     getkey       * get switch key
  82 0000000E C07C001F        and.w   #$001F,d0    * make u/l case into ctrl char
  83 00000012 207C0000003A    move.l  #table3,a0   * setup case switch table
  84 00000018 61000000        bsr     case         * process choices
  85 0000001C 4E75            rts                  * resume editing
  86 0000001E 57696E646F6F772043  w_cmd:  dc.b    'Window Commands: P R E X',0
  86 00000026 6F6D6D616E64733A
  86 0000002E 2050205220452058
  86 00000036 00
  87 00000038
  87 00000038 0000                    dc.w    0

  88          *****************************************************************
  89          * TABLE3 - switch table for group 3 (window) commands
  90          table3:
  91 0000003A 0004            dc.w    4            * four choices
  92 0000003C 0010            dc.w    $10          * ^P - pop new window
  93 0000003E 00000148        dc.l    pop
  94 00000042 0012            dc.w    $12          * ^R - rotate windows
  95 00000044 0000014E        dc.l    rotate
  96 00000048 0005            dc.w    c_up
  97 0000004A 0000005A        dc.l    upleft       * move UL corner of window
  98 0000004E 0018            dc.w    c_down
  99 00000050 00000080        dc.l    lowright     * move LR corner of window
 100 00000054 00000058        dc.l    default      * "others" choice
 101                          default:
 102 00000058 4E75            rts
```

Module GROUP3.PRN (continued)

```
103
104
105          ********************************************************
             * UPLEFT - Moves the upper left corner of the active window
             upleft:
106 0000005A 45ED0032      lea       w_ulbx(a5),a2      * pointer to X left side
107 0000005E 43ED0034      lea       w_ulby(a5),a1      * pointer to Y top
108 00000062 323C0000      move.w    #lim_lx,d1         * X left limit
109 00000066 342D0036      move.w    w_lrbx(a5),d2      * X right limit
110 0000006A 947C000C      sub.w     #12,d2             * must be at least 10 chars wide
111 0000006E 3A3C0004      move.w    #lim_uy,d5         * Y top limit
112 00000072 382D0038      move.w    w_lrby(a5),d4      * Y bottom limit
113 00000076 5544          sub.w     #2,d4              * must be at least 3 high
114 00000078 612C          bsr       mover              * use common code
115 0000007A 610000F2      bsr       refresh            * have to remake screen
116 0000007E 4E75          rts
117
118          ********************************************************
             * LOWRIGHT - moves the lower right corner of the window
             lowright:
120 00000080 45ED0036      lea       w_lrbx(a5),a2      * pointer to X right side
121 00000084 43ED0038      lea       w_lrby(a5),a1      * pointer to Y bottom
122 00000088 343C004F      move.w    #lim_rx,d2         * X right limit
123 0000008C 322D0032      move.w    w_ulbx(a5),d1      * X left limit
124 00000090 D27C000C      add.w     #12,d1             * must be at least 10 chars wide
125 00000094 383C0016      move.w    #lim_ly,d4         * Y bottom limit
126 00000098 3A2D0034      move.w    w_ulby(a5),d5      * Y top limit
127 0000009C 5445          add.w     #2,d5              * must be at least 3 high
128 0000009E 6106          bsr       mover              * use common code
129 000000A0 610000CC      bsr       refresh            * have to remake screen
130 000000A4 4E75          rts
131
132          ********************************************************
             * MOVER - moves the window corners around
             mover:
134 000000A6 3F11          move.w    (a1),-(a7)         * push cursor Y
135 000000A8 3F12          move.w    (a2),-(a7)         * push cursor X
136 000000AA 61000000      bsr       cursor             * move cursor to window corner
137 000000AE 588F          addq.l    #4,a7              * adjust stack
138 000000B0 61000000      bsr       sync_curs          * make sure cursor moves
139 000000B4 61000000      bsr       getkey             * go see what human has in mind
140 000000B8 207C000000C2  move.l    #mtable,a0         * get case switch table ready
141 000000BE 60000000      bra       case               * do what human wants... maybe.
142          ********************************************************
```

```
* MTABLE - window streching case dispatch table
mtable:
143
144
145    000000C2  0009                dc.w    9           * 9 choices for this case
146    000000C4  0005                dc.w    c_up        * cursor up
147    000000C6  000000FE            dc.l    oneup
148    000000CA  0018                dc.w    c_down      * cursor down
149    000000CC  00000106            dc.l    onedn
150    000000D0  0004                dc.w    c_right     * cursor right
151    000000D2  0000010E            dc.l    onert
152    000000D6  0013                dc.w    c_left      * cursor left
153    000000D8  00000116            dc.l    onelf
154    000000DC  0012                dc.w    page_up     * max up
155    000000DE  0000011E            dc.l    allup
156    000000E2  0003                dc.w    page_down   * max down
157    000000E4  00000122            dc.l    alldn
158    000000E8  0006                dc.w    c_w_right   * max right
159    000000EA  0000012C            dc.l    allrt
160    000000EE  0001                dc.w    c_w_left    * max left
161    000000F0  00000126            dc.l    alllf
162    000000F4  000D                dc.w    return      * mods complete
163    000000F6  00000132            dc.l    done
164    000000FA  000000A6            dc.l    mover       * default case (no action)
165    ***************************************************************
166
167    000000FE  BA51        oneup:  cmp.w   (a1),d5     * check top limit
168    00000100  67A4                beq     mover       * branch on limit
169    00000102  5351                sub.w   #1,(a1)     * move up one line
170    00000104  60A0                bra     mover
171    ***************************************************************
172
173    00000106  B851        onedn:  cmp.w   (a1),d4     * check bottom limit
174    00000108  679C                beq     mover       * branch on limit
175    0000010A  5251                addq.w  #1,(a1)     * move down one line
176    0000010C  6098                bra     mover
177    ***************************************************************
178
179    0000010E  B452        onert:  cmp.w   (a2),d2     * check right limit
180    00000110  6794                beq     mover       * branch on limit
181    00000112  5252                addq.w  #1,(a2)     * move one char right
182    00000114  6090                bra     mover
```

Module GROUP3.PRN (*continued*)

```
183
184     ************************************************************
185 00000116 B252    onelf:    cmp.w    (a2),d1    * check left limit
186 00000118 678C              beq      mover      * branch on limit
187 0000011A 5352              subq.w   #1,(a2)    * move left one char
188 0000011C 6088              bra      mover
189     ************************************************************
190
191 0000011E 3285    allup:    move.w   d5,(a1)    * set to upper limit
192 00000120 6084              bra      mover
193     ************************************************************
194
195 00000122 3284    alldn:    move.w   d4,(a1)    * set to lower limit
196 00000124 6080              bra      mover
197     ************************************************************
198
199 00000126 3481    alllf:    move.w   d1,(a2)    * set to left limit
200 00000128 6000FF7C          bra      mover
201     ************************************************************
202
203 0000012C 3482    allrt:    move.w   d2,(a2)    * set to right limit
204 0000012E 6000FF76          bra      mover
205     ************************************************************
206
207 00000132 302D0032  done:   move.w   w_ulbx(a5),d0  * reset window params
208 00000136 322D0034          move.w   w_ulby(a5),d1
209 0000013A 342D0036          move.w   w_lrbx(a5),d2
210 0000013E 362D0038          move.w   w_lrby(a5),d3
211 00000142 61000000          bsr      set_w          * setup new parameters
212 00000146 4E75              rts
213     ************************************************************
214        * POP - opens a new window for editing
215
216 00000148 61000000  pop:    bsr      get_buf    * get new buffer
217 0000014C 4E75              rts
218     ************************************************************
219        * ROTATE - pulls the bottom active screen to the top.
220
221 0000014E 204D    rotate:   move.l   a5,a0      * get active screen
222 00000150 224D              move.l   a5,a1      * prime "last good" pointer
```

```
223
224 00000152 4A90     lp0_rt:  tst.l    (a0)       * is there another window?
225 00000154 6706               beq      sk0_rt     * no, jump out
226 00000156 2248               move.l   a0,a1      * save this pointer
227 00000158 2050               move.l   (a0),a0    * get next window
228 0000015A 60F6               bra      lp0_rt     * keep looping
229
230 0000015C 208D     sk0_rt:  move.l   a5,(a0)    * link to former top window
231 0000015E 23C800000000       move.l   a0,used    * move former bottom to root
232 00000164 2A48               move.l   a0,a5      * make former bottom active
233 00000166 4291               clr.l    (a1)       * mark last window
234 00000168 61000000           bsr      border_w   * re-establish correct frame
235 0000016C 4E75               rts
236
237   *********************************************************** * REFRESH - redraws all screen buffers, leaves a5 set to top win.
238            refresh:
239 0000016E 61000000           bsr      cls        * get rid of stuff on the screen
240 00000172 4241               clr.w    d1         * count the windows to open
241 00000174 2A7C00000000       move.l   #cmd_w,a5  * we have to reopen cmd window
242 0000017A 61000000           bsr      open_w     * so we do.
243 0000017E 2A7900000000       move.l   used,a5    * get first active window address
244
245 00000184 2F0D     lp0_rf:  move.l   a5,-(a7)   * push a window address
246 00000186 6706               beq      sk0_rf     * jump out if null
247 00000188 5241               addq.w   #1,d1      * increment window count
248 0000018A 2A55               move.l   (a5),a5    * get next window address
249 0000018C 60F6               bra      lp0_rf     * and keep on doon it.
250
251 0000018E 588F     sk0_rf:  addq.l   #4,a7      * pop null on top of stack
252 00000190 600A               bra      skl_rf     * do loop test before loop
253
254 00000192 2A5F     lp2_rf:  move.l   (a7)+,a5   * pop the window
255 00000194 61000000           bsr      open_w     * open the window
256 00000198 61000000           bsr      prtscr     * print the contents
257
258 0000019C 51C9FFF4 skl_rf:  dbra     d1,lp2_rf
259 000001A0 4E75               rts
```

Module QUEUE.PRN

```
 1  *********************************************************
 2  * QUEUE - queue manager
 3  *
 4  *
 5  *   queue setup:
 6  *
 7  *          q_len    equ     ?              * size in objects
 8  *          queue:   dc.w    0              * queue head pointer
 9  *                   dc.w    0              * queue tail pointer
10  *                   dc.w    q_len*object   * queue size
11  *                   dc.w    0              * objects in queue
12  *                   ds.obsz q_len          * queue storage
13  *
14  *   procedures:
15  *
16  *          enqueue  - adds a word to queue
17  *             entry: A0.L = queue, D0.W = value
18  *             exit: A0.L = NULL if queue full
19  *
20  *          dequeue  - removes a word from queue
21  *             entry: A0.L = queue
22  *             exit: A0.L = NULL for empty queue, else
23  *                   D0.W = value
24  *
25  *          inquire  - read queue status
26  *             entry: A0.L = queue
27  *             exit: same as 'dequeue', except queue not
28  *                   disturbed.
29  *
30  *********************************************************
31           xdef    enqueue,dequeue,inquire
32  *********************************************************
33  * Queue record offset declarations
34  object   equ     1              * Size of queue object in bytes
35  head     equ     0              * queue head pointer
36  tail     equ     2              * queue tail pointer
37  max      equ     4              * queue maximum size
38  size     equ     6              * current queue count
39  queue    equ     8              * the queue itself
    *********************************************************
    enqueue:
40  00000000 3F01             move.w   d1,-(a7)          * save D1
41  00000002 32280006         move.w   size(a0),d1       * get objects now in queue
42  00000006 B2680004         cmp.w    max(a0),d1        * test for full
43  0000000A 6C1E             bge      sk2_enq           * jump if full
44  0000000C 52680006         addq.w   #object,size(a0)  * increment count
45  00000010 32280000         move.w   head(a0),d1       * get head pointer
46                            ifeq     object-1
47  00000014 11801008         move.b   d0,queue(a0,d1.w) * put value for byte
```

```
48
49        endc
50        ifeq    object-2
          move.w  d0,queue(a0,d1.w)  * put value for word
51        endc
52        ifeq    object-4
          move.l  d0,queue(a0,d1.w)  * put value for longword
53        endc
54
55 00000018 5241       addq.w  #object,d1       * bump head pointer
56 0000001A B2680004   cmp.w   max(a0),d1       * test against queue limit
57 0000001E 6D02       blt     sk1_enq          * jump if no overflow
58 00000020 4241       clr.w   d1               * set back to zero
59
   sk1_enq:
60 00000022 31410000   move.w  d1,head(a0)      * save new head pointer
61
   sk3_enq:
62 00000026 321F       move.w  (a7)+,d1         * restore D1 on exit
63 00000028 4E75       rts
64
   sk2_enq:
65 0000002A 91C8       clr.l   a0               * flag error condition
66 0000002C 60F8       bra     sk3_enq          * exit
67 ****************************************************
68 dequeue:
69 0000002E 3F01       move.w  d1,-(a7)         * save D1
70 00000030 4A680006   tst.w   size(a0)         * see if anything in queue
71 00000034 671E       beq     sk1_deq          * error jump if queue empty
72 00000036 32280002   move.w  tail(a0),d1      * get tail pointer
73        ifeq    object-1
74 0000003A 10301008   move.b  queue(a0,d1.w),d0 * get value for byte
75        endc
76        ifeq    object-2
77        move.w  queue(a0,d1.w),d0 * get value for word
78        endc
79        ifeq    object-4
80        move.l  queue(a0,d1.w),d0 * get value for longword
81        endc
82 0000003E 53680006   subq.w  #object,size(a0) * decrement queue count
83 00000042 5241       addq.w  #object,d1       * move tail pointer
84 00000044 B2680004   cmp.w   max(a0),d1       * test tail against queue size
85 00000048 6D02       blt     sk2_deq          * jump if no overflow
86 0000004A 4241       clr.w   d1               * set back to zero
87
   sk2_deq:
88 0000004C 31410002   move.w  d1,tail(a0)      * save new tail pointer
89
   sk3_deq:
90 00000050 321F       move.w  (a7)+,d1         * restore d1
91 00000052 4E75       rts
92
   sk1_deq:
93 00000054 91C8       clr.l   a0               * flag error
```

Module QUEUE.PRN (*continued*)

```
94 00000056 60F8                    bra      sk3_deq         * exit
95
96                  ***********************************************************
                 inquire:
97 00000058 3F01                    move.w   d1,-(a7)        * save D1
98 0000005A 4A680006                tst.w    size(a0)        * see if queue empty
99 0000005E 670C                    beq      sk1_inq         * jump if queue empty
100 00000060 32280002               move.w   tail(a0),d1     * get tail pointer
101                                  ifeq     object-1
102 00000064 10301008               move.b   queue(a0,d1.w),d0 * get value for byte
103                                  endc
104                                  ifeq     object-2
105                                  move.w   queue(a0,d1.w),d0 * get value for word
106                                  endc
107                                  ifeq     object-4
108                                  move.l   queue(a0,d1.w),d0 * get value for longword
109                                  endc
110              sk3_inq:
111 00000068 321F                   move.w   (a7)+,d1        * restore d1
112 0000006A 4E75                   rts
113              sk1_inq:
114 0000006C 91C8                   clr.l    a0              * flag error
115 0000006E 60F8                   bra      sk3_inq         * exit
116
117 00000070                        end
```

15

The User Interface

In this chapter, we look briefly at the different techniques that can be used generically for user interfaces. Then, we will develop a package to provide edit window support to the text editor.

The classic user interface supported by systems programmers is the teletype model, so named because it can be implemented for the old Model 33 ASR Teletypes. On a CRT device this is sometimes called a "scrolling ASCII" model. Basically, prompting is accomplished by spewing out a line of text at the current cursor position and issuing a carriage return and line feed. Input is by a simple line editor. This model is popular because it is so easy to implement and just about any ASCII terminal device ever made can use it. Programmers involved with the evolution of new systems often use a simple debugging port kludged into the system bus somehow, and this model is suitable for early work. As these systems are upgraded, however, the systems programs developed for the debugging terminal never seem to make it into the revision queue.

With the advent of more powerful personal computers the classic teletype model is gradually disappearing because of user pressure, although it remains entrenched in the mainframe world. We are going to enhance our screen editor YASE with a fairly powerful CRT-based line editor, really an enhancement of the teletype model of input. In YASE we will use it for command dialogue with the user, but the potential goes much further. We mention this line editor here only because an alternative often used in similar editors is sharing the main editing code with the command dialogue editor, an alternative we rejected because of the increased complexity of the code.

We started our line editor specification by combining command techniques from our two personal favorite CRT line editors, WordStar command prompt editing and the MS-DOS public domain key manager DOS-EDIT. What we wanted was a line editor to which we could send a default response if we wanted, one that would allow entry of unprintable characters, that would stay put in its own part of the screen, that would limit the number of characters placed into the target string (keeping a soda can set on the keyboard from trashing your whole data section), and that would allow inserting and deleting within the default or new response. Our code is listed in Module LINEED.PRN.

```
********************************************************************
* CURSOR.H
* Cursor Key Definitions
c_up            equ     5       * move cursor up one line
c_down          equ     24      * move cursor down one line
c_right         equ     4       * move cursor one char right
c_left          equ     19      * move cursor one char left
c_w_right       equ     6       * move cursor one word right
c_w_left        equ     1       * move cursor one word left
return          equ     13      * end-of-line character
backsp          equ     8       * backspace character
left_del        equ     $7F     * delete to the left
right_del       equ     7       * delete to the right
tab             equ     $09     * Tab key
lit_prefix      equ     16      * literal insert prefix character
group1          equ     $11     * ^Q prefix key
group2          equ     $0B     * ^K prefix key
group3          equ     $17     * ^W prefix key
line_del        equ     $19     * ^Y line delete key
page_up         equ     $12     * ^R page up key
page_down       equ     $03     * ^C page down key
repeat          equ     $0C     * ^L repeat find key
insert_key      equ     $16     * ^V insert toggle
ins_line        equ     $0E     * ^N insert line toggle
word_del        equ     $14     * ^T delete word right key

lim_uy          equ     4       * window upper Y limit
lim_ly          equ     23      * window lower Y limit
lim_lx          equ     0       * window left X limit
lim_rx          equ     79      * window right X limit
```

FIGURE 15-1. Module CURSOR.H

Entry requirements are listed in the comment header in lines 2 to 8. The calling sequence is to push first the maximum number of screen columns available for editing, followed by the absolute screen column, then the absolute screen row for character position one of the input window, followed by the address of the target string to receive the prompt. Any default value is placed into the target string before calling the line editor. For example, if the editor is called repeatedly with the same target string address, the default value each time will be the previous response. This requires that the input string be null-terminated before it is passed to the line editor the first time.

Figure 15-1 lists the equates for the cursor movement keys. There are more equates than are used by the line editor because this file is also an "include" input to the editor proper, to keep the definitions consistent. You can, of course, change them to whatever you're used to. Few topics cause more discussion around computer fanatics than the proper key arrangement for cursor control, unless it's whether or not the 6502 is worth using for anything more complex than NC machine controllers.

In Module LINEED entry to the line editor is at line 55. We're pushing the kitchen sink as far as data registers go; we're going to keep information globally to reduce recalculation. An example is the calculation on lines 57 to 59, to decide the maximum CRT column we can use, based on starting column and maximum characters. While in this case it's not a big deal, a lot of these small deals add up.

The main editing loop is quite short, from lines 62 to 67:

```
62   loop:
63          bsr      update        * update display
64          bsr      _getkey       * Get next input key
65          move.l   #dispatch,a0  * setup case statement
66          bsr      case          * case selector already in D0.
67          bra      loop          * end of editing loop.
```

The decision making is all done by a general-purpose procedure "case." We give "case" quite a workout in this book. As might be deduced by the name, "case" simulates a case ("switch" in C) control structure. The dispatch table for the line editor appears as lines 215 to 235:

```
215  dispatch:
216          dc.w     9             * Case options count
217          dc.w     return        * when return => finis
218          dc.l     finis
219          dc.w     c_w_right      * when c_w_right => to_end
220          dc.l     to_end
221          dc.w     c_w_left       * when c_w_right => to_start
222          dc.l     to_start
223          dc.w     c_right        * when c_right => right
224          dc.l     right
225          dc.w     c_left         * when c_left => left
226          dc.l     left
227          dc.w     backsp         * when backsp => left
228          dc.l     left
229          dc.w     left_del       * when left_del => d_left
230          dc.l     d_left
231          dc.w     right_del      * when right_del => d_right
232          dc.l     d_right
233          dc.w     lit_prefix     * when lit_prefix => jamload
234          dc.l     jamload
235          dc.l     others         * default case
```

The code for the "case" module appears in Module CASE.PRN.

The "case" procedure is pretty simple. The case table contains an entry for the number of "arms" in the case structure, and for each arm a word value for the case label and an address to jump to if the case label matches the case selector input in D0.W. A final entry defines the default transfer address in the event that no case label matches the case selector.

In many computer systems (any Z80-based, for example) the use of the case structure can save code space over inline compare-and-branch-equal code. This is not true in the 68K, and in fact using the case structure represents a slight penalty in both code space and execution speed. "So why," you may ask, "is this chump wasting my time?" It's because the case structure has one very nice advantage over most other simple decision schemes: all references to the dispatch table are data references. A case dispatch table can (actually, should) be placed in the data section of your program. What this allows is dynamic reconfiguration. You can even change the size of the table if you want. This makes a fast and reliable way to set up new cursor key configurations from disk files or wherever. There are lots of obscure situations, especially in embedded systems or operating systems, where this dynamic capability is a real lifesaver. It also keeps the anti-self-modifying-code crazies off your back, although we can't see a distinction between patching a case dispatch table and a BEQ instruction.

Incidentally, the subroutine nesting level of "case" is zero. If you use a BSR instruction to get to "case," you need to put a RTS at the end of each of the case arms, and control resumes at the instruction following the call to "case." If you use a BRA or JMP instruction to get to "case," you need to jump back to wherever you're going to resume execution. This second technique can be used to simulate a high level language case structure, with the exit at the bottom.

A disadvantage to our case structure is the use of absolute long addresses. Code referenced by the case structure can't be relocated, unless you go into the case table and tweak the addresses.

Back to the line editor. The line editor is an example of one technique for on-screen editing. Each case arm just makes modifications to the input string or to the input string index D3. A single procedure, "update" (lines 176 to 212) handles any mods to the display caused by the case arms. This technique has the advantage of simplicity, but the disadvantage of rewriting the input window each time the user presses a key. We handle this by using our virtual screen interface, making this rewrite transparent even at very slow terminal rates. If this isn't possible in your case, you need to fall back on a more traditional technique, the "random logic" approach.

With a random logic approach, you keep close track of the cursor each time a key is pressed, to minimize screen access. It's mostly a processor of special cases. This sort of code is typical of a bottom-up design or a design that's been coded by two people not communicating well. Every case arm essentially controls whatever rebuilding is required to maintain the displayed line whenever a change is made. For example, we display nonprintable characters as a circumflex followed by the printable equivalent. Control-B, hex value $02, is displayed as "^B", occupying two character positions. If this character is deleted out of the middle of a line, everything to the right will shift left two character positions, as opposed to the one space shift that deletion of a printable character would cause. If tabs are to be expanded, other logic comes into play.

Random logic's advantage is that fewer screen accesses are required, but at the price of more internal computation and unreadable code. This line editor and the screen editor YASE use a much different approach that relies on the efficiency of the virtual screen interface.

One last thing you'll notice about the main loop. There's no exit. We're using a nasty little technique, of which several variations exist, to get out of the loop. In this variation, since we used a BSR instruction to get the "case," a return address is floating on top of the stack for the case arm to use to return to the edit loop. When the user presses RETURN (or whatever you define the end of string key to be) "case" vectors control to label "finis," line 70:

```
70   finis:
71          clr.b    0(a1,d3.w)        * Terminate input string w/ null
72          addq.l   #4,a7             * Trash last return address
73          movem.l  (a7)+,d0-d7/a0-a3 * Restore caller's register
74          unlk     a6                * Restore caller's stack frame
75          rts
```

Here, we just lift the last return address off the stack, effectively moving us up one sub-routine nesting level. This puts us back to the same logical level as the main editing loop, and we can exit out of the line editor with an RTS instruction.

This is a common practice among the old hands in the assembly language community. It drives structured programmers nuts. The advantage is that you don't have to process a return flag in the edit loop, and you don't need to return a flag from each and every case arm. The disadvantage is when you modify the module a year from now and have forgotten you used this nifty trick and your code blows up.

Let's take a quick look at each case arm before we move on. "to__end" (line 78) is taken when we press the word__right cursor key. This arm moves the cursor to the end of the current input string, or to the end of the displayable area on the screen, whichever is less:

```
78   to_end:
79          tst.b    0(a1,d3.w)        * are we pointing at terminal?
80          beq      skl_te            * yes - no action required
81          addq.w   #1,d3             * move index up one.
82          bra      to_end            * repeat
83   skl_te:
84          rts
```

"to__start" (line 87) is taken when the word__left cursor key is pressed, and moves the cursor to the start of the input string:

```
87   to_start:
88          clr.w    d3                * Set index to start
89          rts
```

"left" (line 92) and "right" (line 100) are taken for the char__left and char__right cursor keys:

```
92   left:
93          tst.w    d3                * are we at start of line?
94          beq      exit_left         * yes, let's blow this popstand
95          subq.w   #1,d3             * Index back one character
96   exit_left:
97          rts
100  right:
101         tst.b    0(a1,d3.w)        * Is there more stuff to display?
102         beq      exit_ri           * Nope, we're done here.
103         addq.w   #1,d3             * add one to character index
104  exit_ri:
105         rts
```

"d__right" (line 108) is taken for the delete-character-right key. "d__left" (line 122) is taken for the delete-character-left key:

```
108   d_right:
109           lea      0(a1,d3.w),a2    * load destination address
110           tst.b    (a2)             * check for end of string
111           beq      exit_dr          * no need to do anything.
112           lea      1(a1,d3.w),a3    * load source address
113           move.w   max(a6),D1       * Get max char count
114           sub      d3,d1            * Compute transfer count
115   lp0_dr:
116           move.b   (a3)+,(a2)+      * start moving the string in
117           dbra     d1,lp0_dr        * do whole string.
118   exit_dr:
119           rts
122   d_left:
123           tst.w    d3               * Are we at start of string?
124           beq      exit_dl          * Yes, no action required.
125           bsr      left             * Move cursor one char left
126           bra      d_right          * re-use d_right code.
127   exit_dl:
128           rts
```

"jamload" (line 131) is taken for the literal__prefix cursor key, and allows us to enter unprintable characters into the input string. Tabs, for example. We're not expanding tabs, and the tab key is normally ignored. If we want a tab character in our input string, we can hit the literal prefix key and then the tab key. Carriage returns and keys considered cursor keys can also be input this way. This routine then branches to arm "othrs" (line 139), the default key handler, just past the test for control characters:

```
131   jamload:
132           bsr      _getkey          * get next key
133           bra      othrs            * shove it in.
```

In this chapter we'll be looking at an application of the line editor within a window application. Before we get there, we'll want to take a look at the window drivers used for YASE, and discuss some design tradeoffs and alternatives.

There are two basic approaches normally taken to windowing. The first, and the one we'll be using for YASE, depends on the fact that we can regenerate all windows on the screen from information contained within the control of the applications program. This approach is suitable only for applications-layer use, and sometimes not even there.

As an example of this, we'll take a look at the YASE window concept. YASE can have a number of windows open at any one time, only one of which is active. One window is a status and dialogue window, and we never let it become obscured by another window. The rest of the windows contain text from files being edited. Because the active edit window is always on top, we never have to worry about characters being written to an obscured window. In addition, when we have to rewrite the screen because a window is deleted or resized, or pull an obscured window to the top, we can reconstruct the contents of the window by looking at the text file associated with the window. Given these conditions, windowing is reasonably simple.

In other cases, it's not so simple. If you install windows at the operating systems level, or in a concurrent environment, or in a case where a window can't easily be reconstructed from internal information, you need to get fancy. In these cases, a full blown window manager is needed.

With a full blown system, a virtual screen for each window is often kept. The virtual screen is the same size as the actual display, because usually the user can resize windows at any time. A complete description of each window's state is kept in a window descriptor record. These window descriptors are usually kept in an ordered list, either a linked list such as we use in YASE, or an array.

When characters are written to a window, the list of windows is searched, starting at the top. At each window, we check first to see if we're looking at the window the character belongs to. If so, we output it to the actual screen and save it in the virtual screen associated with the window. If not, we check to see if this window obscures the position where this character would go on the physical screen. If it's not obscured, we continue the search in lower windows. If it is obscured, we just place the character in its virtual screen.

Because we have a virtual screen reflecting the display as if each window has the whole screen, we can rebuild the physical screen at any time, regardless of how many windows are in use or how we change the size and shape of the windows.

This approach, while more general than the one we chose for YASE, has some drawbacks to it. Each task requiring display resources must be well behaved. Nobody can go around the window manager directly to the display. This approach also takes a lot of memory, although we have as yet been unable to locate anyone who cares how much memory any 68000 program takes. The most serious drawback is that this approach is very slow. You just about have to write this sort of thing in assembler.

Once again, we use Edit.H, the include file we saw in Figure 12-2, on page 142. All of the equates beginning with "w__" are offsets to window parameters in an edit descriptor record. Each window has an edit descriptor associated with it. If we were writing this in C, we would probably separate the window parameters into another structure and keep a pointer to it in the edit descriptor. We don't do that here because the extra level of indirection is unpleasant to deal with. As you try to apply C techniques to assembly language programming, you'll find just how much overhead you can put into a C program without thinking about it. Of course, you gain in coding time what you lose in execution time.

We are describing the shape of a window by identifying the upper left and lower right corners of the window as (X,Y) pairs. We identify the coordinates of both the text area within the window and the outer border, or frame, of the window. While we could generate either from the other pretty easily as we needed them, it's easier and faster to do it once and to keep the results in the edit descriptor.

"w__rows" is a precomputed value and holds the number of text rows in the window. "w__cols" holds the number of text columns in the window. "w__off" is how many columns the left edge of the window is offset as we pan the window to the right over the contents of the buffer.

We have some general-purpose windowing utilities in Module WINDOW.PRN. These are usable with either of the window techniques discussed above.

"set__w" (line 168) does some precalculations on the window corner coordinates from values passed in D0-D3. This routine is called to set initial window parameters, and after resizing a window:

```
168   set_w:
169           movem.w d0-d3,-(a7)       * Save registers
170           move.w  d0,w_ulbx(a5)     * upper left border X
171           move.w  d1,w_ulby(a5)     * upper left border Y
172           move.w  d2,w_lrbx(a5)     * lower right border X
173           move.w  d3,w_lrby(a5)     * lower right border Y
174           subq.w  #1,d2
175           move.w  d2,w_lrcx(a5)     * lower right character X
176           subq.w  #1,d3
177           move.w  d3,w_lrcy(a5)     * lower right character Y
178           sub.w   d0,d2             * calculates usable columns
179           move.w  d2,w_cols(a5)     * window columns
180           sub.w   d1,d3             * calculates usable rows
181           move.w  d3,w_rows(a5)     * window rows
182           addq.w  #1,d0
183           move.w  d0,w_ulcx(a5)     * upper left character X
184           addq.w  #1,d1
185           move.w  d1,w_ulcy(a5)     * upper left character Y
186           movem.w (a7)+,d0-d3       * Restore registers
```

"open__w" (line 71) is called to draw a window on the display. It puts a border on the window and clears the text area to erase any parts of an older window obscured by the new window:

```
71   open_w:
72           bsr     border_w       * make window border
73           bsr     clear_w        * erase window
74           rts
```

"border__w" draws a frame around the window to set it off from any adjacent windows. We are using a character oriented border. The character values for the border characters are set in lines 22 to 27:

```
21   * Character equates for window border characters - IBM-PC
22   ul_cor  equ     201            * Upper left window border char
23   ur_cor  equ     187            * Upper right window border char
24   ll_cor  equ     200            * Lower left window border char
25   lr_cor  equ     188            * Lower right window border char
26   horizn  equ     205            * Horizontal window border char
27   vertic  equ     186            * Vertical window border char
```

These make a nice line display on an IBM-PC monitor. If you have a graphics display, the bordering code should be replaced by line drawing calls to the graphics manager. If you have a standard character display without line fragment characters, plus signs make decent corners, and minus signs and vertical bars make reasonable horizontal and vertical lines.

The code for both "border__w" and "clear__w" (line 145) demonstrate floating a parameter on the stack between calls. This is a good optimization technique. As we start getting into display calls for windows and text, the efficiency of the code becomes critical. Any code you can move out of inner loops to outer loops makes a big difference. Note in lines 156 to 161, where we are outputting a line of blanks, how we have reduced the loop to two instructions:

```
156             move.w  #' ',-(a7)      * push background char - only once
157             subq.w  #1,d2           * adjust for loop index
158     lp2_cw:
159             bsr     putc            * output background char
160             dbra    d2,lp2_cw       * loop
161             addq.l  #2,a7           * pop parameter
```

You really can't make a loop faster. Of course, the code that outputs characters in the routine "putc" will be the driver as far as the speed of this loop, but normally you can't control that.

Module EDIT2.PRN is the screen printer for YASE. "prtscr" is called at the start of each edit loop, just before we wait for a user character, but only if no character is backed up in the keyboard FIFO. It's reasonable to do this when we have the virtual screen interface, because the user will never even notice. Register A5 points to an edit descriptor block on entry. There are no other parameters to this routine.

We start by getting the address of the top left character in the text buffer, stored in top_lef(a5) and initializing the row counter in D3:

```
50      redo:
51              move.l  top_lef(a5),a0  * get starting character for scrn
52              move.w  w_ulcy(a5),d3   * d3 is screen row number
```

From here, we get the precalculated coordinates for the top left character in the window (lines 52 and 54) and place the cursor there (57 to 60). We are also keeping a count of both actual and logical screen columns occupied by the line in registers D4 and D5:

```
53      row_loop:
54              move.w  w_ulcx(a5),d2   * d2 is screen column number
55              clr.w   d5              * D5 is logical column
56              clr.w   d4              * D4 is actual column in line
57              move.w  d3,-(a7)        * Push cursor Y base location
58              move.w  d2,-(a7)        * Push cursor X base address
59              bsr     cursor          * setup cursor location
60              addq.l  #4,a7           * adjust stack
```

The actual column is the column number a given point in a line would have if it was printed on a printer with an arbitrary number of print positions. This differs from the logical column, a number we keep only for the user's convenience, and from the number of printable and unprintable characters from the start of the line to the point in question, which we don't really care about. The logical column and the actual column will diverge whenever we display an expanded control character. We don't count control characters as occupying logical columns, but they do occupy actual columns on the display.

As we outlined in Chapter 12, we are using a gap model for the text editor. Lines 62 to 65 test for the character being printed being at the edge of the gap. This indicates that we are at the cursor position. When we find ourselves at the cursor position, we save the screen coordinates so that we can put the screen cursor back there when we are done. Lines 70 to 81 also test to see that the cursor is within the left and right edges of the display. If not, we drive "w__off" left or right to bring the cursor into the displayed portion of the window:

```
61  chr_loop:
62          cmp.l   b_gap(a5),a0    * Test for gap
63          blt     sk1_ps          * Not at gap, jump by
64          cmp.l   e_gap(a5),a0    * Are we already past gap?
65          bge     sk1_ps          * Yes, jump by
66          move.l  e_gap(a5),a0    * move pointer past gap
67          move.w  d2,scr_col(a5)  * save cursor position
68          move.w  d3,scr_row(a5)
69          move.w  d5,log_col(a5)  * Save logical column
70          cmp.w   w_off(a5),d4    * are we before window edge?
71          bge     sk2_ps          * nope.
72          clr.w   w_off(a5)       * set offset to zero, redraw
73          bra     redo
74  sk2_ps:
75          cmp.w   w_lrcx(a5),d2   * are we past window edge?
76          ble     sk1_ps          * no, continue
77          sub.w   w_lrcx(a5),d4   * subtract difference
78          add.w   w_ulcx(a5),d4   * add screen offset
79          addq.w  #8,d4           * add eight for good measure
80          add.w   d4,w_off(a5)    * set window offset, redraw
81          bra     redo
```

The code to drive "w__off to the right is fairly stupid, and can cause a narrow window to jump as you move the cursor left once you have driven the window contents to the right. This is infrequent and not very annoying to us, so if you can't live with it, you can fix it yourself. As we have mentioned before, code in long programs tends to be a handler of special cases, and this is one special case we decided not to handle.

We're causing the display to be shifted left 8 characters at a time as we move the cursor off the right edge of the window. This limits the number of times we need to do a refresh of the whole window. Because we're re-entering the screen printer when we find we need to scroll horizontally (lines 73 and 81), if there are less than eight positions horizontally in the window, the routine will lock up shifting the window back and forth if the cursor gets out of the window. Take care not to use this code with windows that are too narrow. Our window shrink-and-grow code tests for and will not allow this condition.

Lines 83 to 87 decide if we have any more characters to print in this line. If not, we send blanks to the end of the line. If so, we call "exp__chr" (line 108 to 141) to print the character:

```
83          cmp.l   e_buf(a5),a0    * Test for end of file
84          bgt     sk0_ps          * jump on end of file
85          move.b  (a0)+,d0        * pick up printable character
86          cmp.b   #10,d0          * is this a newline?
87          beq     sk0_ps          * if yes, line is complete
88          bsr     exp_chr         * expand character and print
89          bra     chr_loop        * get next char and repeat
```

"exp__chr" decides if the current character fits horizontally in the window. It also expands tabs and control characters and adjusts the line actual and logical column counters.

```
108    exp_chr:
109            cmp.b    #$9,d0            * Is this a tab character?
110            beq      tabs              * If so, expand tabs.
111            cmp.b    #$20,d0           * is this a control char?
112            blt      control           * If so, expand control char
113            cmp.w    w_off(a5),d4      * are we up to window edge?
114            blt      sk0_ex            * no, skip the printing.
115            cmp.w    w_lrcx(a5),d2     * are we past window edge?
116            bgt      sk0_ex            * if so, skip printing
117            move.w   d0,-(a7)          * just print regular chars
118            bsr      putc
119            addq.l   #2,a7             * adjust stack
120            addq.l   #1,d2             * add 1 to screen column
121    sk0_ex:
122            addq.l   #1,d5             * add 1 to logical column
123            addq.l   #1,d4             * add 1 to line's column count
124            bra      exp_exit          * processing complete
125    tabs:
126            move.b   #' ',d0           * expand with spaces
127            bsr      exp_chr           * call recursively
128            move.w   d5,d1             * get copy of logical column
129            and.w    #7,d1             * check for tab column stop
130            bne      tabs              * repeat as necessary
131            bra      exp_exit          * leave when done
132    control:
133            move.w   d0,-(a7)          * save character
134            move.b   #'^',d0           * pass a circumflex recursively
135            bsr      exp_chr           * go do it
136            move.w   (a7)+,d0          * retrieve character
137            add.b    #$40,d0           * make it printable
138            bsr      exp_chr           * print it out
139            subq.w   #2,d5             * adjust logical column
140    exp_exit:
141            rts
```

A possible improvement to this routine is adding adjustable tab stops.

The routine "stats" (line 158 to 190) is a classic example of "Do what I say, not what I do":

```
158    stats:
159            movem.l  d0/d1/a5,-(a7)
160            tst.w    insert(a5)        * check if insert on or off
161            beq      no_ins
162            move.l   #on,-(a7)         * push "On" message
163            bra      past_ins
164    no_ins:
165            move.l   #off,-(a7)        * push "Off" message
166    past_ins:
167            move.l   e_gap(a5),d0      * compute space available
168            sub.l    b_gap(a5),d0
169            move.w   d0,-(a7)
170            move.l   b_gap(a5),d0      * compute chars behind cursor
171            sub.l    b_buf(a5),d0
172            move.w   d0,-(a7)
```

```
173                move.w  log_col(a5),-(a7)  * print logical column
174                move.w  log_lin(a5),-(a7)  * print logical line
175                pea     fname(a5)          * print filename
176                move.l  #cmd_w,a5          * load up command window desc.
177                move.w  w_ulcy(a5),-(a7)   * push Y position
178                add.w   #1,(a7)            * adjust Y position
179                move.w  w_ulcx(a5),-(a7)   * push X position
180                move.l  #statstr,-(a7)     * push format string address
181                bsr     printf
182                add.l   #24,a7             * adjust stack
183                movem.l (a7)+,d0/d1/a5
184                rts
185    statstr:
186                dc.b    '%vFile: %-14s LN %-5u CO %-5u CH %-5u SP %-5u'
187                dc.b    ' Insert %-3s',0
188    on:         dc.b    'On',0
189    off:        dc.b    'Off',0
190                dc.w    0
```

"stats" is called from the main editing loop and prints statistics about the current window. This procedure doesn't know from chopped liver about the window manager, and just plugs its stuff into the screen in the command I/O window. The reason we're doing this is because otherwise we'd have to modify our general-purpose "printf" routine (Chapter 16) to wire it into the window system. This procedure assumes that there are 78 character positions available for the command I/O window (80-column screen minus 2 border characters). Avoid doing this in your own programs. Ten bucks says we get a nasty letter from some person using an Osborne 1 as a terminal on a 68K system, who learns the hard way why this is such a poor technique.

This essentially concludes what we plan to say about YASE. At the end of the book we have the listings of the parts of the editor not used specifically as examples. It's probably worth your while to type it all in and bring it up on your system, even if you have a good editor already. Typing it in forces you to look at all of the code closely, and any modifications you make will be a good learning experience.

In the next chapters we'll look at some more useful general-purpose procedures that don't fit in with the text editor concept.

Module LINEED.PRN

```
    1      *******************************************************************
    2      * LINEED - Input line editor. Does editing into a string from
    3      * a CRT device. Supports default value prompting.
    4      *
    5      *    ENTRY:   P0.L is the address of the receiving string
    6      *             P1.W is the screen line number to start editing
    7      *             P2.W is the screen column.
    8      *             P3.W is the max number of screen columns allowed
    9
   10      <<include CURSOR.H>>
   40
   41              .xdef    lineed
   42              .xref    case,cursor,putc,_getkey
   43
   44      * The following symbol (and references thereto) required only if
   45      * using the VSCREEN virtual CRT interface.
   46              .xref    sync_curs
   47
   48      string  equ    8            * Stack frame offsets
   49      line    equ    12           * offset to editing line
   50      column  equ    14           * offset to first editing column
   51      max     equ    16           * offset to max editing cols.
   52
   53      *******************************************************************
   54      lineed:
   55 00000000 4E560000          link    a6,#0         * Establish stack frame
   56 00000004 48E7FFF0          movem.l d0-d7/a0-a3,-(a7) * Save caller's registers.
   57 00000008 3E2E0010          move.w  max(a6),d7    * get maximum usable column
   58 0000000C DE6E000E          add.w   column(a6),d7 * compute max crt column
   59 00000010 5347              subq.w  #1,d7         * adjust for tests later
   60 00000012 4243              clr.w   D3            * Initialize string index
   61 00000014 226E0008          move.l  string(a6),a1 * get string base address
   62
   63 00000018 610000C0  loop:   bsr     update        * update display
   64 0000001C 61000000          bsr     _getkey       * Get next input key
   65 00000020 207C0000012A      move.l  #dispatch,a0  * setup case statement
   66 00000026 61000000          bsr     case          * case selector already in D0.
   67 0000002A 60EC              bra     loop          * end of editing loop.
   68      *******************************************************************
   69      * Branches here when human presses RETURN key.
```

Module LINEED.PRN (continued)

```
                       finis:
70
71   0000002C 42313000         clr.b    0(a1,d3.w)              * Terminate input string w/ null
72   00000030 588F             addq.l   #4,a7                   * Trash last return address
73   00000032 4CDF0FFF         movem.l  (a7)+,d0-d7/a0-a3       * Restore caller's register
74   00000036 4E5E             unlk     a6                      * Restore caller's stack frame
75   00000038 4E75             rts
76
77                    * Branches here to display 'old' stuff past cursor.
78                    to_end:
79   0000003A 4A313000         tst.b    0(a1,d3.w)              * are we pointing at terminal?
80   0000003E 6704             beq      skl_te                  * yes - no action required
81   00000040 5243             addq.w   #1,d3                   * move index up one.
82   00000042 60F6             bra      to_end                  * repeat
83                    skl_te:
84   00000044 4E75             rts
85
86                    ***********************************************************
87
88                    * Branches here to return cursor to start of line
                      to_start:
88   00000046 4243             clr.w    d3                      * Set index to start
89   00000048 4E75             rts
90                    ***********************************************************
91                    * branches here to move the cursor one character to the left.
92                    left:
93   0000004A 4A43             tst.w    d3                      * are we at start of line?
94   0000004C 6702             beq      exit_left               * yes, let's blow this popstand
95   0000004E 5343             subq.w   #1,d3                   * Index back one character
96                    exit_left:
97   00000050 4E75             rts
98
99                    ***********************************************************
100                   * Moves the cursor one character to the right.
                      right:
101  00000052 4A313000         tst.b    0(a1,d3.w)              * Is there more stuff to display?
102  00000056 6702             beq      exit_ri                 * Nope, we're done here.
103  00000058 5243             addq.w   #1,d3                   * add one to character index
104                   exit_ri:
105  0000005A 4E75             rts
106
107                   ***********************************************************
108                   * Branch here to delete one character to the right
                      d_right:
109  0000005C 45F13000         lea      0(a1,d3.w),a2           * load destination address
```

```
110  00000060  4A12                  tst.b   (a2)              * check for end of string
111  00000062  6710                  beq     exit_dr           * no need to do anything.
112  00000064  47F13001              lea     1(a1,d3.w),a3     * load source address
113  00000068  322E0010              move.w  max(a6),D1        * Get max char count
114  0000006C  9243                  sub     d3,d1             * Compute transfer count
115
116  0000006E  14DB          lp0_dr: move.b  (a3)+,(a2)+       * start moving the string in
117  00000070  51C9FFFC              dbra    d1,lp0_dr         * do whole string.
118
119  00000074  4E75          exit_dr: rts
120       ************************************************************
121       * Branch here to delete one character to the left
122       d_left:
123  00000076  4A43                  tst.w   d3                * Are we at start of string?
124  00000078  6704                  beq     exit_dl           * Yes, no action required.
125  0000007A  61CE                  bsr     left_             * Move cursor one char left
126  0000007C  60DE                  bra     d_right           * re-use d_right code.
127
128  0000007E  4E75          exit_dl: rts
129       ************************************************************
130       * Branch here to accept next key typed as a literal
131       jamload:
132  00000080  61000000              bsr     getkey            * get next key
133  00000084  6006                  bra     othrs             * shove it in.
134       ************************************************************
135       * Inserts the typed character at the cursor.
136       others:
137  00000086  B03C0020              cmp.b   #' ',d0           * Test for valid character
138  0000008A  6D2A                  blt     exit_ot           * No, less than $20, ignore
139
140  0000008C  322E0010      othrs:  move.w  max(a6),D1        * Get max char count
141  00000090  48C1                  ext.l   d1                * setup for address arithmetic
142  00000092  45E9FFFF              lea     -1(a1),a2         * load source address
143  00000096  D5C1                  add.l   d1,a2             * start at far end of string
144  00000098  47E90000              lea     0(a1),a3          * load destination address
145  0000009C  D7C1                  add.l   d1,a3             * start at far end of string
146  0000009E  9243                  sub.w   d3,d1             * get transfer count
147  000000A0  6002                  bra     sk0_ot            * do dec/tst before first xfer
148
149  000000A2  1722          lp0_ot: move.b  -(a2),-(a3)       * start moving the string out
150
151  000000A4  51C9FFFC      sk0_ot: dbra    d1,lp0_ot         * loop over end of string.
152  000000A8  322E0010              move.w  max(a6),d1        * terminate string, in case of -
153  000000AC  42311000              clr.b   (a1,d1.w)         *   overflow into terminal null
154  000000B0  13803000              move.b  d0,0(a1,d3.w)     * insert new character
155  000000B4  5243                  addq.w  #1,d3             * move string index.
156
157  000000B6  4E75          exit_ot: rts
158       ************************************************************
```

Module LINEED.PRN (continued)

```
159
160      * prints the character in D0, expanding control chars as req.
         c_print:
161 000000B8 3F00           move.w  d0,-(a7)         * save character on stack
162 000000BA B03C0020       cmp.b   #$20,d0          * check if it's a control char
163 000000BE 6C10           bge     sk0_cp           * no, just print it.
164 000000C0 3F3C005E       move.w  #$005E,-(a7)     * push a circumflex for a prefix
165 000000C4 61000000       bsr     putc             * print at cursor.
166 000000C8 548F           addq.l  #2,a7            * restore stack
167 000000CA 06570040       add.w   #$0040,(a7)      * make unprintable printable
168 000000CE 5241           addq.w  #1,d1            * increment column
169      sk0_cp:
170 000000D0 61000000       bsr     putc             * put input char, already on stack
171 000000D4 548F           addq.l  #2,a7            * restore stack
172 000000D6 5241           addq.w  #1,d1            * increment column
173 000000D8 4E75           rts
174
175      ********************************************************
176      * Prints the input string and updates cursor
         update:
177 000000DA 3F2E000C       move.w  line(a6),-(a7)    * set cursor to start of line
178 000000DE 3F2E000E       move.w  column(a6),-(a7)  * this is X, above is Y
179 000000E2 61000000       bsr     cursor            * sets cursor to start
180 000000E6 588F           addq.l  #4,a7             * fix stack
181 000000E8 322E000E       move.w  column(a6),d1      * d1 will be cursor posit
182 000000EC 4244           clr.w   d4                * d4 will be counter
183      lp0_sp:
184 000000EE B644           cmp.w   d4,d3             * are we at cursor?
185 000000F0 6602           bne     sk0_sp            * no, jump
186 000000F2 3A01           move.w  d1,d5             * save screen cursor position
187      sk0_sp:
188 000000F4 10314000       move.b  0(a1,d4.w),d0     * char to print
189 000000F8 6708           beq     sk1_sp            * jump out if it's a null
190 000000FA 61BC           bsr     c_print           * output character
191 000000FC 5244           addq.w  #1,d4             * bump character counter
192 000000FE BE41           cmp.w   d1,d7             * test for end of area
193 00000100 6CEC           bge     lp0_sp            * repeat if there's room.
194      sk1_sp:
195 00000102 B644           cmp     d4,d3             * did we find cursor?
196 00000104 6F06           ble     sk2_sp            * yes, we already found it.
197 00000106 3604           move.w  d4,d3             * reset string counter
198 00000108 5343           subq.w  #1,d3             * adjust because d4 incremented
199 0000010A 60CE           bra     update            * resync all the pointers
200      sk2_sp:
201 0000010C 103C0020       move.b  #' ',d0           * blank rest of edit area
202 00000110 BE41           cmp.w   d1,d7             * did we output enough yet?
203 00000112 6D04           blt     sk3_sp            * jump if we did
204 00000114 61A2           bsr     c_print           * put a blank
205 00000116 60F4           bra     sk2_sp            * try again
```

```
206
207 00000118 3F2E000C    sk3_sp:   move.w   line(a6),-(a7)    * reset cursor
208 0000011C 3F05                   move.w   d5,-(a7)          * this is cursor position
209 0000011E 61000000              bsr      cursor            * now tell the display
210 00000122 588F                   addq.l   #4,a7             * fix stack
211 00000124 61000000              bsr      sync_curs         * only needed if using vscreen
212 00000128 4E75                   rts
213                       **************************************************
214                       * Input character dispatch table
215                       dispatch:
216 0000012A 0009                   dc.w     9                 * Case options count
217 0000012C 000D                   dc.w     return            * when return => finis
218 0000012E 0000002C              dc.l     finis
219 00000132 0006                   dc.w     c_w_right         * when c_w_right => to_end
220 00000134 0000003A              dc.l     to_end
221 00000138 0001                   dc.w     c_w_left          * when c_w_right => to_start
222 0000013A 00000046              dc.l     to_start
223 0000013E 0004                   dc.w     c_right           * when c_right => right
224 00000140 00000052              dc.l     right
225 00000144 0013                   dc.w     c_left            * when c_left => left
226 00000146 0000004A              dc.l     left
227 0000014A 0008                   dc.w     backsp            * when backsp => left
228 0000014C 0000004A              dc.l     left
229 00000150 007F                   dc.w     left_del          * when left_del => d_left
230 00000152 00000076              dc.l     d_left
231 00000156 0007                   dc.w     right_del         * when right_del => d_right
232 00000158 0000005C              dc.l     d_right
233 0000015C 0010                   dc.w     lit_prefix        * when lit_prefix => jamload
234 0000015E 00000080              dc.l     jamload
235 00000162 00000086              dc.l     others            * default case
236
237 00000166                       end
```

Module CASE.PRN

```
     **********************************************************
     *  CASE - Case statement executor
     *
     *     ENTRY:   A0 contains address of case table
     *              D0 contains case selector value
     *
     *     Case Table:
     *              dc.w    number of valid options
     *              dc.w    first match value
     *              dc.l    address of first case arm
     *              dc.w    second match value
     *              dc.l    address of second case arm
     *              . . .
     *              dc.w    n'th match value
     *              dc.l    address of n'th case arm
     *              dc.l    default (no match) arm
     *
     *     EXIT:    A0 is undefined.
     *              D0 retains case selector value.
     *
              .xdef   case

     case:    move.l  d1,-(a7)       * save caller's D1
              move.w  (a0)+,d1       * get case value count
              subq.w  #1,d1          * adjust count value

     loop:    cmp.w   (a0)+,d0       * Check against match value
              beq     done           * found it.
              addq.l  #4,a0          * move past useless case arm
              dbra    d1,loop        * try again

     done:    move.l  (a7)+,d1       * restore caller's d1'
              move.l  (a0),a0        * get jump address
              jmp     (A0)           * go execute case arm.
     *
     *** Note: return from case arm is to statement following ********
     *** the call to this routine *****************************************
```

```
 1
 2
 3
 4
 5
 6
 7
 8
 9
10
11
12
13
14
15
16
17
18
19
20
21
22
23 00000000 2F01
24 00000002 3218
25 00000004 5341
26
27 00000006 B058
28 00000008 6706
29 0000000A 5888
30 0000000C 51C9FFF8
31
32 00000010 221F
33 00000012 2050
34 00000014 4ED0
35
36
37
```

```
 1   * ***************************************************************
 2   * WINDOW.ASM - General purpose window support
 3   *
 4   * OPEN_W: Opens a screen window (borders & clears).
 5   *     ENTRY: A5.L points to an initialized edit descriptor
 6   *
 7   * CLEAR_W: Clears the text area of a window.
 8   *     ENTRY: A5.L points to an initialized edit descriptor
 9   *
10   * BORDER_W: Draws a window border.
11   *     ENTRY: A5.L points to an initialized edit descriptor
12   *
13   * SET_W: Initializes screen parameters in a window descriptor.
14   *     ENTRY: A5.L points to an edit descriptor
15   *         D0.W = upper left corner X position
16   *         D1.W = upper left corner Y position
17   *         D2.W = lower right corner X position
18   *         D3.W = lower right corner Y position
19   *
20   * ***************************************************************
21   * Character equates for window border characters - IBM-PC
22   ul_cor    equ   201     * Upper left window border char
23   ur_cor    equ   187     * Upper right window border char
24   ll_cor    equ   200     * Lower left window border char
25   lr_cor    equ   188     * Lower right window border char
26   horizn    equ   205     * Horizontal window border char
27   vertic    equ   186     * Vertical window border char
28   * ***************************************************************
29   <<include EDIT.H>>
66   * ***************************************************************
67            xdef   open_w,border_w,clear_w,set_w
68            xref   cursor,putc
69   * ***************************************************************
70   * OPEN_W - Opens a screen window.
71   open_w:
72   00000000 6106         bsr    border_w    * make window border
73   00000002 610000C0     bsr    clear_w     * erase window
74   00000006 4E75         rts
75   * ***************************************************************
76   * BORDER_W - borders a window.
77   border_w:
78   00000008 48E7E000     movem.l  d0-d2,-(a7)    * save caller's registers
79   0000000C 610A         bsr    do_top      * draw top of window
80   0000000E 613E         bsr    do_mid      * draw sides and text area
81   00000010 617C         bsr    do_bot      * draw bottom of window
82   00000012 4CDF0007     movem.l  (a7)+,d0-d2    * restore caller's registers
83   00000016 4E75         rts
```

```
84
85  00000018  3F2D0034  do_top:  move.w  w_ulby(a5),-(a7)  * push up/left border Y position
86  0000001C  3F2D0032           move.w  w_ulbx(a5),-(a7)  * push up/left border X position
87  00000020  61000000           bsr     cursor            * set cursor
88  00000024  588F               addq.l  #4,a7             * pop parameter
89  00000026  3F3C00C9           move.w  #ul_cor,-(a7)     * push up/left border char
90  0000002A  61000000           bsr     putc              * output the char
91  0000002E  548F               addq.l  #2,a7             * pop parameter
92  00000030  342D0044           move.w  w_cols(a5),d2     * get column count
93  00000034  3F3C00CD           move.w  #horizn,-(a7)     * push border char - only once
94  00000038  5342               subq.w  #1,d2             * adjust for loop index
95
96  0000003A  61000000  lp0_dt:  bsr     putc              * output horizontal border char
97  0000003E  51CAFFFA           dbra    d2,lp0_dt         * loop
98  00000042  3EBC00BB           move.w  #ur_cor,(a7)      * "push" up/right border char
99  00000046  61000000           bsr     putc              * output it
100 0000004A  548F               addq.l  #2,a7             * pop parameter
101 0000004C  4E75               rts                       * finished
102
103 0000004E  4241      do_mid:  clr.w   d1                * setup line counter
104
105 00000050  5241      lp3_dt:  addq.w  #1,d1             * increment line counter
106 00000052  3F2D0034           move.w  w_ulby(a5),-(a7)  * push up/left border Y position
107 00000056  D357               add.w   d1,(a7)           * add current line number
108 00000058  3F2D0032           move.w  w_ulbx(a5),-(a7)  * push left border X position
109 0000005C  61000000           bsr     cursor            * set cursor
110 00000060  588F               addq.l  #4,a7             * pop parameters
111 00000062  3F3C00BA           move.w  #vertic,-(a7)     * push vertical border char
112 00000066  61000000           bsr     putc              * output the char
113 0000006A  548F               addq.l  #2,a7             * pop parameter
114 0000006C  3F2D0034           move.w  w_ulby(a5),-(a7)  * push up/left border Y position
115 00000070  D357               add.w   d1,(a7)           * add current line number
116 00000072  3F2D0036           move.w  w_lrbx(a5),-(a7)  * push right border X position
117 00000076  61000000           bsr     cursor            * set cursor
118 0000007A  588F               addq.l  #4,a7             * pop parameters
119 0000007C  3F3C00BA           move.w  #vertic,-(a7)     * push vertical border char
120 00000080  61000000           bsr     putc              * output the char
121 00000084  548F               addq.l  #2,a7             * pop parameter
122 00000086  B26D0042           cmp.w   w_rows(a5),d1     * enough?
123 0000008A  6FC4               ble     lp3_dt            * nope, need more lines.
124 0000008C  4E75               rts                       * finished
125
126 0000008E  3F2D0038  do_bot:  move.w  w_lrby(a5),-(a7)  * push low/left border Y position
127 00000092  3F2D0032           move.w  w_ulbx(a5),-(a7)  * push low/left border X position
128 00000096  61000000           bsr     cursor            * set cursor
129 0000009A  588F               addq.l  #4,a7             * pop parameter
130 0000009C  3F3C00C8           move.w  #ll_cor,-(a7)     * push low/left border char
```

```
131  000000A0  61000000           bsr     putc                    * output the char
132  000000A4  548F               addq.l  #2,a7                   * pop parameter
133  000000A6  342D0044           move.w  w_cols(a5),d2           * get column count
134  000000AA  3F3C00CD           move.w  #horizn,-(a7)           * push border char - only once
135  000000AE  5342               subq.w  #1,d2                   * adjust for loop index
136
                        lp2_dt:
137  000000B0  61000000           bsr     putc                    * output horizontal border char
138  000000B4  51CAFFFA           dbra    d2,lp2_dt               * loop
139  000000B8  3EBC00BC           move.w  #lr_cor,(a7)            * "Push" low/right border char
140  000000BC  61000000           bsr     putc                    * output it
141  000000C0  548F               addq.l  #2,a7                   * pop parameter
142  000000C2  4E75               rts                             * finished
143                      *****************************************************
144                      * CLEAR_W - Clears a window to blanks.
                        clear_w:
146  000000C4  48E7E000           movem.l d0-d2,-(a7)             * save callers registers
147  000000C8  4241               clr.w   d1                      * setup line counter
148
                        lp1_cw:
149  000000CA  5241               addq.w  #1,d1                   * increment line counter
150  000000CC  3F2D0034           move.w  w_ulby(a5),-(a7)        * push up/left border Y position
151  000000D0  D357               add.w   d1,(a7)                 * add current line number
152  000000D2  3F2D003A           move.w  w_ulcx(a5),-(a7)        * push left char X position
153  000000D6  61000000           bsr     cursor                  * set cursor
154  000000DA  588F               addq.l  #4,a7                   * pop parameters
155  000000DC  342D0044           move.w  w_cols(a5),d2           * get column count
156  000000E0  3F3C2020           move.w  #' ',-(a7)              * push background char - only once
157  000000E4  5342               subq.w  #1,d2                   * adjust for loop index
158
                        lp2_cw:
159  000000E6  61000000           bsr     putc                    * output background char
160  000000EA  51CAFFFA           dbra    d2,lp2_cw               * loop
161  000000EE  548F               addq.l  #2,a7                   * pop parameter
162  000000F0  B26D0042           cmp.w   w_rows(a5),d1           * enough?
163  000000F4  6DD4               blt     lp1_cw                  * nope, need more lines.
164  000000F6  4CDF0007           movem.l (a7)+,d0-d2             * restore callers registers
165  000000FA  4E75               rts                             * finished
166                      ***************************************************************
167                      * SET_W: Initializes screen parameters in a window descriptor
168                        set_w:
169  000000FC  48A7F000           movem.w d0-d3,-(a7)             * Save registers
170  00000100  3B400032           move.w  d0,w_ulbx(a5)           * upper left border X
171  00000104  3B410034           move.w  d1,w_ulby(a5)           * upper left border Y
172  00000108  3B420036           move.w  d2,w_lrbx(a5)           * lower right border X
173  0000010C  3B430038           move.w  d3,w_lrby(a5)           * lower right border Y
174  00000110  5342               subq.w  #1,d2
175  00000112  3B42003E           move.w  d2,w_lrcx(a5)           * lower right character X
176  00000116  5343               subq.w  #1,d3
177  00000118  3B430040           move.w  d3,w_lrcy(a5)           * lower right character Y
178  0000011C  9440               sub.w   d0,d2                   * calculates usable columns
```

Module WINDOW.PRN (*continued*)

```
179  0000011E  3B420044    move.w   d2,w_cols(a5)    * window columns
180  00000122  9641        sub.w    d1,d3            * calculates usable rows
181  00000124  3B430042    move.w   d3,w_rows(a5)    * window rows
182  00000128  5240        addq.w   #1,d0
183  0000012A  3B40003A    move.w   d0,w_ulcx(a5)    * upper left character X
184  0000012E  5241        addq.w   #1,d1
185  00000130  3B41003C    move.w   d1,w_ulcy(a5)    * upper left character Y
186  00000134  4C9F000F    movem.w  (a7)+,d0-d3      * Restore registers
187  00000138  4E75        rts
188
189  0000013A               end
```

Module EDIT2.PRN

```
   1   ****************************************************************
   2   * EDIT2 - Screen printer. Updates the display after each cursor
   3   * move or file modification.
   4   ****************************************************************
   5
   6                   xref    cursor,putc,printf
   7                   xdef    prtscr,exp_chr,stats,set_edit,cmd_w
   8
  46   <<include EDIT.H>>
  47   ****************************************************************
  48   * PRTSCR - Prints screen from A5
  49  00000000 48E77C80   prtscr:   movem.l  d1-d5/a0,-(a7)
  50                      redo:
  51  00000004 206D0026             move.l   top_lef(a5),a0    * get starting character for scrn
  52  00000008 362D003C             move.w   w_ulcy(a5),d3     * d3 is screen row number
  53                      row_loop:
  54  0000000C 342D003A             move.w   w_ulcx(a5),d2     * d2 is screen column number
  55  00000010 4245                 clr.w    d5                * d5 is logical column
  56  00000012 4244                 clr.w    d4                * D4 is actual column in line
  57  00000014 3F03                 move.w   d3,-(a7)          * Push cursor Y base location
  58  00000016 3F02                 move.w   d2,-(a7)          * Push cursor X base address
  59  00000018 61000000             bsr      cursor            * setup cursor location
  60  0000001C 588F                 addq.l   #4,a7             * adjust stack
  61                      chr_loop:
  62  0000001E B1ED0012             cmp.l    b_gap(a5),a0      * Test for gap
  63  00000022 6D38                 blt      skl_ps            * Not at gap, jump by
  64  00000024 B1ED0016             cmp.l    e_gap(a5),a0      * Are we already past gap?
  65  00000028 6C32                 bge      skl_ps            * Yes, jump by
  66  0000002A 206D0016             move.l   e_gap(a5),a0      * move pointer past gap
  67  0000002E 3B420006             move.w   d2,scr_col(a5)    * save cursor position
  68  00000032 3B430004             move.w   d3,scr_row(a5)
  69  00000036 3B45002E             move.w   d5,log_col(a5)    * Save logical column
  70  0000003A B86D0046             cmp.w    w_off(a5),d4      * are we before window edge?
  71  0000003E 6C06                 bge      sk2_ps            * nope.
  72  00000040 426D0046             clr.w    w_off(a5)         * set offset to zero, redraw
  73  00000044 60BE                 bra      redo
  74                      sk2_ps:
  75  00000046 B46D003E             cmp.w    w_lrcx(a5),d2     * are we past window edge?
  76  0000004A 6F10                 ble      skl_ps            * no, continue
  77  0000004C 986D003E             sub.w    w_lrcx(a5),d4     * subtract difference
  78  00000050 D86D003A             add.w    w_ulcx(a5),d4     * add screen offset
  79  00000054 5044                 addq.w   #8,d4             * add eight for good measure
  80  00000056 D96D0046             add.w    d4,w_off(a5)      * set window offset, redraw
  81  0000005A 60A8                 bra      redo
  82                      skl_ps:
  83  0000005C B1ED001A             cmp.l    e_buf(a5),a0      * Test for end of file
  84  00000060 6E0C                 bgt      sk0_ps            * jump on end of file
  85  00000062 1018                 move.b   (a0)+,d0          * pick up printable character
```

Module EDIT2.PRN (continued)

```
 86  00000064 B03C000A            cmp.b    #10,d0            * is this a newline?
 87  00000068 6704                beq      sk0_ps            * if yes, line is complete
 88  0000006A 6120                bsr      exp_chr           * expand character and print
 89  0000006C 60B0                bra      chr_loop          * get next char and repeat
 90
 91  0000006E 6168       sk0_ps:  bsr      clr_eol           * Clear to end of line
 92
 93  00000070 5243       row_tst: addq.w   #1,d3             * Increment row
 94  00000072 B66D0038            cmp.w    w_lrby(a5),d3     * enough lines to fill window?
 95  00000076 6D94                blt      row_loop          * jump back if not.
 96  00000078 3F2D0004            move.w   scr_row(a5),-(a7) * reset cursor to proper location
 97  0000007C 3F2D0006            move.w   scr_col(a5),-(a7)
 98  00000080 61000000            bsr      cursor            * go set cursor
 99  00000084 588F                addq.l   #4,a7             * adjust stack
100  00000086 4CDF013E            movem.l  (a7)+,d1-d5/a0
101  0000008A 4E75                rts

102  ****************************************************************
103  * EXP_CHR - expands and prints a character
104  *   D0.B is character to print
105  *   D5.W is logical screen column, in/out parameter
106  *   D4.W is column count into line, in/out parameter
107  *   D2.W is actual screen X position, in/out parameter
108  ****************************************************************

109  0000008C B03C0009  exp_chr:  cmp.b    #$9,d0            * Is this a tab character?
110  00000090 6722                beq      tabs              * If so, expand tabs.
111  00000092 B03C0020            cmp.b    #$20,d0           * is this a control char?
112  00000096 6D2C                blt      control           * If so, expand control char
113  00000098 B86D0046            cmp.w    w_off(a5),d4      * are we up to window edge?
114  0000009C 6D10                blt      sk0_ex            * no, skip the printing.
115  0000009E B46D003E            cmp.w    w_lrcx(a5),d2     * are we past window edge?
116  000000A2 6E0A                bgt      sk0_ex            * if so, skip printing
117  000000A4 3F00                move.w   d0,-(a7)          * just print regular chars
118  000000A6 61000000            bsr      putc
119  000000AA 548F                addq.l   #2,a7             * adjust stack
120  000000AC 5282                addq.l   #1,d2             * add 1 to screen column
121
122  000000AE 5285    sk0_ex:     addq.l   #1,d5             * add 1 to logical column
123  000000B0 5284                addq.l   #1,d4             * add 1 to line's column count
124  000000B2 6022                bra      exp_exit          * processing complete
125
126  000000B4 103C0020 tabs:      move.b   #' ',d0           * expand with spaces
127  000000B8 61D2                bsr      exp_chr           * call recursively
128  000000BA 3205                move.w   d5,d1             * get copy of logical column
129  000000BC C27C0007            and.w    #7,d1             * check for tab column stop
130  000000C0 66F2                bne      tabs              * repeat as necessary
131  000000C2 6012                bra      exp_exit          * leave when done
132
133  000000C4 3F00     control:   move.w   d0,-(a7)          * save character
```

```
134 000000C6 103C005E      move.b  #'^',d0        * pass a circumflex recursively
135 000000CA 61C0          bsr     exp_chr        * go do it
136 000000CC 301F          move.w  (a7)+,d0       * retrieve character
137 000000CE D03C0040      add.b   #$40,d0        * make it printable
138 000000D2 61B8          bsr     exp_chr        * print it out
139 000000D4 5545          subq.w  #2,d5          * adjust logical column
140                   exp_exit:
141 000000D6 4E75          rts
142                   *********************************************************
143                   * CLR EOL - Clears to end of line
144                   * D2.W is actual screen column
145                   clr_eol:
146 000000D8 3F3C2020      move.w  #' ',-(a7)     * push spaces
147                   lp0_el:
148 000000DC B46D003E      cmp.w   w_lrcx(a5),d2  * test if we're at end of window
149 000000E0 6E08          bgt     sk0_el         * if so, we're done
150 000000E2 61000000      bsr     putc           * otherwise, print blank
151 000000E6 5242          addq.w  #1,d2          * adjust screen position
152 000000E8 60F2          bra     lp0_el         * and repeat
153                   sk0_el:
154 000000EA 548F          addq.l  #2,a7          * adjust stack (remove blank)
155 000000EC 4E75          rts
156                   *********************************************************
157                   * STATS - prints current file stats in command window
158                   stats:
159 000000EE 48E7C004      movem.l d0/d1/a5,-(a7)
160 000000F2 4A6D0048      tst.w   insert(a5)     * check if insert on or off
161 000000F6 6708          beq     no_ins
162 000000F8 2F3C00000186  move.l  #on,-(a7)      * push "On" message
163 000000FE 6006          bra     past_ins
164                   no_ins:
165 00000100 2F3C00000189  move.l  #off,-(a7)     * push "Off" message
166                   past_ins:
167 00000106 202D0016      move.l  e_gap(a5),d0   * compute space available
168 0000010A 90AD0012      sub.l   b_gap(a5),d0
169 0000010E 3F00          move.w  d0,-(a7)
170 00000110 202D0012      move.l  b_gap(a5),d0   * compute chars behind cursor
171 00000114 90AD000E      sub.l   b_buf(a5),d0
172 00000118 3F00          move.w  d0,-(a7)
173 0000011A 3F2D002E      move.w  log_col(a5),-(a7)  * print logical column
174 0000011E 3F2D0030      move.w  log_lin(a5),-(a7)  * print logical line
175 00000122 486D004A      pea     fname(a5)      * print filename
176 00000126 2A7C00000000  move.l  #cmd_w,a5      * load up command window desc.
177 0000012C 3F2D003C      move.w  w_ulcy(a5),-(a7)  * push Y position
178 00000130 5257          addq.w  #1,(a7)        * adjust Y position
179 00000132 3F2D003A      move.w  w_ulcx(a5),-(a7)  * push X position
180 00000136 2F3C0000014C  move.l  #statstr,-(a7) * push format string address
181 0000013C 61000000      bsr     printf
182 00000140 DFFC00000018  add.l   #24,a7         * adjust stack
```

Module EDIT2.PRN (continued)

```
183  00000146  4CDF2003              movem.l  (a7)+,d0/d1/a5
184  0000014A  4E75                  rts
185
                             statstr:
186  0000014C  25746696C653A20       dc.b     '%vFile: %-14s LN %-5u CO %-5u CH %-5u SP %-5u'
186  00000154  252D31343204C4E
186  0000015C  20252D357520434F
186  00000164  20252D3575204348
186  0000016C  20252D3575205350
186  00000174  20252D3575
187  00000179  20496E7365727420      dc.b     ' Insert %-3s',0
187  00000181  252D337300
                             on:
188  00000186  4F6E00                dc.b     'On',0
                             off:
189  00000189  4F666600              dc.b     'Off',0
190  0000018E  0000                  dc.w     0
191  *********************************************************************
192
193
     * SET_EDIT - initializes edit descriptor file parameters
                             set_edit:
194  00000190  2F08                  move.l  a0,-(a7)              * save caller's a0
195  00000192  426D0004              clr.w   scr_row(a5)           * cursor Y address
196  00000196  426D0006              clr.w   scr_col(a5)           * cursor X address
197  0000019A  426D0008              clr.w   ed_err(a5)            * edit error flag
198  0000019E  426D000A              clr.w   modify(a5)            * file modified flag
199  000001A2  204D                  move.l  a5,a0                 * descriptor base address
200  000001A4  D1FC0000007E          add.l   #buffer,a0            * offset to start of char buffer
201  000001AA  2B48000E              move.l  a0,b_buf(a5)          * buffer start address
202  000001AE  2B480012              move.l  a0,b_gap(a5)          * gap starting address
203  000001B2  2B480026              move.l  a0,top_lef(a5)        * addr of top left character
204  000001B6  204D                  move.l  a5,a0                 * descriptor base address
205  000001B8  D1FC0000FFFF          add.l   #DESC-1,a0            * add offset to end of buffer
206  000001BE  2B48001A              move.l  a0,e_buf(a5)          * buffer end address
207  000001C2  5288                  addq.l  #1,a0                 * gap end address
208  000001C4  2B480016              move.l  a0,e_gap(a5)          * gap ending address
209  000001C8  42AD001E              clr.l   blk_st(a5)            * block start address
210  000001CC  42AD001E              clr.l   blk_end(a5)           * block end address
211  000001D0  42AD002A              clr.l   cur_lin(a5)           * address 1st char, current line
212  000001D4  426D0030              clr.w   log_lin(a5)           * cursor logical line
213  000001D8  426D002E              clr.w   log_col(a5)           * cursor logical column
214  000001DC  426D0046              clr.w   w_off(a5)             * set offset to 0
215  000001E0  3B7CFFFF0048          move.w  #$FFFF,insert(a5)     * turn insert toggle on
216  000001E6  205F                  move.l  (a7)+,a0              * restore caller's a0
217  000001E8  4E75                  rts
218  *********************************************************************
                             cmd_w:
219  00000000                        bss
220  00000000              ds.b      buffer                       * command I/O window
221
222  0000007E                        end
```

16

The Hard Stuff That the Compiler Usually Takes Care Of

This chapter has output support routines that are usually used without giving them much thought when programming in a high level language.

Until you write code in assembler, you don't realize how much help a compiler gives you in terms of the Runtime Support Library (RSL). Operations you have taken for granted in a high level language just aren't there in assembler. Things as simple as printing an integer in ASCII need to be written from scratch.

There is one big advantage to writing your own RSL routines: compactness. A case in point: When C was first becoming popular, a standard benchmark was to write a program that simply printed "Hello, World" to see how large the object code was. Often, it was 10K bytes or more in an 8080 system. For comparison, our YASE editor for the 68K is about 8.5K bytes complete. A Z80 version of YASE (with additional functions, but without windows) weighed in at around 4.8K bytes.

No matter what level of language you choose to implement your program in, there is always a tradeoff between generality and object code size. This tradeoff is functionally equivalent to a tradeoff between size and execution speed of the code versus coding time and reusability of the routine.

These days, with multimegabyte real memories and multigigabyte virtual memories, nobody really cares how big an object module is. It has been observed that as the hardware becomes an order of magnitude faster, the software becomes an order of magnitude slower and larger as software engineers take advantage of the speed differential and automate the code generation process in their quest for the virtual machine. (This observation, paraphrased somewhat, was made to one of the authors by Dr. Paul Stachour—we didn't make it up. We say things like "Geez, this here program don't run no faster than it did on the little computer, does it?")

There are still areas, such as embedded systems, where code size makes a difference. If everything has to fit on a 3-by-5-inch circuit board, managers will be unsympathetic to suggestions that four more ROMs need to be added when your compiler drags in all of the floating-point support and transcendental functions because you used a square root someplace.

Execution speed is always important, no matter what the system. Code size plays some part in execution speed, if for no other reason than that a huge program needs to be paged in and out of memory in a virtual memory system.

Even if a program fits completely in real memory, a compiled program will run slower than a properly designed and coded assembler program. We often hear about optimizers that make smaller and faster code than the best assembly language programmer when fed a reasonably large program, although we've never seen one, let alone used one. The fact is, optimizers are designed by humans and executed by machines. The designer of the optimizer has to be at least twice as smart as you are to write an optimizer that makes code as good as yours. In our case, at least, this is clearly impossible and deserves no further consideration.

The advantage you have over optimizers is that you have a global knowledge of the program. You know the quirks and requirements of imported code modules. As of this writing, the only high order language that can make the same claim is Ada, and Ada is complex enough that really good optimizers won't be available until the middle 1990's. Even then, we'll be willing to go up against an Ada compiler head-to-head, and we're confident that we'll win.

The limiting factor on the really fast assembly language program is the largest program you can write by yourself in about a year. If you can't remember and comprehend every line of code, you'll have to resort to generalizations and standard interfaces, and sooner or later the optimizer will catch up and pass you by.

But enough of this. Part of what we're going to do in this chapter is to give you a generalized output routine with a standard interface. This routine can be used as it stands or can be stripped and tweaked for speed, or expanded and generalized for more features or multiple output streams. It has a possibly familiar name ("printf"), and the listing is in Module PRINTF.PRN.

An Output Routine

"printf" (short for "print-formatted") does much of what the C standard library function of the same name does. We have ouput routines for printing signed and unsigned 16-bit integers, 16- and 32-bit hexadecimal output, strings, characters, a limited signed and unsigned decimal 32-bit integer facility, and, because the YASE editor needs it, the ability to perform direct cursor addressing. For most data types (all excluding "character") the field width and justification can be specified.

The features from the C standard that our version is missing include the ability to ask for leading zeros, and floating-point support.

A brief explanation of the interface is in order for those of you who aren't familiar with C. Output format is controlled by a "formatting" or "control" string. This string is a mixture of printable characters and designated escape codes. The printable characters are output as is. The escape codes tell "printf" the size and type of the data to be printed, and also any special

```
d       print argument as signed 16-bit decimal integer
D       print argument as signed 32-bit decimal integer
u       print argument as unsigned 16-bit decimal integer
U       print argument as unsigned 32-bit decimal integer
x       print argument as 16-bit unsigned hex
X       print argument as 32-bit unsigned hex
s       print argument as string
c       print argument as character
v       argument is special cursor control (X,Y) pair
```

FIGURE 16-1. PRINTF Conversion Characters

formatting instructions. An arbitrary number of data items (including none) can be specified by the control string. The format of the escape code is represented below (Note: braces {} enclose optional elements.):

%{{−}⟨field width⟩}⟨conversion char⟩

Examples:

%d	— use "d" conversion
%8x	— use "x" conversion, 8 character field
%−8D	— use "D" conversion, 8 char field, left justify
%12s	— use "s" conversion, 12 character field

If no field width is specified, the minimum size needed for the ASCII image is used; i.e., no blanks appear on either side of the number. A minus sign before the field width indicates to left justify the item within the field. A minus sign without a field width is legal but meaningless. Fields are padded with blanks on the right if a field width is given and left justify is specified, and on the left if a field width is given by itself. Images too large to fit in the field are printed in their entirety.

The conversion characters supported are case-sensitive, and are listed in Figure 16-1.

When calling "printf," arguments are pushed right to left if you use standard C notation when designing your pseudocode. Take the following call to printf, to print a file name from a string and a file size (in 16-bit unsigned decimal), as written in C notation:

```
char *file_name_ptr;
unsigned file_size;

printf( "Name: %s, size = %u", file_name_ptr, file_size );
```

The arguments would be pushed on the stack in the following order:

> file__size, as a 16-bit value on the stack
> file__name__ptr, as a 32-bit pointer to a string
> address of the format control string, 32 bits
> (BSR PRINTF—outputs the message)
> (ADD.L #10,A7—adjusts the stack)

Most C compilers push arguments right to left (although this is specifically undefined by the language), and in fact, our version of "printf" will work with many C compilers. This right-to-left rule is the secret of how many C compilers, and our code as well, can figure out how many arguments are used, how big and what type the arguments are, and where the arguments are located on the stack when a variable number of parameters are allowed in a procedure call.

The key is the control string. The control string address is pushed last and is always just below (or above, depending on your perspective) the caller's return address on the stack. We always know there will be a control string address and where we can find it. We can then set an argument pointer to the next item down on the stack.

Once we know how to get to the control string, we can just "travel" down the string outputting the literal characters. When we get to a format escape code, the argument pointer tells us where the data is. The format code tells us the size of the data and what to do with it, and also how far to move the argument pointer in preparation for the next format escape code. Since the control string tells us the size and makeup of the stack below the address of the format string, we can have an arbitrary number and makeup of parameters to "printf."

Let's see how this works in practice. There are some other interesting things going on that we'll point out as we go. Refer to the code in Module PRINTF.

Lines 23 to 25 define three equates used as stack frame offsets to local variables. We need some temporary storage for formatting information, and these symbolic names are used to index into the stack to where we keep the local variables. The space for these variables is reserved on line 28, where we link the stack frame to register A6. Throughout the procedure we will use A1 as a pointer to the formatting control string (line 30), and A2 as a pointer to the stack parameters (line 31):

```
27  printf:
28          link    a6,#-6          * make 2 (word) local vars
29          movem.l d0-d6/a0-a2,-(a7)
30          move.l  8(a6),a1        * get control string address
31          lea     12(a6),a2       * get pointer to parameters
```

The main loop of the procedure runs from line 32 to line 66:

```
32  loop:
33          move.b  (a1)+,d0        * get control string character
34          beq     exit            * quit if it's a null.
35          ext.w   d0              * clear high byte
36          cmp.b   #'%',d0         * see if it's control flag
```

```
37              bne     no_ctl          * branch if not
38              clr.w   leftj(a6)       * clear left justify flag
39              clr.w   field(a6)       * clear field width
40              clr.w   signf(a6)       * clear sign flag
41      lp0pf:
42              move.b  (a1)+,d0        * get control string character
43              ext.w   d0              * clear high byte
44              cmp.b   #'-',d0         * is it minus?
45              bne     sk0pf           * no, keep going
46              move.w  #1,leftj(a6)    * set left justify flag
47              bra     lp0pf           * try for next char
48      sk0pf:
49              cmp.b   #'0',d0         * is it smaller than a digit?
50              blt     sklpf           * yes, continue processing
51              cmp.b   #'9',d0         * is it larger than a digit?
52              bgt     sklpf           * yes, continue processing
53              move.w  field(a6),d1    * get current field size
54              mulu    #10,d1          * shift left one decimal digit
55              and.w   #$000F,d0       * make ASCII digit binary
56              add.w   d0,d1           * add current digit
57              move.w  d1,field(a6)    * store answer
58              bra     lp0pf           * get next format char
59      sklpf:
60              move.l  #dispatch,a0    * get case table address for case
61              bra     case            * go do case select.
62      no_ctl:
63              move.w  d0,-(a7)        * push character
64              bsr     putc            * print it
65              addq.l  #2,a7           * trash parameter
66              bra     loop            * do it again.
```

Until we find a lead-in escape code (percent sign), the procedure simply checks the control string for a null, indicating the end of the control string, and then outputs the character.

If we find an escape code, we clear the local variables (lines 38 to 40) and look for the optional justification flag (a minus sign) and field width specifiers (ASCII decimal digits).

String to Binary Conversions

Lines 53 to 57 are of particular interest. This is a general-purpose method of converting a string of ASCII decimal digits to a binary number. This will handle any combination of leading zeros and significant digits, and will be accurate modulo 2**16 (in this case) no matter how many digits you feed it. The number base it recognizes can easily be changed by changing the immediate value in the multiplication on line 54 to the value of the new number base.

Parsing of the optional format parameters continues until we find a character that isn't a digit and isn't a minus sign. At this point we branch to the conversion character dispatching on lines 60 and 61. The dispatch table is at lines 247 to 267. An unrecognized conversion character is printed literally, with any of the optional parameters previously parsed being ignored:

```
247   dispatch:
248             dc.w      9               * number of valid options
249             dc.b      0,'d'           * %d print signed decimal word
250             dc.l      d_arg
251             dc.b      0,'u'           * %u print unsigned decimal word
252             dc.l      u_arg
253             dc.b      0,'D'           * %D print signed decimal longword
254             dc.l      D_arg
255             dc.b      0,'U'           * %U print unsigned decimal longword
256             dc.l      U_arg
257             dc.b      0,'x'           * %x print hex word
258             dc.l      x_arg
259             dc.b      0,'X'           * %X print hex longword
260             dc.l      X_arg
261             dc.b      0,'s'           * %s print null terminated string
262             dc.l      s_arg
263             dc.b      0,'c'           * %c print character
264             dc.l      c_arg
265             dc.b      0,'v'           * %v set cursor (X,Y)
266             dc.l      v_arg
267             dc.l      default   * all unknown cases handled here
```

Handlers exist for each of the recognized conversion characters. The signed and unsigned short and long decimal routines each have a short preamble (lines 72 to 90) that convert the data argument to a common longword absolute value and then branch to shared code ("printdec," line 103) for processing. "printdec" uses an interesting method to convert binary numbers to decimal. In pseudocode, this routine might look like this:

```
printdec( value : unsigned_integer )
begin
    if truncate( value / 10 ) does_not_equal 0 then
        recursively_call printdec( truncate( value / 10 ) );
    end if;
    print_character_val( (value mod 10) + ASCII( 0 ) );
end printdec;
```

This technique makes digits the easy way—by pulling off the least significant digits first. The least significant digit is just the number modulo the number base. Recursion is used to save digits with lesser significance until the more significant digits are output. Most high level implementations that allow recursion will use this technique.

We are using a very similar method in "printdec":

```
103   printdec:
104             clr.w     d1              * output digit count
105   lp0_pd:
106             divu      #10,d0          * divide number by 10
107             bvs       o_flow          * number too large
108             swap      d0              * get remainder in d0.w
109             move.w    d0,-(a7)        * push digit
110             addq.w    #1,d1           * bump digit count
111             clr.w     d0              * get rid of remainder
112             swap      d0              * put quotient into d0.w
113             tst.w     d0              * zero means we're done
114             bne       lp0_pd          * jumps if not done.
115             move.w    d1,d6           * used for field adjust
116             bsr       prefix          * do prefix spaces
```

```
117          subq.w  #1,d1            * adjust loop index counter
118  lp2_pd:
119          add.w   #$30,(a7)        * make digit TOS into ASCII
120          bsr     putc             * output digit
121          addq.l  #2,a7            * eat digit from TOS
122          dbra    d1,lp2_pd        * output all digits
123          bsr     postfix          * do postfix spaces
124          bra     loop             * exit to control parser
125  o_flow:
126          move.l  #oflowstr,-(a7)  * push control string address
127          bsr     printf           * print it
128          addq.l  #4,a7            * adjust stack
129          bra     loop             * continue
130  oflowstr:
131          dc.w    '*overflow*',0
```

The difference is that we're not using recursion to save digits as we make them—we're just pushing them onto the stack as we make them, and popping them as we need them. This saves whole bunches of subroutine-call overhead. We're also saving a count of how many digits are generated, to use with the field padding routines "prefix," line 154, and "postfix," line 161.

The limitation alluded to earlier with respect to long integers comes from the technique we're using to generate the digits—a division, saving the remainder as the basis for the digit. The 68K requires that the quotient after an unsigned division be less than 65,536. Since we are dividing by 10, the dividend must then be less than 655,360, and this is the limit on the value of the number printed by this routine. If larger numbers need to be printed, an alternative method of converting from binary must be used. (The 68020 has an extended-precision divide that will allow this technique to be used on 32-bit integers.)

For example, a long integer division routine can be written specially and used with the same algorithm. If you already have a long divide in the program somewhere, use it. Another alternative is one often used on machines that don't have hardware divide instructions. This method involves a table of powers of 10. Starting with the largest power of 10 that is less than the maximum representable in the data type in question, subtractions are made (and counted) until the power of 10 no longer "goes into" the value. Then we repeat with the next largest power of 10, and so on. For example, with a 16-bit unsigned integer, we start by counting how many times we can subtract 10,000 from the value. This count becomes the ten-thousands place digit. Next we see how many times we can subtract 1,000, then 100, then 10, and then 1. This method requires no division and can be used on any size number, but is slow and inelegant. For smaller numbers, the first method is faster even though it uses the divide instruction. The second method also requires cobbling in leading zero suppression.

The hexadecimal output routines "x__arg" (line 173) and "X__arg" (line 180) have a structure similar to the decimal routines. Data is converted to a common format and an output driver ("printhex", line 187) is shared between the two.

Hex output is easier to make than decimal. All we have to do is strip off groups of 4 bits and use this value to index into a lookup table for digits. What could be easier:

```
187   printhex:
188           bsr     prefix              * output prefix spaces
189   lp0ph:
190           move.l  #hexdigits,a0       * address of translate table
191           rol.l   #4,d2               * put MSD in low four bits
192           move.w  d2,d0               * we're only interested in LSD
193           and.w   #$000F,d0           * so we hack off all but LSD
194           move.b  0(a0,d0.w),d0       * get digit
195           move.w  d0,-(a7)            * push for output
196           bsr     putc                * output it
197           addq.l  #2,a7               * trash parameter
198           dbra    d1,lp0ph            * loop for next digit
199           bsr     postfix             * do postfix spaces
200           bra     loop                * return to control string parser
201   hexdigits:
202           dc.w    '0123456789ABCDEF'
```

As it happens, if leading zero suppression is added to "printhex", these routines will also work very nicely for BCD numbers. As far as output is concerned, the only difference between converting hex and BCD to ASCII images is that some digits never occur in BCD.

String output ("s__arg", line 204) is straightforward. The length of the string is calculated for padding purposes, any prefix pad is output, then the string, then any postfix pad:

```
204   s_arg:
205           move.l  (a2),a0             * get string address from stack
206           clr.w   d6                  * get strlen for field adjust
207   slen:
208           tst.b   (a0)+               * look for terminal null
209           beq     sk0_sa              * jump if found
210           addq.w  #1,d6               * increment string length counter
211           bra     slen                * look at next byte
212   sk0_sa:
213           move.l  (a2)+,a0            * get string address again
214           bsr     prefix              * print prefix spaces
215   lp0_sa:
216           tst.b   (a0)                * end of string?
217           bne     sk1_sa              * no, keep going
218           bsr     postfix             * print postfix spaces
219           bra     loop                * continue parsing format string
220   sk1_sa:
221           move.b  (a0)+,d0            * get char from string
222           move.w  d0,-(a7)            * push for output
223           bsr     putc                * output it
224           addq.l  #2,a7               * adjust stack
225           bra     lp0_sa              * continue
```

Character output ("c __ arg", line 227) is even simpler.

```
227   c_arg:
228           move.w  (a2)+,-(a7)         * get argument
229           bsr     putc                * send it out
230           addq.l  #2,a7               * adjust stack
231           bra     loop                * continue
```

The part of "printf" most likely to be removed is the cursor addressing feature ("v__arg", line 233):

```
233  v_arg:
234         move.l   (a2)+,-(a7)    * move both args at once
235         bsr      cursor         * perform function
236         addq.l   #4,a7          * adjust stack
237         bra      loop           * continue parse of control str
```

A purist would not include this in a routine like "printf" because it doesn't support a "virtual terminal" concept—it won't be portable, and it doesn't work at all with redirection. We put it in because we're not purists, and we assume purists won't be reading this book. Purists are more likely to be writing "Towers of Hanoi" or "Sieve" benchmarks in Pascal and arguing about structured programs.

The cursor addressing feature is activated by pushing the cursor "Y," or row, address as a 16-bit integer, followed by the cursor "X," or column, address, also a 16-bit integer. The "v" escape code triggers the cursor addressing. More than one cursor addressing sequence can be used in a single control string.

If a lot of absolute cursor addressing to fixed areas of the screen is used, you may want to consider adding an enhancement that would allow the cursor address to be encoded in ASCII as part of the optional escape format parameters. For example, you may want to format your control string like this, assuming you add a format control code "y".

```
dc.b    "%0,0yUpper Left%23,68yLower Right",0
```

Since we already have an ASCII-to-binary converter as part of the control string escape optional argument parser in lines 41 to 58, all you have to do is add another temporary variable and a little logic. The existing code will convert the left-hand argument to binary and leave it in the local variable "field." When you encounter a comma in the argument, transfer the value in "field" to the new temporary variable you added, clear "field" to zero, and continue. When you get to the "y" handler, the left-hand cursor address will be in the new variable, and the right-hand argument will be in "field." We'll leave this as an exercise for the reader.

While the "printf" routine is useful as it is, we encourage you to modify the code to fit your application, especially for realtime or size-sensitive software. For example, in a small program that only outputs a couple of numbers, you can remove the unused conversions and the control string parser, and make direct calls to the remaining conversion routines.

For an example of how "printf" is used, see the "stats" routine in the previous chapter.

Module PRINTF.PRN

```
  1  ****************************************************************
  2  * PRINTF - subset/superset of C printf standard I/O function
  3  * Control args:
  4  *
  5  *          push last parameter in control string first, then next-to
  6  *          last, etc.  Push address of control string last.
  7  *
  8  *     %d: print signed decimal word
  9  *     %u: print unsigned decimal word
 10  *     %D: print signed decimal longword
 11  *     %U: print unsigned decimal longword
 12  *     %x: print hexadecimal word
 13  *     %X: print hexadecimal longword
 14  *     %s: print null terminated string
 15  *     %c: print character
 16  *     %v: cursor (x,y) - push Y, then X, as words.
 17  *     %default: print next character as literal
 18  ****************************************************************
 19           xdef    printf
 20           xref    case,putc,cursor
 21  ****************************************************************
 22  * Local variable displacement definitions
 23  leftj    equ    -2              * left justify displacement
 24  field    equ    -4              * field width displacement
 25  signf    equ    -6              * sign flag
 26  ****************************************************************
 27  printf:
 28  00000000  4E56FFFA          link    a6,#-6           * make 2 (word) local vars
 29  00000004  48E7FEE0          movem.l d0-d6/a0-a2,-(a7)
 30  00000008  226E0008          move.l  8(a6),a1         * get control string address
 31  0000000C  45EE000C          lea     12(a6),a2        * get pointer to parameters
 32  loop:
 33  00000010  1019              move.b  (a1)+,d0         * get control string character
 34  00000012  675A              beq     exit             * quit if it's a null.
 35  00000016  4880              ext.w   d0               * clear high byte
 36  00000016  B03C0025          cmp.b   #'%',d0          * see if it's control flag
 37  0000001A  6648              bne     no_ctl           * branch if not
 38  0000001C  426EFFFE          clr.w   leftj(a6)        * clear left justify flag
 39  00000020  426EFFFC          clr.w   field(a6)        * clear field width
 40  00000024  426EFFFA          clr.w   signf(a6)        * clear sign flag
 41  lp0pf:
 42  00000028  1019              move.b  (a1)+,d0         * get control string character
 43  0000002A  4880              ext.w   d0               * clear high byte
 44  0000002C  B03C002D          cmp.b   #'-',d0          * is it minus?
 45  00000030  6608              bne     sk0pf            * no, keep going
 46  00000032  3D7C0001FFFE      move.w  #1,leftj(a6)     * set left justify flag
 47  00000038  60EE              bra     lp0pf            * try for next char
```

```
48                     sk0pf:  cmp.b   #'0',d0             * is it smaller than a digit?
49   0000003A B03C0030         blt     sklpf               * yes, continue processing
50   0000003E 6D1A             cmp.b   #'9',d0             * is it larger than a digit?
51   00000040 B03C0039         bgt     sklpf               * yes, continue processing
52   00000044 6E14             move.w  field(a6),d1        * get current field size
53   00000046 322EFFFC         mulu    #10,d1              * shift left one decimal digit
54   0000004A C2FC000A         and.w   #$000F,d0           * make ASCII digit binary
55   0000004E C07C000F         add.w   d0,d1               * add current digit
56   00000052 D240             move.w  d1,field(a6)        * store answer
57   00000054 3D41FFFC         bra     lp0pf               * get next format char
58   00000058 60CE
59
60   0000005A 207C000001DE sklpf:  move.l  #dispatch,a0    * get case table address for case
61   00000060 60000000         bra     case                * go do case select.
62                     no_ctl:
63   00000064 3F00             move.w  d0,-(a7)            * push character
64   00000066 61000000         bsr     putc                * print it
65   0000006A 548F             addq.l  #2,a7               * trash parameter
66   0000006C 60A2             bra     loop                * do it again.
67                     exit:
68   0000006E 4CDF077F         movem.l (a7)+,d0-d6/a0-a2
69   00000072 4E5E             unlk    a6
70   00000074 4E75             rts
71   ********************************************************
72                     d_arg:
73   00000076 301A             move.w  (a2)+,d0            * get value, move pointer
74   00000078 48C0             ext.l   d0                  * convert to common format
75   0000007A 6116             bsr     sign                * print sign, if any, take abs()
76   0000007C 6026             bra     printdec            * go print value
77   ********************************************************
78                     u_arg:
79   0000007E 301A             move.w  (a2)+,d0            * get value, move pointer
80   00000080 C0BC0000FFFF     and.l   #$0000FFFF,d0       * zero out high word
81   00000086 601C             bra     printdec            * go print value
82   ********************************************************
83
84   00000088 201A     D_arg:  move.l  (a2)+,d0            * get value, move pointer
85   0000008A 6106             bsr     sign                * print sign, if any, take abs()
86   0000008C 6016             bra     printdec            * go print value
87   ********************************************************
88                     U_arg:
89   0000008E 201A             move.l  (a2)+,d0            * get value, move pointer
90   00000090 6012             bra     printdec            * print decimal value
91   ********************************************************
92   * SIGN - print sign if needed and takes abs() of value
93                     sign:
94   00000092 4A80             tst.l   d0                  * is it negative?
95   00000094 6A0C             bpl     sk0_sg              * exit if not
96   00000096 3D7CFFFFFFFA     move.w  #-1,signf(a6)       * flag sign needed
```

Module PRINTF.PRN (continued)

```
 97  0000009C 536EFFFC        subq.w  #1,field(a6)    * take away one for sign
 98  000000A0 4480            neg.l   d0              * change the sign
 99
100  000000A4 4E75    sk0_sg: rts
101                   *****************************************************
102                   * printdec - common decimal output routine. Value in D0.
103                   *****************************************************
104  000000A4 4241    printdec:
                              clr.w   d1              * output digit count
105                   lp0_pd:
106  000000A6 80FC000A        divu    #10,d0          * divide number by 10
107  000000AA 6928            bvs     o_flow          * number too large
108  000000AC 4840            swap    d0              * get remainder in d0.w
109  000000AE 3F00            move.w  d0,-(a7)        * push digit
110  000000B0 5241            addq.w  #1,d1           * bump digit count
111  000000B2 4240            clr.w   d0              * get rid of remainder
112  000000B4 4840            swap    d0              * put quotient into d0.w
113  000000B6 4A40            tst.w   d0              * zero means we're done
114  000000B8 66EC            bne     lp0_pd          * jumps if not done.
115  000000BA 3C01            move.w  d1,d6           * used for field adjust
116  000000BC 6132            bsr     prefix          * do prefix spaces
117  000000BE 5341            subq.w  #1,d1           * adjust loop index counter
118                   lp2_pd:
119  000000C0 06570030        add.w   #$30,(a7)       * make digit TOS into ASCII
120  000000C4 61000000        bsr     putc            * output digit
121  000000C8 548F            addq.l  #2,a7           * eat digit from TOS
122  000000CA 51C9FFF4        dbra    d1,lp2_pd       * output all digits
123  000000CE 615C            bsr     postfix         * do postfix spaces
124  000000D0 6000FF3E        bra     loop            * exit to control parser
125
126  000000D4 2F3C000000E4 o_flow:
                              move.l  #oflowstr,-(a7) * push control string address
127  000000DA 6100FF24        bsr     printf          * print it
128  000000DE 588F            addq.l  #4,a7           * adjust stack
129  000000E0 6000FF2E        bra     loop            * continue
130
131  000000E4 2A6F76657266C6F oflowstr:
131  000000EC 772A0000        dc.w    '*overflow*',0
132
133                   *****************************************************
134                   * PREFIX - outputs prefix spaces and/or sign
                      prefix:
135  000000F0 4A6EFFFC        tst.w   field(a6)       * check if field nonzero
136  000000F4 6F20            ble     chksign         * if zero, just boogie on out
137  000000F6 4A6EFFFE        tst.w   leftj(a6)       * left justify selected?
138  000000FA 661A            bne     chksign         * jump if no
139  000000FC 9D6EFFFC        sub.w   d6,field(a6)    * digits allowed - digits actual
140  00000100 6F14            ble     chksign         * exit if no spaces needed
141
142  00000102 3F00    lp0_pr: move.w  d0,-(a7)        * save d0 across call to _put
```

```
143  00000104  3F3C2020              move.w  #' ',-(a7)      * space to output
144  00000108  61000000              bsr     putc            * output the space
145  0000010C  548F                  addq.l  #2,a7           * adjust stack
146  0000010E  301F                  move.w  (a7)+,d0        * retrieve d0
147  00000110  536EFFFC              subq.w  #1,field(a6)    * decrement loop index
148  00000114  66EC                  bne     lp0_pr          * do again if more spaces needed
149                          chksign:
150  00000116  4A6EFFFA              tst.w   signf(a6)       * sign needed?
151  0000011A  670E                  beq     chkexit         * jump if no
152  0000011C  2400                  move.l  d0,d2           * save d0 across call to _put
153  0000011E  3F3C202D              move.w  #'-',-(a7)      * push sign
154  00000122  61000000              bsr     putc            * output it
155  00000126  548F                  addq.l  #2,a7           * adjust stack
156  00000128  2002                  move.l  d2,d0           * retrieve argument
157                          chkexit:
158  0000012A  4E75                  rts
159                          *******************************************
160                          * POSTFIX - prints postfix spaces in field
161                          postfix:
162  0000012C  9D6EFFFC              sub.w   d6,field(a6)    * digits allowed - digits actual
163  00000130  6F10                  ble     skl_po          * exit if no spaces needed
164                          lp0_po:
165  00000132  3F3C2020              move.w  #' ',-(a7)      * space to output
166  00000136  61000000              bsr     putc            * output the space
167  0000013A  548F                  addq.l  #2,a7           * adjust stack
168  0000013C  536EFFFC              subq.w  #1,field(a6)    * decrement loop index
169  00000140  66F0                  bne     lp0_po          * do again if more spaces needed
170                          skl_po:
171  00000142  4E75                  rts
172                          *******************************************
173                          x_arg:
174  00000144  323C0003              move.w  #3,d1           * number of digits to print
175  00000148  3C3C0004              move.w  #4,d6           * used for field adjust
176  0000014C  341A                  move.w  (a2)+,d2        * transfer output value
177  0000014E  4842                  swap    d2              * position output value
178  00000150  600A                  bra     printhex        * go print it
179                          *******************************************
180                          X_arg:
181  00000152  323C0007              move.w  #7,d1           * number of digits to print
182  00000156  3C3C0008              move.w  #8,d6           * used for field adjust
183  0000015A  241A                  move.l  (a2)+,d2        * transfer output value
184                                  bra     printhex        * go print it
185                          *******************************************
186                          * PRINTHEX - outputs value held in D2 in hex. D1 is digit count
187                          printhex:
188  0000015C  6192                  bsr     prefix          * output prefix spaces
189                          lp0ph:
190  0000015E  207C00000182          move.l  #hexdigits,a0   * address of translate table
191  00000164  E99A                  rol.l   #4,d2           * put MSD in low four bits
```

Module PRINTF.PRN (continued)

```
192  00000166  3002                  move.w   d2,d0               * we're only interested in LSD
193  00000168  C07C000F              and.w    #$000F,d0           * so we hack off all but LSD
194  0000016C  10300000              move.b   0(a0,d0.w),d0       * get digit
195  00000170  3F00                  move.w   d0,-(a7)            * push for output
196  00000172  61000000              bsr      putc                * output it
197  00000176  548F                  addq.l   #2,a7               * trash parameter
198  00000178  51C9FFE4              dbra     d1,lp0ph            * loop for next digit
199  0000017C  61AE                  bsr      postfix             * do postfix spaces
200  0000017E  6000FE90              bra      loop                * return to control string parser
201
202  00000182  3031323334353637      hexdigits:  dc.w  '0123456789ABCDEF'
202  0000018A  3839414243444546

203
204  ****************************************************************
205  00000192  2052         s_arg:   move.l   (a2),a0             * get string address from stack
206  00000194  4246                  clr.w    d6                  * get strlen for field adjust
207
208  00000196  4A18         slen:    tst.b    (a0)+               * look for terminal null
209  00000198  6704                  beq      sk0_sa              * jump if found
210  0000019A  5246                  addq.w   #1,d6               * increment string length counter
211  0000019C  60F8                  bra      slen                * look at next byte
212
213  0000019E  205A         sk0_sa:  move.l   (a2)+,a0            * get string address again
214  000001A0  6100FF4E              bsr      prefix              * print prefix spaces
215
216  000001A4  4A10         lp0_sa:  tst.b    (a0)                * end of string?
217  000001A6  6606                  bne      skl_sa              * no, keep going
218  000001A8  6182                  bsr      postfix             * print postfix spaces
219  000001AA  6000FE64              bra      loop                * continue parsing format string
220
221  000001AE  1018         skl_sa:  move.b   (a0)+,d0            * get char from string
222  000001B0  3F00                  move.w   d0,-(a7)            * push for output
223  000001B2  61000000              bsr      putc                * output it
224  000001B6  548F                  addq.l   #2,a7               * adjust stack
225  000001B8  60EA                  bra      lp0_sa              * continue
226
227  ****************************************************************
228  000001BA  3F1A         c_arg:   move.w   (a2)+,-(a7)         * get argument
229  000001BC  61000000              bsr      putc                * send it out
230  000001C0  548F                  addq.l   #2,a7               * adjust stack
231  000001C2  6000FE4C              bra      loop                * continue
232
233  ****************************************************************
234  000001C6  2F1A         v_arg:   move.l   (a2)+,-(a7)         * move both args at once
235  000001C8  61000000              bsr      cursor              * perform function
236  000001CC  588F                  addq.l   #4,a7               * adjust stack
237  000001CE  6000FE40              bra      loop                * continue parse of control str
238  ****************************************************************
```

```
239                   * DEFAULT: user has specified unknown control argument
240                   default:
241 000001D2 3F00             move.w  d0,-(a7)    * we'll just print it.
242 000001D4 61000000         bsr     putc        * so there it goes!
243 000001D8 548F             addq.l  #2,a7       * adjust stack
244 000001DA 6000FE34         bra     loop        * that's all for here
245                   ********************************************************
246                   * Case dispatch table for printf
247                   dispatch:
248 000001DE 0009             dc.w    9           * number of valid options
249 000001E0 0064             dc.b    0,'d'       * %d print signed decimal word
250 000001E2 00000076         dc.l    d_arg
251 000001E6 0075             dc.b    0,'u'       * %u print unsigned decimal word
252 000001E8 0000007E         dc.l    u_arg
253 000001EC 0044             dc.b    0,'D'       * %D print signed decimal longword
254 000001EE 00000088         dc.l    D_arg
255 000001F2 0055             dc.b    0,'U'       * %U print unsigned decimal longword
256 000001F4 0000008E         dc.l    U_arg
257 000001F8 0078             dc.b    0,'x'       * %x print hex word
258 000001FA 00000144         dc.l    x_arg
259 000001FE 0058             dc.b    0,'X'       * %X print hex longword
260 00000200 00000152         dc.l    X_arg
261 00000204 0073             dc.b    0,'s'       * %s print null terminated string
262 00000206 00000192         dc.l    s_arg
263 0000020A 0063             dc.b    0,'c'       * %c print character
264 0000020C 000001BA         dc.l    c_arg
265 00000210 0076             dc.b    0,'v'       * %v set cursor (X,Y)
266 00000212 000001C6         dc.l    v_arg
267 00000216 000001D2         dc.l    default     * all unknown cases handled here
268
269 0000021A                  end
```

17
Bit Mapped Graphics

The 68000 has a well-deserved reputation as a good graphics processor. This is primarily due to its high speed, large address space, and extensive implementation of bit manipulation instructions. Another contributing factor is the large number of registers—it makes the sorts of calculations required for bit graphics much faster.

There are a lot of ways to implement graphics, especially when dealing with display terminals that nowadays include graphics coprocessors to assist the CPU with graphics presentation. For example, the NEC 7220 Graphics Display Controller manages the display memory and hardware, accepts fairly high level graphics commands from the CPU, and has a programmer learning curve of only a man-month or two. (At least, it took us a couple of months to learn it.)

However, there are many instances in which a graphics coprocessor isn't available or can't be used. Low end personal computers (IBM PC, Macintosh) tend to leave graphics to the CPU. Preparing graphics images for printers and other hardcopy devices is another example.

Even though we want to avoid using the CPU as a graphics processor if at all possible, there are times when we can't. Once the decision is made to use the CPU as a graphics engine, though, there's no reason to be chintzy about it. Some reasonably fast general-purpose graphics routines can be built up by making use of the 68000's bit instructions.

We're going to present our solution to "the graphics problem" in this chapter. Our solution will be for a raster-type graphics image in memory. This image may or may not be associated with video display hardware to produce a video image, or may be output to hardcopy devices.

Most graphics displays are raster scanned. For those of you who didn't go to TV school, that means video images are generated a line at a time, starting at the top of the screen. A line is scanned from left to right. Due to the messy details of how video hardware works, it's easier to generate a raster line if adjacent bits are in the same memory location. That way, the video hardware can just reach in and grab a byte or a word and then crank the bits out one at a time as pixels while the CPU goes about its business.

Cheap video controllers are usually 8-bit chips, so we will design our graphics package

```
        Memory layout for an M wide x N high pixel graphics image
           Note that bits are reversed from "normal" orientation

        bit               bit                 bit                bit
   |0 1 2 3 4 5 6 7|0 1 2 3 4 5 6   0 1 2 3 4 5 6 7|0 1 2 3 4 5 6 7|
   |                                                                
   +-+-+-+-+-+-+-+-+-+-+-+-+-+-+-+   -+-+-+-+-+-+-+-+-+-+-+-+-+-+-+-+
   | |byte 0 | | | | | | | | | | |  - | | | | | | | | |byte (M-1)/8| |
   +-+-+-+-+-+-+-+-+-+-+-+-+-+-+-+   +-+-+-+-+-+-+-+-+-+-+-+-+-+-+-+-+
   | |byte M / 8 | | | | | | | | |  - | | | | | | | | |byte (2M-1)/8 |
   +-+-+-+-+-+-+-+-+-+-+-+-+-+-+-+   +-+-+-+-+-+-+-+-+-+-+-+-+-+-+-+-+
   | |byte 2M / 8 | | | | | | | |   - | | | | | | | | |byte (3M-1)/8 |
   +-+-+-+-+-+-+-+-+-+-+-+-+-+-+-+   +-+-+-+-+-+-+-+-+-+-+-+-+-+-+-+-+
   | |byte 3M / 8| | | | | | | | |  - | | | | | | | | |byte (4M-1)/8 |
   -+-+-+-+-+-+-+-+-+-+-+-+-+-+-+-+   +-+-+-+-+-+-+-+-+-+-+-+-+-+-+-+-+
   |        *              *         -       *                *      |
   +-+-+-+-+-+-+-+-+-+-+-+-+-+-+-+   +-+-+-+-+-+-+-+-+-+-+-+-+-+-+-+-+
   | |byte (N-1)M/8| | | | | | | |  - | | | | | | | | | | | | | | | |
   +-+-+-+-+-+-+-+-+-+-+-+-+-+-+-+-   +-+-+-+-+-+-+-+-+-+-+-+-+-+-+-+-+
```

FIGURE 17-1. Raster

around a byte oriented image. This also helps us with the memory-addressed operand bit instructions, which operate on bytes. Figure 17-1 shows the bit and byte alignment for an **M** by
N bit graphic image.

In designing graphics drivers, there's a tradeoff between generality and speed. A very
general purpose solution, e.g., one that allows multiple images of arbitrary size and alignment,
will be slower than a specific solution to support a single image of a fixed size. We're going to
give you something between these extremes, and you can tailor it up or down to suit
your needs.

Our package will work on a single monochrome image (color display techniques require
multiple bits per pixel, in several schemes, and will unnecessarily complicate the discussion) of
a fixed size in a fixed location. That location will be fixed at linktime. We are requiring that
each raster line of the image contains a multiple of 16 bits.

Figure 17-2 is a common header file included in all files accessing graphics primitives.
The equates "hor__w" and "vert" set the size of the graphic image, and so are fixed at assemble time. The equates "jam__m", "comp__m", "set__m," and "clr__m" set the write modes

```
***************************************************************
* BIT MAPPED GRAPHICS HEADER
hor_w     equ     20              * words in horizontal row
hor_b     equ     hor_w*16        * bits in horizontal row
vert      equ     200             * number of rows of pixels
jam_m     equ     $01             * jam mode value
comp_m    equ     $02             * complement mode value
set_m     equ     $04             * set mode value
clr_m     equ     $08             * clear mode value
```

FIGURE 17-2. Module BIT.H

```
                   "Jam" Mode
+----------+----------+----------+
| Original | Value    | New      |
| Pixel    | Written  | Pixel    |
+----------+----------+----------+
|    0     |    0     |    0     |
|    1     |    0     |    0     |
|    0     |    1     |    1     |
|    1     |    1     |    1     |
+----------+----------+----------+

                   "Set" Mode
+----------+----------+----------+
| Original | Value    | New      |
| Pixel    | Written  | Pixel    |
+----------+----------+----------+
|    0     |    0     |    0     |
|    1     |    0     |    1     |
|    0     |    1     |    1     |
|    1     |    1     |    1     |
+----------+----------+----------+

                 "Complement" Mode
+----------+----------+----------+
| Original | Value    | New      |
| Pixel    | Written  | Pixel    |
+----------+----------+----------+
|    0     |    0     |    0     |
|    1     |    0     |    1     |
|    0     |    1     |    1     |
|    1     |    1     |    0     |
+----------+----------+----------+

                  "Clear" Mode
+----------+----------+----------+
| Original | Value    | New      |
| Pixel    | Written  | Pixel    |
+----------+----------+----------+
|    0     |    0     |    0     |
|    1     |    0     |    1     |
|    0     |    1     |    0     |
|    1     |    1     |    0     |
+----------+----------+----------+
```

FIGURE 17-3. Mode Truth Tables

for the graphics primitives, and are modeled after the NEC 7220 modes. Figure 17-3 shows the truth tables for installing "1" or "0" pixels over a current image.

"Jam" mode means that image fragments are jammed in on top of the rest of the image. For example, if a checkerboard image is imposed on another image, the checkerboard pattern will be inserted as is.

"Complement" mode means that image fragments are exclusive-or'ed with the previous contents of the image. Imposing a "1" pixel on the image results in the previous pixel value being inverted. Complement mode is very useful for superimposing temporary fragments like mouse pointers and crosshairs, because if the same fragment is complemented twice, it disappears, leaving no trace. Also, you can always see a complemented line or block, no matter what it's superimposed on.

"Set" mode works just like "jam" mode for all of the primitives, but we'll see its use in a more complex function later in the chapter. "Set" is a logical-or function of the current pixel and the new pixel. If we tried to superimpose a checkerboard pattern on another image, in "set" mode all the "1" pixels of the checkerboard would be set, while all the "0" bits of the checkerboard would remain unaffected in the image. If a graphics character is superimposed in "set" mode, it is transparent (the background shows through the white space) whereas in "jam" mode, the graphics character would be opaque.

"Clear" mode causes all "1" pixels of the new fragment to show as "0" in the image, while "0" pixels have no effect on the image. We are not supplying a "reset pixel" procedure, but setting the mode to "clear" and doing a "set pixel" has the same effect.

We have developed the following bit primitive functions, all of which conform to the mode conventions just presented: "g__mode," a procedure to set the current mode of the primitives; "g__pix," to set pixels; "g__vector," to draw lines from one point to another; "g__circle," to draw a circle; "g__clear," to provide a fast way to erase the image; and "g__fill," to fill a rectangular area given diagonal corners. The only basic function missing (mostly because we never use it anyhow) is a procedure to draw an arc.

Module BITPRIM.PRN (Figure 17-2) is the listing of our graphics primitive procedures. The "g__pix" (set pixel) procedure appears as lines 18 to 50. The first four lines check the clipping rectangle, to make sure that we hit within the boundaries of the image:

```
22          cmp.w     #hor_b,d0      * check clipping horizontal
23          bcc       sk0_sp         * exit on over X
24          cmp.w     #vert,d1       * check clipping vertical
25          bcc       sk0_sp         * exit on over Y
```

If this were to be generalized, a test for lower bounds could be added and the limits kept in static storage at the expense of some speed. However, since "g__pix" is a basic and often used procedure, it pays to make this as fast as possible.

Lines 26 to 33 calculate the address of the pixel:

```
27          move.l    #image,a0      * get base of image area
28          mulu      #(hor_w*2),d1  * get vertical offset to line
29          add.l     d1,a0          * and add to base address
30          move.w    d0,d1          * save X for later
31          lsr.w     #3,d0          * get number of bytes to pixel
32          add.w     d0,a0          * add to pointer
33          and.w     #$0007,d1      * strip all but bit number
```

Note that an "X" pixel bit address is the address of the byte containing the pixel, obtained by shifting the pixel address 3 bits right, and the bit address within the byte, obtained by stripping all but the lower 3 bits of the pixel address. If hardware or other constraints force you to number your bits from left-to-right, instead of our right-to-left system, the bit address may be obtained by inverting the lower 3 bits of the pixel address.

Note the multiply at line 28. You can save about 65 clock cycles per pixel if you constrain the horizontal dimension of the image to a power-of-2 number of bytes. Then you can use a shift instruction in place of the multiply.

Lines 34 to 40 figure out what mode we're in:

```
34              move.w  mode,d0         * get mode flag
35              lsr.w   #1,d0           * pop bit 0 into carry flag
36              bcs     sk1_sp          * jam mode jump
37              lsr.w   #1,d0           * pop bit 1 into carry flag
38              bcs     sk2_sp          * complement mode jump
39              lsr.w   #1,d0           * pop bit 2 into carry flag
40              bcs     sk3_sp          * set mode jump
41              bclr    d1,(a0)         * falls thru to clear mode
42              bra     sk0_sp          * so we're done
```

We chose values for the mode equates so that the technique shown works. Lines 261 to 266 show an alternate technique:

```
260             and.b   d6,d4           * combine the two masks
261             btst    #0,mode+1       * look for jam mode
262             bne     sk4_fil         * go jam
263             btst    #1,mode+1       * look for complement mode
264             bne     sk5_fil         * go complement
265             btst    #2,mode+1       * look for set mode
266             bne     sk4_fil         * it's the same as jam here
```

We test for the most common choices (set and complement) first, to speed things up just a tad more. The actual bit fiddling takes place on lines 41, 45 and 48:

```
43  sk1_sp:
44  sk3_sp:
45              bset    d1,(a0)         * jam and set are the same here
46              bra     sk0_sp          * now we're done
47  sk2_sp:
48              bchg    d1,(a0)         * complement mode
```

We provided (and use) a procedure to set the mode (lines 53 to 55) rather than having the application stuff a value directly into memory just in case you decide to port this code to a machine with hardware support for graphics.

Things get interesting when we come to the procedure "g__vector," lines 59 to 136. This is an example of the principle that it's better to spend twice as long setting up a loop if it cuts

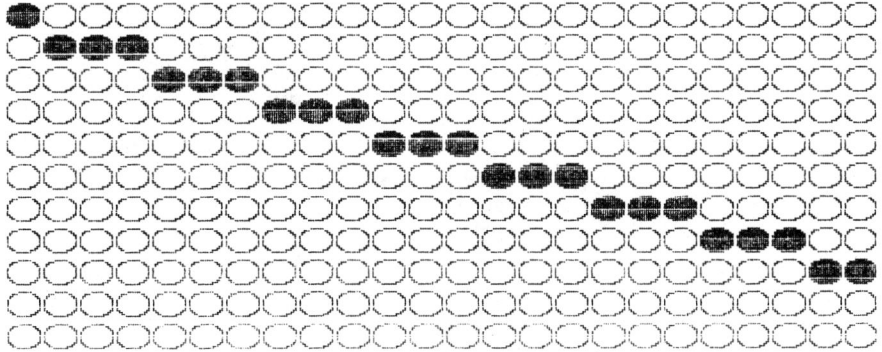

FIGURE 17-4.   Pixels

the loop body by even one instruction. "g—vector" is also a good example of how to represent fractional values on a binary machine. If we had floating-point hardware this procedure could be about half as long. (But even with floating-point hardware this routine would be slower than with integer representation because of type conversions. In general, floating point should be avoided if at all possible, if only because even implementing some bizarre integer scheme as opposed to simple floating point will usually save 10 to 50 percent in development time, and add two to four years to your life.)

The algorithm is fairly simple. The idea is to get a line of pixels such that pixels are adjacent either directly or diagonally (see Figure 17-4). The number of pixels required to make a line is the greater of the X run or the Y run ("run" is a projection of the distance between two points projected onto one of the axes). What we do is determine the maximum run, either X or Y, and make this our independent axis. The other axis becomes the dependent axis. We output a number of pixels equal to the magnitude of the independent axis. If we start at one end of the line, the location of the next pixel is plus or minus one pixel along the independent axis, and some fractional value along the dependent axis. After we determine the values of the pixel-to-pixel increments, outputting the next pixel becomes a matter of simply adding to the coordinates of the previous pixel.

Lines 63 to 68 set up the origin of the vector:

```
62            move.w   d0,d4          * setup base for X
63            swap     d4             * scale x 2^16
64            clr.w    d4             * make even number
65            move.w   d1,d5          * setup base for Y
66            swap     d5             * scale x 2^16
67            clr.w    d5             * make even number
```

The scaling mentioned in the comments will be covered shortly. Lines 69 to 82 determine absolute and signed differences along the X and Y axis and the dependent axis:

```
69            sub.w    d0,d2          * find difference in X
70            move.w   d2,d0          * save signed difference
71            bpl      sk1_vec        * skip X absolute value convert
72            neg.w    d0             * D0 is X absolute distance
73     ****** Determine absolute and signed run in Y *****************
74     sk1_vec:
75            sub.w    d1,d3          * find difference in Y
76            move.w   d3,d1          * save signed difference
77            bpl      sk2_vec        * skip Y absolute value convert
78            neg.w    d1             * D1 is Y absolute distance
79     ****** Determine independent (larger) and dependent axis ******
80     sk2_vec:
```

We need the absolute difference to tell whether X or Y is the independent axis, and for pixel counters, and we need the signed difference to give a direction to the line.

Once we have determined the independent axis, we have to calculate the increment for the dependent axis. The two blocks of code at lines 84 to 100 and 102 to 118 are essentially identical, differing only in the reversal of X and Y, so we will explain only one of them.

The independent axis will always be incremented in steps of 1 pixel, and since the dependent run is always less than or equal to the independent run, the dependent axis step will always be less than or equal to 1. The problem is representing a fraction with an integer register.

To solve the problem, we are scaling the values by 65,536, or 2**16. For example, "1" is represented as $10000. 0.5 or one half of "1," is represented as $8000. 0.25 is represented as $4000, and so on. We are keeping all our numbers as scaled fixed-point values throughout the procedure. Note in lines 86 and 89 the assignments of 1 and −1.

```
84              tst.w   d2              * check sign of X run
85              bmi     sk3_vec         * jump if negative
86              move.l  #$00010000,d6   * setup X step = 1.0
87              bra     sk4_vec         * jump to Y setup
88      sk3_vec:
89              move.l  #$FFFF0000,d6   * setup Y step = -1.0
90      ******* Determine Y step as scaled fixed point longword *********
91      sk4_vec:
92              swap    d3              * Scale up
93              clr.w   d3              * make longword
94              asr.l   #2,d3           * take out two bits of precision
95              divs    d0,d3           * divide by independent axis
96              ext.l   d3              * make long again
97              asl.l   #2,d3           * put two precisions bits back
98              move.l  d3,d7           * D7 is signed Y step
99              move.w  d0,d2           * get independant axis counter
```

The determining of the dependent step is more difficult. The precision of the dependent step is limited by the 16-bit precision of the hardware divide instruction. Since we need the signed value to maintain the line direction, this amounts to plus or minus 15 bits. In line 94 we are taking out 2 more bits of precision so that we can do a signed division of the scaled dependent run by the unscaled independent run, returning the pixel-to-pixel increment (step) of the dependent run. This bit of code depends on the fact that the dependent run is always less than or equal to the independent run. If the dependent run was allowed to be larger, the division would overflow.

The minimum precision required for the dependent step is a function of the maximum line length required. If a line is allowed to be as long as possible within the limits of the image, the greater of the horizontal or vertical pixel count can be used to find the limit on precision. With the 13 bits of accuracy in our vector procedure, the absolute maximum size of an image is 8K by 8K. At the absolute maximum size, the slope of certain worst-case diagonal lines will be somewhat ragged. With the 1K or 2K image areas we have used, line imperfections are practically nonexistent.

Once the axis steps are found, the output of the pixels (lines 121 to 135) is trivial:

```
121     sk7_vec:
122             bra     sk8_vec         * do loop test before body
123     lp0_vec:
124             move.l  d4,d0           * get scaled X position
125             add.l   #$00008000,d0   * round up by adding 0.5
126             swap    d0              * scale X down for output
127             move.l  d5,d1           * get scaled Y position
128             add.l   #$00008000,d1   * round up by adding 0.5
129             swap    d1              * scale Y down for output
130             bsr     g_pix           * put the pixel
131             add.l   d6,d4           * add X step
```

```
132              add.l    d7,d5              * add Y step
133  sk8_vec:
134              dbra     d2,lp0_vec         * loop around
135              movem.l  (a7)+,d0-d7        * restore registers
```

Each time we need to output a pixel, we simply add the steps computed earlier to the current pixel position. We are rounding up at lines 125 and 128 to make the lines transition pixel boundaries as close as possible to where they ought to be. Note the use of the "g__pix" routine to preserve correct write mode operation and the clipping rectangle.

A word of caution: "g__vector" will blow up with a divide-by-zero exception if a zero length line is requested. We decided that the amount of code needed to trap this was unreasonable. You may think differently.

Our "fast circle" procedure begins on line 139. The circle code is more straightforward than the vector, but it uses the same scaling principle. There is less setup possible for a circle, so we have more computation within the pixel output loop.

The general equation for a circle centered at (0,0) is $X**2 + Y**2 = radius**2$. When this equation is rearranged and solved for X, we find that for each X there are two Y solutions. Similarly, for each Y there are two X solutions. It can also be shown that for any point (X,Y) that falls on the circle, there is another point (−X,−Y) 180 degrees away. "So what?", you might say, "If I cared about trig I would have gone back to school." Good point. The bottom line is that we only need to compute one eighth of the points around the circle—we can get the other seven eighths of the pixels by "reflecting" each of the computed pixels around the circumference.

The number of pixels needed for one eighth circle is the number of pixels in a 45-degree arc of the circle. This number is equal to the radius divided by the square root of 2. We determine this number in lines 147 to 149. The strange constant $B504 in line 147 is the square root of 2 shifted left 15 bits.

The way the rest of the procedure works is this: We will calculate an X value for each Y value in the 45-degree arc from 0 to 45 degrees. The X value is equal to the square root of the difference between the radius squared and the Y value squared—the old Pythagoras stuff. This computation is performed in lines 151 to 156 as part of the circle loop (the function "sqrt" is listed in Appendix B):

```
151              move.w   d2,d4              * d4 is a scratch register
152              mulu     d4,d4              * d4 is (rise**2)
153              move.l   d3,d0              * d0 is   scratch register
154              sub.l    d4,d0              * d0 is (run**2)
155              bsr      sqrt               * after call, d0 = (run)
```

Because the square of the radius is a constant throughout each invocation of the circle procedure, it is calculated outside the loop at lines, 143 to 144:

```
143              move.w   d2,d3              * get copy of radius
144              mulu     d3,d3              * d3.1 is radius squared
```

The rest of the procedure is just the reflection of the rise (the Y value) and the run (the X value) around the circle. Again, we are using the "g__pix" procedure to preserve the write mode operation and clipping rectangle.

Our procedure "g__clear" begins on line 211. This procedure clears the graphics image to all zeros, regardless of the current write mode setting. A fill command could also be used, but would be slower. The only thing of note about this procedure is the use of a longword loop counter. A 16-bit counter would allow a maximum image size of 4 megapixels. The rest of the procedures are good to about 32K pixels in either direction, except for the vector procedure.

The "g__fill" rectangular area fill procedure (line 222), on the other hand, is another one of those complicated deals. A very reasonable solution would have been to loop through the vector procedure and compose the rectangle of a number of lines. Reasonable solutions are for reasonable people, though, and we're maniacs. We want to avoid a whole bunch of overhead associated with the pixel and vector routines. The way we picked is much, much, much faster than the reasonable solution, but takes more code.

Our fill routine depends on the fact that an area can be considered a range of columns within a range of rows. We are using this fact to develop a set of masks that fit over the range of affected columns in a single row, and then we are applying this set of masks to a series of rows.

Lines 225 to 231 shuffle the X and Y values such that we know for sure that the X value in D0 is smaller than the X value in D2, and the Y value in D1 is smaller than D3:

```
225             cmp.w    d0,d2            * Who's bigger?
226             bge      skl_fil          * jump if d2 is bigger
227             exg      d0,d2            * swap if not
228   skl_fil:
229             cmp.w    d1,d3            * Who's bigger here?
230             bge      sk2_fil          * jump if d3 is bigger
231             exg      d1,d3            * swap if not
```

Once this is done, we know that the point (D0,D1) is the upper-left corner of the rectangle, and the point (D2,D3) is the lower-right corner of the rectangle.

Lines 234 to 241 determine the number of rows affected, and the address of the first affected byte:

```
233   ****** Calculate (number of rows) - 1, save in D7
234             move.w   d3,d7            * uses D7 as accumulator
235             sub.w    d1,d7            * D7 is (#rows-1)
236   ****** Calculate first byte address in A0
237             move.l   #image,a0        * A0 is base of image memory
238             mulu     #(hor_w*2),d1    * D1 is row offset from zero
239             move.w   d0,d3            * D3 is a scratch register
240             asr.w    #3,d3            * D3 is number of bytes into row
241             add.w    d3,d1            * D1 is bytes into image
```

Once this is done, we have no further use for the Y parameters.

Our masks are computed next (see Figure 17-5). The mask model we picked uses a fragment of 0 to 8 bits to cover bits in the left-hand byte of the affected columns, 0 or more whole bytes of affected pixels, and a fragment of 0 to 8 bits to cover bits in the right-hand byte of the affected columns. A special case occurs when the affected columns are all contained in the same byte, and this special case is handled separately.

Once the masks are computed, we take six different branches depending on special or

```
                 Example 1: normal, large area fill
Left mask ->    0 0 0 0 1 1 1 1                                = $F0
Center mask ->                  1 1 1 1 1 1 1 1                 = $FF
Right Mask ->                                  1 1 0 0 0 0 0 0  = $03

0 1 2 3 4 5 6 7 0 1 2 3 4 5 6 7 0 1 2 3 4 5 6 7 0 1 2 3 4 5 6 7
- - - - - - - - - - - - - - - - - - - - - - - - - - - - - - - -
- - - - - - - - - - - - - - - - - - - - - - - - - - - - - - - -
- - - - - - - - - - - - * * * * * * * * * * * * * * * * - - - - - -
- - - - - - - - - - - - * * * * * * * * * * * * * * * * - - - - - -
- - - - - - - - - - - - * * * * * * * * * * * * * * * * - - - - - -
- - - - - - - - - - - - * * * * * * * * * * * * * * * * - - - - - -
- - - - - - - - - - - - * * * * * * * * * * * * * * * * - - - - - -
- - - - - - - - - - - - * * * * * * * * * * * * * * * * - - - - - -
- - - - - - - - - - - - - - - - - - - - - - - - -  - - - - - - -
- - - - - - - - - - - - - - - - - - - - - - - - - - - - - - - -


             Example 2: Normal case, two bytes only affected
Left Mask ->    0 0 0 0 0 0 1 1                     = $C0
(No Center Mask)
Right Mask ->                   1 1 1 1 1 0 0 0     = $1F

0 1 2 3 4 5 6 7 0 1 2 3 4 5 6 7 0 1 2 3 4 5 6 7 0 1 2 3 4 5 6 7
- - - - - - - - - - - - - - - - - - - - - - - - - - - - - - - -
- - - - - - - - - - - - - - - - - - - - - - - - - - - - - - - -
- - - - - - - - - - - - - - * * * * * * * - - - - - - - - - - - -
- - - - - - - - - - - - - - * * * * * * * - - - - - - - - - - - -
- - - - - - - - - - - - - - * * * * * * * - - - - - - - - - - - -
- - - - - - - - - - - - - - - - - - - - - - - - - - - - - - - -
- - - - - - - - - - - - - - - - - - - - - - - - - - - - - - - -


        Example 3: Special case: all affected bits within one byte
Left Mask ->                    0 0 1 1 1 1 1 1     = $FC
(No Center Mask)
Right Mask ->                   1 1 1 1 1 1 0 0     = $3F
Special Case Mask ->            0 0 1 1 1 1 0 0     = $3C

0 1 2 3 4 5 6 7 0 1 2 3 4 5 6 7 0 1 2 3 4 5 6 7 0 1 2 3 4 5 6 7
- - - - - - - - - - - - - - - - - - - - - - - - - - - - - - - -
- - - - - - - - - - - - - - - - - - - - - - - - - - - - - - - -
- - - - - - - - - - - - - - - - - - * * * * - - - - - - - - - - -
- - - - - - - - - - - - - - - - - - * * * * - - - - - - - - - - -
- - - - - - - - - - - - - - - - - - * * * * - - - - - - - - - - -
- - - - - - - - - - - - - - - - - - * * * * - - - - - - - - - - -
- - - - - - - - - - - - - - - - - - * * * * - - - - - - - - - - -
- - - - - - - - - - - - - - - - - - - - - - - - - - - - - - - -
- - - - - - - - - - - - - - - - - - - - - - - - - - - - - - - -
```

FIGURE 17-5. Masks

normal case and the selected write mode (we can treat "set" and "jam" mode the same, because "fill" is considered to mean "fill with ones"). The normal case is to apply the left-hand mask, then any whole byte masks, then the right-hand mask, to each affected row. The special case just combines the left- and right-hand masks and applies this combined mask to each affected row.

Once you set up a graphic image, it's nice to be able to see it. The ideal, of course, is to see it on a video display. Lacking that, you can display it on a printer.

Most of the dot-matrix printers on the market are capable of some sort of graphics output. We have an old Okidata Microline 83A with Okigraph ROMs installed. (Actually, if we'd been on the ball, we would have gotten the publisher to buy us a shiny new PC-Graphics compatible printer on the grounds that it's much more common than the ol' Oki. This is the sort of idea that occurs to us programmer types way too late to do anything about.) While the chances are good that you have a different printer, the chances are also good that your printer will use a similar scheme.

The big problem is that printers usually want to print seven or eight (with seven being the most common) rows of dots on each pass, and they want data as one column of seven rows per byte output. As we mentioned earlier, most graphics images are generated to make raster scans easily. The result is that we need bits from 7 different bytes for each byte of data sent to the printer.

Module OKI.PRN is our solution to the problem. It's pretty simple, but illustrates our idea of good function partitioning. The printer drivers are pulled out of the mainline code to make maintenance easier. That way, when the Oki printers you ordered come in as Brand X printers (because procurement has a corporate purchasing agreement with the distributor, and a printer's a printer, right?), you don't have to hunt through the code looking for embedded control sequences. With suitable modifications to the printer interface, this procedure should be usable with most of the printers on the market.

Lines and circles and rectangular fills are fine, but after the first couple of pictures, you'll begin to want a little more sophisticated stuff, especially if you're planning to make a paint program. The world desperately needs another paint program, and you're just the person to do it.

A favorite feature of paint programs is the "creep" function, usually iconized as a paint bucket or a paint roller. The user selects a point on the display, clicks the mouse, and "paint" spreads out along adjacent white space until it encounters a barrier of set pixels. If the perimeter isn't solid, "paint" leaks all over the image, making a mess.

Module CREEP.PRN is the listing of our "creep" procedure. It is a single-case procedure—it operates only on light areas bordered by dark areas. If you need both, it is better to write a whole new procedure, reversing the senses of the tests, than to build in decision logic—it keeps the speed up. Our "creep" also works correctly only if the original pixel given it is not set, and the current write mode is "jam," "set," or "complement." Within these restrictions, it works very well and reasonably fast.

Lines 19 to 39 run left and right down the row containing the original pixel, setting pixels to the edge of the image or until a perimeter pixel is found:

```
20              move.w   d0,d2          * save pixel X
21              move.w   d1,d3          * save pixel Y
22    lpl_cp:
23              bsr      tstpix         * check this pixel
24              bne      skl_cp         * we're done if this one set
25              bsr      g_pix          * set this pixel
26              subq.w   #1,d0          * move left one pixel
27              bra      lpl_cp         * do it 'til we boink
```

```
28  skl_cp:
29           addq.w   #1,d0          * adjust right end X position
30           exg      d0,d2          * save leftmost, get original
31           addq.w   #1,d0          * move left of original
32  lp2_cp:
33           bsr      tstpix         * check this pixel
34           bne      sk2_cp         * we're done if this one set
35           bsr      g_pix          * set this pixel
36           addq.w   #1,d0          * move right one pixel
37           bra      lp2_cp         * keep on to the right end
38  sk2_cp:
```

The endpoints of the line are saved. This code is supported by the procedure "tstpix,"
lines 66 to 91:

```
66  tstpix:
67           movem.l  d0/d1/a0,-(a7)  * save caller's registers
68  ******  See if X and Y are valid addresses *********************
69           tst.w    d0             * look for off left edge
70           bmi      skl_pix        * error out if so
71           tst.w    d1             * look for off top
72           bmi      skl_pix        * error out if so
73           cmp.w    #hor_b,d0      * look for off right edge
74           bge      skl_pix        * error out if so
75           cmp.w    #vert,d1       * look for off bottom
76           bge      skl_pix        * error out if so
77  ******  pixel (X,Y) is valid; check value of pixel **************
78           move.l   #image,a0      * get base of image area
79           mulu     #(hor_w*2),d1  * get vertical offset to line
80           add.l    d1,a0          * and add to base address
81           move.w   d0,d1          * save X for later
82           lsr.w    #3,d0          * get number of bytes to pixel
83           add.w    d0,a0          * add to pointer
84           and.w    #$0007,d1      * strip all but bit number
85           btst     d1,(a0)        * test the bit
86           bra      sk2_pix        * and exit
87  skl_pix:
88           andi     #$FB,ccr       * errors always show set pixel
89  sk2_pix:
90           movem.l  (a7)+,d0/d1/a0  * restore caller's registers
91           rts
```

"tstpix" takes a pixel address and first checks for the address being valid within the
defined image. If the address isn't valid, "tstpix" returns a value as if the pixel is set. Since a set
pixel always indicates a perimeter, this has the effect of placing a perimeter line all the way
around the edge of the image. If the address is valid, "tstpix" calculates the pixel position and
tests the pixel, using logic block-copied from the "g—pix" procedure. "tstpix" returns its
result in the zero flag, with non-zero (FALSE) meaning a set pixel, and zero (TRUE) meaning
a reset pixel.

Once the endpoints of the new pixels in the current row are determined, we need to run
down the pixels on each side of the new pixels looking for white space. Lines 42 to 49 set up
for the procedure "run" (lines 54 to 62, which does the looking). When "run" finds a clear
pixel, it calls "creep" recursively with the address of the clear pixel:

```
54   run:
55           bsr      tstpix           * check this pixel
56           bne      sk4_cp           * set, no need to worry
57           bsr      creep            * set the new line
58   sk4_cp:
59           addq.w   #1,d0            * move right one pixel
60           cmp.w    d0,d4            * test against right limit
61           bge      run              * loop if more to check
62           rts
```

The largest contributor to the inefficiency of this procedure is the requirement to look at both sides of a newly set line. If you want to be sure that the "paint" leaks through every gap, you pretty much have to. For example, if a barrier extends from the top center of the image to the middle of the image, and "creep" is seeded with a pixel in the upper-right quadrant of the image, the "paint" will spread downward on the right half of the image until it slips left under the barrier. At this point, you want the paint flow up over the upper-left quadrant of the image. If you're using a smart algorithm that only looks in the direction of flow, this won't happen.

If speed is absolutely essential, the direction and endpoints of the parent line could be passed to "creep" on the recursive call and this area could be excluded from testing by "run." The amount of added overhead and complexity would only result in a marginal gain in speed, however, and it adds to the effect if the end user can see the process as it happens.

As long as we're talking about paint programs, we might as well go the whole hog and talk about icons. Icons are a throwback to the pictographs used when man (or should it be "person"?) hadn't yet developed a written language. They are ideal for the average user, who can't read and comprehend the words "press the letter corresponding to your choice." Icons also make nice companions for your mouse, if you can get it unstuck from the residue left by your soda cans.

To support icons, we have the procedure "icon" at lines 86–142 of Module OLAY.PRN. We also have two sample icons, a 10 by 10-pixel arrow (lines 19 to 38) useful for a mouse pointer, and a 32 by 32-pixel snarl face (lines 40 to 83) to accompany the "close the disk drive door, you idiot!" message.

The icon procedure takes five parameters. Two of them (D0.W and D1.W) are the pixel address of the upper-left corner of the icon position. D2.W contains a count of pixels in the icon's horizontal dimension, with an upper limit of 32 pixels. D3.W contains a count of pixels in the pixel's vertical dimension. The limit in the vertical dimension is the vertical size of the image.

A0.L is the last parameter to "icon"; it points to an array of longwords, one for each row of the icon, containing a bit pattern of the icon. The pattern is left-justified for icons of less than 32 pixels horizontally.

The "arrow" and "snarl" procedures do nothing more than set up the parameters to "icon," and save registers. Note that "icon" trashes a whole bunch of registers. Seeing that we have the horizontal and vertical counts embedded in the icon bit tables, you might ask why we didn't put the acquistion logic for these values in the "icon" procedure. The reason we didn't is because someday we are going to add a character generator, and the icon code will serve nicely. The only thing we need to create is a bit table for the font, and a quick calculation to point A0 at the pattern for the correct character.

Regardless of how the pattern is obtained, "icon" will not place a partial icon (one that hangs over an edge) onto the image. Lines 87 to 98 trap out these partial icons and return silently.

There are several ways to merge two graphics images. Our method is a compromise between complexity and inefficiency, and is reasonably close to the fastest possible method.

We keep the speed up by writing new set-pixel and reset-pixel procedures. Our general-case pixel procedure "g__pix" can't make assumptions about the history or validity of a pixel operation. That's not the case here. Most of the time, a pixel being operated on is one pixel to the right of the previous pixel. We also know that a pixel is on the image because illegal pixels were screened by the icon check in lines 87 to 98. We need only make a full pixel address calculation once, in lines 100 to 108, and from then on we can get the next address by simple addition (lines 125 to 128 and 135).

The merging of the two images is also simple. We have two loops. An outer loop (lines 109 to 139), picks up one longword of the icon pattern on each iteration. The inner loop (lines 115 to 131) cranks the pattern out to the left one bit a time, processing each bit.

The procedures "pix__off" (lines 145 to 151) and "pix__on" (lines 154 to 168) process pattern pixels that are "off" and "on," respectively.

The icon procedure is the only one of the graphics procedures in this book that makes a distinction between the "jam" and "set" write modes. In jam mode, zero pixels in the icon pattern are cleared in the image. In set mode, as well as complement and clear modes, zero pixels in the icon pattern are ignored.

By now, you've either gotten bored and quit reading this, or you're ready to see the results of all these routines. Figure 17-6 is an actual dump from the Oki, and has an example of each of the procedures discussed in this chapter. It's not pretty, but it can answer most of the questions you may have had about the operation of our graphics procedures.

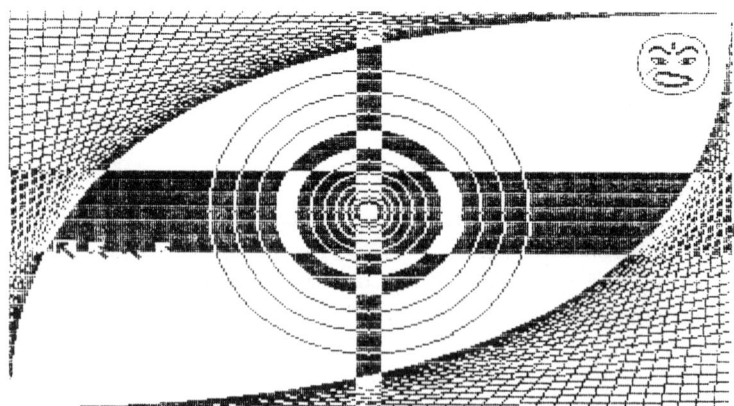

FIGURE 17-6. Output of DEMO program.

Figure 17-6 was produced by the program in Module DEMO.PRN. In case you're wondering just how fast our graphics procedures are, the program in Module DEMO runs in just a hair under one second on our 10 MHz. 68000 machine. For the amount of junk in the picture, that's fast. It's quite gratifying to see this run on a memory-mapped video display.

To see how the write modes work, if you're still not sure, notice the arrow icon tests in lines 62 to 78 of Module DEMO. The arrow icons are written on the intersection of a dark area and a light area, and are written in all four modes.

That concludes our dissertation on graphics. Next chapter, we leave this sissy icon stuff behind and get to the stuff the Real Programmer does best: programming on the bare metal.

Module BITPRIM.PRN

```
 1
 2          * BITPRIM - bit mapped graphics primitives
 3          ****************************************************************
 4          <<include BIT.H>>
12
13                    xref    image,sqrt
14                    xdef    g_pix,g_mode,g_vector,g_circle,g_clear,g_fill
15                    xdef    mode
16
17          ****************************************************************
18          * SET_PIX - sets the pixel where D0.W = X and D1.W = Y
19          g_pix:
20  00000000 48E7C080     movem.l  d0/d1/a0,-(a7)    * save caller's registers
21                   *
22  00000004 B07C0140     cmp.w    #hor_b,d0         * check clipping horizontal
23  00000008 6438         bcc      sk0_sp            * exit on over X
24  0000000A B27C00C8     cmp.w    #vert,d1          * check clipping vertical
25  0000000E 6432         bcc      sk0_sp            * exit on over Y
26                   *
27  00000010 207C00000000 move.l   #image,a0         * get base of image area
28  00000016 C2FC0028     mulu     #(hor_w*2),d1     * get vertical offset to line
29  0000001A D1C1         add.l    d1,a0             * and add to base address
30  0000001C 3200         move.w   d0,d1             * save X for later
31  0000001E E648         lsr.w    #3,d0             * get number of bytes to pixel
32  00000020 D0C0         add.w    d0,a0             * add to pointer
33  00000022 C27C0007     and.w    #$0007,d1         * strip all but bit number
34  00000026 30390000000  move.w   mode,d0           * get mode flag
35  0000002C E248         lsr.w    #1,d0             * pop bit 0 into carry flag
36  0000002E 650C         bcs      sk1_sp            * jam mode jump
37  00000030 E248         lsr.w    #1,d0             * pop bit 1 into carry flag
38  00000032 650C         bcs      sk2_sp            * complement mode jump
39  00000034 E248         lsr.w    #1,d0             * pop bit 2 into carry flag
40  00000036 6504         bcs      sk3_sp            * set mode jump
41  00000038 0390         bclr     d1,(a0)           * falls thru to clear mode
42  0000003A 6006         bra      sk0_sp            * so we're done
43          sk1_sp:
44          sk3_sp:
45  0000003C 03D0         bset     d1,(a0)           * jam and set are the same here
46  0000003E 6002         bra      sk0_sp            * now we're done
47          sk2_sp:
```

```
48  00000040  0350                bchg    d1,(a0)              * complement mode
49
50  00000042  4CDF0103            movem.l (a7)+,d0/d1/a0       * restore caller's registers
51  00000046  4E75                rts
52
53  * SET MODE - Sets mode to value contained in D0.W
54  g_mode:
55  00000048  33C000000000        move.w  d0,mode
56  0000004E  4E75                rts
57
58  * G_VECTOR - draws a vector from (D0.W,D1.W) to (D2.W,D3.W)
59
60  00000050  48E7FF00    g_vector:
                                  movem.l d0-d7,-(a7)          * Save registers
61  ******** Scale and save vector origin coordinates **********************
62  00000054  3800                move.w  d0,d4                * setup base for X
63  00000056  4844                swap    d4                   * scale x 2^16
64  00000058  4244                clr.w   d4                   * make even number
65  0000005A  3A01                move.w  d1,d5                * setup base for Y
66  0000005C  4845                swap    d5                   * scale x 2^16
67  0000005E  4245                clr.w   d5                   * make even number
68  ******** Determine absolute and signed run in X ***********************
69  00000060  9440                sub.w   d0,d2                * find difference in X
70  00000062  3002                move.w  d2,d0                * save signed difference
71  00000064  6A02                bpl     skl_vec              * skip X absolute value convert
72  00000066  4440                neg.w   d0                   * D0 is X absolute distance
73  ******** Determine absolute and signed run in Y ***********************
74  skl_vec:
75  00000068  9641                sub.w   d1,d3                * find difference in Y
76  0000006A  3203                move.w  d3,d1                * save signed difference
77  0000006C  6A02                bpl     sk2_vec              * skip Y absolute value convert
78  0000006E  4441                neg.w   d1                   * D1 is Y absolute distance
79  ******** Determine independent (larger) and dependent axis ********
80  sk2_vec:
81  00000070  B240                cmp.w   d0,d1                * see if X dif > y dif
82  00000072  6E24                bgt     Y_bigger             * jump if y is bigger
83  ******** X is independent axis - determine X step as +/- 1.0 ******
84  00000074  4A42                tst.w   d2                   * check sign of X run
85  00000076  6B08                bmi     sk3_vec              * jump if negative
86  00000078  2C3C00010000        move.l  #$00010000,d6        * setup X step = 1.0
87  0000007E  6006                bra     sk4_vec              * jump to Y setup
```

```
88
89  00000080  2C3CFFFF0000  sk3_vec:  move.l  #$FFFF0000,d6  * setup Y step = -1.0
90            ******* Determine Y step as scaled fixed point longword **********
91            sk4_vec:
92  00000086  4843                    swap    d3              * Scale up
93  00000088  4243                    clr.w   d3              * make longword
94  0000008A  E483                    asr.l   #2,d3           * take out two bits of precision
95  0000008C  87C0                    divs    d0,d3           * divide by independent axis
96  0000008E  48C3                    ext.l   d3              * make long again
97  00000090  E583                    asl.l   #2,d3           * put two precisions bits back
98  00000092  2E03                    move.l  d3,d7           * D7 is signed Y step
99  00000094  3400                    move.w  d0,d2           * get independant axis counter
100 00000096  6022                    bra     sk7_vec         * go do output
101           ******* Y is independent axis - setup Y step as +/- 1.0 **********
102           Y_bigger:
103 00000098  4A43                    tst.w   d3              * check sign of Y run
104 0000009A  6B08                    bmi     sk5_vec         * jump if step negative
105 0000009C  2E3C00010000            move.l  #$00010000,d7   * make Y step 1.0
106 000000A2  6006                    bra     sk6_vec         * jump to X setup
107
108 000000A4  2E3CFFFF0000  sk5_vec:  move.l  #$FFFF0000,d7   * make Y step -1.0
109           ******* Determine X step as scaled fixed point longword **********
110           sk6_vec:
111 000000AA  4842                    swap    d2              * Scale up
112 000000AC  4242                    clr.w   d2              * make longword
113 000000AE  E482                    asr.l   #2,d2           * Take out two bits of precision
114 000000B0  85C1                    divs    d1,d2           * divide by independent axis
115 000000B2  48C2                    ext.l   d2              * make long again
116 000000B4  E582                    asl.l   #2,d2           * put back the precision
117 000000B6  2C02                    move.l  d2,d6           * D6 is signed X step
118 000000B8  3401                    move.w  d1,d2           * get independant axis counter
119           *
120           ******* Pixel output loop *******************************************
121
122 000000BA  601C          sk7_vec:  bra     sk8_vec         * do loop test before body
123           lp0_vec:
124 000000BC  2004                    move.l  d4,d0           * get scaled X position
125 000000BE  D0BC00008000            add.l   #$00008000,d0   * round up by adding 0.5
126 000000C4  4840                    swap    d0              * scale X down for output
127 000000C6  2205                    move.l  d5,d1           * get scaled Y position
```

```
128  000000C8  D2BC00008000  add.l   #$00008000,d1   * round up by adding 0.5
129  000000CE  4841          swap    d1              * scale Y down for output
130  000000D0  6100FF2E      bsr     g_pix           * put the pixel
131  000000D4  D886          add.l   d6,d4           * add X step
132  000000D6  DA87          add.l   d7,d5           * add Y step
133
     sk8_vec:
134  000000D8  51CAFFE2      dbra    d2,lp0_vec      * loop around
135  000000DC  4CDF00FF      movem.l (a7)+,d0-d7     * restore registers
136  000000E0  4E75          rts
137
138 ***********************************************************
* Draws a circle around (D0.W,D1.W) of radius D2.W
     g_circle:
139
140  000000E2  48E7FF00      movem.l d0-d7,-(a7)     * Save registers
141  000000E6  3C00          move.w  d0,d6           * d6 will be X base pixel
142  000000E8  3E01          move.w  d1,d7           * d7 will be Y base pixel
143  000000EA  3602          move.w  d2,d3           * get copy of radius
144  000000EC  C6C3          mulu    d3,d3           * d3.l is radius squared
145  000000EE  4842          swap    d2              * make into scaled longword
146  000000F0  4242          clr.w   d2              * truncate
147  000000F2  84FCB504      divu    #$B504,d2       * radius / (sqr(2) << 15)
148  000000F6  5242          add.w   #1,d2           * round up
149  000000F8  E282          asr.l   #1,d2           * align D2 because sqr(2) scaled
150
     lp0_cir:
151  000000FA  3802          move.w  d2,d4           * d4 is a scratch register
152  000000FC  C8C4          mulu    d4,d4           * d4 is (rise**2)
153  000000FE  2003          move.l  d3,d0           * d0 is scratch register
154  00000100  9084          sub.l   d4,d0           * d0 is (run**2)
155  00000102  61000000      bsr     sqrt            * after call, d0 = (run)
156  00000106  3800          move.w  d0,d4           * save run
157
* ******* Quadrant I, counterclockwise
158  00000108  3006          move.w  d6,d0           * X center
159  0000010A  3207          move.w  d7,d1           * Y center
160  0000010C  D044          add.w   d4,d0           * add run
161  0000010E  D242          add.w   d2,d1           * add rise
162  00000110  6100FEEE      bsr     g_pix
163
* ******* Quadrant I, clockwise
164  00000114  3006          move.w  d6,d0           * X center
165  00000116  3207          move.w  d7,d1           * Y center
166  00000118  D244          add.w   d4,d1           * add rise
167  0000011A  D042          add.w   d2,d0           * add run
```

Module BITPRIM.PRN (continued)

```
168  0000011C 6100FEE2          bsr       g_pix

169  ******** Quadrant II, counterclockwise
170  00000120 3006              move.w    d6,d0       * X center
171  00000122 3207              move.w    d7,d1       * Y center
172  00000124 9042              sub.w     d2,d0       * add rise
173  00000126 D244              add.w     d4,d1       * add run
174  00000128 6100FED6          bsr       g_pix

175  ******** Quadrant II, clockwise
176  0000012C 3006              move.w    d6,d0       * X center
177  0000012E 3207              move.w    d7,d1       * Y center
178  00000130 D242              add.w     d2,d1       * add rise
179  00000132 9044              sub.w     d4,d0       * add run
180  00000134 6100FECA          bsr       g_pix

181  ******** Quadrant III, counterclockwise
182  00000138 3006              move.w    d6,d0       * X center
183  0000013A 3207              move.w    d7,d1       * Y center
184  0000013C 9242              sub.w     d2,d1       * add rise
185  0000013E 9044              sub.w     d4,d0       * add run
186  00000140 6100FEBE          bsr       g_pix

187  ******** Quadrant III, clockwise
188  00000144 3006              move.w    d6,d0       * X center
189  00000146 3207              move.w    d7,d1       * Y center
190  00000148 9042              sub.w     d2,d0       * add rise
191  0000014A 9244              sub.w     d4,d1       * add run
192  0000014C 6100FEB2          bsr       g_pix

193  ******** Quadrant IV, counterclockwise
194  00000150 3006              move.w    d6,d0       * X center
195  00000152 3207              move.w    d7,d1       * Y center
196  00000154 D042              add.w     d2,d0       * add rise
197  00000156 9244              sub.w     d4,d1       * add run
198  00000158 6100FEA6          bsr       g_pix

199  ******** Quadrant IV, clockwise
200  0000015C 3006              move.w    d6,d0       * X center
201  0000015E 3207              move.w    d7,d1       * Y center
202  00000160 D044              add.w     d4,d0       * add run
203  00000162 9242              sub.w     d2,d1       * add rise
204  00000164 6100FE9A          bsr       g_pix
205  00000168 51CAFF90          dbra      d2,lp0_cir  * loop for next set
206  0000016C 4CDF00FF          movem.l   (a7)+,d0-d7 * Restore registers
207  00000170 4E75              rts
     *****************************************************************
     * Clears the graphics image area
208  
209  g_clear:
210  
211  00000172 48E78080          movem.l   a0/d0,-(a7) * save registers
```

```
212 00000176 207C00000000          move.l   #image,a0          * Get image area base address
213 0000017C 203C000007D0          move.l   #(vert*hor_w/2),d0
214                        lp0_cl:
215 00000182 4298                   clr.l    (a0)+              * zero out byte
216 00000184 5380                   subq.l   #1,d0              * pop counter
217 00000186 66FA                   bne      lp0_cl             * loop for next
218 00000188 4CDF0101               movem.l  (a7)+,a0/d0        * restore registers
219 0000018C 4E75                   rts
220                        ************************************************************
221                        * Fills the area bounded by (D0.W,D1.W) and (D2.W,D3.W)
222                        g_fill:
223 0000018E 48E7FFC0               movem.l  d0-d7/a0/a1,-(a7)  save callers registers
224                        ******** Adjust so that D2.W >= D0.W and D3.W >= D1.W
225 00000192 B440                   cmp.w    d0,d2              * Who's bigger?
226 00000194 6C02                   bge      skl_fil            * jump if d2 is bigger
227 00000196 C142                   exg      d0,d2              * swap if not
228                        skl_fil:
229 00000198 B641                   cmp.w    d1,d3              * Who's bigger here?
230 0000019A 6C02                   bge      sk2_fil            * jump if d3 is bigger
231 0000019C C343                   exg      d1,d3              * swap if not
232                        sk2_fil:
233                        ******** Calculate (number of rows) - 1, save in D7
234 0000019E 3E03                   move.w   d3,d7              * uses D7 as accumulator
235 000001A0 9E41                   sub.w    d1,d7              * D7 is (#rows-1)
236                        ******** Calculate first byte address in A0
237 000001A2 207C00000000           move.l   #image,a0          * A0 is base of image memory
238 000001A8 C2FC0028               mulu     #(hor_w*2),d1      * D1 is row offset from zero
239 000001AC 3600                   move.w   d0,d3              * D3 is a scratch register
240 000001AE E643                   asr.w    #3,d3              * D3 is number of bytes into row
241 000001B0 D243                   add.w    d3,d1              * D1 is bytes into image
242 000001B2 D0C1                   add.w    d1,a0              * A0 is now address of first byte
243                        ******** Make mask for left fragment in D4.B
244 000001B4 3200                   move.w   d0,d1              * D1 is scratch register
245 000001B6 C27C0007               and.w    #$0007,d1          * D1 is pixel address
246 000001BA 383C00FF               move.w   #$00FF,d4          * D4 will be fragment mask
247 000001BE E32C                   lsl.b    d1,d4              * move mask to correct pixels
248                        ******** Make mask for right fragment in D6.B
249 000001C0 3202                   move.w   d2,d1              * D1 is scratch register
250 000001C2 C27C0007               and.w    #$07,d1            * D1 is pixel address
251 000001C6 3C3CFE01               move.w   #$FE01,d6          * D6 will be fragment mask
252 000001CA E37E                   rol.w    d1,d6              * move mask to correct pixels
253                        ******** Compute distance 'twixt start and end byte in row
```

Module BITPRIM.PRN (continued)

```
254 000001CC E648                  lsr.w   #3,d0           * get starting offset into row
255 000001CE E64A                  lsr.w   #3,d2           * get ending offset into row
256                        ******* Test for special case - left and right frags in same byte
257 000001D0 9440                  sub.w   d0,d2           * are they the same?
258 000001D2 6652                  bne     sk3_fil         * jump if not...
259                        ******* process start/end in same byte
260 000001D4 C806                  and.b   d6,d4           * combine the two masks
261 000001D6 0839000000000001      btst    #0,mode+1       * look for jam mode
262 000001DE 6626                  bne     sk4_fil         * go jam
263 000001E0 0839000100000001      btst    #1,mode+1       * look for complement mode
264 000001E8 662C                  bne     sk5_fil         * go complement
265 000001EA 0839000200000001      btst    #2,mode+1       * look for set mode
266 000001F2 6612                  bne     sk4_fil         * it's the same as jam here
267                        ******* must be clear mode, special case. Let's do it! (yay!) ***
268 000001F4 4604                  not.b   d4              * invert the mask
269                        lp1_fil:
270 000001F6 C910                  and.b   d4,(a0)         * reset the right bits
271 000001F8 D1FC00000028          add.l   #(hor_w*2),a0   * move the address to next row
272 000001FE 51CFFFF6              dbra    d7,lp1_fil      * and repeat as necessary
273 00000202 6000009C              bra     ex_fill         * finished!
274                        ******* jam or set mode, special case ****************************
275                        sk4_fil:
276 00000206 8910                  or.b    d4,(a0)         * set the right bits
277 00000208 D1FC00000028          add.l   #(hor_w*2),a0   * move the address to next row
278 0000020E 51CFFFF6              dbra    d7,sk4_fil      * and repeat
279 00000212 6000008C              bra     ex_fill         * exit
280                        ******* complement mode, special case ****************************
281                        sk5_fil:
282 00000216 B910                  eor.b   d4,(a0)         * complement the right bits
283 00000218 D1FC00000028          add.l   #(hor_w*2),a0   * move the address to next row
284 0000021E 51CFFFF6              dbra    d7,sk4_fil      * repeat
285 00000222 6000007C              bra     ex_fill         * exit
286                        ******* normal (multi-byte/row) fill case continued *************
287                        sk3_fil:
288 00000226 5342                  subq.w  #1,d2           * d2 is now number of whole bytes
289 00000228 0839000000000001      btst    #0,mode+1       * look for jam mode
290 00000230 6634                  bne     sk6_fil         * go jam
291 00000232 0839000100000001      btst    #1,mode+1       * look for complement mode
292 0000023A 6648                  bne     sk7_fil         * go complement
293 0000023C 0839000200000001      btst    #2,mode+1       * look for set mode
294 00000244 6620                  bne     sk6_fil         * it's the same as jam here
295                        ******* Must be clear mode, normal case *********************
296 00000246 4604                  not.b   d4              * invert start mask
297 00000248 4606                  not.b   d6              * invert end mask
298                        lp2_fil:
299 0000024A 3A02                  move.w  d2,d5           * Have to save d2
300 0000024C 2248                  move.l  a0,a1           * A1 can be modified, A0 can't.
```

```
301 0000024E C919            and.b   d4,(al)+        * catch left-hand bits
302 00000250 6002            bra     sk8_fil         * do loop test before body
303
304 00000252 4219    lp3_fil: clr.b  (al)+           * zero out middle bytes
305                  sk8_fil:
306 00000254 51CDFFFC        dbra    d5,lp3_fil      * repeat for middle bytes
307 00000258 CD11            and.b   d6,(al)         * get right-hand bits
308 0000025A D1FC00000028    add.l   #(hor_w*2),a0   * move to next row
309 00000260 51CFFFE8        dbra    d7,lp2_fil      * repeat for all rows
310 00000264 603A            bra     ex_fill         * and quit
311
312      ******** Jam or Set mode, normal case *******************************
313 00000266 3A02    sk6_fil: move.w d2,d5           * Have to save d2
314 00000268 2248            move.l  a0,al           * Al can be modified, A0 can't.
315 0000026A 8919            or.b    d4,(al)+        * catch left-hand bits
316 0000026C 6004            bra     sk9_fil         * do loop test before body
317                  lp4_fil:
318 0000026E 12FC00FF        move.b  #$FF,(al)+      * set middle bytes
319                  sk9_fil:
320 00000272 51CDFFFA        dbra    d5,lp4_fil      * repeat for middle bytes
321 00000276 8D11            or.b    d6,(al)         * get right-hand bits
322 00000278 D1FC00000028    add.l   #(hor_w*2),a0   * move to next row
323 0000027E 51CFFFE6        dbra    d7,sk6_fil      * repeat for all rows
324 00000282 601C            bra     ex_fill         * and quit
325
326      ******** Complement mode, normal case *******************************
327 00000284 3A02    sk7_fil: move.w d2,d5           * Have to save d2
328 00000286 2248            move.l  a0,al           * Al can be modified, A0 can't.
329 00000288 B919            eor.b   d4,(al)+        * catch left-hand bits
330 0000028A 6004            bra     skl0_fil        * do loop test before body
331                  lp5_fil:
332 0000028C 0A1900FF        eor.b   #$FF,(al)+      * zero out middle bytes
333                  skl0_fil:
334 00000290 51CDFFFA        dbra    d5,lp5_fil      * repeat for middle bytes
335 00000294 BD11            eor.b   d6,(al)         * get right-hand bits
336 00000296 D1FC00000028    add.l   #(hor_w*2),a0   * move to next row
337 0000029C 51CFFFE6        dbra    d7,sk7_fil      * repeat for all rows
338      ******** fill procedure common exit *********************************
339                  ex_fill:
340 000002A0 4CDF03FF        movem.l (a7)+,d0-d7/a0/al restore registers
341 000002A4 4E75            rts
342      ********************************************************************
343
344 00000000        mode    data
345 00000000 0001           dc.w    jam_m           * start in jam mode
346
347 00000002                end
```

Module OKI.PRN

```
 1                       *****************************************************
 2                       * OKIDATA graphics printer interface
 3                       *
 4                       <<include BIT.H>>

13                                 xref    image
14                                 xdef    dump
15
16                       *****************************************************
17                       * Column offsets into graphics image area
18     row1      equ     hor_w*2
19     row2      equ     hor_w*4
20     row3      equ     hor_w*6
21     row4      equ     hor_w*8
22     row5      equ     hor_w*10
23     row6      equ     hor_w*12
24     *****************************************************
25     * Prints the graphic image on the ol' Okidata ML-83A
26     dump:
27
28     00000000 48E7FF80          movem.l d0-d7/a0,-(a7)    * Save all registers
29     00000004 61000080          bsr     setup_lst         * set up printer
30     00000008 303C001C          move.w  #((vert/7)),d0    D0 will be row loop counter
31     ******** Outer loop: prints 7 rows per pass thru this loop ********
32     outer:
33     0000000C 4840              swap    d0                * keep counter in hi word
34     0000000E 207C00000000      move.l  #image,a0         * a0 will be image base
35     00000014 2E00              move.l  d0,d7             * bring row counter into d7
36     00000016 4847              swap    d7                * D7.W is row counter
37     00000018 9E7C001C          sub.w   #((vert/7)),d7    adjust for reverse direction
38     0000001C 4447              neg.w   d7                * take absolute value
39     0000001E CEFC0118          mulu    #(hor_w*14),d7    * get offset to this row
40     00000022 D1C7              add.l   d7,a0             * A0 points at correct top row
41     00000024 323C0027          move.w  #((2*hor_w)-1),d1 d1 will be word loop counter
42     ******** Middle loop: Picks up 7 vertically aligned bytes per pass
43     middle:
44     00000028 4841              swap    d1                * keep counter in hi word
45     0000002A 3E3C0007          move.w  #7,d7             * d7 will be bit counter
46     0000002E 1010              move.b  (a0),d0           * get top (row 1 ) bits
47     00000030 12280028          move.b  row1(a0),d1       * Get row 2 bits
48     00000034 14280050          move.b  row2(a0),d2       * Get row 3 bits
```

```
49 00000038 16280078            move.b   row3(a0),d3    * Get row 4 bits
50 0000003C 182800A0            move.b   row4(a0),d4    * Get row 5 bits
51 00000040 1A2800C8            move.b   row5(a0),d5    * Get row 6 bits
52 00000044 1C2800F0            move.b   row6(a0),d6    * Get bottom (row 7) bits
53         ********* Inner loop: Cranks out one graphic byte per pass *********
54 inner:
55 00000048 4847               swap    d7              * keep counter in high word
56 0000004A E216               roxr.b  d6              * position bottom (row 7) bit
57 0000004C E317               roxl.b  d7              * pull extend flag into d7
58 0000004E E215               roxr.b  d5              * position row 6 bit in ext flag
59 00000050 E317               roxl.b  d7              * pull extend flag into d7
60 00000052 E214               roxr.b  d4              * position row 5 bit in ext flag
61 00000054 E317               roxl.b  d7              * pull extend flag into d7
62 00000056 E213               roxr.b  d3              * position row 4 bit in ext flag
63 00000058 E317               roxl.b  d7              * pull extend flag into d7
64 0000005A E212               roxr.b  d2              * position row 3 bit in ext flag
65 0000005C E317               roxl.b  d7              * pull extend flag into d7
66 0000005E E211               roxr.b  d1              * position row 2 bit in ext flag
67 00000060 E317               roxl.b  d7              * pull extend flag into d7
68 00000062 E210               roxr.b  d0              * position top (row 1) bit
69 00000064 E317               roxl.b  d7              * pull extend flag into d7
70 00000066 6134               bsr     putd7           * output byte in d7
71 00000068 4847               swap    d7              * bring bit cntr into position
72 0000006A 51CFFFDC           dbra    d7,inner        * loop for the next col
73         ******** end of inner loop  ********************************
74 0000006E 5288               addq.l  #1,a0           * bump word pointer
75 00000070 4841               swap    d1              * bring word cntr into position
76 00000072 51C9FFB4           dbra    d1,middle       * loop for the next word
77         ******** end of middle loop ********************************
78 00000076 6146               bsr     gcrlf           * graphics return/line feed
79 00000078 4840               swap    d0              * bring row cntr into position
80 0000007A 51C8FF90           dbra    d0,outer        * loop for next rows
81         ******** end of outer loop  ********************************
82 0000007E 610E               bsr     unset_lst       * reset printer
83 00000080 4CDF01FF           movem.l (a7)+,d0-d7/a0  * restore all registers
84 00000084 4E75               rts
85         ***********************************************************
86         * Puts printer into graphics mode
87 setup_lst:
88 00000086 323C0003           move.w  #3,d1           * OKI enter graphics command
```

Module OKI.PRN (*continued*)

```
89  0000008A 6148                  bsr     lst_out     * printer output
90  0000008C 4E75                  rts
91  ********************************************************
92  * Removes printer from graphics mode
93                         unset_lst:
94  0000008E 323C0003              move.w  #3,d1       * OKI graphics escape
95  00000092 6140                  bsr     lst_out     * printer output
96  00000094 323C0002              move.w  #2,d1       * OKI exit graphics command
97  00000098 613A                  bsr     lst_out     * printer output
98  0000009A 4E75                  rts
99  ********************************************************
100 * Outputs byte in D7 as graphics byte - traps escape byte
101                        putd7:
102 0000009C 48E7C000              movem.l d0/d1,-(a7) * save registers
103 000000A0 3207                  move.w  d7,d1       * get output byte lined up
104 000000A2 C27C007F              and.w   #$007F,d1   * off with its head!
105 000000A6 B23C0003              cmp.b   #3,d1       * test for graphics escape char
106 000000AA 660A                  bne     skip_put    * jump if not escape char
107 000000AC 323C0003              move.w  #3,d1       * escape cancel prefix
108 000000B0 6122                  bsr     lst_out     * output to printer
109 000000B2 323C0003              move.w  #3,d1       * reload esacpe char
110                        skip_put:
111 000000B6 611C                  bsr     lst_out     * output to printer
112 000000B8 4CDF0003              movem.l (a7)+,d0/d1 * restore registers
113 000000BC 4E75                  rts
114 ********************************************************
115 * Outputs a return/linefeed sequence in graphics mode
116                        gcrlf:
117 000000BE 48E7C000              movem.l d0/d1,-(a7) * Save registers
118 000000C2 323C0003              move.w  #3,d1       * graphics escape code
119 000000C6 610C                  bsr     lst_out     * output to printer
120 000000C8 323C000E              move.w  #14,d1      * grpahics return/line feed
121 000000CC 6106                  bsr     lst_out     * output to printer
122 000000CE 4CDF0003              movem.l (a7)+,d0/d1 * restore registers
123 000000D2 4E75                  rts
124 ********************************************************
125 * Outputs byte in D1 to CP/M LST: device
126 * destroys D0 and D1
127                        lst_out:
128 000000D4 303C0005              move.w  #5,d0       * CP/M LST: device output code
129 000000D8 4E42                  trap    #2          * Call CP/M BDOS
130 000000DA 4E75                  rts
131
132 000000DC                       end
```

Module CREEP.PRN

```
                              ********************************************************************
 1                            * CREEP - Does a "spreading dot" trick
 2                            ********************************************************************
 3
 4                                    <<include BIT.H>>
12
13                                    xdef    creep
14                                    xref    g_pix,image
15
16                            ********************************************************************
17                            * CREEP - Fills all "white" space adjacent to pixel (D0.W,D1.W)
18                            creep:
19  00000000  48A7F800                movem.w d0-d4,-(a7)
20  00000004  3400                    move.w  d0,d2           * save pixel X
21  00000006  3601                    move.w  d1,d3           * save pixel Y
22                            lpl_cp:
23  00000008  6142                    bsr     tstpix          * check this pixel
24  0000000A  6608                    bne     skl_cp          * we're done if this one set
25  0000000C  61000000                bsr     g_pix           * set this pixel
26  00000010  5340                    subq.w  #1,d0           * move left one pixel
27  00000012  60F4                    bra     lpl_cp          * do it 'til we boink
28                            skl_cp:
29  00000014  5240                    addq.w  #1,d0           * adjust right end X position
30  00000016  C142                    exg     d0,d2           * save leftmost, get original
31  00000018  5240                    addq.w  #1,d0           * move left of original
32                            lp2_cp:
33  0000001A  6130                    bsr     tstpix          * check this pixel
34  0000001C  6608                    bne     sk2_cp          * we're done if this one set
35  0000001E  61000000                bsr     g_pix           * set this pixel
36  00000022  5240                    addq.w  #1,d0           * move right one pixel
37  00000024  60F4                    bra     lp2_cp          * keep on to the right end
38                            sk2_cp:
39  00000026  5340                    subq.w  #1,d0           * adjust left end X position
40  00000028  3800                    move.w  d0,d4           * save left end X position
41
42  0000002A  3002                    move.w  d2,d0           * get left end X position
43  0000002C  5241                    addq.w  #1,d1           * move down to next row
44  0000002E  610E                    bsr     run             * check the run for adjacent pixs
45
46  00000030  3002                    move.w  d2,d0           * get right end X limit
47  00000032  3203                    move.w  d3,d1           * get original Y
```

Module CREEP.PRN (continued)

```
48  00000034  5341            subq.w  #1,d1               * move up one row
49  00000036  6106            bsr     run                 * check for adjacent white pixels
50
51  00000038  4C9F001F        movem.w (a7)+,d0-d4
52  0000003C  4E75            rts
53              ***********************************************************
54
    run:
55  0000003E  610C            bsr     tstpix              * check this pixel
56  00000040  6602            bne     sk4_cp              * set, no need to worry
57  00000042  61BC            bsr     creep               * set the new line
58
    sk4_cp:
59  00000044  5240            addq.w  #1,d0               * move right one pixel
60  00000046  B840            cmp.w   d0,d4               * test against right limit
61  00000048  6CF4            bge     run                 * loop if more to check
62  0000004A  4E75            rts
63              ***********************************************************
64              * TSTPIX - tests the pixel where D0.W = X and D1.W = Y
65              *          returns zero flag TRUE if pixel not set
66
    tstpix:
67  0000004C  48E7C080        movem.l d0/d1/a0,-(a7)      * save caller's registers
68              ******* See if X and Y are valid addresses ****************
69  00000050  4A40            tst.w   d0                  * look for off left edge
70  00000052  6B2A            bmi     skl_pix             * error out if so
71  00000054  4A41            tst.w   d1                  * look for off top
72  00000056  6B26            bmi     skl_pix             * error out if so
73  00000058  B07C0140        cmp.w   #hor_b,d0           * look for off right edge
74  0000005C  6C20            bge     skl_pix             * error out if so
75  0000005E  B27C00C8        cmp.w   #vert,d1            * look for off bottom
76  00000062  6C1A            bge     skl_pix             * error out if so
77              ******* pixel (X,Y) is valid; check value of pixel *******
78  00000064  207C00000000    move.l  #image,a0           * get base of image area
79  0000006A  C2FC0028        mulu    #(hor_w*2),d1       * get vertical offset to line
80  0000006E  D1C1            add.l   d1,a0               * and add to base address
81  00000070  3200            move.w  d0,d1               * save X for later
82  00000072  E648            lsr.w   #3,d0               * get number of bytes to pixel
83  00000074  D0C0            add.w   d0,a0               * add to pointer
84  00000076  C27C0007        and.w   #$0007,d1           * strip all but bit number
85  0000007A  0310            btst    d1,(a0)             * test the bit
86  0000007C  6004            bra     sk2_pix             * and exit
87
    skl_pix:
88  0000007E  023C00FB        andi    #$FB,ccr            * errors always show set pixel
89
    sk2_pix:
90  00000082  4CDF0103        movem.l (a7)+,d0/d1/a0      * restore caller's registers
91  00000086  4E75            rts
92              ***********************************************************
93  00000088                  end
```

Module OLAY.PRN

```
 1
 2                ************************************************************
 3                * OLAY - Overlay a bit image
 4                ************************************************************
 5
12                      <<include BIT.H>>
13
14                      xref    image,mode
15                      xdef    arrow,snarl
16
17                ************************************************************
18                * ARROW - draws an arrow at (D0.W,D1.W)
                  arrow:
19 00000000 48E7F880     movem.l  d0-d4/a0,-(a7)    * save registers
20 00000004 207C00000018 move.l   #arrowdef,a0      * pick up arrow definition
21 0000000A 3418         move.w   (a0)+,d2          * pick up horizontal count
22 0000000C 3618         move.w   (a0)+,d3          * pick up vertical count
23 0000000E 610000D0     bsr      icon             * go put icon
24 00000012 4CDF011F     movem.l  (a7)+,d0-d4/a0    * restore registers
25 00000016 4E75         rts
26                arrowdef:
27 00000018 000A         dc.w    10                * horizontal count
28 0000001A 000A         dc.w    10                * vertical count
29 0000001C 00000000     dc.l    $00000000         * . . . . . . . . . .
30 00000020 7E000000     dc.l    $7E000000         * . * * * * * * . . .
31 00000024 7E000000     dc.l    $7E000000         * . * * * * * * . . .
32 00000028 78000000     dc.l    $78000000         * . * * * * . . . . .
33 0000002C 7C000000     dc.l    $7C000000         * . * * * * * . . . .
34 00000030 6E000000     dc.l    $6E000000         * . * * . * * * . . .
35 00000034 67000000     dc.l    $67000000         * . * * . . * * * . .
36 00000038 03800000     dc.l    $03800000         * . . . . . . * * . .
37 0000003C 01C00000     dc.l    $01C00000         * . . . . . . . * * .
38 00000040 00800000     dc.l    $00800000         * . . . . . . . . * .
39
                ************************************************************
40                * SNARL - puts a snarl face icon at (D0.W,D1.W)
                  snarl:
41
42 00000044 48E7F880     movem.l  d0-d4/a0,-(a7)    * save registers
43 00000048 207C0000005C move.l   #snarldef,a0      * pick up arrow definition
44 0000004E 3418         move.w   (a0)+,d2          * pick up horizontal count
45 00000050 3618         move.w   (a0)+,d3          * pick up vertical count
46 00000052 6100008C     bsr      icon             * go put icon
```

Module OLAY.PRN (continued)

```
47  00000056  4CDF011F            movem.l  (a7)+,d0-d4/a0   * restore registers
48  0000005A  4E75                rts
49                      snarldef:
50  0000005C  0020                dc.w  32                 * horizontal count
51  0000005E  0020                dc.w  32                 * vertical count
52  00000060  000FF000            dc.l  $000FF000
53  00000064  00700E00            dc.l  $00700E00
54  00000068  038001C0            dc.l  $038001C0
55  0000006C  04000020            dc.l  $04000020
56  00000070  08000010            dc.l  $08000010
57  00000074  10018008            dc.l  $10018008
58  00000078  20018004            dc.l  $20018004
59  0000007C  21E18784            dc.l  $21E18784
60  00000080  23F18FC0            dc.l  $23F18FC0
61  00000084  46181862            dc.l  $46181862
62  00000088  440E7022            dc.l  $440E7022
63  0000008C  40066002            dc.l  $40066002
64  00000090  80000001            dc.l  $80000001
65  00000094  83F00FC1            dc.l  $83F00FC1
66  00000098  82781E41            dc.l  $82781E41
67  0000009C  81742E81            dc.l  $81742E81
68  000000A0  80F81F01            dc.l  $80F81F01
69  000000A4  80000001            dc.l  $80000001
70  000000A8  81800001            dc.l  $81800001
71  000000AC  82000001            dc.l  $82000001
72  000000B0  447E0001            dc.l  $447E0001
73  000000B4  48FFE002            dc.l  $48FFE002
74  000000B8  4083FE02            dc.l  $4083FE02
75  000000BC  21001F04            dc.l  $21001F04
76  000000C0  21800384            dc.l  $21800384
77  000000C4  20F00E04            dc.l  $20F00E04
78  000000C8  107FFE08            dc.l  $107FFE08
79  000000CC  080FF010            dc.l  $080FF010
80  000000D0  04000020            dc.l  $04000020
81  000000D4  038001C0            dc.l  $038001C0
82  000000D8  00700E00            dc.l  $00700E00
83  000000DC  000FF000            dc.l  $000FF000
84
85                      * ICON - puts an icon on the graphic image.
86                      icon:
```

```
 87  000000E0  4A40          tst.w   d0                * check for off left edge
 88  000000E2  6B66          bmi     ex_icon           * quit if off left edge
 89  000000E4  4A41          tst.w   d1                * check for off top
 90  000000E6  6B62          bmi     ex_icon           * quit if off top
 91  000000E8  383C00C8      move.w  #vert,d4          * get maximum vertical
 92  000000EC  9843          sub.w   d3,d4             * less vertical count
 93  000000EE  B841          cmp.w   d1,d4             * check for off bottom
 94  000000F0  6D58          blt     ex_icon           * quit if off bottom
 95  000000F2  383C0140      move.w  #hor_b,d4         * get maximum horizontal
 96  000000F6  9842          sub.w   d2,d4             * less horizontal count
 97  000000F8  B840          cmp.w   d0,d4             * check for off right edge
 98  000000FA  6D4E          blt     ex_icon           * jump if off right edge
 99  ********  output image pixels - first get base addresses ************
100  000000FC  227C00000000  move.l  #image,a1         * get image base address
101  00000102  3801          move.w  d1,d4             * D4 is scratch register
102  00000104  C8FC0028      mulu    #hor_w*2,d4       * D4 is offset to row
103  00000108  D3C4          add.l   d4,a1             * A1 is address of pixel row
104  0000010A  3800          move.w  d0,d4             * D4 is scratch register
105  0000010C  E644          asr.w   #3,d4             * get byte offset to pixel
106  0000010E  D2C4          add.w   d4,a1             * A1 is byte address of first pix
107  00000110  C07C0007      and.w   #$0007,d0         * strip pixel address
108  ********  main (row) output loop starts here ******************
109  00000114  6030          bra     sk4_ico           * loop test before body
110
111  00000116  3F02   lp1_ico:  move.w  d2,-(a7)       * save horizontal count
112  00000118  3F00          move.w  d0,-(a7)          * save starting pixel address
113  0000011A  2F09          move.l  a1,-(a7)          * save byte address
114  0000011C  2818          move.l  (a0)+,d4          * get image row
115  ********  inner (column) output loop starts here *****************
116  0000011E  6016          bra     sk9_ico           * loop test before body
117
118  00000120  E384   lp2_ico:  asl.l   #1,d4          * get one pixel to carry flag
119  00000122  6504          bcs     sk3_ico           * jump if set
120  00000124  6126          bsr     pix_off           * otherwise reset pixel
121  00000126  6002          bra     sk2_ico           * and continue
122
123  00000128  6132   sk3_ico:  bsr     pix_on         * set this pixel
124
125  0000012A  5240   sk2_ico:  addq.w  #1,d0          * increment horizontal
126  0000012C  B07C0008      cmp.w   #8,d0             * look for overrun to next byte
```

Module OLAY.PRN (continued)

```
127 00000130 6D04                blt      sk9_ico        * jump if no overrun
128 00000132 4240                clr.w    d0             * set D0 back to zero
129 00000134 5289                addq.l   #1,a1          * move to next byte
130                     sk9_ico:
131 00000136 51CAFFE8            dbra     d2,lp2_ico     * end of horizontal loop
132         ******** end of inner loop ************************************
133                     sk1_ico:
134 0000013A 225F                move.l   (a7)+,a1       * retrieve byte address
135 0000013C D3FC00000028        add.l    #hor_w*2,a1    * go to next pixel row
136 00000142 301F                move.w   (a7)+,d0       * reset horizontal position
137 00000144 341F                move.w   (a7)+,d2       * reset horizontal count
138
139 00000146 51CBFFCE            dbra     d3,lp1_ico     * end of vertical loop
140         ******** end of outer loop ************************************
141                     ex_icon:
142 0000014A 4E75                rts
143
144         *****************************************************************
145         * PIX_OFF - processes zero bits in overlaid image
                         pix_off:
146 0000014C 0839000000000001    btst     #0,mode+1      * look for jam mode
147 00000154 6602                bne      sk1_poff       * branch if jam mode
148 00000156 4E75                rts                     * jam is only reset mode acted on
149                     sk1_poff:
150 00000158 0191                bclr     d0,(a1)        * reset pixel
151 0000015A 4E75                rts
152         *****************************************************************
153         * PIX_ON - processes one bits in overlaid image
                         pix_on:
154
155 0000015C 0839000000000001    btst     #0,mode+1      * look for jam mode
156 00000164 6618                bne      sk1_pon        * branch if jam mode
157 00000166 0839000100000001    btst     #1,mode+1      * look for complement mode
158 0000016E 6612                bne      sk2_pon        * branch if complement mode
159 00000170 0839000200000001    btst     #2,mode+1      * look for set mode
160 00000178 6604                bne      sk1_pon        * same as jam mode
161 0000017A 0191                bclr     d0,(a1)        * must be clear mode
162 0000017C 4E75                rts
163                     sk1_pon:
164 0000017E 01D1                bset     d0,(a1)        * turn on pixel
165 00000180 4E75                rts
166                     sk2_pon:
167 00000182 0151                bchg     d0,(a1)        * complement pixel
168 00000184 4E75                rts
169
170 00000186                     end
```

Module DEMO.PRN

```
 1                      * Graphics test
 2                      ********************************************************************
 3                      <<include BIT.H>>
11
12                              xref    g_pix,g_clear,g_vector,g_mode,g_circle,g_fill
13                              xref    creep,dump,arrow,snarl
14                              xdef    image
15
16  00000000  303C0001          move.w  #jam_m,d0
17  00000004  61000000          bsr     g_mode
18  00000008  61000000          bsr     g_clear     * clear up screen
19                      ******** Draw distorted crosshatch ******************************
20  0000000C  303C0000          move.w  #0,d0        * set initial moving X
21  00000010  363C00C7          move.w  #vert-1,d3   * set initial moving Y
22
23  00000014  4241      lpx:    clr.w   d1           * set stationary Y
24  00000016  4242              clr.w   d2           * set stationary X
25  00000018  61000000          bsr     g_vector     * draw line
26  0000001C  323C00C7          move.w  #vert-1,d1   * go across image for stationary
27  00000020  343C013F          move.w  #hor_b-1,d2  * X and Y
28  00000024  61000000          bsr     g_vector     * draw reflected line
29  00000028  5040              add.w   #8,d0        * move the moving X
30  0000002A  5B43              sub.w   #5,d3        * move the moving Y
31  0000002C  B07C0140          cmp.w   #hor_b,d0    * check for limit
32  00000030  6DE2              blt     lpx          * loop if we aren't at limit
33                      ******** circle test - concentric circles ***********************
34  00000032  303C00A0          move.w  #hor_b/2,d0  * center the circles in the image
35  00000036  323C0064          move.w  #vert/2,d1
36  0000003A  343C0005          move.w  #5,d2        * start with a tiny radius
37  0000003E  363C0001          move.w  #1,d3        * this will be incrementer
38
39  00000042  61000000  lpc:    bsr     g_circle     * draw the circle
40  00000046  D443              add.w   d3,d2        * double the radius
41  00000048  5243              addq.w  #1,d3        * increment the incrementer
42  0000004A  B47C004B          cmp     #75,d2       * check that we don't get too big
43  0000004E  6DF2              blt     lpc          * if not, make more circles
44                      ******** fill in between two of the circles *********************
45  00000050  323C0041          move.w  #65,d1       * pick Y to start creep
46  00000054  61000000          bsr     creep        * do creep
47                      ******** mode check - set mode to complement for next tests ******
```

Module DEMO.PRN (continued)

```
48  00000058  303C0002          move.w  #comp_m,d0
49  0000005C  61000000          bsr     g_mode
50            ******* fill test *****************************************
51  00000060  303C0000          move.w  #0,d0              * make a vertical bar down the
52  00000064  323C0050          move.w  #(vert/2-20),d1    * center
53  00000068  343C013F          move.w  #hor_b-1,d2
54  0000006C  363C0078          move.w  #(vert/2+20),d3
55  00000070  61000000          bsr     g_fill
56  00000074  303C009B          move.w  #(hor_b/2-5),d0    * make a horizontal bar across
57  00000078  323C0000          move.w  #0,d1              * the center
58  0000007C  343C00A5          move.w  #(hor_b/2+5),d2
59  00000080  363C00C7          move.w  #vert-1,d3
60  00000084  61000000          bsr     g_fill
61            ******* Arrow icon test ************************************
62  00000088  303C0001          move.w  #jam_m,d0          * test first in jam mode
63  0000008C  61000000          bsr     g_mode
64  00000090  303C0014          move.w  #20,d0             * put way over on left
65  00000094  323C0073          move.w  #(vert/2+15),d1    * and half on filled area
66  00000098  61000000          bsr     arrow             * put arrow
67  0000009C  303C0002          move.w  #comp_m,d0         * next test complement mode
68  000000A0  61000000          bsr     g_mode            * set comp code
69  000000A4  303C0023          move.w  #35,d0             * put next arrow just right
70  000000A8  61000000          bsr     arrow             * put arrow
71  000000AC  303C0004          move.w  #set_m,d0          * next try set mode
72  000000B0  61000000          bsr     g_mode            * set set mode
73  000000B4  303C0032          move.w  #50,d0             * put next arrow just right
74  000000B8  61000000          bsr     arrow             * put arrow
75  000000BC  303C0008          move.w  #clr_m,d0          * last, try clear mode
76  000000C0  61000000          bsr     g_mode            * set clear mode
77  000000C4  303C0041          move.w  #65,d0             * put last arrow to the right
78  000000C8  61000000          bsr     arrow             * put arrow
79            ******* Snarl icon test ***********************************
80  000000CC  303C0001          move.w  #jam_m,d0          * reset to jam mode
81  000000D0  61000000          bsr     g_mode            * set mode
82  000000D4  303C0116          move.w  #278,d0            * put way over on right
83  000000D8  323C000A          move.w  #10,d1             * and down a little from top
84  000000DC  61000000          bsr     snarl             * put snarl icon
85            ******* now we dump our picture to the printer ***********
86  000000E0  61000000          bsr     dump
87  000000E4  4E75
88            *********************************************************
89  00000000
90                      bss
91  00000000  image:    ds.b    vert*hor_w   * This is the global image memory
92
93  00000FA0            end
```

18

On the Bare Metal

Every assembly language programmer who wants to earn his/her wings must at one time or another write code to talk to hardware devices. The ultimate goal of any Real Programmer is to be good enough to get a Zilog 8230 Serial Communications Controller talking over a half duplex data bus in SDLC mode at 38.4 kilobaud. Few, if any, reach this goal. After reading this chapter, however, you will know how to make a Motorola MC68681 Dual Universal Asyncronous Receiver Transmitter (DUART, or two-channel serial I/O peripheral chip) talk over two channels in interrupt driven mode. We won't give an exhaustive treatment of the MC68681 by any means (that would take about half of this book), but given this chapter and the data book for the chip you should have little trouble making a '681 work. We chose the '681 as an example because you are likely to find this device in 68K systems. We will also discuss some of the perils of interrupt-driven programmable peripherals in general.

There are two general methods of device I/O available to computer designers, "polled" and "interrupt-driven." The polled method is hardly ever used anymore because it is very inefficient. In a polled I/O system, the operating system (or whatever executive is handling I/O) needs to get control of the system often enough to check all of the devices to see if data is ready, and everything stops and waits while I/O takes place.

If you ever have the chance to crash a hardware design review for a new computer (you'll have to crash it; software types are never invited to hardware design reviews for two reasons. First, reviews are usually held in small rooms and software types are not reknowned for their personal hygiene, and second, software types tend to complain a lot about the hardware configuration) and someone suggests a polled system, start whining about cost and schedule impact until they shut up. Polled systems are actually easier to write code for, but you'll be ashamed of the system throughput.

The more commonly used method for device I/O is the interrupt driven system. When a device needs service, it generates a special type of exception known as an "interrupt." This exception is serviced as if it was a trap-type instruction jammed into the user application code at the point where the code was executing when the interrupting device decided it needed service. It is important for someone learning about how interrupts work to realize that the user code needn't make any special provisions to allow interrupts to occur—they just do, no matter what user code is executing. It is the responsibility of the supervisor code to allow interrupts to happen, and to do something about them when they do. Once turned on by the supervisor, interrupts take place without user code having any control over them whatsoever, and if properly designed, without the user code having any knowledge of them.

There are three ways a device interrupt can be translated into an exception vector. The simplest from the hardware designer's viewpoint is the spurious interrupt exception (vector $24). The way this works is the hardware designer hooks all of the devices that can generate an interrupt together. When a device interrupts, there isn't any special extra hardware out there to say "Me! Me!," and a bus error occurs. Exception $24 is taken for bus errors during an interrupt acknowledge. Then, you put code at the end of vector $24 that looks at each and every device to see who wants service.

From the standpoint of good software design, the spurious interrupt system is only one notch above polled I/O.

The two other interrupt methods are to use the 68K "autovector" interrupts (vectors 25 to 31) or a device-supplied vector. The choice is fixed when the hardware is designed. The autovectors are used when there are relatively few devices in a system. The device-supplied vectors are used when "smart" hardware is available to put a vector on the bus at the right time. The only difference between the two from a software standpoint is that you need to tell smart peripherals what their vector numbers are when you initialize them. (68K family peripherals will place the "uninitialized interrupt" vector, vector 15, on the bus if no vector is programmed into them.) Otherwise, the difference between the two techniques is just a matter of which vector is taken when the interrupt is serviced.

Some peripheral chips are capable of operating in several different interrupt modes. For example, the 68681 DUART we're using in this chapter is a two channel serial I/O chip. It can generate a single interrupt signal suitable for use as a spurious or autovector input, or can be programmed to put a vector on the bus in a device-supplied-vector system, or external pins on the chip can be programmed to generate separate interrupts for each of the conditions that can cause an interrupt to occur, to be resolved into separate vectors.

In the last case, another chip called an "interrupt controller" needs to go between the 68681 and the 68K to sort things out. Again, unless you can get in on the design meeting, these choices are fixed by the time you get to write code. Given a choice, taking a separate vector for each possible source of interrupts is the preferred method, because you don't need to waste time trying to figure out why an interrupt happened. If only one thing can cause an interrupt, you'll know it happened by the simple fact that the interrupt handler is being executed.

When designing an interrupt handler, the very first thing to do is to find out how the hardware folks mapped the interrupts into the 68K. This sometimes isn't a trivial undertaking, but it does have to be done first. A good understanding of the entire interrupt structure of the machine is crucial to a good design.

Pay particular attention to the priorities assigned to each device. The priority of the interrupt determines what device gets serviced first when more than one wants service at once. The order of servicing may not make any difference at all to your design, but then again, it may make a big difference.

For example, let us suppose that you have a system that includes a DMA controller and a disk controller. The DMA controller can be programmed to transfer data between the disk controller and memory, and both of them can cause an interrupt when the transfer is complete. If the DMA interrupt is recognized first, you may want to be able to quickly program it to send more data to the disk controller. If the disk controller is recognized first you may want to shut down the DMA channel before it interrupts so that you don't pay the overhead of another interrupt service routine when you don't have to.

As another example of priorities affecting the design, suppose a serial I/O controller is assigned to a lower priority than another device. You need to design the service routine for the higher priority device such that the "latency," or maximum time from the service request to recognizing and servicing the serial I/O interrupt is short enough that you won't miss incoming characters.

Once you have the interrupt structure down, you then need to read the device data sheet to see the capabilities of the particular device. This can range from a ten-minute job to a two-week ordeal. Today's chips are becoming unreasonably complicated. For example, an older chip, the Intel 8251 UART, a nice little one-channel serial chip and the workhorse of the CP/M world, has a control register, a status register, a data transmit register, and a receive data register. A two-page data sheet will tell you everything you need to know about programming it. Contrast this with the Zilog 8230 SCC, with umpteen registers and a 40-page data book in which each sentence needs to be read and the full ramifications of that sentence understood and related to the rest of the data book. Of course, the SCC is a much more powerful chip than the 8251, with dual channels, synchronous and asynchronous modes, and a programmable interrupt system.

The MC68681 DUART falls between the 8251 and the SCC in complexity. The 68681 is a 68000-family peripheral. From a software point of view, whether or not a chip belongs to the processor family doesn't make a whole lot of difference, except that when the hardware designer is trying to get a nonfamily chip glued into the 68K bus and debugged you get to sit in the lab and make helpful remarks like "Gee, Bill, how about if we like, you know, stick a PAL in there or, like, maybe try one of these buggers right . . . here . . . (fzzzzzzzzzzzt)." Hardware folks are known for their appreciation of constructive criticism and helpful suggestions when debugging hardware.

The '681 has 16 read and 16 write registers associated with it, two of which are "do not access" registers—reading them sends the chip off into the tall weeds. Aside from this, the registers are fairly straightforward (for a programmable peripheral), and are remarkably tolerant of the order of programming.

As part of the preparations for an interrupt handler, we recommend writing a header file for each peripheral chip, as we did in Figure 18-1. This file should have equates for all register addresses associated with the chip, preferably referenced to an offset such as our equate "base." Assuming the hardware folks assigned bus addresses to the '681 address pins in the logical manner, this file (and code faithfully depending on it) can be moved to any machine by changing the "base" equate and the "vector" equate.

We also have symbolic names assigned to the programming codes for most of the register contents. For example, the "Mode Register 1" equates are grouped into six bunches. To make a control word for mode register 1, all we have to do is add together one equate from each

```
***********************************************************************
* MC68681 DUART Register Definition Header

******* Address Equates ******************************************
base      equ   $FF0001 * Base address of MC68681 DUART
mode_a    equ   base+0  * (R/W) Mode Register A
stat_a    equ   base+2  * (R/O) Status Register A
clock_a   equ   base+2  * (W/O) Clock Select Register A
cmd_a     equ   base+4  * (W/O) Command Register A
rba_a     equ   base+6  * (R/O) Receive Data Buffer A
tba_a     equ   base+6  * (W/O) Transmit Data Buffer A
ipcr      equ   base+8  * (R/O) Input Port Change Register
acr       equ   base+8  * (W/O) Auxiliary Control Register
isr       equ   base+10 * (R/O) Interrupt Status Register
imr       equ   base+10 * (W/O) Interrupt Mask Register
count_h   equ   base+12 * (R/W) Counter High Byte
count_l   equ   base+14 * (R/W) Counter Low Byte
mode_b    equ   base+16 * (R/W) Mode Register B
stat_b    equ   base+18 * (R/O) Status Register B
clock_b   equ   base+18 * (W/O) Clock Select Register B
cmd_b     equ   base+20 * (W/O) Command Register B
rba_b     equ   base+22 * (R/O) Receive Data Buffer B
tba_b     equ   base+22 * (W/O) Transmit Data Buffer B
ivr       equ   base+24 * (R/W) Interrupt Vector Register
ipu       equ   base+26 * (R/O) Input Port (Unlatched)
opcr      equ   base+26 * (W/O) Output Port Config. Register
srt_cnt   equ   base+28 * (R/O) Start Counter address trigger
stp_cnt   equ   base+30 * (R/O) Stop Counter address trigger
bit_set   equ   base+28 * (W/O) OPR Bit Set address trigger
bit_res   equ   base+30 * (W/O) OPR Bit Reset address trigger
vector    equ   29      * Autovector 5, address $74
******* Mode Register 1 equates ***************************
******* Group 1 - use 1 command from each group
RxRTS     equ   $80     * Use Rx RTS handshake for flow control
NO_RRTS   equ   $00     * Don't use RTS Handshake
******* Group 2
RI_RDY    equ   $00     * Receive Interrupt on RxRDY
RI_FFUL   equ   $40     * Receive Interrupt on FIFO full
******* Group 3
C_ERR     equ   $00     * Character Mode Error Reporting
B_ERR     equ   $20     * Block Mode Error Reporting
******* Group 4
WTH_PAR   equ   $00     * With Parity
FORCE_P   equ   $08     * Force Parity
NO_PAR    equ   $10     * No Parity
MULTI     equ   $18     * Multidrop Mode
******* Group 5
EVEN_P    equ   $00     * Even Parity
ODD_P     equ   $04     * Odd Parity
M_DATA    equ   $00     * Multidrop Data
M_ADDR    equ   $04     * Multidrop Address
******* Group 6
BITS_5    equ   $00     * 5 bits/character
BITS_6    equ   $01     * 6 bits/character
BITS_7    equ   $02     * 7 bits/character
BITS_8    equ   $03     * 8 bits/character
******* Mode Register 2 equates *********************************
******* Group 1 - use 1 command from each group
```

FIGURE 18-1. Module MC68681.H

```
NOR_OP    equ    $00    * Normal Operation
ECHO      equ    $40    * Automatic Echo Mode
LLOOP     equ    $80    * Local Loopback Mode
RLOOP     equ    $C0    * Remote Loopback
******* Group 2
TxRTS     equ    $20    * Use Tx RTS handshake for flow control
NO_TRTS   equ    $00    * Don't use Tx RTS
******* Group 3
CTS       equ    $10    * Use CTS to enable transmitter
NO_CTS    equ    $00    * Don't use CTS
******* Group 4
STOP_1    equ    $07    * One Stop Bit
STOP_2    equ    $0F    * Two Stop Bits
******* Clock Select Register equates - Tx and Rx same rates ****
** Baud rates prefixed with "B1" must use "SET_1" ACR equate.
** Baud rates prefixed with "B2" must use "SET_2" ACR equate.
** Baud rates prefixed with "B_" may use either equate.
B1_50     equ    $00    * 50    baud
B2_75     equ    $00    * 75    baud
B_110     equ    $11    * 110   baud
B_134     equ    $22    * 134.5 baud
B2_150    equ    $33    * 150   baud
B1_200    equ    $33    * 200   baud
B_300     equ    $44    * 300   baud
B_600     equ    $55    * 600   baud
B_1200    equ    $66    * 1200  baud
B1_1050   equ    $77    * 1050  baud
B2_1800   equ    $AA    * 1800  baud
B2_2000   equ    $77    * 2000  baud
B_2400    equ    $88    * 2400  baud
B_4800    equ    $99    * 4800  baud
B1_7200   equ    $AA    * 7200  baud
B_9600    equ    $BB    * 9600  baud
B2_19K    equ    $CC    * 19.3K baud
B1_38K    equ    $CC    * 38.4K baud
B_TIMER   equ    $DD    * Use timer output as clock
B_IP16X   equ    $EE    * Input Pin @ 16x clock
B_IP1X    equ    $FF    * Input Pin @ 1x clock
******* Command Register Command Equates ***********************
*******     Use one command from each group
******* Group 1 - Miscellaneous Commands
NO_CMD    equ    $00    * No Command
POINT_1   equ    $10    * Point to Mode Register 1
RST_RX    equ    $20    * Reset Receiver
RST_TX    equ    $30    * Reset Transmitter
RST_ERR   equ    $40    * Reset Error Status
RST_INT   equ    $50    * Reset Break-Change Interrupt
BRK_ON    equ    $60    * Start Break
BRK_OFF   equ    $70    * Stop Break
******* Group 2 - Transmitter Commands
T_NO_OP   equ    $00    * No operation
T_EN      equ    $04    * Enable Transmitter
T_DIS     equ    $08    * Disable Transmitter
******* Group 3 - Receiver Commands
R_NO_OP   equ    $00    * No operation
R_EN      equ    $01    * Enable Receiver
R_DIS     equ    $02    * Disable Receiver
******* Output Port Configuration Register ********************
```

FIGURE 18-1, cont'd.

```
B_TXRDY   equ    $80    * Use OP7 as channel B TXRDY interrupt
A_TXRDY   equ    $40    * Use OP6 as channel A TXRDY interrupt
B_RXINT   equ    $20    * Use OP5 as Ch. B RXRDY/FFULL interrupt
A_RXINT   equ    $10    * Use OP4 as Ch. A RXRDY/FFULL interrupt
CT_OUT    equ    $04    * Use OP3 as Counter/Timer output
TXCB      equ    $08    * Use OP3 as channel B 1x Tx Clock output
RXCB      equ    $0C    * Use OP3 as channel B 1x Rx Clock output
TXCA_16   equ    $01    * Use OP2 as channel A 16X Tx Clk output
TXCA      equ    $02    * Use OP2 as channel A 1x Tx Clock output
RXCA      equ    $03    * Use OP2 as channel A 1x Rx Clock output
ALL_OUT   equ    $00    * All OP pins are general purpose outputs
******* Auxiliary Control Register equates ********************
******* Group 1 - use 1 command from each group
SET_1     equ    $00    * Use Baud Rate Set 1
SET_2     equ    $80    * Use Baud Rate Set 2
******* Group 2
CNT_IP2   equ    $00    * Counter mode, uses IP2 as input
CNT_TXA   equ    $10    * Counter mode, input is 1x Ch. A Tx Clk
CNT_TXB   equ    $20    * Counter mode, input is 1x Ch. B Tx Clk
CNT_XTL   equ    $30    * Counter mode, input is crystal / 16
TMR_IP2   equ    $40    * Timer mode, input is 1x IP2
TMR_P2    equ    $50    * Timer mode, input is IP2 / 16
TMR_XTL   equ    $60    * Timer mode, input is 1x crystal
TMR_XXX   equ    $70    * Timer mode, input is crystal / 16
******* Group 3 - use 0 to 4 of these. Also set IN_CHNG in IMR
del_IP3   equ    $08    * Change of State IP3 interrupt enabled
del_IP2   equ    $04    * Change of State IP2 interrupt enabled
del_IP1   equ    $02    * Change of State IP1 interrupt enabled
del_IP0   equ    $01    * Change of State IP0 interrupt enabled
******* Interrupt Mask Register/Interrupt Status Register *******
IN_CHNG   equ    $80    * Enable Input Port Change Interrupt
INCHNG    equ    $07    * bit number for above
DELTA_B   equ    $40    * Enable delta-break B interrupt
DELTAB    equ    $06    * bit number for above
I_RX_B    equ    $20    * Enable RXRDY/FFULL B interrupt
IRX_B     equ    $05    * bit number for above
I_TX_B    equ    $10    * Enable TXRDY B interrupt
ITX_B     equ    $04    * bit number for above
I_CNTR    equ    $08    * Enable Counter/Timer Ready interrupt
ICNTR     equ    $03    * bit number for above
DELTA_A   equ    $04    * Enable delta-break A interrupt
DELTAA    equ    $02    * bit number for above
I_RX_A    equ    $02    * Enable RXRDY/FFULL A interrupt
IRX_A     equ    $01    * bit number for above
I_TX_A    equ    $01    * Enable TXRDY A interrupt
ITX_A     equ    $00    * bit number for above
NO_INTS   equ    $00    * All interrupts disabled
******* Status Register Bits ***********************************
break     equ    $80    * Received Break
frame     equ    $40    * Framing Error
parity    equ    $20    * Parity Error
overrun   equ    $10    * Overrun Error
txempty   equ    $08    * Transmitter Empty
txready   equ    $04    * Transmitter Ready
ffull     equ    $02    * FIFO Full
rxready   equ    $01    * Received Character Ready
******* Input Port Change Register equates *********************
delta_3   equ    $80    * Change-of-State detected on IP3
delta_2   equ    $40    * Change-of-State detected on IP2
```

FIGURE 18-1, cont'd.

```
delta_1 equ    $20     * Change-of-State detected on IP1
delta_0 equ    $10     * Change-of-State detected on IP0
level_3 equ    $08     * Current level of IP3
level_2 equ    $04     * Current level of IP2
level_1 equ    $02     * Current level of IP1
level_0 equ    $01     * Current level of IP0
```

FIGURE 18-1,   cont'd.

group. We'll see how this works in practice in a moment. It's a real pain writing a 180-line header file for the chip, especially when you know you'll never use half the stuff in it, but it's a great aid when debugging. When writing interrupt handlers, you need to take every advantage possible, and even then it's not enough. In the case of the header file for this chip, the pain of typing it in is more than made up for by the reduction in errors. Interrupt code is always debugged late at night (it's the law), and it's very, very easy to bitpack a control word incorrectly when jacked up on a couple of gallons of coffee. Just one little bit in the wrong place makes the problem you're working go away while a new one takes over. Using symbolic names from the header makes it kind of self-documenting, too. Just be damn sure you type the header in correctly in the first place. Of course, you're typing the table when you still think the whole thing's a piece of cake, so the pressure's off and it's easier to be accurate.

The next trick is to get the initialization constants into one place where you can see them all at one time. Our procedure "sinit" in Module SINIT.PRN accomplishes this by using a table. The table consists of two longwords per source line, one being the address of the register and the other being the constant to store into the register. The register constant only needs to be 8 bits; we are storing it as a longword so that the register name can be on the same source line as the register name.

Picking the order for initializing a peripheral is mostly an art—unless an explicit order is given in the data sheet. The '681 data sheet doesn't have a recommended order of programming, so we just picked a logical order and it worked. For example, we start by disabling the interrupts before fooling with the other registers. Next we set the modes for each channel. The '681 has a timer feature than we opted to use as a 10mS heartbeat interrupt to run a clock, and it is initialized next. The next thing we do is reset both channels, enable the receivers and disable the transmitters. Finally, we enable the interrupts. When we're finished, both channels are set to 8 bits, no parity, one stop bit, 1200 baud, no handshaking.

It is important that the interrupt vectors are pointed towards interrupt handler code before a chip's interrupts are enabled. The same executive that called "sinit" would be responsible for setting up the interrupt vector. We have a sample executive that we'll present later.

When bringing up a device driver for the first time, it is best to start with a simple case, get it working, test it thoroughly, and then start adding features. Let us give an example. The initialization we chose for this chip is about as simple as we could make it. Note that we set it up for no handshaking. The '681 will automatically handshake with other hardware using the standard RS-232 handshake lines if the hardware designer implemented the necessary handshake lines and the proper initialization constants are programmed into the '681. You might be tempted to use this hardware handshake, believing that it will make your life easier.

However, starting out with the hardware handshake enabled will introduce variables into the problem space. You could spend days trying to get the chip to talk before discovering that the hardware team forgot an inverter somewhere, or that the RS-232 cable you're using is wired for something else and doesn't have all the wires, or the terminal you're testing with didn't have the right switches set. Keep it simple—start with no handshake at all and get that working. Once you do, you can add one direction of handshake to one channel at a time and test as you go. Note the last line of the initialization code—we set all the outputs true "just in case." This isn't superfluous in our case—it's there because we spent three days trying to get our '681 to receive, and discovered (after locating and using an RS-232 breakout box) that our test terminal was looking for a hardware handshake back before it would send. This was the same terminal that we *knew* for *sure* didn't look for a handshake.

The same principles apply to other peripherals. Start with the simplest operation you can find and get that working. On a disk controller, for example, just get it to step back and forth a couple of tracks before you try the "format track" function.

Once you do get something going, however, go for broke until you get all of the functions working and tested, expecially with newly built hardware. You have all the fixes to the earlier problems fresh in your mind, and you can catch hardware quirks early. A peripheral may appear to work for simple functions and then fail on more complicated ones.

Module SERINT.PRN illustrates an interrupt service routine for the '681, and two other important routines. These three routines match the initialization parameters just presented.

The first, "s__vector" on line 189, installs a vector into the exception vector table to vector the interrupt to the service routine. We are saving the old vector, so we can replace it when we're done. Actually, this is not a "well-behaved" routine. Most operating systems provide a service call to install vectors into the table. These routines should be used if at all possible. For example, CP/M-68K for the 68010 will do some processing on the interrupt exception stack before your routine gets it, to simulate the 68000 exception stack, but only if you use the operating system service call to set the vector. If you just bang a vector into memory, CP/M can't get its hooks into the vector and hence never sees the exception. If you're working on an embedded system, or are at the operating system level, you can use the same code we have. "s__vector" must be called before initializing the '681, to make sure that any interrupt is properly handled.

The second routine, "r__vector" at line 196, restores the vector that "s__vector" saved, and also makes sure that the '681 has had its interrupts disabled. The same comments about using operating system services apply here. "r__vector" should be called when the program using the '681 is finished with it.

Before looking at the interrupt handler, we should review interrupt exception processing.

An interrupt will be recognized if the current interrupt mask in the supervisor portion of the status word is less than the priority of the interrupt requesting service. When the interrupt is recognized, the status word and the program counter are pushed on the supervisor stack, the processor is forced into supervisor mode, and the corresponding vector from the exception vector table is loaded into the program counter. The key point to remember is that exception handlers in general and interrupt handlers in particular execute in supervisor mode.

Interrupts do one thing more that general-purpose exceptions don't—the interrupt mask field in the status word is set to the level of the interrupt just recognized. This means that another interrupt of the same or lower priority (including the interrupt under service) cannot interrupt the interrupt handler. When an RTE instruction is executed, the interrupt mask will be set to the value it had upon entry to the interrupt handler, allowing new interrupts of the same or lower priority. This brings up rule number one for interrupt handlers:

- An interrupt handler MUST make the hardware interrupt signal "go away," or an endless loop will result. If the interrupt signal is not removed, every time the RTE instruction is executed, the interrupt handler will be re-entered.

A symptom of violating rule number one is when the system hangs immediately after enabling an interrupt. Even tracing with a debugger won't prevent this from happening, because the trace bit is pushed with the rest of the status word and reset when the interrupt is recognized. Your debugger loses control. (Hardware debuggers do not have this limitation.)

Because interrupts are asynchronous, the user code executing when the interrupt occurs has no advance knowledge of it. An interrupt handler has to leave the processor state exactly the way it was on entry to the handler, rule number two:

- An interrupt handler MUST save and restore any register it uses.

An interrupt service routine really needs to be completely transparent, because interrupts are recognized between any two instructions. The interrupt handler needs to be written so that you could insert TRAP instructions calling it between every instruction in all your programs and (other than the speed penalty) see no effect on the execution of your program.

Interrupt handlers frequently need to interact with non-interrupt code, to pass messages or data between the handler and the mainline code. For example, a serial receiver needs to tell somebody that it has data ready, and a serial transmitter needs to tell somebody that it's ready to send more data. Some sort of communication needs to be set up, usually a shared data structure. If only a single access to the shared data is required, as in the case of a realtime clock (the interrupt handler needs only increment the clock, and the application needs only read the clock), there isn't normally any problem. If the shared access is to a complex shared data structure such as a queue or a heap, however, we need rule number three:

- Mutual exclusion needs to be provided for shared data structures.

Normally, the interrupt service routine provides intrinsic exclusion on its end. If a shared structure is used only by one interrupt handler, there's no problem in the interrupt end, because the application code can't interrupt the interrupt handler. If, however, more than one service routine uses a data structure (as when more than one service routine calls the heap manager), exclusion must be provided for in the interrupt handlers as well.

Let's take a look at the interrupt handler "isrtn" on line 202 of Module SERINT and see one way all of these rules can be implemented.

Our initialization sets up the '681 with transmitters disabled, receivers enabled, and the on-chip timer set to interrupt every 10mS. There are three more interrupts possible from the '681, two "break change" (an interrupt when either the start or the end of a received break signal is detected) and an "input port change" (an interrupt when input handshaking lines change state). These extra three interrupts are masked in the chip by our initialization constants, but we have provided handlers for them to satisfy rule number one. If in the future, either by design or accident, we unmask these interrupts, and they have no handlers, we will unleash a subtle and horrible bug. Turning a terminal attached to the '681 on or off in this situation will cause the system to die silently as the interrupt service routine is called repeatedly without resetting the interrupt signal to the CPU.

As we enter the service routine we save registers D0 and A0 to satisfy rule number two (line 203). These two registers are the only ones the service routine will use. They are restored on line 222, just before the RTE instruction terminates the service routine.

Next, on line 204, we read the '681 interrupt status register (ISR). This register displays potential sources of interrupts. This brings up another subtle potential problem, that of servicing a non-interrupt. The ISR only displays potential interrupts. An interrupt may be displayed as potential in the ISR but masked by the on-chip interrupt mask register (IMR). It's very possible to read a pending interrupt in the ISR and attempt to service it, when in fact that interrupt is masked and not the cause of the interrupt in the first place. To be completely safe, in the case of the '681, we should AND the contents of the ISR with the value we stored into the IMR. This would leave us only actual interrupts, instead of potential interrupts.

Unfortunately, the value in the IMR cannot be read directly from the '681.To implement this safeguard, we would have to save a copy of the IMR in memory somewhere, and update it each time we change the mask. This mask then becomes a shared resource and needs to be managed with mutual exclusion.

In our routine, we use a careful order to test the ISR, and a trick with the transmitter servicing to make sure we only service valid interrupts. Once we decide that we have an interrupt, we branch to the service routine to handle the interrupt.

The routines "rx__a," line 225, and "rx__b," line 231, service receiver interrupts. We are using the queue managers from Chapter 14 to queue the data as it comes in. Note that we don't take any corrective action if the receive queue is full. There's really nothing that can be done if there isn't room for more characters, so we do nothing.

The transmitter service routines "tx__a", line 237, and "tx__b", line 253, are somewhat more complicated. In most (but not all) serial chips, an interrupt can be programmed to occur when the transmitter buffer is empty (meaning it wants another character to transmit), or the interrupt can be masked somehow. In the transmitter routines here,we check to see if another character is available, and if one is, it is sent and the service routine exited.

Where it gets complicated is if another character isn't ready to transmit. In this case we can't make the interrupt go away by feeding the chip a new character. If we just exit without doing anything else, we violate rule number one, and the system will hang up in a loop. With the '681, we have two ways to remove the transmitter empty interrupt without sending another character. Both ways take about the same amount of overhead.

The way we did not choose is to keep a copy of the interrupt mask in memory somewhere and set and reset the transmitter interrupt bit as required. This method would be appropriate if we already had a copy floating around (e.g., to AND with the ISR register as discussed earlier).

The way we did choose, because it is a more general solution, is to disable the transmitter when no characters are ready to send. The '681 will not show the transmitter buffer empty bit in the ISR if the transmitter is disabled. This still doesn't get us completely out of the mutual exclusion bind, however. We'll see the rest of the transmitter controls when we look at our sample executive. First let's look at the rest of the interrupt service routine.

"delt__a," line 269, "delt__b," line 273, and "in__change," line 277, are included to reset interrupt sources in the unlikely event that they get enabled accidentally. In a debug setting you would most likely make arrangements for error flags to be set or error messages to be printed if these branches are taken in the interrupt handler. Because these interrupts are relatively low frequency, it won't matter much if they are enabled and do go off occasionally. In a system with potential interrupts at high frequency, however, system throughput will suffer if extraneous interrupts are being serviced.

The "clock" routine at line 282 just increments a memory longword designated as the realtime clock. Depending on how the realtime clock is used, this location can be maintained in binary, as we do, or it can be maintained in BCD. If, for example, the realtime clock is displayed on the screen continuously, a BCD representation will simplify conversion to ASCII. If the clock is to be used to measure intervals, a binary representation is more suitable.

All of the service routines use the common exit at line 221. A design decision can be made to re-enter the poll at line 204 instead of exiting right away if it is likely that more than one interrupt will be pending at one time, as when a heavy volume of receiver traffic is expected at high baud rates. You have to balance the relatively high interrupt acknowledge overhead for a separate invocation of the service routine for each interrupt source against the longer execution of the service routine each time. In the case of the '681, which has a 3 byte receiver FIFO built in, a high interrupt latency can be compensated for by re-entering the poll loop after each service routine, or adjusting the routine so that only receiver interrupts are repolled.

Module ECH.PRN is a simple executive program to test and demonstrate the serial I/O routines. This program simply echoes to the output whatever comes in the receiver. Note that this procedure must execute in supervisor mode, as evidenced by the operating system service call at lines 12 and 13. This is a consequence of the method we have chosen for mutual exclusion on the queue managers. We also do a little dancing with the stack here; this is needed in CP/M but probably not elsewhere.

We next install the serial I/O interrupt vector (line 17), before we call the serial initialization (line 18). This is so any interrupts lurking in the serial chip will be properly vectored. When writing code for interrupts handlers, the absolute worst scenario must always be imagined and planned for.

The main loop just checks each receiver FIFO via a call to the local "d__queue" routine, and if a character is waiting, sends it to the transmitter via the local routines "a__xmit" and "b__xmit." These local routines are of interest because they implement the host end of mutual exclusion for the data areas shared with the interrupt handlers.

The transmitters check the busy flag associated with the transmitter, and if not busy, set the flag (this is all accomplished by the TAS instructions on lines 44 and 58) and then transmit the character directly. If the transmitter is already busy, the character is placed in the transmit queue. We are providing exclusion by disabling the interrupts while we check the data structures. This code works—let's analyze it a bit and see what could go wrong if we change it. We'll use the "tx__a" routine as an example, as "tx__b" is essentially identical.

First of all, it is a basic assumption that interrupts should be disabled for as short a time as possible, to decrease latency. The most obvious modification is to move closer together the points at which we disable and re-enable interrupts or to disable/re-enable more than once, to provide an interruptable window between the areas where interrupts are disabled.

In line 44, we check the busy flag. We're using a TAS (Test-and-Set) instruction both to set the flag and to test its prior value. This may be somewhat misleading, as TAS is often used to implement a mutual exclusion scheme, where in this case it is only used to save an instruction in a larger implementation.

TAS can only help us in a case where two (or more) concurrent processes share a flag somewhere. The key to TAS working as it was designed to is to allow all processes competing for the resource to "go around" if the resource is in use. If process A is using a resource and process B uses the TAS instruction to test if it is busy (and at the same time mark the resource as reserved), process B must be able to let process A complete its use of the resource and then mark it as clear. This doesn't work in the case of an interrupt when the user code has locked the resource, because the interrupt service routine has no way of relinquishing the processor to allow the user code to clear the resource lock, and then regaining control of the processor. The only viable alternative here is to disable the interrupts.

But we digress—we were looking at moving the interrupt disable. If we placed the disable interrupt just after the TAS on line 44, we run into an intermittent and very hard to trace bug. Once every blue moon, we will test the flag and find it busy. At the same instant, a transmitter interrupt will occur and the queue will be empty. The service routine will obligingly shut down the transmitter interrupt and clear the busy flag. Returning from the interrupt, the user code still thinks the transmitter is busy and will enqueue the character. The character sits in the queue, awaiting an interrupt that never comes if no more characters are sent out by the application code. If another character does come through, it goes out before the queued character. The net result is an occasional transposed character pair, or the system hanging before printing the last character in a string.

Another point in the code where a mistimed interrupt can get us is in the queue manager (its code is in Chapter 14). If an interrupt blows through while we're fooling with either the queue count or the pointers, we'll occasionally either miss characters or have doubled characters, or the characters will get a little out of sync—on the echo program, for example, the echoed key might be garbage, or very old stuff from the queue, or just one or two keystrokes old.

On the other hand, you can get in trouble by going too far the other way with disabled interrupts. For example, if you're looping on a receive FIFO and you don't enable interrupts at least once during the loop, the queue can never be filled. Luckily, this is a reasonably easy problem to diagnose.

All in all, interrupt driven devices and the servicing code for them are tricky beasts. Experienced systems programmers writing service routines for devices they are familiar with, on systems they know well, still have trouble. Standard procedure for interrupt debugging is to write the code, try it once (it won't work, of course), and then go home and get some sleep. The next day, you lay on plenty of Twinkies, get a pile of change for the coffee machine, and talk the program managers into buying pizza for the duration. Everything after the first three days is a haze, but somehow at the end of it the system works.

Systems code, such as interrupt drivers, is the place for assembly language programming. Nobody really expects to write a data base manager or a payroll program in assembly language anymore—it's just not practical.

However, even a well-written serial driver will take 10 percent or more of the available CPU time when operating continuously at 9600 baud. 9600 baud is an interrupt 960 times per second! With this sort of overhead, you can't afford to use a high level system language (C, for example) that's "almost" as good as assembler. Just because of the structure of the language (passing parameters on the stack, being well behaved with registers, needs calls to assembly language routines to fool with the interrupt mask, etc.), a good assembly language programmer not following a rigid structure can get at least twice the speed, and usually more, with assembler than with C. A difference of 10 percent or more in total CPU load is well worth the extra effort needed for assembly language.

```
   1
   2
   3
   4
 184
 185
 186  00000000  48E7C0C0          *************************************************
 187  00000004  207C00000020      * Serial I/O initialization - MC68681 DUART
 188  0000000A  303C001A          <<include MC68681.H>>
 189  0000000E  6006
 190                                      xdef    sinit
 191  00000010  2258
 192  00000012  2218              sinit:
 193  00000014  1281                      movem.l d0/d1/a0/a1,-(a7)    Save registers
 194                                      move.l  #table,a0           * get init parameter table base
 195  00000016  51C8FFF8                  move.w  #size,d0            * get count of parameters
 196  0000001A  4CDF0303                  bra     sk0_init            * do loop test before loop body
 197  0000001E  4E75
 198                              lp0_init:
 199                                      move.l  (a0)+,al            * Get register address
 200  00000020  00FF000B00000000          move.l  (a0)+,d1            * Get register contents
 201  00000028  00FF000000000010          move.b  d1,(al)             * Put command
 202  00000030  00FF000100000013
 203  00000038  00FF000100000007  sk0_init:
 204                                      dbra    d0,lp0_init         * Loop test
 205  00000040  00FF001500000010          movem.l (a7)+,d0/d1/a0/al   Restore registers
 206  00000048  00FF001100000013          rts
 207  00000050  00FF001100000007
 208                              table:
 209  00000058  00FF000D00000047  ******** Set mode of channel A ***********************
 210  00000060  00FF000F000000FE          dc.l    imr,NO_INTS
 211  00000068  00FF000900000060          dc.l    cmd_a,POINT_1       * Point to mode register 1
 212                                      dc.l    mode_a,NO_RRTS+RI_RDY+C_ERR+NO_PAR+BITS_8
 213  00000070  00FF001B00000000          dc.l    mode_a,NOR_OP+NO_TRTS+NO_CTS+STOP_1
 214                              ******** Set mode of channel B ***********************
 215  00000078  00FF000500000020          dc.l    cmd_b,POINT_1       * Point to mode register 1
 216  00000080  00FF000500000030          dc.l    mode_b,NO_RRTS+RI_RDY+C_ERR+NO_PAR+BITS_8
 217  00000088  00FF000500000040          dc.l    mode_b,NOR_OP+NO_TRTS+NO_CTS+STOP_1
 218  00000090  00FF000500000050  ******** Setup real time clock for 10mS heartbeat ****
 219  00000098  00FF000500000079          dc.l    count_h,$47
                                          dc.l    count_l,$FE
                                          dc.l    acr,SET_1+TMR_XTL
                                  ******** Set Output Port Config Register *************
                                          dc.l    opcr,ALL_OUT
                                  ******** Reset and Enable channel A ******************
                                          dc.l    cmd_a,RST_RX        * reset receiver
                                          dc.l    cmd_a,RST_TX        * reset transmitter
                                          dc.l    cmd_a,RST_ERR       * reset error status
                                          dc.l    cmd_a,RST_INT       * reset interrupts
                                          dc.l    cmd_a,BRK_OFF+T_DIS+R_EN
```

```
220 000000A0 00FF000300000066    dc.l   clock_a,B_1200
221                  ********* Reset and Enable channel B **********************************
222 000000A8 00FF001500000020    dc.l   cmd_b,RST_RX          * reset receiver
223 000000B0 00FF001500000030    dc.l   cmd_b,RST_TX          * reset transmitter
224 000000B8 00FF001500000040    dc.l   cmd_b,RST_ERR         * reset error status
225 000000C0 00FF001500000050    dc.l   cmd_b,RST_INT         * reset interrupts
226 000000C8 00FF001500000079    dc.l   cmd_b,BRK_OFF+T_DIS+R_EN
227 000000D0 00FF001300000066    dc.l   clock_b,B_1200
228                  ********* Turn on Interrupts ***************************************
229 000000D8 00FF00190000001D    dc.l   ivr,vector
230 000000E0 00FF000B0000003B    dc.l   imr,I_RX_A+I_TX_A+I_CNTR+I_RX_B+I_TX_B
231                  ********* Set up output pins **********************************
232 000000E8 00FF001D000000FF    dc.l   bit_set,$FF           * set outputs TRUE just in case
233          size    equ    (*-table)/8
234
235 000000F0                     end
```

Module SERINT.PRN

```
   1
   2        <<include MC68681.H>>

 183              xref     sinit,enqueue,dequeue
 184              xref     a_busy,b_busy,rafifo,rbfifo,tafifo,tbfifo
 185              xdef     time,a_busy,b_busy,s_vector,r_vector
 186              xdef     send_a,send_b
 187        ***********************************************************
 188        * S_VECTOR - sets up interrupt vector - saves old vector
 189        s_vector:
 190 00000000 23F900000074000000004   move.l   vector*4,o_vect  * save old vector
 191 0000000A 23FC0000002A00000074    move.l   #isrtn,vector*4  * setup interrupt vector
 192 00000014 4E75                    rts
 193        ***********************************************************
 194        * R_VECTOR - replaces original interrupt vector and shuts down
 195        *            interrupts
 196        r_vector:
 197 00000016 13FC000000FF000B        move.b   #NO_INTS,imr     * kill interrupts
 198 0000001E 23F900000004000000074   move.l   o_vect,vector*4  * replace old vector
 199 00000028 4E75                    rts
 200        ***********************************************************
 201        * ISRTN - Interrupt Service Routine for 68681
 202        isrtn:
 203 0000002A 48E78080                movem.l  d0/a0,-(a7)      * save D0 and A0
 204 0000002E 103900FF000B            move.b   isr,d0           * Get Interrupt Status Register
 205 00000034 08000001                btst     #IRX_A,d0        * look for RX first
 206 00000038 663A                    bne      rx_a
 207 0000003A 08000005                btst     #IRX_B,d0        * Look for B RX
 208 0000003E 6646                    bne      rx_b
 209 00000040 08000000                btst     #ITX_A,d0        * Next look for TX
 210 00000044 6652                    bne      tx_a
 211 00000046 08000004                btst     #ITX_B,d0        * look for B TX
 212 0000004A 66000082                bne      tx_b
 213 0000004E 08000003                btst     #ICNTR,d0        * Check for counter/timer
 214 00000052 660000D4                bne      clock
 215 00000056 08000002                btst     #DELTAA,d0       * check deltas just in case
 216 0000005A 660000AA                bne      delt_a
 217 0000005E 08000006                btst     #DELTAB,d0       * check delta B
 218 00000062 660000AE                bne      delt_b
 219 00000066 08000007                btst     #INCHNG,d0       * check input port change
 220 0000006A 660000B2                bne      in_change
```

```
221
222  0000006E  4CDF0101      isrtn2:  movem.l  (a7)+,d0/a0      * get registers back
223  00000072  4E73                   rte                       * done with ISR
224  ***************************************************************************
225
226  00000074  103900FF0007  rx_a:    move.b   rba_a,d0         * get character
227  0000007A  207C00000000           move.l   #rafifo,a0       * get right fifo
228  00000080  61000000               bsr      enqueue          * enqueue character
229  00000084  60E8                   bra      isrtn2           * recheck for more pending
230
231  ***************************************************************************
232  00000086  103900FF0017  rx_b:    move.b   rba_b,d0         * get character
233  0000008C  207C00000000           move.l   #rbfifo,a0       * get right fifo
234  00000092  61000000               bsr      enqueue          * enqueue character
235  00000096  60D6                   bra      isrtn2           * check for more pending
236  ***************************************************************************
237
238  00000098  207C00000000  tx_a:    move.l   #tafifo,a0       * get fifo
239  0000009E  61000000               bsr      dequeue          * dequeue character
240  000000A2  B1FC00000000           cmp.l    #0,a0            * test A0 for empty return
241  000000A8  6704                   beq      close_a          * if no char available, jump
242  000000AA  6112                   bsr      send_a           * otherwise, send character
243  000000AC  60C0                   bra      isrtn2           * and check for more pending
244
245  000000AE  427900000008  close_a: clr.w    a_busy           * reset busy flag
246  000000B4  13FC000800FF0005        move.b  #T_DIS,cmd_a     * shut down TX
247  000000BC  60B0                   bra      isrtn2           * and check for more pending
248
249  000000BE  13FC000400FF0005 send_a: move.b #T_EN,cmd_a      * make sure transmitter enabled
250  000000C6  13C000FF0007           move.b   d0,tba_a         * load character up
251  000000CC  4E75                   rts
252  ***************************************************************************
253
254  000000CE  207C00000000  tx_b:    move.l   #tbfifo,a0       * get fifo
255  000000D4  61000000               bsr      dequeue          * dequeue character
256  000000D8  B1FC00000000           cmp.l    #0,a0            * test A0 for empty return
257  000000DE  6704                   beq      close_b          * if no char available, jump
258  000000E0  6114                   bsr      send_b           * otherwise, send character
259  000000E2  608A                   bra      isrtn2           * and check for more pending
260                         close_b:
```

Module SERINT.PRN (continued)

```
261  000000E4  42790000000A              clr.w    b_busy             * reset busy flag
262  000000EA  13FC000800FF0015          move.b   #T_DIS,cmd_b       * shut down TX
263  000000F2  6000FF7A                  bra      isrtn2             * and check for more pending
264                               send_b:
265  000000F6  13FC000400FF0015          move.b   #T_EN,cmd_b        * make sure transmitter enabled
266  000000FE  13C00FF0017               move.b   d0,tba_b           * load character up
267  00000104  4E75                      rts
268                               ***************************************************************
269                               delt_a:
270  00000106  13FC005000FF0005          move.b   #RST_INT,cmd_a     * reset break-change interrupt
271  0000010E  6000FF5E                  bra      isrtn2
272                               ***************************************************************
273                               delt_b:
274  00000112  13FC005000FF0015          move.b   #RST_INT,cmd_b     * reset break-change interrupt
275  0000011A  6000FF52                  bra      isrtn2
276                               ***************************************************************
277                               in_change:
278  0000011E  4A3900FF0009              tst.b    ipcr               * clear interrupt status
279  00000124  6000FF48                  bra      isrtn2
280                               ***************************************************************
281                               * CLOCK - increments 10mS real time clock
282                               clock:
283  00000128  4A3900FF001F              tst.b    stp_cnt            * reset clock interrupt
284  0000012E  52B900000000              addq.l   #1,time            * increment time
285  00000134  6000FF38                  bra      isrtn2             * get out
286                               ***************************************************************
287                                        data
288  00000000  00000000         time:    dc.l     0                 * real time clock
289  00000004  00000000         o_vect:  dc.l     0                 * old interrupt vector
290  00000008  0000             a_busy:  dc.w     0                 * A transmitter in use
291  0000000A  0000             b_busy:  dc.w     0                 * B transmitter in use
292
293  0000000C                            end
```

Module ECH.PRN

```
 1          ********************************************************
 2          xref    s_vector,r_vector,enqueue,dequeue,send_a,send_b
 3          xref    a_busy,b_busy,sinit
 4
 5          xdef    rafifo,rbfifo,tafifo,tbfifo
 6
 7
 8  q_size  equ     100
 9
10          ********************************************************
11
12 00000000 303C003E    echo:   move.w  #$3E,d0     * CP/M request supervisor state
13 00000004 4E42                 trap    #2
14 00000006 2C4F                 move.l  a7,a6       * save supervisor stack
15 00000008 4E6F                 move.l  usp,a7      * get back to our regular stack
16 0000000A 2F0E                 move.l  a6,-(a7)    * put old ssp on user stack
17 0000000C 61000000             bsr     s_vector    * install serial I/O vector
18 00000010 61000000             bsr     sinit       * setup serial chip
19
20 00000014 207C0000000  lpl:    move.l  #rafifo,a0  * check for chars waiting on A
21 0000001A 61000078             bsr     d_queue     * check queue
22 0000001E B1FC00000000         cmp.l   #0,a0       * check for error return
23 00000024 6708                 beq     skl_eko     * jump if no chars waiting
24 00000026 B03C001A             cmp.b   #$1a,d0     * look for exit flag
25 0000002A 671C                 beq     sk2_eko     * exit in ^Z received
26 0000002C 6122                 bsr     a_xmit      * transmit D0.W otherwise
27
28 0000002E 207C0000006C skl_eko: move.l #rbfifo,a0  * check for B chars received
29 00000034 615E                 bsr     d_queue     * check queue
30 00000036 B1FC00000000         cmp.l   #0,a0       * check for error return
31 0000003C 67D6                 beq     lpl         * restart on error
32 0000003E B03C001A             cmp.b   #$1a,d0     * look for exit flag
33 00000042 6704                 beq     sk2_eko     * exit in ^Z received
34 00000044 612C                 bsr     b_xmit      * send the data
35 00000046 60CC                 bra     lpl         * and repeat
36
37 00000048 61000000     sk2_eko: bsr    r_vector    * replace old vector
38 0000004C 4240                 clr.w   d0          * set reset system function
39 0000004E 4E42                 trap    #2          * return to CP/M system
40          ********************************************************
```

Module ECH.PRN (continued)

```
41
42  00000050  40E7          a_xmit:  move.w  sr,-(a7)          * save status register
43  00000052  007C0700               ori     #$0700,sr         * disable interrupts
44  00000056  4AF900000000           tas     a_busy            * is the transmitter active?
45  0000005C  670C                   beq     skl_sa            * no, go send it
46  0000005E  207C000000D8           move.l  #tafifo,a0        * need to enqueue it
47  00000064  61000000               bsr     enqueue           * so we do.
48  00000068  6004                   bra     sk2_sa            * exit
49
50  0000006A  61000000      skl_sa:  bsr     send_a            * prime the transmitter
51
52  0000006E  46DF          sk2_sa:  move.w  (a7)+,sr          * restore status & ints
53  00000070  4E75                   rts
54
55  ********************************************************************
56  00000072  40E7          b_xmit:  move.w  sr,-(a7)          * save status register
57  00000074  007C0700               ori     #$0700,sr         * disable interrupts
58  00000078  4AF900000000           tas     b_busy            * is the transmitter active?
59  0000007E  670C                   beq     skl_sb            * no, go send it
60  00000080  207C00000144           move.l  #tbfifo,a0        * need to enqueue it
61  00000086  61000000               bsr     enqueue           * so we do.
62  0000008A  6004                   bra     sk2_sb            * exit
63
64  0000008C  61000000      skl_sb:  bsr     send_b            * prime the transmitter
65
66  00000090  46DF          sk2_sb:  move.w  (a7)+,sr          * restore status & ints
67  00000092  4E75                   rts
68
69  ********************************************************************
70  00000094  40E7          d_queue: move.w  sr,-(a7)          * save status register
71  00000096  007C0700               ori.w   #$0700,sr         * disable interrupts
72  0000009A  61000000               bsr     dequeue           * check queue
73  0000009E  46DF                   move.w  (a7)+,sr          * restore status & ints
74  000000A0  4E75                   rts
75
76  ********************************************************************
                              * Serial I/O Queues
                              data
77  00000000
78
79  00000000  0000          rafifo:  dc.w    0
80  00000002  0000                   dc.w    0
```

```
 81 00000004 0064              dc.w    q_size
 82 00000006 0000              dc.w    0
 83 00000008                   ds.b    q_size
 84                            even
 85
 86 0000006C 0000    rbfifo:   dc.w    0
 87 0000006E 0000              dc.w    0
 88 00000070 0064              dc.w    q_size
 89 00000072 0000              dc.w    0
 90 00000074                   ds.b    q_size
 91                            even
 92
 93 000000D8 0000    tafifo:   dc.w    0
 94 000000DA 0000              dc.w    0
 95 000000DC 0064              dc.w    q_size
 96 000000DE 0000              dc.w    0
 97 000000E0                   ds.b    q_size
 98                            even
 99
100 00000144 0000    tbfifo:   dc.w    0
101 00000146 0000              dc.w    0
102 00000148 0064              dc.w    q_size
103 0000014A 0000              dc.w    0
104 0000014C                   ds.b    q_size
105                            even
106
107 000001B0                   end
```

19

The 68010
and 68020 Processors

In this chapter we expand the 68000 instruction set to include the similar but more powerful 68010 and 68020 processors. We do this not to provide a comprehensive reference to these two processors, but to allow you to plan for code transportability. Ideally, this chapter will also tie together and reinforce some of the asides we've placed in the earlier chapters.

We have included substantially more detail on the 68010, as this chip is a pin-for-pin replacement for the 68000. If you already have a 68000, you are more likely to see an upgrade from a 68000 to a 68010 than you are from 68000/68010 to 68020. The 68020 is packaged in a 120-pin pin grid array ("bed of nails") package and has some substantial data and address bus differences from its siblings. While the 68010 can be covered reasonably well in a single chapter, the 68020 needs a more exhaustive treatment to do it justice.

The 68010 Processor

The 68000 has one flaw that prevents it from running as a virtual system: the MOVE from SR instruction is not privileged. Because this instruction isn't privileged, any program can tell at any time if the CPU is in system mode or user mode. This prevents you from loading several operating systems in at a time and running them independently in their own memory and processing time partitions as user programs, with a "super operating system" supervising the whole process. The 68010 corrects this flow and adds other features as well.

Most of the enhancements to the 68010 are designed to improve the performance of a virtual system. If you aren't planning on using these features, or aren't writing exception handlers for eventual use on a 68010, just detach this chapter from the binding and use it to line your bird cage.

Except for a difference in stack format for BUS ERROR and ADDRESS ERROR exceptions, code that runs on a 68000 will run unchanged on a 68010.

Additions to the 68010

The 68010 has three more registers than the 68000. They are the Vector Base Register (VBR), the Source Function Code (SFC) register, and the Destination Function Code (DFC) register. These registers, as well as the User Stack Pointer (USP), are all accessed with the privileged instruction MOVEC (Move Control).

Other features of the 68010 include a Return and Deallocate instruction, two stack formats, and hardware loop optimization.

The Vector Base Register

The VBR is used to map the vector table into different portions of memory. On hardware reset, this register is set to zero, and if the VBR is never changed, the 68010 acts just like the 68000. If you want to map the vector table to another part of memory, you can load a new address into the VBR, and all exception vectors will have this value added to the computed vector address.

This feature allows multiple operating systems to each have their own vector tables. In the 68000, each time the operating system context is changed, you would have to save and reload the vector table, or else instruct a memory management unit (MMU) to translate addresses for you. Either way adds appreciably to the overhead in a context switch.

In order to fully utilize this feature of the 68010, you need to have a memory management unit protecting the memory from $000000 to $0003FF. Otherwise, operating systems (which have an irritating habit of fooling with the vector table) running in your virtual machine will update their table in the wrong place. By simulating a failed access to the "standard" vector table, the 68010 can place a vector into the correct virtual table for the operating system currently in control.

The Source and Destination Function Code Registers

(Much of this narrative is simply untrue. It is a particularly dry subject, and we got carried away while trying to spice it up a little. As the technical information is correct, we decided to leave it as it is. We hope that you—and the folks at Motorola—take this in the spirit in which it is intended.)

As you may or may not remember, while discussing exception stack formats in Chapter 11, we briefly touched on a hardware feature of the 68000 regarding function codes. The 68000 and the 68010 have three output pins called FC0, FC1, and FC2. These pins provide external hardware with information about what sort of memory reference is being made. In the 68000 and 68010, four unique codes tell the outside world whether the access is from supervisor or user code, and whether the access is to program or data memory. Normally, these pins are connected to a memory management unit, or left unconnected.

It seems that the hardware types who wrote the 68000 manual, who really don't care what kind of hoops we software types have to jump through, thought that they could hang 64 megabytes of memory on a 68000 by decoding these function code pins into four 16-megabyte banks, one for user program, one for user data, one for supervisor program, and one for supervisor data. They probably talked some poor Pascal programmer, who of course didn't know any better, into coming to Management with them when they presented the idea. No doubt the guy who had the idea in the first place came over from Intel. (You old timers may remember an obscure passage in the 8080 manual along the same lines. That was what led to the glut of 256K 8080 systems.)

The problem, of course, is that there's no way to move data between these banks. For example: The supervisor drags a hunk of user program in from disk, into its data space. Then it tries to load it into the user program space using a MOVE (A0)+, (A1)+ sort of loop. The external hardware sees a supervisor data function code, and writes into the supervisor data area. Murphy's Law says it has to hit in the active part of the supervisor stack, and your supervisor program takes off into never-never land.

Never daunted, the hardware types at Motorola get another whack at it when they design the 68010. "I know what we'll do," exclaims the guy who had the function code bank switching idea in the first place, "we'll add a couple of instructions that will assert arbitrary function codes when we do data moves to memory!"

Grabbing the poor Pascal programmer again, who by now has graduated from Pascal to Ada, off they go to Management. Thus was born the Move Address Space (MOVES) instruction and the SFC and DFC registers.

The two registers, each 3 bits long, contain the function codes to assert on the function code pins when the MOVES instruction makes a memory reference. MOVES is a privileged instruction.

By the way, since there are three pins, with eight combinations of states, and only five assigned address spaces, you could have another 48 megabytes of RAM out there accessible only to a MOVES instruction . . . Oh golly, what fun.

Actually, there are very useful purposes to these function codes. For example, one of the big complaints about the earlier Motorola processors was the lack of an I/O address space like the Intel processor had. The 8080 has a special status output when the IN port and OUT port instructions are executed, so that port $20 is distinct from address $20. Without this I/O address space, the already limited 64K memory map has devices mapped into it, making those addresses unavailable for RAM or ROM.

If you stop and think about it, unused 68010 function codes can be assigned to an I/O address space, and the MOVES instruction is then very similar to the Intel IN and OUT instructions. Because there are three unassigned function codes, this still leaves two function codes for whatever bizarre extended memory scheme your hardware folks slap together.

Doing this makes the I/O map privileged, of course, but that's consistent with the 68K family protection schemes anyhow, and can probably be considered a feature rather than a drawback.

The RTD Instruction

Apparently taking a page from the Intel 8086 manual (Intel apparently took a page from the Motorola 68000 manual with the ENTER and LEAVE 80286 instructions), Motorola added the Return and Deallocate (RTD) Instruction to the 68010. This instruction pops the return address after a subroutine, then pops a specified number of parameters from the top of the stack before returning to the caller, cleaning up after the subroutine call.

This works great if you're using a high level language like Pascal that has a fixed number of parameters in a subprogram call, but is not so great for a language like C that allows a variable number of parameters to a function call. In assembler you make your own rules, of course.

The tradeoff is code size against subroutine flexibility. Without the RTD instruction, if you call a subroutine 500 times, you need stack cleanup in 500 places. With the RTD instruction, you are constrained to a fixed number of parameters to a subroutine.

Our preference is to not use the RTD type instructions and to handle cleanup after the call. Besides, if you remember our discussion of parameter passing, in most cases you can just leave the stuff on the stack anyhow. It'll go away when you unlink the calling subroutine.

The 68010 Exception Stack

As with the 68000, the 68010 has two different stack formats. Unfortunately, the 68010's formats are not exactly the same as the 68000's.

The short form stack (see Figure 19-1) is similar to the 68000's short form stack, and is used for all exceptions except for BUSERR and ADDRESS ERROR. The difference in the 68010 stack frame is the addition of one more word, at the bottom of the stack. This word has a special flag in bits 31 through 28, used by the RTE instruction, and in bits 27 through 0 the processor places the the displacement into the exception vector table.

This displacement allows a system program to install a single default vector to catch unhandled exceptions. The default handler can determine from the displacement what vector was taken. At three in the morning, it's infinitely preferable to have an error message of "Unhandled Exception $FE" as opposed to "Unhandled Exception—Try and Guess Which One" (or worse, no message at all).

As long as 68000 code doesn't depend on the supervisor stack being only three words deep on an exception (for example, if parameters are pushed before a TRAP instruction), exception handlers for the short form exceptions will run on either a 68000 or 68010.

The long form stack (see Figure 19-2) is much different from the 68000 stack. First, the top of the stack is identical to the short format, with a different flag placed into the high nibble of word +6 of the stack frame.

```
              15  14  13  12  11  10  9   8   7   6   5   4   3   2   1   0
       +----------------------------------------------------------------------+
    +0 | Status Register (before exception)                                   |
       +----------------------------------------------------------------------+
    +2 |                                  High                                 |
       + - Program Counter - - - - - - - - - - - - - - - - - - - - - - - - - +
    +4 |                                  Low                                  |
       +---+---+---+---+------------------------------------------------------+
    +6 | 0 | 0 | 0 | 0 |              Vector Offset                           |
       +---+---+---+---+------------------------------------------------------+
```

FIGURE 19-1.   68010 Exception Stack – Short Format

```
              15  14  13  12  11  10  9   8   7   6   5   4   3   2   1   0
       +----------------------------------------------------------------------+
    +0 | Status Register (before exception)                                   |
       +----------------------------------------------------------------------+
    +2 |                                  High                                 |
       + - Program Counter - - - - - - - - - - - - - - - - - - - - - - - - - +
    +4 |                                  Low                                  |
       +---+---+---+---+------------------------------------------------------+
    +6 | 1 | 0 | 0 | 0 |              Vector Offset                           |
       +---+---+---+---+---+---+---+---+---+--------------------+-------------+
    +8 |R/R|   |I-F|D-F|RMW|H-B|BYT|R/W|                    | Fnct. Cd    |
       +---+---+---+---+---+---+---+---+--------------------+-------------+
   +10 | Fault Address High Word                                              |
       +----------------------------------------------------------------------+
   +12 | Fault Address Low Word                                               |
       +----------------------------------------------------------------------+
   +14 | Reserved                                                             |
       +----------------------------------------------------------------------+
   +16 | Data Output Buffer                                                   |
       +----------------------------------------------------------------------+
   +18 | Reserved                                                             |
       +----------------------------------------------------------------------+
   +20 | Data Input Buffer                                                    |
       +----------------------------------------------------------------------+
   +22 | Reserved                                                             |
       +----------------------------------------------------------------------+
   +24 | Instruction Input Buffer                                             |
       +----------------------------------------------------------------------+
   +26 | Internal Information ends                                            |
       +----------------------------------------------------------------------+
       |             |                |                |                      |
       +----------------------------------------------------------------------+
   +56 | Internal Information ends                                            |
       +----------------------------------------------------------------------+
```

Special Status Word (+8) Definitions

```
R/R   Re-Run Failed Access.
I-F   Instruction Fetch: 1 = Instruction Buffer input.
D-F   Data Fetch: 1 = Data buffer I/O.
RMW   Read-Modify-Write: 1 = RMW failed.
H-B   High Byte: 1 = High byte, 0 = Low byte.
BYT   Byte access: 1 = Byte access failed, 0 = Word access failed.
R/W   Read/Write: 1 = Read failed, 0 = Write Failed.
```

FIGURE 19-2.   68010 Exception Stack–Long Format

Second, and more important, the processor dumps a lot of extra information on the stack for bus errors and address errors. This extra information makes it easy to manage a virtual memory machine. Two options are available to a virtual machine: an access can be simulated, or it can be rerun (presumably after correcting whatever problem caused the access failure).

Using the failure status word (+6) the cause of a failure can be determined. There is enough information in this status word to correct or simulate failed accesses.

The Rerun bit is cleared when the stack is set up by the processor. If this bit is clear when the RTE is executed, the processor will attempt to rerun the failed access. If the Rerun bit is set, the processor assumes the access has been simulated.

The Instruction Fetch bit indicates that the processor was loading the instruction buffer when the failure occurred. When simulating accesses, the instruction buffer in the stack must be loaded with the simulated data.

The Data Fetch bit indicates that the processor was loading the data input buffer. When simulating the access, you have to load the data input buffer in the stack with the simulated data.

Instruction Fetch and Data Fetch are not mutually exclusive. If both are set, both buffers must be loaded.

The Byte Access bit is set if the failed access was a byte. If the Byte Access flag is set, the High Byte flag tells you whether the byte is the high byte or low byte.

The RMW (Read-Modify-Write) bit indicates a failed RMW cycle. TAS is one instruction that uses an RMW cycle, MOVE from SR is another. If the instruction is rerun, the entire RMW cycle repeats. If simulating this access, you need to load the simulated data into the input buffer on the stack, plus you need to set the condition codes image on the stack and the memory operand to the values appropriate to the instruction.

The function codes (bits 2 through 0) are the same as for the 68000. These codes are useful if external hardware decodes these bits for multiple address spaces, or if a MMU is present.

68010 Loop Speedup

Another optimization for the 68010 is the hardware loop mode optimization. A two-instruction sequence consisting of a one-word instruction and a DBcc instruction with a displacement of −4 is executed entirely without refetching the two instructions. This lets you write some loops that really scream. Memory block moves and searches are obvious candidates.

Additions to the 68010 Instruction Set

The MOVE from CCR Instruction

MOVE from CCR moves the CCR to a word-sized effective address operand. The high byte of the effective address destination is set to zeros.

Addressing modes allowed for the effective address operand are all except PC-relative and Immediate. No condition codes are affected.

Assembler Syntax:

```
MOVE. W    CCR, ⟨EA⟩
```

The MOVE Control Register Instruction

MOVEC (MOVE Control Register) is a privileged instruction. This copies data between any of the control register VBR, DFC, USP, or SFC and any data or address registers. The operation size is always 32 bits. When copying from the 3-bit registers, bits 3 to 31 are zeroed. No condition codes are affected.

Assembler Syntax:

```
MOVEC. L    Rc, Rn
MOVEC. L    Rn, Rc
```

The MOVE Address Space Instruction

MOVES (Move to/from Address Space) is a privileged instruction. A transfer is made between memory and any address or data register. If memory is used as a source, the function codes asserted externally are taken from the SFC register, if memory is the destination the function codes are taken from the DFC register. No condition codes are affected, but all other standard rules for MOVE apply (e.g., no byte operations on address registers).

Assembler Syntax:

[NOTE: . s = { . B .W. L}]

MOVES. s   Rn, ⟨EA⟩

MOVES. s   ⟨EA⟩, Rn

Addressing Modes for ⟨EA⟩:

		(An)	(An)+
−(An)	d(An)	d(An, xi)	xxx. W
xxx. L			

The RTD Instruction

RTD (Return and Deallocate) executes a subroutine return, and also adjusts the stack pointer to deallocate parameters pushed by the caller. A 16-bit displacement is sign-extended and added to the stack pointer after the return address is popped. Note that due to sign extension the maximum displacement is +32766. Note also that a negative displacement will cause days of bug-hunting. Also, take care to use even displacements only. No condition codes are affected.

Assembler Syntax:

RTD   #xxx

The 68020 Processor

As we indicated in the introduction to this chapter, this section will be fairly brief. It's essentially a listing of the enhancements included in the 68020, with some notes on the impact to code you want to eventually port to a 68020.

Address/Data Bus

The 68020 has a 32-bit address bus, as opposed to the 24-bit bus of the 68000/68010. This means that the upper byte of addresses is now significant, where before this byte was discarded. This may cause trouble in certain cases where you were getting away with leaving garbage in the top byte of address registers, although these cases will be rare. You really would have had to work at sloppy or convoluted code (not that this is rare among assembly language programmers).

It is also possible that you'll need to reassemble or recompile source code, if you made absolute references to high memory locations in a 68000/68010. Most assemblers will convert absolute references to the top 32K of memory to absolute short addressing. These are not the same absolute addresses in the 68020. Again, this is rare.

The 68020 also has a dynamically sized data bus of up to 32 bits wide. This shouldn't present any problems with upward compatibility. However, when they put in the new bus interface they also eliminated all alignment restrictions except that instructions must still be on even addresses, so code may run fine on a 68020 but give address error exceptions when ported down to a 68000/68010.

Instruction Cache

The 68020 includes an on-chip 256-byte instruction cache. This cache stores instructions within a page of code, and can speed up small loops quite a bit. Caching only speeds things up; there is never a speed penalty because of the cache. The only thing to watch out for is self-modifying code. If you do manage to write code that depends on self-modification, it may fail because the modified code is never refetched.

Self-modifying code is generally frowned upon anyhow. It's about as popular with the 68K designers as the thought of CP/M-68K on the Macintosh is with the folks at Apple—the design philosophies just don't mesh.

Two new cache registers have been added to the 68020 to control the cache operation.

New Addressing Modes

Six new addressing modes have also been added. They are all based on address register indirect or PC-relative modes, and offer scaling of data sizes when using an index, larger displacements, and a memory-indirect mode. These modes are useful mostly for handling arrays and table-based software.

Trace Bits

A new trace bit has been added to allow a different level of control when tracing. Trace bit T1, bit 15 of the status register, is the same as the 68000/68010 T bit, also bit 15 of SR. When set, trace bit T0, bit 14 of SR, will generate a trace exception only when a change in program control occurs, such as a branch or subroutine call.

Coprocessor Support

The 68020 includes new instructions with the necessary hardware interaction to support coprocessors.

When a coprocessor is present, function code 111 is used to signal coprocessor communications, and is not available for other uses.

The coprocessor instructions use op code $Fxxx, an unimplemented instruction on the 68000/68010. Op code $Fxxx is sometimes used for simulated instructions or for debugger breakpoints on the 68000/68010.

Emulators for the coprocessors can be written for any of the 68K family processors if desired.

Master Bit

A new mode control bit has been added to supplement the user/supervisor. This bit essentially controls what stack is used by interrupt service routines. The supervisor stack pointer of the 68000/68010 has been replaced by two new stacks, a master stack pointer and an interrupt stack pointer.

Displacements

The PC relative branch instructions (BRA, Bcc, BSR) now support 8-, 16-, and 32-bit displacements. The assembler will usually choose the most efficient displacement mode for the job, although external references will most likely be given 32-bit displacements. With the 32-bit displacements it is much easier to write very large relocatable code modules. With the 68000/68010, a maximum displacement of $7FFF was allowed; with the 68020, a displacement can reach any point in memory. Due to the way this feature is implemented, your code should be recompiled with a 68020 assembler.

The LINK instruction is also extended to allow a 32-bit displacement if desired.

Division and Multiplication

The divide and multiply instructions have been extended to allow larger operands. The multiply instructions can multiply two 32-bit numbers to produce a 64-bit number, and the divide instructions can divide a 64-bit number by a 32-bit number. Several intermediate enhancements to the 68000/68010 multiply and divide operand formats are also available.

Sign Extension

A new instruction allows sign-extending a byte to a longword. This requires two instructions on the 68000/68010.

Addressing modes for TST and CMPI

The legal addressing modes for CMPI and TST have been extended to allow the PC-relative and address register direct modes.

Miscellaneous New Instructions and Enhancements

The CHK instruction has been expanded to support features found in new high level languages (such as Ada). CHK will now test a longword, and a new CHK2 instruction will test against an upper and lower bound in one instruction.

A CMP2 instruction has been added to compare a register against two bounds, as the CHK2 instruction does, except that CMP2 sets flags instead of taking a CHK exception.

Two new instructions, CAS and CAS2, are used in mutual exclusion schemes for multitasking or multiprocessor systems. These instructions are extensions to the TAS instruction.

A conditional TRAP instruction, TRAPcc, has been added, also presumably to support high level language constructs. This instruction uses the same formats as the Bcc instruction.

Instructions to pack and unpack ASCII or EBCDIC-coded numbers into BCD format are also provided.

Perhaps the most interesting new instructions are the bit-field instructions. Eight new instructions operate on a range of bits from either a data register or a memory byte. Four instructions are extensions to the bit instructions (bit-field-set, bit-field-clear, bit-field-test-and-complement, and bit-field-test), and the other four insert and extract signed or unsigned bit fields. Bit fields are 1 to 32 bits wide, and can be aligned arbitrarily within the operand. For example, the second byte of D0 could be extracted and moved to memory with the following instruction:

```
BFEXTU    DO[8:15], (AO)
```

These bit-field instructions can greatly speed up the operation of languages like Ada and C, that allow bit fields to be specified as part of the language standard. These constructions allow for writing device drivers in high level languages and for dense memory usage without resorting to strange, error-prone and time consuming tricks, not to mention the advantages in more applications-oriented problems like bit-mapped graphics.

The 68020 is a fast and fun processor, and our treatment of it here in no way covers it in detail. We suggest that you obtain the manufacturer's data book if you are fortunate enough to have one of these processors available to play with.

20

The Last Step

The last step in program development is the debugging of the program. (Actually, it's customer support, but who wants to quibble?) Like any other processor, the 68000 is susceptible to its own peculiar programming errors, as well as the standard mistakes everyone makes on all processors. This chapter provides a checklist for debugging, and a look at some of the hardware and software tools used in the debugging process.

Let's start with programming errors. We find that we can read a list of potential problems many times, and it still doesn't sink in. Some late night we'll still make the same dumb mistakes, and we'll look at the code, and we won't see the problem for a couple of days. Usually the hardest bugs to find are the simplest, or they're caused by the assembler or linker.

Here are some of the common errors we make, with the symptoms the computer displays when the bug manifests itself.

The Unbalanced Stack

This is the stupidest error of all, and probably the most common. You push one more thing than you pop, or vice-versa. The symptom is usually an address error exception when you run through the routine that unbalances the stack, although really odd things will happen if you accidentally pop the return address and there's another valid return address underneath.

The Unsized Instruction

This is a devious error caused by forgetting to put a size attribute on an instruction mnemonic. For example, the following instruction:

```
MOVE    DO, AO
```

Usually, the assembler will default the size attribute to "word." The example above will probably be converted to:

```
MOVE. W    DO, AO
```

This may or may not be what you intended. If the address in D0 is in the lowest or highest 32K of the address space, there won't be any problem. If the address is outside this space, only the word portion of D0 is used, but it's sign-extended to 32 bits. This error doesn't have any typical symptoms, and usually can only be found by looking through your code at least ten times.

A less common but even harder to find error is the wrongly sized instruction—you didn't forget the size attribute, you just used the wrong one.

The Backwards Compare

Because the 68000 syntax puts the source operand to the left of the destination operand, the sense of the compare instructions seems to be backwards. This will cause program control to seem to be working backwards. If you're even slightly dyslexic, as we are, this problem will plague you as long as you program the 68K—it doesn't get better, you just get used to it.

The Backwards Operand

This problem usually happens to programmers used to writing in Intel or Zilog assembly languages. It normally occurs when the mind wanders when coding a simple and well-understood solution. About halfway through the code, your fingers go on automatic and take over. What happens is your fingers, being used to a source operand to the right and a destination operand to the left sort of syntax, start putting the operand backwards. When you come to and realize what they've done, you go back and correct most of the mistakes, but you miss one or two.

The Misaligned Instruction

Most 68000 assemblers are designed as the back end of a C compiler, and don't get much of a workout from actual assembly language programmers—they usually are just fed the output of a C code generator. Code generators don't usually do much fancy stuff, and so the code for one program is usually pretty similar to the code from another. This means that all the bugs aren't wrung out of the assembler.

One of the places this will show up is in instruction alignments. If an odd number of byte constants (such as strings) are assembled, most assemblers are supposed to realign the instruction counter on an even address after the byte constants. In some cases, though, this doesn't happen, and instructions get aligned on odd addresses. The symptom is an address error exception. Most often this will occur as the first procedure in a source module is called, although if you interleave constants and procedures in a source module, it can happen as you call any procedure that follows constant data. In the case where the first procedure in the source module is blowing up as you call it, the problem is usually in the module immediately preceeding the subject module in the link list.

It is a good idea to follow every byte constant definition with an alignment-forcing pseudo-op, usually called "EVEN" or "ALIGN." In the YASE examples in this book, we have also used a "DC.W 0" after each of our byte constant definitions, because we port our 68K code between two assemblers that have different alignment pseudo-ops. The definition of the word constant seems to force realignment in both assemblers.

The Loop-Off-by-One Syndrome

A common problem is a loop executing one too many times, or one too few times. This is normally a conceptual error and not much can be done to guard against it. One thing that helps some is to always construct a DBRA-type loop so that the entry into the loop is by jumping to the DRBA, and not by falling in at the top. This at least ensures that the register that controls the loop will contain the number of times the loop body is to be executed, and not that number plus one.

The Inconsistent Definition

This problem is not unique to assembler—in fact, the only computer language that really addresses this problem by providing specific language constructs is Ada. The problem comes from declaring constants or other values in more than one source module, and failing to update all copies when one gets changed.

For example, suppose you declare equates to define a record structure in several different source files, or even worse, you hard-code literal offsets in effective addresses. Later, you find that you need to change one component of the record from word to longword. You then update the equates in most of the places, but forget one source file. The forgotten code will be thinking apples when the rest of the program is thinking oranges.

This is a particularly hard problem to find, because as you read the source code you will see the right things in the part of the code you're looking at—who ever goes back to look at constants?

The cure is relatively simple. You rigorously and dogmatically adhere to the principle that objects are to be declared in one and only one spot, and you never make an exception to this rule. This means that you will have to write "include," or "header," files to declare all the equates that are used by more than one source module.

In the case of the CP/M-68K assembler, and probably others, this is more difficult than it may seem. The CP/M-68K assembler does not allow for included files, and a preprocessor needs to be written to merge header files into the source before feeding them to the assembler. This is relatively easy. Some people use the C preprocessor to manage this process, thereby also gaining the C macro capability as well. However, the C preprocessor will leave its own marks on the file, in the form of #line directives to resync the source line numbers to the master source file, and these need to be disabled by a command line switch (if available), or a second preprocessor has to be written to remove the new directives from the file.

It's not good enough just to read the header file into the source file with your text editor, either. This still leaves you with the update problem as the include file is changed—you have to go back through all the sources deleting and rereading whenever the header file is changed.

If you do write a preprocessor, take our advice and write it in C. This is the sort of program that C is really good at, is not time-critical, and can be written in an hour or so. We have a listing of the preprocessor we wrote in Figure 20-1. It just looks for a pound sign in column 1 of the assembly source code. When it finds one, it considers the rest of the line to be a filename for an include file, and opens and reads in the include file. This is recursive—include files can be nested until the C runtime runs out of file control blocks.

Debugging Tools

These are not all of the possible errors that can occur when writing assembler code—they are just the most common semantic errors we encounter when we write code. You will doubtless have your own favorite errors that you develop as you write code, and you'll have to become good at finding out why your program fails, and where it's failing. There are a number of tools available for debugging.

There are three basic aids to the solitary debugging of assembly language programs: software probes; software debuggers; and hardware debuggers. We'll look at each of these three basic alternatives. If you aren't alone, a really valuable technique is the "fresh look" by an uninvolved party—the "code walkthrough." We won't go into this fourth alternative, as we find that most of our debugging is done at times and in places where uninvolved parties are not available. Well, we will say one thing—if you do use an outsider to review your code, don't hang over their shoulder pointing out the code flow. Many times, you have overlooked a simple problem over and over, and with your prompting, the outsider will also overlook it.

```
/* ASM file preprocessor         */

#include <stdio.h>
FILE *fopen();

main( argc, argv )
    int argc;
    char *argv[];
{
    FILE *output;

        if( argc != 3 )
        {
                printf( "\nError: Two args only" );
                exit( 0 );
        }
        if( (output = fopen( argv[ 2 ], "w" )) == NULL )
        {
                printf( "\nError: Can't open %s", argv[ 2 ] );
                exit( 0 );
        }
        copy( argv[ 1 ], output );
        fclose( output );
}

copy( str, stream )
    char *str;
    FILE *stream;
{
    FILE *input;
    char input_line[ 132 ];

        if( (input = fopen( str, "r" )) == NULL )
        {
                printf( "\nError: Can't open %s", argv[ 1 ] );
                fclose( output );
                exit( 0 );
        }
        for( ; ; )
        {
                if( fgets( input_line, 132, input ) == NULL )
                {
                        fclose( input );
                        return;
                }
                if( input_line[ 0 ] == '#' )
                        copy( input_line+1, output );
                else
                        fputs( input_line, output );

        }
}
```

FIGURE 20-1. AP.C

Software Debug Probes

When things aren't going right in a particular piece of code, one way to find out why is with a software probe—one or more pieces of code embedded in the problem area to dump out results, or to trap conditions and somehow display them to you.

For example, suppose you have a simple routine to compute square roots. Every now and then, you think it is computing an incorrect solution, but you're not sure, and you think the code is correct. You could install a probe to print the parameter on entry to the routine, and the answer on exit. Then, you run the program and watch the output as the routine is called, and check the results of each computation.

Take another case: you think that a decision path is being incorrectly executed. You can install a probe to dump the criterion for the decision just before the path branches, and then print "I'm here" messages at the top of each of the path branches.

Software probes are much less useful in assembly language than in a high order language. The major problem is that they are intrusive—they change the timing of the routine, and they can potentially introduce more errors as flags or registers get stepped on by accident. A high order language takes care of the flags and registers for you, so software probes make more sense.

Perhaps a better solution is to make sure that the bugs don't occur. Write a test executive for each module, and test and debug at the module level. We realize that you probably won't—there's something about assembler programmers that resists validation testing. Just a thought. Assembler programmers are more likely to use the next debugging aid—the software debugger.

Software Debuggers

Anyone who spends any amount of time writing assembly language programs will become intimately familiar with the system software debugger. A software debugger is a debugger that runs in supervisor mode and allows your program to run underneath it. The features of these debuggers can vary widely, but all of them have certain things in common.

The single most valuable feature of a software debugger is the ability to single-step a program. When single-stepping, the debugger executes one instruction of the target program, and then stops and lets you look at and/or change the registers or memory. Most debuggers will also step over calls to subroutines with a special command or switch, so you can start tracing your program at the top level, and narrow the problem down quickly to a module. You then repeat at the top level of the suspect module until you get to the lowest level of the program.

A feature similar to the single step, but implemented differently, is the breakpoint. A breakpoint is a place in the program where you decide that execution should stop. For example, if you are still having trouble with that pesky square root function, you could set a breakpoint at the start of the square root function. You then start the program at the normal entry point, and when the square root function is called, execution halts. At this point you can examine or change registers and memory, just as for single step, or set another breakpoint. Or, you may want to go through the routine in single-step to verify that the flow goes the way you designed it.

Breakpoints are implemented in software debuggers by placing illegal instructions at the address you specify as the breakpoint. Most debuggers allow more than one breakpoint, and most make a distinction between a temporary breakpoint, which "goes away" the first time you break on it, and permanent breakpoints, which stay put until you request their removal. The debugger will replace the original contents of the breakpointed instructions each time execution stops, so if you examine the memory it has the right stuff there.

Note that because of this technique, you must place a breakpoint on top of a valid instruction that is executed as an instruction. If the breakpoint is not fetched as an op code, it won't cause a breakpoint exception. Common things that can cause the breakpoint to not be fetched as an op code include operator error (you tell the assembler the wrong spot) and jumps that land on the extension words of the previous instruction, causing the breakpoint to be fetched as an extension word.

Most debuggers will also disassemble code for you too. Many times you can find problems by comparing the disassembled code to the source. This is how we usually find the "unsized instruction" problem. This will also show you the effects of "loose pointers," that spray garbage into your code space and corrupt the program.

Certain types of programs are hard to debug with a software debugger. Unfortunately, these are the types of programs that almost have to be coded in assembler. Interrupt service routines (ISRs) are a prime example. You can't single-step up to an ISR, because the recognition of the interrupt disables the trace flag in the status register.

If you need to debug an ISR (and trust us, if you write one you *will* need to debug it), you almost are forced to use breakpoints to regain control when the ISR is executed. By the time you can respond to the breakpoint, the exception being serviced will almost certainly be stale.

Take a serial I/O driver, for example. If you break on the entry to the received-data ISR, by the time the breakpoint message is displayed the receiver will probably have been overrun by subsequent characters. If you break on the transmitter buffer empty interrupt, the transmitter shift register will also be empty by the time you can read the status register from the debugging console, or can single-step through the code in the ISR that reads the status register. This changes the problem. It is better either to design the ISR with testability in mind, or to modify the code slightly to provide good targets for breakpoint instructions. If you do modify the code, leave the modifications in, if at all possible, after testing is completed.

While not as intrusive as software probes, software debuggers are somewhat intrusive because of the way breakpoints are implemented. For example, it is very common in military applications to run a checksum or CRC on the code of the program. If breakpoints are installed, the checksum or CRC will be incorrect, causing error handlers to be called when in fact nothing is really wrong.

Software debugging also does not work on ROM-based code. Single-stepping will work, if the exception vector table is either in RAM or has the debugger hooks installed in ROM, but breakpoints don't work. There are software debuggers that will single-step up to breakpoints, but these can't run in realtime, or trace through TRAPs or exceptions. For these types of problems, you need to move up to the next level of debuggers: the hardware debugger.

The Hardware Debugger

Hardware debugging systems represent the ultimate debugging aid. (Excepting, of course, junior engineers, if you have some available to do the debugging for you.) Hardware debuggers in their minimal configuration usually consist of a host machine of some sort, with a debugging console, a mass-storage device for the code under test, and an emulation pod of some sort.

The emulation pod is a device that plugs into the target computer in place of the processor. The pod can be made to act just like a 68000, including all bus signals, and can operate at the normal speed of the processor. In addition, it has the ability to download code from the host machine into the target memory, or to provide simulated memory to take the place of ROM in the target's address map. The most important feature is extra instrumentation added to the pod to cause hardware breakpoints, and to record bus cycles.

Of course, this stuff isn't cheap. Hardware debuggers in any sort of useful configuration are not likely to be found in the home. If you plan on any sort of commercial venture involving embedded or realtime processing, though, it's well worth the cost. A good hardware debugger will cut the amount of time spent in integration and final debug by at least 500 percent over the next-best alternative.

The reason hardware debuggers are so good is because they can provide completely nonintrusive debugging. Take our serial interrupt service routine as an example. If it seems not to be working for some reason, a hardware trace can be set up to trigger on the fetch of the interrupt vector, or the execution of the first instruction in the ISR, or in some cases, on the assertion of an interrupt request from the serial chip. The hardware trace is a snapshot of the bus over a period of time. All bus transactions are recorded in realtime. After the event happens, you can scroll through the bus record, looking at what instructions were executed, and in what order.

What a hardware trace will not tell you is the contents of the registers at each step. This can usually be inferred from the instruction stream, though, and is not normally a problem.

An emulator can also cut down on the amount of time spent loading new code into embedded systems. If you have ever debugged a ROM-based system without a hardware emulator, you know that most of your time is spent burning EPROMs. A good emulator will have overlay memory you can load your code into a fraction of the time it takes to burn EPROMs. Sections of memory can also be made read-only or illegal-access, too, and will cause breakpoints if an attempt is made to write into code space, or to access in any way illegal sections of memory. This allows you to quickly track down memory errors.

A
The Rest of YASE

This appendix contains the parts of the YASE editor not printed in earlier chapters. It also contains a list of all the parts needed to make the editor work and what page each piece can be found on. Last, it contains instructions on operating the version of YASE shown in this book—we find that it's often easier to understand how a program works if you have some sort of clue as to what it does.

Pieces Necessary for YASE

CRT.PRN	CRT interface	163
CASE.PRN	Case statement dispatcher	216
CURSOR.H	Cursor Key equates	200
EDIT.H	Window & buffer equates	142
EDIT0.PRN	Editor file I/O routines	323
EDIT1.PRN	Editor file I/O routines	174
EDIT2.PRN	Editing display manager	221
EDIT3.PRN	Main keystroke dispatcher	326
EDIT4.PRN	Misc. support routines	337
ERRORS.PRN	Error messages	341
EXEC.PRN	Editor executive	145
FCB.H	File Control Block equates	156
FILEPRIM.PRN	File I/O primitives	168
GROUP1.PRN	Group 1 (Quick) commands	343
GROUP2.PRN	Group 2 (Block) commands	348
GROUP3.PRN	Group 3 (Window) commands	191
GROUP4.PRN	Group 4 (PC Keyboard)	354
LINEED.PRN	Command input editor	211

PRINTF.PRN	Formatted numeric I/O	234
VSCREEN.PRN	Virtual display interface	165
WINDOW.PRN	Windowing primitives	217

YASE (Yet Another Screen Editor, pronounced "Yeow-Sah") is a small (8.5K) full-screen windowing text editor designed for use with nondocument files, such as program source code files.

YASE is remotely descended from a public domain editor called VDO. VDO was designed for the TRS-80 model I, and has since been transported to many CP/M machines, including the Commodore 64 CP/M version.

YASE is a memory-based editor. The file being edited and the editor itself both reside completely in memory. Each open window requires 64K for the editing buffer, with a maximum file size of just under 64K.

Where possible, the keystrokes to active a YASE operation are exactly the same as for WordStar. WordStar is "the" editor for CP/M and MSDOS, and we felt that using compatible commands would ease the transition between different systems. Of course, WordStar is much more powerful than YASE, but then YASE doesn't take 80K of your disk and load overlays every other keystroke, either.

YASE lacks many of the sophisticated document editing and text formatting features found in WordStar and other editors. However, the most commonly used nondocument (text) editing features are implemented. Additionally, windowing capability makes it possible to edit a number of files at once, and to cut and paste text between files.

Operation of YASE

YASE does not read the command line for a file name; this is a possible area for enhancements. YASE will ask for a filename and attempt to load the file as its first action. If the file does not exist, an error message will be displayed and a new window opened for inserting text.

YASE has only a few commands, broken into four major groups:

Cursor Controls
Quick Commands
Block Commands
Window Commands

Several minor commands are also implemented. Any control character that can't be interpreted as a command will be ignored.

Cursor Controls

The standard WordStar cursor controls ^A, ^S, ^D, ^F, ^E, ^X, ^R, ^C are all implemented. These work well for a touch typist, as all of the controls can be operated with the left hand. If you refer to the list below, you'll see that the basic cursor keys are in a diamond-shaped configuration. These keystrokes are also terminal-independent. Following is a list of cursor key definitions:

^S	moves cursor one character to the left
^D	moves cursor one character to the right
^A	moves cursor one word to the left
^F	moves cursor one word to the right
^E	moves cursor up one line
^X	moves cursor down one line
^R	moves cursor up 18 lines
^C	moves cursor down 18 lines

When lines are too long to fit the window width, the contents of the window will scroll to the left and right to keep the cursor on the display. Scrolling is done in jumps of eight columns.

Single Keystroke Commands

These commands are all activated by single keystrokes:

RETURN	causes and end-of-line. The cursor moves to the next line.
TAB	moves the cursor to the next tab stop. Tab stops are set to multiples of 8 columns.
^L	repeats the last ^QF or ^QA (see Quick commands).
^P	enters a printer code—the next character typed will be entered into the text as is, even if it normally has other significance (e.g., ^P ^L will enter a ^L, which is a printer form-feed, into the text file rather than doing a "repeat find" operation). Control characters in the text are displayed as a normal character with an up-arrow to the left of it.
^V	toggles the Insert mode on or off. When Insert mode is ON, new text is inserted into the file at the cursor position. Existing text is pushed ahead by the added characters. When Insert mode is OFF, old text is overtyped, with the exception of carriage returns, which are pushed ahead as if Insert mode was in operation.
^N	inserts a carriage return to the right of the cursor.

^T	deletes one "word" to the right of the cursor.
^Y	deletes the entire line containing the cursor, and pulls any following lines up one line.
^G	deletes the character to the right of (under) cursor.

Quick Commands

The Quick Commands are all accessed by typing a Control-Q, followed by a single keystroke subcommand. The Quick Commands all move the cursor through the text quickly.

^QR	places the cursor at the start (beginning) of the text.
^QC	places the cursor at the bottom (end) of the text.
^QB	places the cursor at the marker for the beginning of the block, if this marker is set (see ^KB).
^QK	places the cursor at the marker for the end of the block, if this marker is set (see ^KK).
^QF	allows you to specify a string to search for in the text. This operation is currently an exact match search, with upper and lower case being considered different.
^QA	Find-and-replace. Works just like ^QF, except when the string is found, a string of your choice is substituted for the target string. Note: To repeat a ^QF or ^QA operation, just type ^L.

Block Commands

The Block Commands are all accessed by typing ^K (Control-K), followed by a single key-stroke subcommand. A "Block" is a section of text beginning with the Block Start marker, and ending with the Block End marker, which you set. A block may be marked anywhere in the file. If either the beginning or end is not marked, or if the block end marker appears earlier in the file than the block start marker, or if you attempt to move a block inside itself, YASE will signal the error with a message.

In this version of YASE, block markers disappear whenever the text is modified (any inserts or deletes remove the markers), and the marked block is not highlighted. Both of these shortcomings are areas of possible enhancement.

^KB	sets Block Start marker. Marks the start of the block at the current cursor position.
^KK	sets Block End marker. Marks the end of the block at the current position.

^KC	copies the marked block to the cursor position. The text is also placed into the paste buffer, overwriting any previous contents.
^KV	moves the marked block to the cursor position. The marked block is removed from its position and appears at the cursor. The text is also placed into the paste buffer, overwriting any previous contents.
^KP	copies the contents of the paste buffer to the cursor position.
^KY	deletes the marked block. The marked block is removed from the file and the cursor remains where it is.
^KW	writes the marked block into a file of its own. You specify the new filename.
^KR	reads a file into the current file at the cursor position. You specify the filename.
^KX	end of Edit. Saves the file and closes the window. Does not keep a backup copy; an excellent area for enhancements.
^KQ	abandons (Quits) file—unsaved changes to the file are abandoned after asking for confirmation (if file has been modified; if file is unchanged it is just abandoned).
^KS	Save and continue. Saves the file as it appears in memory, and continues the editing session.

Window Commands

Window commands are activated by typing ^W (Control-W) followed by a single keystroke subcommand.

^WP	Pops a new window. The editor will ask for a filename, just as it does when you first enter the editor.
^WR	rotates the windows and refreshes the display. The bottom editing window is brought to the top of the display, and becomes the active window.
^WE	allows repositioning of the active window's upper-right corner. The cursor will be placed on the upper-left corner of the window, and the following cursor keys allow you to move the cursor to the desired position:

^E	up one line
^X	down one line
^R	to top of display
^C	to bottom of display
^F	to maximum possible right-hand column
^A	to maximum possible left-hand column

^S   left one column
^D   right one column
RETURN marks the current cursor position and returns to editing.

^WX   allows repositioning of the active window's lower-right corner. The cursor will be placed on the lower-right hand corner. Position proceeds as above, using the same keys.

The Status Line

YASE maintains a status line in a window at the top of the display. The first item on the status line is the name of the file being edited. If no name was specified on the command line when YASE was invoked, this area will be blank and YASE will ask for a filename when you exit with ^KX.

The LN and CO headings stand for Line Number and COlumn number, and show the line and logical column of the cursor. If a control character is embedded in the text, or if the screen has scrolled, the count on the status line may not agree with the screen column position. Control characteristics are ignored in the counting process; scrolling, of course, moves other columns onto the screen. The line number is always accurate. Line and column numbering begins at zero.

The SP entry tells you the remaining space in the edit buffer. The state of the insert toggle is displayed to the far right of the status window.

There is plenty of room for improvement in this editor, although we use the current version for all of our programming needs. If you do make improvements, please release them into the public domain.

Module EDIT0.PRN

```
  1                     ************************************************
  2                     * FILE I/O ROUTINES
  3                     ************************************************
  4                             xref    open_w,lineed,printf,read_in,prompt
  5                             xref    write_out,set_w,ask,cmd_w
  6                             xdef    readfile,writefile,filenm
  7
  8                     <<include EDIT.H>>
 46                     ************************************************
 47                     * Asks for a filename and reads it into current editing buffer
 48                     * ENTRY:  A5.L points to edit buffer window descriptor file
 49                     *         sets ed_err(a5) on error
 50                     readfile:
 51 00000000 48E760FC          movem.l d1/d2/a0-a5,-(a7)  * Save caller's registers
 52 00000004 207C0000005C      move.l  #fprompt,a0        * setup prompt address
 53 0000000A 227C00000000      move.l  #filenm,a1         * setup input string address
 54 00000010 61000000          bsr     ask               * output prompt
 55 00000014 207C00000000      move.l  #filenm,a0         * setup for file read
 56 0000001A 246D0012          move.l  b_gap(a5),a2       * save current start of gap
 57 0000001E 61000000          bsr     read_in            * try to read file
 58 00000022 266D0012          move.l  b_gap(a5),a3       * get new start of gap
 59 00000026 2B4A0012          move.l  a2,b_gap(a5)       * save gap start point
 60
                       loop_point:
 61 0000002A 220B              move.l  a3,d1              * check how many chars read
 62 0000002C 928A              sub.l   a2,d1              * d1 is now number of chars read
 63 0000002E 246D0016          move.l  e_gap(a5),a2       * get end of gap address
 64 00000032 6002              bra     loop_test          * this is a check-first loop·
 65
 66 00000034 1523              move.b  -(a3),-(a2)        * transfer chars to end of gap
 67                     loop_test:
 68 00000036 51C9FFFC          dbra    d1,loop_point
 69 0000003A 2B4A0016          move.l  a2,e_gap(a5)       * save new gap end address
 70 0000003E 4A40              tst.w   d0                 * check if file was read
 71 00000040 6714              beq     exit               * just leave if we read it
 72 00000042 B03C0001          cmp.b   #1,d0              * is it file-not-found error?
 73 00000046 6708              beq     sk0_rf             * yes, go tell user
 74 00000048 3B7C00050008      move.w  #5,ed_err(a5)      * was file-too-large error
 75 0000004E 6006              bra     exit               * print error
 76
 77 00000050 3B7C00060008      sk0_rf: move.w  #6,ed_err(a5)  * new file message address
```

Module EDIT0.PRN (*continued*)

```
78
79  00000056  4CDF3F06              exit:      movem.l  (a7)+,d1/d2/a0-a5  * restore caller's registers
80  0000005A  4E75                             rts

81
82  0000005C  496E707574204669      fprompt:   dc.b     'Input Filename: ',0
82  00000064  6C656E616D653A20
82  0000006C  00
83  0000006E
83  0000006E  0000                             dc.w     0

84
85  ****************************************************************
86  * WRITEFILE - writes a block to disk
87  * ENTRY: A1.L points to start of data buffer
88  *        D1.W holds number of bytes to write
89  * EXIT:  D0.W = 0 for success
90  *             = 1 for failure
    *
91  00000070  48E76084             writefile: movem.l  d1/d2/a0/a5,-(a7)  * Save caller's registers
92  00000074  2A7C00000000                    move.l   #cmd_w,a5          * get command I/O window desc.
93  0000007A  61000000                        bsr      open_w             * open command window
94  0000007E  3F2D003C                        move.w   w_ulcy(a5),-(a7)   * setup prompt Y position
95  00000082  3F2D003A                        move.w   w_ulcx(a5),-(a7)   * setup prompt X position
96  00000086  2F3C000000E6                     move.l   #wprompt,-(a7)     * setup prompt address
97  0000008C  61000000                        bsr      printf             * output prompt
98  00000090  508F                            addq.l   #8,a7              * fix the stack
99  00000092  302D003A                        move.w   w_ulcx(a5),d0      * input line X position
100 00000096  D07C0011                        add.w    #17,d0             * new X position for input line
101 0000009A  342D003E                        move.w   w_lrcx(a5),d2      * calculate max. line length for
102 0000009E  9440                            sub.w    d0,d2              * ... input line editor
103 000000A0  3F02                            move.w   d2,-(a7)           * push max editing lines
104 000000A2  3F00                            move.w   d0,-(a7)           * push starting screen column
105 000000A4  3F2D003C                        move.w   w_ulcy(a5),-(a7)   * push screen row
106 000000A8  2F3C00000000                    move.l   #filenm,-(a7)      * push string address
107 000000AE  61000000                        bsr      lineed             * get input line with filename
108 000000B2  DFFC0000000A                    add.l    #10,a7             * pop lineed parameters
109
110 000000B8  207C00000000                    move.l   #filenm,a0         * setup for file write
111 000000BE  61000000                        bsr      write_out          * try to read file
112 000000C2  4A40                            tst.w    d0                 * check if file was written
113 000000C4  671A                            beq      wexit              * just leave if we wrote it
114 000000C6  3F2D003C                        move.w   w_ulcy(a5),-(a7)   * push message Y position - 1
```

```
115 000000CA 5257           addq.w  #1,(a7)              * adjust for correct position
116 000000CC 3F2D003A       move.w  w_ulcx(a5),-(a7)     * push x position
117 000000D0 2F3C000000FA   move.l  #cant_rite,-(a7)     * push message string address
118 000000D6 61000000       bsr     printf               * tell user
119 000000DA 508F           addq.l  #8,a7                * fix stack
120 000000DC 303C0001       move.w  #1,d0                * set error code
121
122 000000E0 4CDF2106  wexit:   movem.l (a7)+,d1/d2/a0/a5  * restore caller's registers
123 000000E4 4E75           rts
124                     wprompt:
125 000000E6 25764F7574707574   dc.b    '%vOutput Filename: ',0
125 000000EE 2046696C656E616D
125 000000F6 653A2000
126                     cant_rite:
127 000000FA 25762A202A202A20   dc.b    '%v* * * Error writing file * * *',0
127 00000102 4572726F72207772
127 0000010A 6974696E67206669
127 00000112 6C65202A202A202A
127 0000011A 00
128 0000011C                    dc.w    0
128 0000011C 0000
129
    ***************************************************************
130 00000000              bss
131 00000000  filenm: ds.b    80                       * current filename buffer
132
133 00000050              end
```

Module EDIT3.PRN

```
 1      *****************************************************************
 2      * Editor Dispatcher
 3      *****************************************************************
 4              xref    prtscr,stats,getkey,sync_curs,case,cursor
 5              xref    keyhit,group_1,group_2,group_4,refind,errors
 6              xref    prompt
 7              xdef    up,down,right,left,down_page,up_page,del_left
 8              xdef    toggle,eol,sol,dirty
 9              xdef    edit
10
11              <<include EDIT.H>>
42              <<include CURSOR.H>>
79      *****************************************************************
80      * EDIT - Main editor dispatcher and executive.
81      *****************************************************************
        edit:
82      00000000 61000000           bsr     keyhit          * see if we're busy
83      00000004 4A40               tst.w   d0              * d0 is nonzero if we're busy
84      00000006 6626               bne     sklexec         * we skip refresh if busy
85      00000008 61000346           bsr     align_scr       * make sure cursor's on screen
86      0000000C 61000000           bsr     prtscr          * Print current buffer
87      00000010 61000000           bsr     stats           * Print editing stats
88      00000014 302D0008           move.w  ed_err(a5),d0   * Get edit error flag
89      00000018 48C0               ext.l   d0              * make into longword
90      0000001A E588               lsl.l   #2,d0           * multiply by four
91      0000001C 207C00000000       move.l  #errors,a0      * get error message lookup table
92      00000022 D1C0               add.l   d0,a0           * get offset
93      00000024 2050               move.l  (a0),a0         * get error string address
94      00000026 61000000           bsr     prompt          * output message (or blank old)
95      0000002A 426D0008           clr.w   ed_err(a5)      * mark "no errors"
        sklexec:
97      0000002E 3F2D0004           move.w  scr_row(a5),-(a7)   put cursor where it belongs
98      00000032 3F2D0006           move.w  scr_col(a5),-(a7)
99      00000036 61000000           bsr     cursor
100     0000003A 588F               addq.l  #4,a7           * adjust stack
101     0000003C 61000000           bsr     sync_curs       * Put cursor where it belongs
102     00000040 61000000           bsr     getkey          * get input
103     00000044 4880               ext.w   d0              * make into a word
104     00000046 207C00000052       move.l  #dispatch,a0    * load up case table
105     0000004C 61000000           bsr     case            * perform required operation
106
```

```
107 00000050 60AE              bra     edit            * repeat
108                   *****************************************************************
109                   * Top Level Editor Dispatch Table
110                   dispatch:
111 00000052 0017              dc.w    23              * Number of valid options
112 00000054 0009              dc.w    tab             * Tab
113 00000056 0000026E          dc.l    in_chr
114 0000005A 0000              dc.w    0               * PC cursor key prefix
115 0000005C 00000000          dc.l    group_4
116 00000060 0005              dc.w    c_up            * Cursor up one line
117 00000062 00000138          dc.l    up
118 00000066 0018              dc.w    c_down          * Cursor down one line
119 00000068 00000148          dc.l    down
120 0000006C 0004              dc.w    c_right         * Cursor one char right
121 0000006E 000000E8          dc.l    right
122 00000072 0013              dc.w    c_left          * Cursor one char left
123 00000074 00000110          dc.l    left
124 00000078 0006              dc.w    c_w_right       * Cursor one word right
125 0000007A 00000154          dc.l    w_right
126 0000007E 0001              dc.w    c_w_left        * Cursor one word left
127 00000080 00000174          dc.l    w_left
128 00000084 000D              dc.w    return          * Return Key
129 00000086 0000023C          dc.l    ret
130 0000008A 0008              dc.w    backsp          * Backspace Key
131 0000008C 00000110          dc.l    left
132 00000090 007F              dc.w    left_del        * Left Delete Character
133 00000092 000001EE          dc.l    del_left
134 00000096 0007              dc.w    right_del       * Right Delete Character
135 00000098 000001DC          dc.l    del_right
136 0000009C 0010              dc.w    lit_prefix      * Literal Insertion Prefix
137 0000009E 00000236          dc.l    prefix
138 000000A2 0014              dc.w    word_del        * Right Delete Word
139 000000A4 00000224          dc.l    del_word
140 000000A8 0011              dc.w    group1          * Group 1 Commands prefix
141 000000AA 00000000          dc.l    group_1
142 000000AE 000B              dc.w    group2          * Group 2 Commands prefix
143 000000B0 00000000          dc.l    group_2
144 000000B4 0017              dc.w    group3          * Group 3 Commands prefix
145 000000B6 000000E2          dc.l    group_3
146 000000BA 0019              dc.w    line_del        * Delete line key
```

Module EDIT3.PRN (continued)

```
147  000000BC 00000200              dc.l    del_line
148  000000C0 0012                  dc.w    page_up        * Page Up key
149  000000C2 00000196              dc.l    up_page
150  000000C6 0003                  dc.w    page_down      * Page Down key
151  000000C8 000001BA              dc.l    down_page
152  000000CC 000C                  dc.w    repeat         * Repeat Find key
153  000000CE 00000000              dc.l    refind
154  000000D2 0016                  dc.w    insert_key     * Insert Toggle Key
155  000000D4 00000242              dc.l    toggle
156  000000D8 000E                  dc.w    ins_line       * Insert Line key
157  000000DA 00000248              dc.l    line_ins
158  000000DE 00000268              dc.l    ins_chr        * default - insert character
159                          *****************************************************
160                          * GROUP 3 - group 3 (window) commands
161                          group_3:
162  000000E2 70FF                  move.l  #-1,d0          * Set "continue" flag
163  000000E4 588F                  addq.l  #4,a7           * lift one return address
164  000000E6 4E75                  rts                     * return to caller of "edit"
165                          *****************************************************
166                          * RIGHT - Moves cursor right. Returns byte moved in D0.
167                          right:
168  000000E8 4240                  clr.w   d0              * setup fake return value
169  000000EA 206D0016              move.l  e_gap(a5),a0    * check if we can move left
170  000000EE B1ED001A              cmp.l   e_buf(a5),a0    * we look at the end of buffer
171  000000F2 6E1A                  bgt     sk0_rt          * jump if we can't move
172  000000F4 226D0012              move.l  b_gap(a5),a1    * get destination for char
173  000000F8 1010                  move.b  (a0),d0         * save the byte to return it
174  000000FA 0C10000A              cmp.b   #10,(a0)        * check for line crossing
175  000000FE 6604                  bne     sk1_rt          * skip if not line crossing
176  00000100 526D0030              addq.w  #1,log_lin(a5)  * add one to line count
177                          sk1_rt:
178  00000104 12D8                  move.b  (a0)+,(a1)+     * move the byte across gap
179  00000106 52AD0016              addq.l  #1,e_gap(a5)    * move end pointer
180  0000010A 52AD0012              addq.l  #1,b_gap(a5)    * move start pointer
181                          sk0_rt:
182  0000010E 4E75                  rts
183                          *****************************************************
184                          * LEFT - moves cursor left. Returns byte moved in D0.
185                          left:
186  00000110 4240                  clr.w   d0              * setup fake return value
```

```
187 00000112 206D0012   move.l    b_gap(a5),a0      * check if we can move right
188 00000116 B1ED000E   cmp.l     b_buf(a5),a0      * we look at the start of buffer
189 0000011A 6F1A       ble       sk0_lf            * jump if we can't move
190 0000011C 226D0016   move.l    e_gap(a5),a1      * get destination for char
191 00000120 1320       move.b    -(a0),-(a1)       * move the byte across gap
192 00000122 1011       move.b    (a1),d0           * save the byte to return it
193 00000124 0C11000A   cmp.b     #10,(a1)          * check for line crossing
194 00000128 6604       bne       sk1_lf            * jump if not line crossing
195 0000012A 536D0030   subq.w    #1,log_lin(a5)    * bump down current line counter
196
197 0000012E 53AD0016 sk1_lf: subq.l    #1,e_gap(a5)   * move end pointer
198 00000132 53AD0012         subq.l    #1,b_gap(a5)   * move start pointer
199
200 00000136 4E75     sk0_lf: rts

201
202 ***********************************************************************
203 * UP - moves cursor up one line
204 00000138 610001B4  up:    bsr       sol               * move to start of this line
205 0000013C 61D2             bsr       left              * move back over newline
206 0000013E 610001AE         bsr       sol               * move to start of this line
207 00000142 610001D2         bsr       outline           * put cursor out into line
208 00000146 4E75             rts
209
210 ***********************************************************************
211 * DOWN - moves cursor down one line
212 00000148 610001B8 down:   bsr       eol               * move to end of line
213 0000014C 619A             bsr       right             * jump over newline
214 0000014E 610001C6         bsr       outline           * put cursor out into line
215 00000152 4E75             rts
216
217 ***********************************************************************
218 * W_RIGHT - Moves the cursor one word right
219 00000154 6192     w_right: bsr      right             * start right
220 00000156 4A00             tst.b     d0                * look for end-of-file
221 00000158 6718             beq       sk0_wr            * outta here if end of file
222 0000015A 61000168         bsr       isdelim           * look for delimiter
223 0000015E 4A00             tst.b     d0                * check return value
224 00000160 67F2             beq       w_right           * loop until we find delimiter
225
226 00000162 6184     lp0_wr:  bsr      right             * start right
```

Module EDIT3.PRN (continued)

```
227 00000164 4A00      tst.b   d0              * look for end-of-file
228 00000166 670A      beq     sk0_wr          * outta here if end of file
229 00000168 6100015A  bsr     isdelim         * look for delimiter
230 0000016C 4A00      tst.b   d0              * check return value
231 0000016E 66F2      bne     lp0_wr          * loop until we finish delimiters
232 00000170 619E      bsr     left            * back off one
233
234 00000172 4E75    sk0_wr:  rts
235 *********************************************************
236
237 * W_LEFT - move the cursor one word to the left
    w_left:
238 00000174 619A      bsr     left            * start left
239 00000176 4A00      tst.b   d0              * look for start-of-file
240 00000178 671A      beq     sk0_wl          * outta here if start of file
241 0000017A 61000148  bsr     isdelim         * look for delimiter
242 0000017E 4A00      tst.b   d0              * check return value
243 00000180 66F2      bne     w_left          * loop while no delimiter
244
    lp0_wl:
245 00000182 618C      bsr     left            * start left
246 00000184 4A00      tst.b   d0              * look for start-of-file
247 00000186 670C      beq     sk0_wl          * outta here if start of file
248 00000188 6100013A  bsr     isdelim         * look for delimiter
249 0000018C 4A00      tst.b   d0              * check return value
250 0000018E 67F2      beq     lp0_wl          * loop until we hit delimiters
251 00000190 6100FF56  bsr     right           * back off one
252
253 00000194 4E75    sk0_wl:  rts
254 *********************************************************
255
256 * UP_PAGE - moves cursor up one page
    up_page:
257 00000196 322D0042  move.w  w_rows(a5),d1   * calculate number of lines
258 0000019A 5541      subq.w  #2,d1           * leave two rows for context
259 0000019C 6E02      bgt     sk0_up          * check if we still have some
260 0000019E 4241      clr.w   d1              * we need at least one...
261
    sk0_up:
262 000001A0 6100014C  bsr     sol             * move to start of this line
263 000001A4 6100FF6A  bsr     left            * back up over newline
264 000001A8 4A40      tst.w   d0              * check for top of file
265 000001AA 6708      beq     skl_up          * break out if top of file
266 000001AC 51C9FFF2  dbra    d1,sk0_up       * loop 'lines' times
```

```
267  000001B0  6100FF36   skl_up:   bsr    right          * move over current newline
268
269  000001B4  61000160             bsr    outline        * move cursor out into line
270  000001B8  4E75                 rts
271                       **********************************************************
272                       * DOWN_PAGE - moves cursor down one page
273                       down_page:
274  000001BA  322D0042             move.w  w_rows(a5),d1   * calculate number of lines
275  000001BE  5741                 subq.w  #3,d1           * leave two rows for context
276  000001C0  6E04                 bgt     sk0_dn          * check if we still have some
277  000001C2  323C0000             move.w  #0,d1           * we need at least one...
278                       sk0_dn:
279  000001C6  6100013A             bsr    eol              * move to end of this line
280  000001CA  6100FF1C             bsr    right            * skip over newline
281  000001CE  51C9FFF6             dbra   d1,sk0_dn        * loop 'lines' times
282  000001D2  6100011A             bsr    sol              * move to start of this line
283  000001D6  6100013E             bsr    outline          * move cursor out into line
284  000001DA  4E75                 rts
285
286                       **********************************************************
287                       * DEL_RIGHT - delete one character to the right
288  000001DC  6100FF0A   del_right:
                                    bsr    right            * try to move right
289  000001E0  4A00                 tst.b  d0               * is there anything there?
290  000001E2  6708                 beq    sk0dr            * jump if not
291  000001E4  53AD0012             subq.l #1,b_gap(a5)     * delete character
292  000001E8  61000000             bsr    dirty            * set modified flags
293
294  000001EC  4E75       sk0dr:    rts
295
296                       **********************************************************
297                       * DEL_LEFT - delete one character to the left
298  000001EE  6100FF20   del_left:
                                    bsr    left             * try to move left
299  000001F2  4A00                 tst.b  d0               * is there anything there?
300  000001F4  6708                 beq    sk0dl            * jump if not
301  000001F6  52AD0016             addq.l #1,e_gap(a5)     * delete character
302  000001FA  61000000             bsr    dirty            * set modified flags
303
304  000001FE  4E75       sk0dl:    rts
305
306                       **********************************************************
                          * DEL_LINE - deletes line that cursor is on
```

Module EDIT3.PRN (continued)

```
307
308    00000200  610000EC    del_line:
309    00000204  2F2D0012               bsr       sol              * move to start of this line
310    00000208  610000F8               move.l    b_gap(a5),-(a7)  * save gap start address
311    0000020C  6100FEDA               bsr       eol              * move to end of this line
312    00000210  B03C000A               bsr       right            * and one more for newline
313    00000214  6604                   cmp.b     #10,d0           * make sure we got a newline
314    00000216  536D0030               bne       sk0ld            * jump if not
315                                     subq.w    #1,log_lin(a5)   * adjust line count
316    0000021A  2B5F0012    sk0ld:
317    0000021E  61000000               move.l    (a7)+,b_gap(a5)  * poof! line's gone.
318    00000222  4E75                   bsr       dirty            * set modified flags
319                                     rts
320                         del_word:
321    00000224  2F2D0012               move.l    b_gap(a5),-(a7)  * Save gap pointer
322    00000228  6100FF2A               bsr       w_right          * move cursor one word right
323    0000022C  2B5F0012               move.l    (a7)+,b_gap(a5)  * restore pointer, word vanishes
324    00000230  61000000               bsr       dirty            * set modified flags
325    00000234  4E75                   rts
326
327                         * PREFIX - Allows human to inser next char typed as literal
328                         prefix:
329    00000236  61000000               bsr       getkey           * take the next keystroke as-is
330    0000023A  6032                   bra       in_chr           * insert whatever comes in
331                         *****************************************************************
332                         ret:
333    0000023C  103C000A               move.b    #10,d0           * load up a newline
334    00000240  602C                   bra       in_chr           * go insert it
335                         *****************************************************************
336                         toggle:
337    00000242  466D0048               not.w     insert(a5)       * complement insert toggle
338    00000246  4E75                   rts
339                         *****************************************************************
340                         line_ins:
341    00000248  206D0016               move.l    e_gap(a5),a0     * get begin gap pointer
342    0000024C  B1ED0012               cmp.l     b_gap(a5),a0     * see if there's room
343    00000250  6F0E                   ble       sk0_lns          * jump if no room
344    00000252  113C000A               move.b    #10,-(a0)        * put in newline
345    00000256  53AD0016               subq.l    #1,e_gap(a5)     * adjust end pointer
346    0000025A  61000000               bsr       dirty            * set modified flags
```

```
347  0000025E 4E75                  rts                             * exit
348                    sk0_lns:
349  00000260 3B7C00020008          move.w  #2,ed_err(a5)           * error 2 - no more room
350  00000266 4E75                  rts
351  ***********************************************************************
352
353  00000268 B03C0020      ins_chr:  cmp.b   #$20,d0               * check if char out of range
354  0000026C 6D46                    blt     sk1_ins               * if out, goto error
355                    in_chr:
356  0000026E 4A6D0048                tst.w   insert(a5)            * is insert toggle on?
357  00000272 6620                    bne     sk2_ins               * jump if yes
358  00000274 206D0016                move.l  e_gap(a5),a0          * get end-of-gap address
359  00000278 B1ED001A                cmp.l   e_buf(a5),a0          * check if at end of buffer
360  0000027C 6E16                    bgt     sk2_ins               * yes, go insert
361  0000027E 0C10000A                cmp.b   #10,(a0)              * see if next char is newline
362  00000282 6710                    beq     sk2_ins               * yes, go insert
363  00000284 206D0012                move.l  b_gap(a5),a0          * we need to replace...
364  00000288 1080                    move.b  d0,(a0)               * emplace new character
365  0000028A 52AD0012                addq.l  #1,b_gap(a5)          * move begin gap pointer
366  0000028E 52AD0016                addq.l  #1,e_gap(a5)          * move end gap pointer
367  00000292 601A                    bra     sk4_ins               * exit
368                    sk2_ins:
369  00000294 206D0012                move.l  b_gap(a5),a0          * get begin gap pointer
370  00000298 B1ED0016                cmp.l   e_gap(a5),a0          * look see if there's room
371  0000029C 6C1E                    bge     sk3_ins               * jump if no room
372  0000029E 1080                    move.b  d0,(a0)               * insert character
373  000002A0 52AD0012                addq.l  #1,b_gap(a5)          * move gap pointer
374  000002A4 B03C000A                cmp.b   #10,d0                * check for newline
375  000002A8 6604                    bne     sk4_ins               * skip if not
376  000002AA 526D0030                addq.w  #1,log_lin(a5)        * increment logical line count
377                    sk4_ins:
378  000002AE 61000000                bsr     dirty                 * set modified flags
379  000002B2 4E75                    rts                           * That's it.
380                    sk1_ins:
381  000002B4 3B7C00010008            move.w  #1,ed_err(a5)         * error #1 - char out of range
382  000002BA 4E75                    rts
383                    sk3_ins:
384  000002BC 3B7C00020008            move.w  #2,ed_err(a5)         * error #2 - no room
385  000002C2 4E75                    rts
386  ***********************************************************************
```

Module EDIT3.PRN (continued)

```
387
388                               * ISDELIM - returns TRUE if char in D0 matches delimiter list
                                  isdelim:
389  000002C4  207C000002E0                 move.l  #delim,a0        * get delimiter list address
390  000002CA  323C000C                     move.w  #d_cnt,d1        * get delimiter count
391                               lp0_dm:
392  000002CE  B018                          cmp.b   (a0)+,d0         * look for a match
393  000002D0  6708                          beq     d_true           * found one, jump out
394  000002D2  51C9FFFA                      dbra    d1,lp0_dm        * check all cases
395  000002D6  4240                          clr.w   d0               * return FALSE
396  000002D8  4E75                          rts
397                               d_true:
398  000002DA  303CFFFF                      move.w  #$FFFF,d0        * return TRUE
399  000002DE  4E75                          rts
400
401  000002E0  090A202C2E2D2B2F     delim:   dc.b    9,10,' ,.-+/><()'
401  000002E8  3E3C2829
402                               d_cnt      equ     *-delim
403  000002EC  0000                           dc.w    0
404                               *********************************************************
405                               * SOL - moves cursor to start of line
406                               sol:
407  000002EE  6100FE20                      bsr     left             * try one char back
408  000002F2  4A00                          tst.b   d0               * check if at top of file
409  000002F4  670A                          beq     sk0sol           * jump out if at top of file
410  000002F6  B03C000A                      cmp.b   #10,d0           * is this a newline?
411  000002FA  66F2                          bne     sol              * back up to start of this line
412  000002FC  6100FDEA                      bsr     right            * re-adjust cursor
413                               sk0sol:
414  00000300  4E75                          rts
415                               *********************************************************
416                               * EOL - moves cursor to end of line
417                               eol:
418  00000302  6100FDE4                      bsr     right            * try one char forward
419  00000306  4A00                          tst.b   d0               * check if at end of file
420  00000308  670A                          beq     sk0eol           * jump out if at end of file
421  0000030A  B03C000A                      cmp.b   #10,d0           * check for newline
422  0000030E  66F2                          bne     eol              * loop if not newline
423  00000310  6100FDFE                      bsr     left             * put cursor behind newline
424                               sk0eol:
425  00000314  4E75                          rts
```

```
                                                    * ***************************************************************
                                                    * OUTLINE - moves cursor to current logical column
                                                    * outline:
426
427
428
429  00000316  4242           clr.w   d2                * d2 is column accumulator
430                   lp0_ol:
431  00000318  6100FDCE       bsr     right             * try to move right
432  0000031C  4A00           tst.b   d0                * check if end-of-file
433  0000031E  672E           beq     sk1_ol            * exit if end-of-file
434  00000320  B03C000A       cmp.b   #10,d0            * check for end of line
435  00000324  6724           beq     sk0_ol            * done if end-of-line
436  00000326  5242           addq.w  #1,d2             * start with one column
437  00000328  B03C0020       cmp.b   #$20,d0           * see if control char
438  0000032C  6C16           bge     sk2_ol            * if not, we're done with char
439  0000032E  B03C0009       cmp.b   #tab,d0           * is char a tab?
440  00000332  6704           beq     sk3_ol            * jump if tab
441  00000334  5382           subq.l  #1,d2             * take away column for ctrl char
442  00000336  600C           bra     sk2_ol            * make loop test
443                   sk3_ol:
444  00000338  3002           move.w  d2,d0             * make a copy of column count
445  0000033A  C07C0007       and.w   #$0007,d0         * check for correct tab column
446  0000033E  6704           beq     sk2_ol            * if so, make loop test
447  00000340  5242           addq.w  #1,d2             * otherwise, add one space to col
448  00000342  60F4           bra     sk3_ol            * and keep expanding tab
449                   sk2_ol:
450  00000344  B46D002E       cmp.w   log_col(a5),d2    * are we far enough out?
451  00000348  6FCE           ble     lp0_ol            * no, keep trying
452                   sk0_ol:
453  0000034A  6100FDC4       bsr     left              * back up to correct position
454                   sk1_ol:
455  0000034E  4E75           rts
                                                    * ***************************************************************
                                                    * ALIGN_SCR - Handles vertical cursor alignment. Puts the cursor
                                                    * on the screen if it's off.
456                   align_scr:
457
458
459
460  00000350  206D0012       move.l  b_gap(a5),a0      * Get start of gap (cursor loc.)
461  00000354  B1ED0026       cmp.l   top_lef(a5),a0    * see if cursor's off top
462  00000358  6C20           bge     sk0_as            * jump if not off the top
463                   lp0_as:
464  0000035A  5388           subq.l  #1,a0             * start backing off
465  0000035C  B1ED000E       cmp.l   b_buf(a5),a0      * don't go under start of file
```

Module EDIT3.PRN (*continued*)

```
466  00000360  6708      beq    sk1_as           * jump if at start of file
467  00000362  0C10000A  cmp.b  #10,(a0)         * look for newline
468  00000366  66F2      bne    lp0_as           * not newline, try again
469  00000368  5288      addq.l #1,a0            * ok, move past newline
470
              sk1_as:
471  0000036A  B1ED000E  cmp.l  b_buf(a5),a0     * one last check for nasties
472  0000036E  6C04      bge    sk5_as           * no nasties
473  00000370  206D000E  move.l b_buf(a5),a0     * start at top
474
              sk5_as:
475  00000374  2B480026  move.l a0,top_lef(a5)   * reset top of screen
476  00000378  6032      bra    sk3_as           * exit
477
              sk0_as:
478  0000037A  91ED0026  sub.l  top_lef(a5),a0   * A0 is now chars-to-cursor
479  0000037E  2008      move.l a0,d0            * we need count in data register
480  00000380  206D0026  move.l top_lef(a5),a0   * A0 is where we start looking
481  00000384  4241      clr.w  d1               * d1 will be newline count
482  00000386  6008      bra    sk2_as           * do loop test before check
483
              lp1_as:
484  00000388  0C18000A  cmp.b  #10,(a0)+        * look for newlines
485  0000038C  6602      bne    sk2_as           * if not newline, don't care
486  0000038E  5241      addq.w #1,d1            * if newline, increment count
487
              sk2_as:
488  00000390  51C8FFF6  dbra   d0,lp1_as        * loop test
489  00000394  926D0042  sub.w  w_rows(a5),d1    * see if more newlines than rows
490  00000398  6D12      blt    sk3_as           * if not, we're ok
491  0000039A  206D0026  move.l top_lef(a5),a0   * get starting point
492
              lp3_as:
493  0000039E  0C18000A  cmp.b  #10,(a0)+        * we need to skip newlines
494  000003A2  66FA      bne    lp3_as           * if not newline, we don't care
495
              sk4_as:
496  000003A4  51C9FFF8  dbra   d1,lp3_as        * loop for (d1+1) newlines
497  000003A8  2B480026  move.l a0,top_lef(a5)   * save new top left corner
498
              sk3_as:
499  000003AC  4E75      rts
500
501  000003AE            end
```

Module EDIT4.PRN

```
 1
 2                     *****************************************************
 3                     * Editor Auxiliary Functions
 4                             xref    cmd_w,lineed,printf,to_end,write_out
 5                             xdef    prompt,dirty,ask,eof,cnt_nl,seek,chk_blk,default
 6                             xdef    putfile
 7
 8                             <<include EDIT.H>>
46                     *****************************************************
47                     * EOF - moves cursor to end of file
48                     eof:
49 00000000 61000000          bsr     to_end          * move everything before cursor
50 00000004 6102              bsr     cnt_nl          * count newlines behind cursor
51 00000006 4E75              rts
52                     *****************************************************
53                     * CNT_NL - count newlines behind cursor
54                     cnt_nl:
55 00000008 206D000E          move.l  b_buf(a5),a0    * a0 is search start address
56 0000000C 202D0012          move.l  b_gap(a5),d0    * compute number of bytes
57 00000010 9088              sub.l   a0,d0           * d0 is number of file bytes
58 00000012 4241              clr.w   d1              * d1 is newline counter
59 00000014 143C000A          move.b  #10,d2          * do register compare - faster
60 00000018 6006              bra     sk0_nl          * loop test before loop body
61                     lp0_nl:
62 0000001A B418              cmp.b   (a0)+,d2        * look for newline
63 0000001C 6602              bne     sk0_nl          * nope.
64 0000001E 5241              addq.w  #1,d1           * increment line counter
65                     sk0_nl:
66 00000020 51C8FFF8          dbra    d0,lp0_nl       * loop test
67 00000024 3B410030          move.w  d1,log_lin(a5)  * save new logical line count
68 00000028 4E75              rts
69                     *****************************************************
70                     * DIRTY - marks file as modified, and clears block markers
71                     dirty:
72 0000002A 42AD001E          clr.l   blk_st(a5)      * reset block start marker
73 0000002E 42AD0022          clr.l   blk_end(a5)     * reset block end marker
74 00000032 3B7CFFFF000A      move.w  #-1,modify(a5)  * set file modified flag
75 00000038 4E75              rts
76                     *****************************************************
77                     * SEEK - moves the cursor to the location in d0
```

Module EDIT4.PRN (*continued*)

```
78
79  0000003A 206D0012            seek:    move.l  b_gap(a5),a0    * gap start address in A0
80  0000003E 226D0016                     move.l  e_gap(a5),a1    * gap end location in A1
81  00000042 9088                         sub.l   a0,d0           * calculate characters to dest.
82  00000044 6E0E                         bgt     sk1_sk          * move towards end of file
83  00000046 4440                         neg.w   d0              * take abs() of char count
84  00000048 6002                         bra     sk2_sk          * loop test before branch
85
86  0000004A 1320            lp0_sk:      move.b  -(a0),-(a1)     * move towards start of file
87
88  0000004C 51C8FFFC        sk2_sk:      dbra    d0,lp0_sk       * to start of file loop
89  00000050 6006                         bra     sk0_sk          * get out
90
91  00000052 10D9            lp1_sk:      move.b  (a1)+,(a0)+     * move towards end of file
92
93  00000054 51C8FFFC        sk1_sk:      dbra    d0,lp1_sk       * to end of file loop
94
95  00000058 2B480012        sk0_sk:      move.l  a0,b_gap(a5)    * reset gap start address
96  0000005C 2B490016                     move.l  a1,e_gap(a5)    * reset gap end address
97  00000060 4E75                         rts
98
99  *************************************************************
    * CHK_BLK - checks for valid block markers
    chk_blk:
100
101 00000062 4AAD001E                     tst.l   blk_st(a5)      * check if start is marked
102 00000066 6714                         beq     sk0_cb          * branch if not
103 00000068 4AAD0022                     tst.l   blk_end(a5)     * check if end is marked
104 0000006C 6716                         beq     sk1_cb          * branch if not
105 0000006E 202D0022                     move.l  blk_end(a5),d0  * check if end is after start
106 00000072 B0AD001E                     cmp.l   blk_st(a5),d0
107 00000076 6F14                         ble     sk3_cb          * branch if mismarked
108 00000078 4240                         clr.w   d0              * get "ok" return code
109 0000007A 6016                         bra     sk2_cb          * branch out
110
111 0000007C 3B7C00070008    sk0_cb:      move.w  #7,ed_err(a5)   * show start not marked error
112 00000082 600E                         bra     sk2_cb
113
114 00000084 3B7C00080008    sk1_cb:      move.w  #8,ed_err(a5)   * show end not marked error
115 0000008A 6006                         bra     sk2_cb
116
117 0000008C 3B7C00090008    sk3_cb:      move.w  #9,ed_err(a5)   * show mismark error
```

```
118
119 00000092 4E75            sk2_cb:  rts
120
121          ****************************************************************
122          * DEFAULT: User hits unspecified subcommand key
123 00000094 4E75            default: rts
124          ****************************************************************
125          * PUTFILE - puts the file to disk - returns D0 nonzero on error
126                          putfile:
127 00000096 61000000                bsr    to_end          * move all text behind cursor
128 0000009A 41ED004A                lea    fname(a5),a0     * load name for file write
129 0000009E 226D000E                move.l b_buf(a5),a1     * start of data to write
130 000000A2 222D0012                move.l b_gap(a5),d1     * calculate number of bytes
131 000000A6 9289                    sub.l  a1,d1            * D1 is numbers of bytes to write
132 000000A8 61000000                bsr    write_out        * write the file to disk
133 000000AC 4A40                    tst.w  d0               * check return code
134 000000AE 6706                    beq    sk0_pf           * skip error message with no err
135 000000B0 3B7C00030008            move.w #3,ed_err(a5)    * load edit error code
136                          sk0_pf:
137 000000B6 4E75                    rts
138
139          ****************************************************************
140          * PROMPT - outputs a prompt in command window. A0 points to prmt
                          prompt:
141 000000B8 2F08                    move.l a0,-(a7)         * push parameter string address
142 000000BA 207C00000000            move.l #cmd_w,a0        * get command window address
143 000000C0 3F28003C                move.w w_ulcy(a0),-(a7) * push Y screen address
144 000000C4 3F28003A                move.w w_ulcx(a0),-(a7) * push X screen address
145 000000C8 2F3C000000D8            move.l #p_str,-(a7)     * push format string address
146 000000CE 61000000                bsr    printf           * output prompt
147 000000D2 508F                    addq.l #8,a7            * adjust stack
148 000000D4 205F                    move.l (a7)+,a0         * restore a0
149 000000D6 4E75                    rts
150 000000D8 2576252D37387300 p_str: dc.b   '%v%-78s',0
151 000000E0 0000                    dc.w   0
152          ****************************************************************
153          * ASK - prompts human for string input - A0 is prompt string,
154          *        A1 is input string
155
                          ask:
156 000000E2 61D4                    bsr    prompt           * output prompt string
157 000000E4 247C00000000            move.l #cmd_w,a2        * a2 has output limits
```

Module EDIT4.PRN (*continued*)

```
158 000000EA 302A003A            move.w    w_ulcx(a2),d0     * d0 will count be X offset
159
                          lp0_ask:
160 000000EE 4A18                 tst.b     (a0)+             * see if we have a null
161 000000F0 6704                 beq       sk0_ask           * jump out if null
162 000000F2 5240                 addq.w    #1,d0             * increment X position
163 000000F4 60F8                 bra       lp0_ask           * loop again for strlen
164                       sk0_ask:
165 000000F6 322A003E             move.w    w_lrcx(a2),d1     * d1 is input window right edge
166 000000FA 9240                 sub.w     d0,d1             * d1 is now max chars in input
167 000000FC 3F01                 move.w    d1,-(a7)          * push max number for lineed
168 000000FE 3F00                 move.w    d0,-(a7)          * push screen column
169 00000100 3F2A003C             move.w    w_ulcy(a2),-(a7)  * push screen line
170 00000104 2F09                 move.l    a1,-(a7)          * push input string address
171 00000106 61000000             bsr       lineed            * go edit input line
172 0000010A DFFC0000000A         add.l     #10,a7            * adjust stack
173 00000110 4E75                 rts
174
175 00000112                      end
```

Module ERRORS.PRN

```
  1                                   *************************************************************
  2                                   * Editor error messages
  3                                   *************************************************************
  4
  5                                           xdef    errors
  6 00000000 0000003400000035        errors: dc.l    err_0,err_1,err_2,err_3,err_4,err_5,err_6
  6 00000008 0000004C00000059
  6 00000010 0000007C0000008E
  6 00000018 000000AC
  7 0000001C 000000BC000000D8                dc.l    err_7,err_8,err_9,err_10,err_11,err_12
  7 00000024 000000F200000120
  7 0000002C 0000013B00000152
  8
  9 00000034 00                      err_0:  dc.b    0
 10 00000035 556E7265636F676E        err_1:  dc.b    'Unrecognized Character',0
 10 0000003D 697A656420436861
 10 00000045 72616374657200
 11 0000004C 4E6F204D6F726520        err_2:  dc.b    'No More Room',0
 11 00000054 526F6F6D00
 12 00000059 46696C6520777269        err_3:  dc.b    'File write error, file not written',0
 12 00000061 7465206572726F72
 12 00000069 2C2066696C65206E
 12 00000071 6F74207772697474
 12 00000079 656E00
 13 0000007C 426C6F636B206E6F        err_4:  dc.b    'Block not marked.',0
 13 00000084 74206D61726B6564
 13 0000008C 2E00
 14 0000008E 46696C6520657863        err_5:  dc.b    'File exceeds available memory',0
 14 00000096 6565647320617661
 14 0000009E 696C61626C65206D
 14 000000A6 656D6F727900
 15 000000AC 46696C65206E6F74        err_6:  dc.b    'File not found.',0
 15 000000B4 20666F756E642E00
 16 000000BC 426C6F636B205374        err_7:  dc.b    'Block Start Marker not set.',0
 16 000000C4 617274204D61726B
 16 000000CC 6572206E6F742073
 16 000000D4 65742E00
 17 000000D8 426C6F636B20456E        err_8:  dc.b    'Block End Marker not set.',0
 17 000000E0 64204D61726B6572
 17 000000E8 206E6F7420736574
```

```
17  000000F0  2E00
18  000000F2  426C6F636B20456E         err_9:    dc.b    'Block End Marker preceeds Block Start Marker.',0
18  000000FA  64204D61726B6572
18  00000102  2070726563656564
18  0000010A  7320426C6F636B20
18  00000112  5374617274204D61
18  0000011A  726B65722E00
19  00000120  426C6F636B206973         err_10:   dc.b    'Block is too large to fit.',0
19  00000128  20746F6F206C6172
19  00000130  676520746F206669
19  00000138  742E00
20  0000013B  5061737465204275         err_11:   dc.b    'Paste Buffer is empty.',0
20  00000143  6666657220697320
20  0000014B  656D7074792E00
21  00000152  5365617263682073         err_12:   dc.b    'Search string not found.',0
21  0000015A  7472696E67206E6F
21  00000162  7420666F756E642E
21  0000016A  00
22  0000016C                            dc.w    0
22  0000016C  0000
23
24  0000016E                            end
```

Module GROUP1.PRN

```
                ********************************************************
                * GROUP 1 (Quick) Commands                            *
                ********************************************************
                        xref    _getkey,ask,case,cnt_nl,default,dirty,eol,findpat
                        xref    prompt,repflag,reppat,seek,sol
                        xdef    group_1,refind,to_end,home

                <<include EDIT.H>>
                <<include CURSOR.H>>
                ********************************************************
                * GROUP_1 - group 1 (quick) commands
                group_1:
78  00000000  207C0000001C    move.l  #q_cmd,a0    * load up prompt address
79  00000006  61000000        bsr     prompt       * output prompt
80  0000000A  61000000        bsr     getkey       * get switch key
81  0000000E  C07C001F        and.w   #$001F,d0    * make u/l, l/c letters cntrl
82  00000012  207C0000003E    move.l  #table1,a0   * load up case table address
83  00000018  60000000        bra     case         * returns to caller of group_2
84  0000001C  5175696364436F  q_cmd:  dc.b  'Quick Command: A B C D F K R S',0
84  00000024  6D6D616E643A2041
84  0000002C  2042204320442046
84  00000034  204B2052205300
85  0000003C
85  0000003C  0000            dc.w    0

                ********************************************************
                * TABLE_1 - switch table for group 1 commands         *
                table1:
90  0000003E  0008            dc.w    8
91  00000040  0001            dc.w    $01
92  00000042  00000098        dc.l    find_repl    * ^A find/replace
93  00000046  0002            dc.w    $02
94  00000048  00000188        dc.l    find_b_s     * ^B find block start
95  0000004C  0003            dc.w    $03
96  0000004E  000001B8        dc.l    to_end       * ^C to end of file
97  00000052  0006            dc.w    $06
98  00000054  00000074        dc.l    find         * ^F find
99  00000058  000B            dc.w    $0B
100 0000005A  000001A0        dc.l    find_b_e     * ^K find block end
101 0000005E  0004            dc.w    $04          * ^D end of line
```

Module GROUP1.PRN (continued)

```
102  00000060 00000000              dc.l     eol
103  00000064 0012                  dc.w     $12
104  00000066 00000162              dc.l     home
105  0000006A 0013                  dc.w     $13           * ^R top of file
106  0000006C 00000000              dc.l     sol
107  00000070 00000000              dc.l     default       * ^S start of line
108
         ***********************************************************
109
110  00000074 207C0000008E  find:   move.l   #fwhat,a0     * prompt string address
111  0000007A 227C00000000          move.l   #findpat,a1   * find pattern string address
112  00000080 61000000              bsr      ask           * see what human wants
113  00000084 42790000000           clr.w    repflag       * zero "replace" flag
114  0000008A 6144                  bsr      refind        * go find it
115  0000008C 4E75                  rts
116  0000008E 46696E643A2000 fwhat:  dc.b    'Find: ',0
117  00000096 0000                  dc.w     0
118
         ***********************************************************
119
120  00000098 207C0000008E  find_repl:  move.l  #fwhat,a0  * prompt string address
121  0000009E 227C00000000          move.l   #findpat,a1   * find pattern string address
122  000000A4 61000000              bsr      ask           * see what human wants
123  000000A8 207C000000C4          move.l   #rwhat,a0     * prompt string address
124  000000AE 227C00000000          move.l   #reppat,a1    * replace pattern string address
125  000000B4 61000000              bsr      ask           * get reply
126  000000B8 33FCFFFF00000000      move.w   #-1,repflag   * set "replace" flag
127  000000C0 610E                  bsr      refind        * go find it
128  000000C2 4E75                  rts
129  000000C4 5265706C6163653A rwhat:  dc.b  'Replace: ',0
130  000000CC 2000
130  000000CE 0000                  dc.w     0
131
         ***********************************************************
132
133  000000D0 202D001A  refind:  move.l   e_buf(a5),d0    * calculate bytes past cursor
134  000000D4 90AD0016          sub.l    e_gap(a5),d0     * D0 is bytes +1
135  000000D8 5280              addq.l   #1,d0            * adjust byte count to actual
136  000000DA 206D0016          move.l   e_gap(a5),a0     * a0 will be search location
137  000000DE 023C00FB          andi     #$FB,ccr         * reset zero flag
138  000000E2 600A              bra      sk0_ref          * do loop test before looping
139                      lp0_ref:
```

```
140  000000E4  227C00000000    move.l   #findpat,a1     * a1 will be search pattern
141  000000EA  5288            addq.l   #1,a0           * bump start pointer
142  000000EC  6162            bsr      instr           * do instring compare
143                        sk0_ref:
144  000000EE  57C8FFF4        dbeq     d0,lp0_ref      * loop if (d0) AND not zero flag
145  000000F2  6650            bne      sk1_ref         * jump if not found
146  000000F4  246D0016        move.l   e_gap(a5),a2    * setup to move cursor
147  000000F8  202D0012        move.l   b_gap(a5),d0    * calculate bytes to move
148  000000FC  91CA            sub.l    a2,a0           * a0 holds bytes to move
149  000000FE  D088            add.l    a0,d0           * a1 is desired cursor location
150  00000100  61000000        bsr      seek            * move cursor
151  00000104  4A7900000000    tst.w    repflag         * see if we're replacing
152  0000010A  673E            beq      sk2_ref         * jump if no.
153                        * replace
154  0000010C  61000000        bsr      dirty           * mark file as modified
155  00000110  227C00000000    move.l   #findpat,a1     * we'll use brute force
156  00000116  206D0016        move.l   e_gap(a5),a0    * get end-of-gap
157                        lp1_ref:
158  0000011A  4A19            tst.b    (a1)+           * look for end-of-find-pattern
159  0000011C  6704            beq      sk3_ref         * jump out at end of pattern
160  0000011E  5288            addq.l   #1,a0           * pop character out of file
161  00000120  60F8            bra      lp1_ref         * keep it up
162                        sk3_ref:
163  00000122  2B480016        move.l   a0,e_gap(a5)    * delete "found" pattern
164                        * insert replacement string
165                        * we really ought to check for room here....
166  00000126  227C00000000    move.l   #reppat,a1      * replacement string address
167  0000012C  206D0012        move.l   b_gap(a5),a0    * destination for string
168  00000130  2008            move.l   a0,d0           * save cursor position for later
169                        lp2_ref:
170  00000132  4A11            tst.b    (a1)            * see if we have stuff to insert
171  00000134  6704            beq      sk4_ref         * nope, all done.
172  00000136  10D9            move.b   (a1)+,(a0)+     * transfer a byte
173  00000138  60F8            bra      lp2_ref         * try for next byte
174                        sk4_ref:
175  0000013A  2B480012        move.l   a0,b_gap(a5)    * reset gap position
176  0000013E  61000000        bsr      seek            * fix cursor position
177  00000142  6006            bra      sk2_ref         * finished.
178                        sk1_ref:
179  00000144  3B7C000C0008    move.w   #12,ed_err(a5)  * string-not-found error
```

```
180
181 0000014A 61000000     sk2_ref:
                                  bsr     cnt_nl          * adjust line counter
182 0000014E 4E75                 rts
183                        ***********************************************************
184                        * INSTR - tests if a string in contained in the buffer.
185
186 00000150 4281         instr:   clr.l   d1              * d1 is compare count
187
188 00000152 4A11         lp0_str:
                                   tst.b   (a1)            * at end of pattern string?
189 00000154 6706                  beq     sk0_str         * jump if yes (we found it)
190 00000156 5281                  addq.l  #1,d1           * increment compare count
191 00000158 B109                  cmp.b   (a1)+,(a0)+     * check a byte - equal?
192 0000015A 67F6                  beq     lp0_str         * jump if no - no match
193
194 0000015C 91C1         sk0_str:
                                   sub.l   d1,a0           * reset compare pointer
195 0000015E 93C1                  sub.l   d1,a1           * reset source pointer
196 00000160 4E75                  rts
197                        ***********************************************************
198                        * HOME - moves cursor to top of file
199
200 00000162 202D0012     home:
                                   move.l  b_gap(a5),d0    * get number of bytes to xfer
201 00000166 90AD000E             sub.l   b_buf(a5),d0    * d0 is number of bytes
202 0000016A 206D0012             move.l  b_gap(a5),a0    * a0 is source address
203 0000016E 226D0016             move.l  e_gap(a5),a1    * a1 is destination address
204 00000172 6002                 bra     sk0_hm          * loop test before 1st transfer
205
206 00000174 1320         lp0_hm:  move.b  -(a0),-(a1)     * transfer across cursor gap
207
208 00000176 51C8FFFC     sk0_hm:  dbra    d0,lp0_hm       * loop for all chars
209 0000017A 2B480012             move.l  a0,b_gap(a5)    * save ending positions
210 0000017E 2B490016             move.l  a1,e_gap(a5)
211 00000182 426D0030             clr.w   log_lin(a5)     * reset current line counter
212 00000186 4E75                 rts
213                        ***********************************************************
214                        * FIND_B_S - move the cursor to the beginning of the block
215                        find_b_s:
216 00000188 202D001E             move.l  blk_st(a5),d0   * load marker
217 0000018C 670A                 beq     sk0_fbs         * if zero, there's an error
218 0000018E 61000000             bsr     seek            * go find the spot
219 00000192 61000000             bsr     cnt_nl          * reset line count
```

```
220  00000196  4E75
221
222  00000198  3B7C00040008   sk0_fbs:  move.w  #4,ed_err(a5)   * mark edit error #4 (block mark)
223  0000019E  4E75                     rts
224
225  ****************************************************************
226  * FIND_B_E - move the cursor to the end of the block
227  000001A0  202D0022   find_b_e:  move.l  blk_end(a5),d0   * load marker
228  000001A4  670A                  beq     sk0_fbe          * if zero, block's not marked.
229  000001A6  61000000              bsr     seek             * go to the spot
230  000001AA  61000000              bsr     cnt_nl           * reset line count
231  000001AE  4E75                  rts
232
233  000001B0  3B7C00040008  sk0_fbe:  move.w  #4,ed_err(a5)   * mark edit error #4 (block mark)
234  000001B6  4E75                   rts
235  ****************************************************************
236  * TO_END - moves cursor to end of file
237  to_end:
238  000001B8  202D001A   move.l  e_buf(a5),d0   * get number of bytes to xfer
239  000001BC  90AD0016   sub.l   e_gap(a5),d0   * d0 is number of bytes + 1
240  000001C0  206D0016   move.l  e_gap(a5),a0   * a0 is source address
241  000001C4  226D0012   move.l  b_gap(a5),a1   * a1 is destination address
242  000001C8  5280       addq.l  #1,d0          * adjust index for cursor update
243  000001CA  6002       bra     sk0_te         * loop test before 1st transfer
244
245  000001CC  12D8   lp0_te:  move.b  (a0)+,(a1)+    * transfer across cursor gap.
246
247  000001CE  51C8FFFC   sk0_te:  dbra    d0,lp0_te      * loop for all chars
248  000001D2  2B480016            move.l  a0,e_gap(a5)   * save ending positions
249  000001D6  2B490012            move.l  a1,b_gap(a5)
250  000001DA  61000000            bsr     cnt_nl         * count lines to cursor
251  000001DE  4E75                rts
```

Module GROUP2.PRN

```
  1      ****************************************************************
  2      * GROUP 2 (Block) Commands
  3      ****************************************************************
  4              xref    _getkey,ask,case,chk_blk,cnt_nl,default,dirty
  5              xref    p_buf,p_cnt,prompt,putfile,query,readfile,seek
  6              xref    writefile
  7              xdef    group_2
  8
 46      <<include EDIT.H>>
 76      <<include CURSOR.H>>
 77      ****************************************************************
 78      * GROUP_2 - group 2 (block) commands
         group_2:
 79 00000000 207C0000001C          move.l  #k_cmd,a0        * load up prompt address
 80 00000006 61000000              bsr     prompt           * output prompt
 81 0000000A 61000000              bsr     getkey           * get switch key
 82 0000000E C07C001F              and.w   #$001F,d0        * make u/l, l/c letters cntrl
 83 00000012 207C00000044          move.l  #table2,a0       * load up case table address
 84 00000018 60000000              bra     case             * returns to caller of group_2
 85 0000001C 426C6F636B20436F  k_cmd:  dc.b    'Block Command: B C D P Q R S V W Y X',0
 85 00000024 6D6D616E643A2042
 85 0000002C 204320442050204C
 85 00000034 2052205320562057
 85 0000003C 2059205800
 86 00000042 0000
 86 00000042              dc.w    0
 87
 88      ****************************************************************
 89      * TABLE2 - switch table for group 2 commands
         table2:
 90 00000044 000C                  dc.w    12               * number of case options
 91 00000046 000B                  dc.w    $0B              * ^K mark block end
 92 00000048 00000092              dc.l    mark_end
 93 0000004C 0002                  dc.w    $02              * ^B mark block start
 94 0000004E 0000009A              dc.l    mark_start
 95 00000052 0003                  dc.w    $03              * ^C copy block to cursor
 96 00000054 000000B0              dc.l    copy
 97 00000058 0004                  dc.w    $04              * ^D end edit and save
 98 0000005A 0000022A              dc.l    end_save
 99 0000005E 0013                  dc.w    $13              * ^S save and resume
100 00000060 000001CA              dc.l    save
```

```
101 00000064 0019                    dc.w    $19           * ^Y cut block
102 00000066 000000F0                dc.l    delete
103 0000006A 0010                    dc.w    $10           * ^P Paste block
104 0000006C 0000014E                dc.l    paste
105 00000070 0011                    dc.w    $11           * ^Q abandon file
106 00000072 000001DA                dc.l    abandon
107 00000076 0017                    dc.w    $17           * ^W write block
108 00000078 0000019C                dc.l    write
109 0000007C 0012                    dc.w    $12           * ^R read file
110 0000007E 00000000                dc.l    readfile
111 00000082 0016                    dc.w    $16           * ^V move block
112 00000084 000000A2                dc.l    mblock
113 00000088 0018                    dc.w    $18           * ^X end edit and save
114 0000008A 0000022A                dc.l    end_save
115 0000008E 00000000                dc.l    default       * all other options
116
117 *************************************************************
118 * MARK_END - marks the gap as the end of the block
119 00000092 2B6D00120022 mark_end:  move.l  b_gap(a5),blk_end(a5)
120 00000098 4E75                    rts
121
122 *************************************************************
123 * MARK_START - marks the gap as the beginning of the block
124 0000009A 2B6D0012001E mark_start: move.l b_gap(a5),blk_st(a5)
125 000000A0 4E75                    rts
126
127 *************************************************************
128 * MBLOCK - moves the marked block to the cursor
129 000000A2 614C        mblock:     bsr     delete        * cut block
130 000000A4 4A6D0008                tst.w   ed_err(a5)    * check for errors
131 000000A8 6604                    bne     sk0_mbl       * exit on error
132 000000AA 610000A2                bsr     paste         * insert block here
133
134 000000AE 4E75        sk0_mbl:    rts
135
136 *************************************************************
137 * COPY - copies the marked block to the cursor
138 000000B0 61000000    copy:       bsr     chk_blk       * look for valid block
139 000000B4 4A6D0008                tst.w   ed_err(a5)    * look for error code
140 000000B8 6634                    bne     sk0_cpy       * error jump out
```

Module GROUP2.PRN (continued)

```
141 000000BA 2F2D0012      move.l   b_gap(a5),-(a7)        * save current cursor position
142 000000BE 202D0022      move.l   blk_end(a5),d0         * we want to have cursor at end
143 000000C2 61000000      bsr      seek                   * move to end of block
144 000000C6 206D001E      move.l   blk_st(a5),a0          * load source address
145 000000CA 227C00000000  move.l   #p_buf,a1              * load destination address
146 000000D0 202D0022      move.l   blk_end(a5),d0         * calculate number of bytes
147 000000D4 9088          sub.l    a0,d0                  * d0 is number of bytes
148 000000D6 2200          move.l   d0,d1                  * save number of bytes
149 000000D8 6002          bra      sk1_cpy                * loop test before loop
150
151              lp0_cpy:
    000000DA 12D8          move.b   (a0)+,(a1)+            * transfer bytes
152
153              skl_cpy:
    000000DC 51C8FFFC      dbra     d0,lp0_cpy             * loop test
154 000000E0 201F          move.l   (a7)+,d0               * get old cursor position
155 000000E2 33C100000000  move.w   d1,p_cnt               * save byte count
156 000000E8 61000000      bsr      seek                   * go back to old cursor position
157 000000EC 6160          bsr      paste                  * get stuff in
158
159              sk0_cpy:
    000000EE 4E75          rts
160 ***********************************************************
161
162              * DELETE - cuts marked block and puts into paste buffer
                 delete:
163 000000F0 61000000      bsr      chk_blk                * look for valid block
164 000000F4 4A6D0008      tst.w    ed_err(a5)             * look for error code
165 000000F8 6652          bne      sk0_del                * error jump out
166 000000FA 2F2D0012      move.l   b_gap(a5),-(a7)        * save current cursor position
167 000000FE 202D0022      move.l   blk_end(a5),d0         * we want to have cursor at end
168 00000102 61000000      bsr      seek                   * move to end of block
169 00000106 206D001E      move.l   blk_st(a5),a0          * load source address
170 0000010A 227C00000000  move.l   #p_buf,a1              * load destination address
171 00000110 202D0022      move.l   blk_end(a5),d0         * calculate number of bytes
172 00000114 9088          sub.l    a0,d0                  * d0 is number of bytes
173 00000116 2200          move.l   d0,d1                  * save number of bytes
174 00000118 6002          bra      skl_del                * loop test before loop
175
176              lp0_del:
    0000011A 12D8          move.b   (a0)+,(a1)+            * transfer bytes
177
178              skl_del:
    0000011C 51C8FFFC      dbra     d0,lp0_del             * loop test
179 00000120 2B6D001E0012  move.l   blk_st(a5),b_gap(a5)   ** erase block
180 00000126 201F          move.l   (a7)+,d0               * get old cursor position
```

```
181  00000128 B0AD0012      cmp.l  b_gap(a5),d0     * were we past cursor?
182  0000012C 6D0C          blt    sk2_del          * yes.
183  0000012E 9081          sub.l  d1,d0            * adjust for missing bytes
184  00000130 B0AD0012      cmp.l  b_gap(a5),d0     * were we in gap?
185  00000134 6C04          bge    sk2_del          * no, we're ok still
186  00000136 202D0012      move.l b_gap(a5),d0     * fake it.
187                 sk2_del:
188  0000013A 33C100000000  move.w d1,p_cnt         * save byte count
189  00000140 61000000      bsr    seek             * go back to old cursor position
190  00000144 61000000      bsr    cnt_nl           * adjust line count
191  00000148 61000000      bsr    dirty            * mark file as modified
192                 sk0_del:
193  0000014C 4E75          rts
194  ***********************************************************
195  * PASTE - pulls whatever's in paste buffer into cursor gap
196                 paste:
197  0000014E 4A7900000000  tst.w  p_cnt            * check if paste buffer used
198  00000154 673E          beq    sk0_pas          * jump if empty
199  00000156 202D0016      move.l e_gap(a5),d0     * check for room.
200  0000015A 90AD0012      sub.l  b_gap(a5),d0     * calculate gap size
201  0000015E B079000000000 cmp.w  p_cnt,d0         * test againt paste buffer
202  00000164 6526          bcs    sk2_pas          * jump on error
203  00000166 61000000      bsr    dirty            * mark file as modified
204  0000016A 206D0012      move.l b_gap(a5),a0     * get load address
205  0000016E 227C00000000  move.l #p_buf,a1        * get source address
206  00000174 303900000000  move.w p_cnt,d0         * get byte count
207  0000017A 6002          bra    sk3_pas          * loop test before move
208                 lp0_pas:
209  0000017C 10D9          move.b (a1)+,(a0)+       * transfer byte
210                 sk3_pas:
211  0000017E 51C8FFFC      dbra   d0,lp0_pas       * loop for all bytes in p_buf
212  00000182 2B480012      move.l a0,b_gap(a5)     * save new gap start pointer
213  00000186 61000000      bsr    cnt_nl           * reset line count
214  0000018A 600E          bra    sk1_pas
215                 sk2_pas:
216  0000018C 3B7C000A0008  move.w #10,ed_err(a5)   * load "block too large" code
217  00000192 6006          bra    sk1_pas          * jump out
218                 sk0_pas:
219  00000194 3B7C000B0008  move.w #11,ed_err(a5)   * load "paste buffer empty" code
220                 sk1_pas:
```

Module GROUP2.PRN (continued)

```
221 0000019A 4E75              rts
222              ***********************************************************
223              * WRITE - writes a marked block to disk
224              write:
225 0000019C 61000000          bsr      chk_blk          * check for valid blocks
226 000001A0 4A6D0008          tst.w    ed_err(a5)       * look at return code
227 000001A4 6622              bne      sk0_wrt          * error jump
228 000001A6 2F2D0012          move.l   b_gap(a5),-(a7)  * save cursor position
229 000001AA 202D0022          move.l   blk_end(a5),d0   * setup for seek
230 000001AE 61000000          bsr      seek             * seek end of block
231 000001B2 226D001E          move.l   blk_st(a5),a1    * setup for file write
232 000001B6 222D0022          move.l   blk_end(a5),d1   * compute number of bytes to write
233 000001BA 92AD001E          sub.l    blk_st(a5),d1    * D1 is number of bytes in block
234 000001BE 61000000          bsr      writefile        * go try to write file
235 000001C2 201F              move.l   (a7)+,d0         * now put cursor back
236 000001C4 61000000          bsr      seek
237              sk0_wrt:
238 000001C8 4E75              rts
239              ***********************************************************
240              * SAVE - Saves file and resumes editing
241              save:
242 000001CA 2F2D0012          move.l   b_gap(a5),-(a7)  * save current gap position
243 000001CE 61000000          bsr      putfile          * save out the file
244 000001D2 201F              move.l   (a7)+,d0         * setup for seek
245 000001D4 61000000          bsr      seek             * put cursor back
246 000001D8 4E75              rts
247              ***********************************************************
248              * ABANDON - abondon file being edited
249              abandon:
250 000001DA 4A6D000A          tst.w    modify(a5)       * check for changes
251 000001DE 6606              bne      sk0_abn          * confirm if modified
252              lp0_abn:
253 000001E0 4280              clr.l    d0
254 000001E2 588F              addq.l   #4,a7            * pop top return address
255 000001E4 4E75              rts                       * returns to 'edit's caller
256              sk0_abn:
257 000001E6 207C0000020A      move.l   #confirm,a0      * confirm prompt
258 000001EC 227C00000000      move.l   #query,a1        * general purpose response area
259 000001F2 61000000          bsr      ask              * check with the human
260 000001F6 0239005F00000000  and.b    #$5F,query       * make uppercase
```

```
261 000001FE 0C39005900000000     cmp.b   #'Y',query     * test for 'Y' or 'y'
262 00000206 67D8                  beq     lp0_abn        * human says ok, so dump it.
263 00000208 4E75                  rts                    * failed abandon exit
264                       confirm:
265 0000020A 4162616E646F6E20      dc.b    'Abandon modified file? (Y/N) ',0
265 00000212 6D6F646966696564
265 0000021A 2066696C653F2028
265 00000222 592F4E292000
266 00000228 0000                  dc.w    0
267          **********************************************************
268                       end_save:
269 0000022A 61000000              bsr     putfile        * write the file to disk
270 0000022E 4A40                  tst.w   d0             * check return code
271 00000230 6606                  bne     sk0_ener       * jump if error
272 00000232 4280                  clr.l   d0             * mark as don't resume editing
273 00000234 588F                  addq.l  #4,a7          * pop top return address
274 00000236 4E75                  rts                    * returns to caller of EDIT
275                       sk0_ener:
276 00000238 4E75                  rts                    * and back to edit main loop
277
278 0000023A                       end
```

Module GROUP4.PRN

```
 1
 2
 3                      ********************************************************************
 4                      * GROUP 4 (PC Function Key) Commands
 5
 6                                xref    getkey,case,up,down,right,left,down_page,up_page
 7                                xref    del_left,toggle,home,eof,default
 8                                xdef    group_4
 9
10                      ********************************************************************
11                      * GROUP 4 - group 4 (PC Cursor) commands
12   00000000  61000000  group_4:
13   00000004  207C0000000E          bsr     getkey        * get switch key
     0000000A  60000000             move.l  #table4,a0    * load up case table address
14                                   bra     case          * returns to caller of group_2
15                      ********************************************************************
16                      * TABLE_4 - switch table for group 4 commands
17   0000000E  000A      table4:    dc.w    10            * 10 choices
18   00000010  0048                 dc.w    $48           * cursor up key
19   00000012  00000000             dc.l    up
20   00000016  0050                 dc.w    $50           * cursor down key
21   00000018  00000000             dc.l    down
22   0000001C  004D                 dc.w    $4D           * cursor right key
23   0000001E  00000000             dc.l    right
24   00000022  004B                 dc.w    $4B           * cursor left key
25   00000024  00000000             dc.l    left
26   00000028  0051                 dc.w    $51           * PgDn key
27   0000002A  00000000             dc.l    down_page
28   0000002E  0049                 dc.w    $49           * PgUp key
29   00000030  00000000             dc.l    up_page
30   00000034  0053                 dc.w    $53           * Del key
31   00000036  00000000             dc.l    del_left
32   0000003A  0052                 dc.w    $52           * Ins key
33   0000003C  00000000             dc.l    toggle
34   00000040  0047                 dc.w    $47           * Home key
35   00000042  00000000             dc.l    home
36   00000046  004F                 dc.w    $4F           * End key
37   00000048  00000000             dc.l    eof
38   0000004C  00000000             dc.l    default
39
40   00000050                       end
```

B

Math Routines

Module BCD.PRN

```
     1    **********************************************************************
     2    *                                                                    *
     3    *     BCD Arithmetic Multiple Precision Routines  -  CP/M-69K AS68    *
     4    *                                                                    *
     5    *     All routines operate on n-digit BCD numbers stored in memory.  *
     6    *     'n' is set by an equate, and assembled in. 'n' must be even.    *
     7    *                                                                    *
     8    *     Routines:       BCD_ADD   Adds two n-digit BCD numbers          *
     9    *                     BCD_SUB   Subtracts two n-digit BCD numbers     *
    10    *                     BCD_NEG   Negates two n-digit BCD numbers       *
    11    *                     BCD_MOVE  Moves an n-digit BCD number           *
    12    *                                                                    *
    13    *     Constants:      BCD_ZERO  zero, in n-digit BCD format           *
    14    *                     BCD_ONE   one, in n-digit BCD format            *
    15    *                     BCD_NONE  minus one, in n-digit BCD format      *
    16    *                                                                    *
    17    *     Calling Conventions:                                            *
    18    *                     A0 points to source operand in memory.          *
    19    *                     A1 points to destination operand in memory.     *
    20    *                     (A0 not used for single operand calls)          *
    21    *                                                                    *
    22    *     Exit Conditions:                                                *
    23    *                     A0 points to source operand in memory (if used).*
    24    *                     A1 points to (modified) destination operand in memory.*
    25    *                                                                    *
    26    *     Exit Flags:     N   Set if result BCD negative.                 *
    27    *                     Z   Clear if result non-zero, set if result zero.*
    28    *                     V   Undefined.                                  *
    29    *                     C   Set on BCD borrow/carry                     *
    30    *                     X   Same as C-flag.                             *
    31    *                                                                    *
    32    DIGITS   equ    10/2
    33    *
    34 00000000         even
    35                  text               * begin program section
    36                  .xdef  BCD_ADD,BCD_SUB,BCD_NEG,BCD_ONE,BCD_ZERO,BCD_NONE
    37    **********************************************************************
    38    * General-Purpose BCD Constants
    39 00000000 00000000000000000 BCD_ZERO:
    40                  DC.W   0,0,0,0          * Good for n <= 16 digits
         BCD_NONE:
```

```
41  00000008  9999                          DC.W      $9999              * Good for n <= 16 digits
42  0000000A  9999                          DC.W      $9999
43  0000000C  9999                          DC.W      $9999
44  0000000E  9999                          DC.W      $9999
45
46  00000010  00000000      BCD_ONE:        DC.W      $0,0               * Good only for n = 10
47  00000014  0100                          DC.W      $0100
48                          *
49                          ************************************************
50                          * Adds n-digit BCD numbers.
51                          ************************************************
52  00000016  2F09          BCD_ADD:        MOVE.L    A1,-(A7)           * Save Destination pointer
53  00000018  2F00                          MOVE.L    D0,-(A7)           * Save loop counter register
54  0000001A  5A88                          ADDQ.L    #DIGITS,A0         * Move past source operand
55  0000001C  5A89                          ADDQ.L    #DIGITS,A1         * Move past dest operand
56  0000001E  7004                          MOVEQ.L   #DIGITS-1,D0       * Set loop counter
57  00000020  44FC0004                      MOVE.W    #$04,CCR           * Preset flags
58                          *
59  00000024  C308          ADD_LOOP:       ABCD      -(A0),-(A1)        * Actual addition here...
60  00000026  51C8FFFC                      DBRA      D0,ADD_LOOP        * Decrement D0/branch not -1
61  0000002A  6046                          BRA       BCD_OUT            * Clean up flags & exit
62                          *
63                          ************************************************
64
65  0000002C  2F09          BCD_SUB:        MOVE.L    A1,-(A7)           * Save Destination pointer
66  0000002E  2F00                          MOVE.L    D0,-(A7)           * Save loop counter register
67  00000030  5A88                          ADDQ.L    #DIGITS,A0         * Move past source operand
68  00000032  5A89                          ADDQ.L    #DIGITS,A1         * Move past dest operand
69  00000034  7004                          MOVEQ.L   #DIGITS-1,D0       * Setup loop counter
70  00000036  44FC0004                      MOVE.W    #$04,CCR           * Preset flags
71                          *
72  0000003A  8308          SUB_LOOP:       SBCD      -(A0),-(A1)        * Actual subtraction...
73  0000003C  51C8FFFC                      DBRA      D0,SUB_LOOP        * Decrement D0/Branch not -1
74  00000040  6030                          BRA       BCD_OUT            * Clean up flags and exit
75                          *
76                          ************************************************
77
78  00000042  2F09          BCD_NEG:        MOVE.L    A1,-(A7)           * Push dest pointer
79  00000044  2F00                          MOVE.L    D0,-(A7)           * Save loop counter register
80  00000046  5A89                          ADDQ.L    #DIGITS,A1         * Move past dest operand
```

```
                              MOVEQ.L #DIGITS-1,D0    * Setup loop counter
81 00000048 7004              MOVE.W  #$04,CCR        * Preset flags
82 0000004A 44FC0004
83
84 0000004E 4821     NEG_LOOP:  NBCD  -(A1)           * Negation
85 00000050 51C8FFFC            DBRA  D0,NEG_LOOP     * Decrement D0, branch not -1
86 00000054 601C               BRA   BCD_OUT         * Clean up flags and exit
87
88              *********************************************************
89
90 00000056 2F09     BCD_MOVE:  MOVE.L A1,-(A7)       * Push caller's A1
91 00000058 2F00               MOVE.L D0,-(A7)        * Push loop counter register
92 0000005A 2F08               MOVE.L A0,-(A7)        * Push caller's A0
93 0000005C 3F3C0000           MOVE.W #0,-(A7)        * Make a temporary flag var
94 00000060 7004               MOVEQ.L #DIGITS-1,D0   * Setup loop counter
95
96 00000062 12D8     MOVE_LOOP: MOVE.B (A0)+,(A1)+    * Copy bytes
97 00000064 6704               BEQ   MOVE_TEST        * Check for zero flag
98 00000066 3EBC00FF           MOVE.W #$00FF,(A7)     * Mark flag non-zero
99
100 0000006A 51C8FFF6 MOVE_TEST: DBRA D0,MOVE_LOOP    * Decrement D0, branch not -1
101 0000006E 301F               MOVE.W (A7)+,D0       * Pop temp to set Z, C flags
102 00000070 205F               MOVE.L (A7)+,A0       * Pop caller's A0
103
104              *********************************************************
105              * Simulates binary arithmetic flag action for BCD arithmetic, also
106              * pops D0, A1 saved previously.
107              BCD_OUT:
108 00000072 226F0004          MOVE.L 4(A7),A1        * Retrieve Destination pointer
109 00000076 40E7              MOVE.W SR,-(A7)        * Push Flags
110 00000078 1011              MOVE.B (A1),D0         * Get high byte of result
111 0000007A C03C00F0          AND.B  #$F0,D0         * Mask out low digit
112 0000007E 0C000090          CMPI.B #$90,D0         * Is high digit negative (9)?
113 00000082 6708              BEQ    IS_NEG          * Yes, jump to set N flag
114 00000084 44DF              MOVE.W (A7)+,CCR       * Pop old flags
115 00000086 023C00F7          ANDI.W #$00F7,CCR      * Clear N flag
116 0000008A 6006              BRA    DONE            * get outta here
117
118 0000008C 44DF     IS_NEG:  MOVE.W (A7)+,CCR       * Pop old flags
119 0000008E 003C0008          ORI.W  #$0008,CCR      * Set N flag
120
121 00000092 225F     DONE:    MOVE.L (A7)+,A1        * Pop caller's D0 and EXG to
122 00000094 C189              EXG    A1,D0           *   avoid trashing flags.
123 00000096 225F              MOVE.L (A7)+,A1        * Retrieve caller's A1
124 00000098 4E75              RTS                    * Common exit
125 0000009A                   END
```

Module SQRT.PRN

```
1                   **********************************************************
2                   * SQRT - Integer floored square root
3                   *       Entry:  D0.L = number to take root of
4                   *       Exit:   D0.L = square root
5
6                           xdef    sqrt
7
8
9   00000000 48E77000 sqrt:   movem.l d1-d3,-(a7)
10  00000004 4281             clr.l   d1              * D1 will be test case root
11  00000006 343C8000         move.w  #$8000,d2       * D2 is succ. aprox. mask
12
13  0000000A 8242     lpl:    or.w    d2,d1           * load in mask value
14  0000000C 3601             move.w  d1,d3           * d3 is a scratch register
15  0000000E C6C3             mulu    d3,d3           * make a try
16  00000010 B083             cmp.l   d3,d0           * take a look - how'd we do?
17  00000012 6206             bhi     skl             * try less than goal - keep bit
18  00000014 4642             not.w   d2              * we need to mask bit out
19  00000016 C242             and.w   d2,d1           * take out trial bit
20  00000018 4642             not.w   d2              * fix mask
21
22  0000001A E24A     skl:    lsr.w   #1,d2           * move mask down
23  0000001C 64EC             bcc     lpl             * mask mot done - go around.
24
25  0000001E 2001     sq_exit: move.l  d1,d0          * transfer answer
26  00000020 4CDF000E         movem.l (a7)+,d1-d3     * restore registers
27  00000024 4E75             rts
```

Module SQRT2.PRN

```
 1                        ************************************************************
 2                        * SQRT - Integer floored square root
 3                        *     Entry: D0.L = number to take root of
 4                        *     Exit:  D0.L = square root
 5                        *
 6                                xdef    sqrt
 7
 8                        sqrt:
 9  00000000 48E77000            movem.l d1-d3,-(a7)
10  00000004 4281                clr.l   d1               * D1 will be test case root
11  00000006 343C000F            move.w  #15,d2           * D2 is succ. aprox. mask
12                        lpl:
13  0000000A 05C1                bset    d2,d1            * load in mask value
14  0000000C 3601                move.w  d1,d3            * d3 is a scratch register
15  0000000E C6C3                mulu    d3,d3            * make a try
16  00000010 B083                cmp.l   d3,d0            * take a look - how'd we do?
17  00000012 6202                bhi     skl              * try less than goal - keep bit
18  00000014 0581                bclr    d2,d1            * we need to reset bit
19                        skl:
20  00000016 5342                subq.w  #1,d2            * move mask down
21  00000018 6CF0                bge     lpl              * mask not done - go around.
22                        sq_exit:
23  0000001A 2001                move.l  d1,d0            * transfer answer
24  0000001C 4CDF000E            movem.l (a7)+,d1-d3      * restore registers
25  00000020 4E75                rts
```

Module SQRT3.PRN

```
1
2   ******************************************************************
3   * SQRT - Integer floored square root
4   *       Entry:  D0.L = number to take root of
5   *       Exit:   D0.L = square root
6   *       xdef    sqrt
7
    sqrt:
8  00000000 48E77000    movem.l  d1-d3,-(a7)
9  00000004 343C8000    move.w   #$8000,d2    * D2 is succ. aprox. mask
10 00000008 2200        move.l   d0,d1        * copy argument
11 0000000A 6724        beq      zer_exit     * exit if zero
12
    lp0:
13 0000000C E389        lsl.l    #1,d1        * look for non-zero bit...
14 0000000E 6508        bcs      sk2          * jump if we find one
15 00000010 E389        lsl.l    #1,d1        * look for non-zero bit...
16 00000012 6504        bcs      sk2          * jump if we find one
17 00000014 E24A        lsr.w    #1,d2        * shift test mask
18 00000016 60F4        bra      lp0          * repeat for new bit
19
    sk2:
20 00000018 4281        clr.l    d1           * D1 will be test case root
21
    lpl:
22 0000001A 8242        or.w     d2,d1        * load in mask value
23 0000001C 3601        move.w   d1,d3        * d3 is a scratch register
24 0000001E C6C3        mulu     d3,d3        * make a try
25 00000020 B083        cmp.l    d3,d0        * take a look - how'd we do?
26 00000022 6206        bhi      skl          * try less than goal - keep bit
27 00000024 4642        not.w    d2           * we need to mask bit out
28 00000026 C242        and.w    d2,d1        * take out trial bit
29 00000028 4642        not.w    d2           * fix mask
30
    skl:
31 0000002A E24A        lsr.w    #1,d2        * move mask down
32 0000002C 64EC        bcc      lpl          * mask mot done - go around.
33
    sq_exit:
34 0000002E 2001        move.l   d1,d0        * transfer answer
35
    zer_exit:
36 00000030 4CDF000E    movem.l  (a7)+,d1-d3  * restore registers
37 00000034 4E75        rts
```

C

Instruction Format Summary *

C.1 INTRODUCTION

This appendix provides a summary of the first word in each instruction of the instruction set. Table C-1 is an operation code (op-code) map which illustrates how bits 15 through 12 are used to specify the operations. The remaining paragraph groups the instructions according to the op-code map.

Table C-1. Operation Code Map

Bits 15 through 12	Operation	Bits 15 through 12	Operation
0000	Bit Manipulation/MOVEP/Immediate	1000	OR/DIV/SBCD
0001	Move Byte	1001	SUB/SUBX
0010	Move Long	1010	(Unassigned)
0011	Move Word	1011	CMP/EOR
0100	Miscellaneous	1100	AND/MUL/ABCD/EXG
0101	ADDQ/SUBQ/Scc/DBcc	1101	ADD/ADDX
0110	Bcc/BSR	1110	Shift/Rotate
0111	MOVEQ	1111	(Unassigned)

Table C-2. Effective Address Encoding Summary

Addressing Mode	Mode	Register
Data Register Direct	000	register number
Address Register Direct	001	register number
Address Register Indirect	010	register number
Address Register Indirect with Postincrement	011	register number
Address Register Indirect with Predecrement	100	register number
Address Register Indirect with Displacement	101	register number
Address Register Indirect with Index	110	register number
Absolute Short	111	000
Absolute Long	111	001
Program Counter with Displacement	111	010
Program Counter with Index	111	011
Immediate or Status Register	111	100

*Courtesy of Motorola, Inc.

Table C-3. Conditional Tests

Mnemonic	Condition	Encoding	Test
T	true	0000	1
F	false	0001	0
HI	high	0010	$\overline{C} \cdot \overline{Z}$
LS	low or same	0011	$C + Z$
CC(HS)	carry clear	0100	$\overline{C}$
CS(LO)	carry set	0101	C
NE	not equal	0110	$\overline{Z}$
EQ	equal	0111	Z
VC	overflow clear	1000	$\overline{V}$
VS	overflow set	1001	V
PL	plus	1010	$\overline{N}$
MI	minus	1011	N
GE	greater or equal	1100	$N \cdot V + \overline{N} \cdot \overline{V}$
LT	less than	1101	$N \cdot \overline{V} + \overline{N} \cdot V$
GT	greater than	1110	$N \cdot V \cdot \overline{Z} + \overline{N} \cdot \overline{V} \cdot \overline{Z}$
LE	less or equal	1111	$Z + N \cdot \overline{V} + \overline{N} \cdot V$

OR Immediate

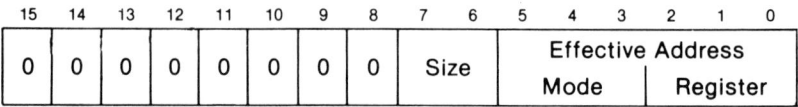

15	14	13	12	11	10	9	8	7	6	5	4	3	2	1	0
0	0	0	0	0	0	0	0	Size		Effective Address Mode			Register		

Size field: 00 = byte
01 = word
10 = long

OR Immediate to CCR

15	14	13	12	11	10	9	8	7	6	5	4	3	2	1	0
0	0	0	0	0	0	0	0	0	0	1	1	1	1	0	0

OR Immediate to SR

15	14	13	12	11	10	9	8	7	6	5	4	3	2	1	0
0	0	0	0	0	0	0	0	0	1	1	1	1	1	0	0

Dynamic Bit

15	14	13	12	11 10 9	8	7 6	5 4 3	2 1 0
0	0	0	0	Data Register	1	Type	Effective Address Mode	Register

Type field: 00 = TST
01 = CHG
10 = CLR
11 = SET

MOVEP

15	14	13	12	11 10 9	8 7 6	5	4	3	2 1 0
0	0	0	0	Data Register	Op-Mode	0	0	1	Address Register

Op-Mode field: 100 = transfer word from memory to register
101 = transfer long from memory to register
110 = transfer word from register to memory
111 = transfer long from register to memory

AND Immediate

15	14	13	12	11	10	9	8	7 6	5 4 3	2 1 0
0	0	0	0	0	0	1	0	Size	Effective Address Mode	Register

Size field: 00 = byte
01 = word
10 = long

AND Immediate to CCR

15	14	13	12	11	10	9	8	7	6	5	4	3	2	1	0
0	0	0	0	0	0	1	0	0	0	1	1	1	1	0	0

AND Immediate to SR

15	14	13	12	11	10	9	8	7	6	5	4	3	2	1	0
0	0	0	0	0	0	1	0	0	1	1	1	1	1	0	0

SUB Immediate

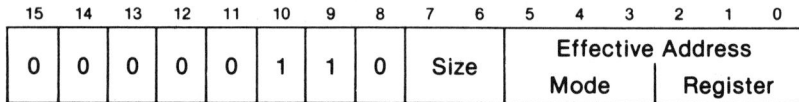

15	14	13	12	11	10	9	8	7	6	5	4	3	2	1	0
0	0	0	0	0	1	0	0	Size		Effective Address					
										Mode			Register		

Size field: 00 = byte
01 = word
10 = long

ADD Immediate

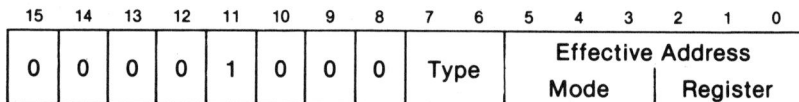

15	14	13	12	11	10	9	8	7	6	5	4	3	2	1	0
0	0	0	0	0	1	1	0	Size		Effective Address					
										Mode			Register		

Size field: 00 = byte
01 = word
10 = long

Static Bit

15	14	13	12	11	10	9	8	7	6	5	4	3	2	1	0
0	0	0	0	1	0	0	0	Type		Effective Address					
										Mode			Register		

Type field: 00 = TST
01 = CHG
10 = CLR
11 = SET

EOR Immediate

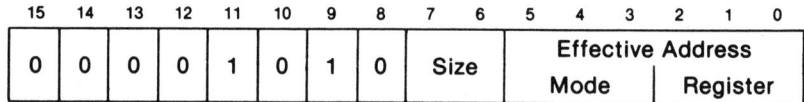

15	14	13	12	11	10	9	8	7	6	5	4	3	2	1	0
0	0	0	0	1	0	1	0	Size		Effective Address					
										Mode			Register		

Size field: 00 = byte
01 = word
10 = long

EOR Immediate to CCR

15	14	13	12	11	10	9	8	7	6	5	4	3	2	1	0
0	0	0	0	1	0	1	0	0	0	1	1	1	1	0	0

EOR Immediate to SR

15	14	13	12	11	10	9	8	7	6	5	4	3	2	1	0
0	0	0	0	1	0	1	0	0	1	1	1	1	1	0	0

CMP Immediate

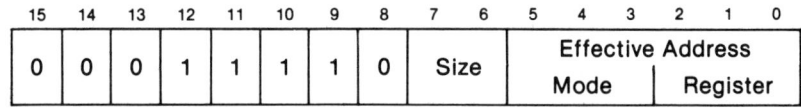

15	14	13	12	11	10	9	8	7	6	5	4	3	2	1	0
0	0	0	0	1	1	0	0	Size		Effective Address					

15	14	13	12	11	10	9	8	7	6	5	4	3	2	1	0
0	0	0	0	1	1	0	0	Size		Effective Address					
										Mode			Register		

Size field: 00 = byte
01 = word
10 = word

MOVES   MC68010

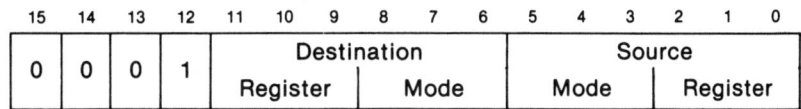

15	14	13	12	11	10	9	8	7	6	5	4	3	2	1	0
0	0	0	1	1	1	1	0	Size		Effective Address					
										Mode			Register		

Size field: 00 = byte
01 = word
10 = long

MOVE Byte

15	14	13	12	11	10	9	8	7	6	5	4	3	2	1	0
0	0	0	1	Destination						Source					
				Register			Mode			Mode			Register		

Note register and mode locations

MOVEA Long

14	14	13	12	11 10 9	8	7	6	5 4 3	2 1 0
0	0	1	0	Destination Register	0	0	1	Source Mode	Source Register

MOVE Long

15	14	13	12	11 10 9	8 7 6	5 4 3	2 1 0
0	0	1	0	Destination Register	Destination Mode	Source Mode	Source Register

Note register and mode locations

MOVEA Word

15	14	13	12	11 10 9	8	7	6	5 4 3	2 1 0
0	0	1	1	Destination Register	0	0	1	Source Mode	Source Register

MOVE Word

15	14	13	12	11 10 9	8 7 6	5 4 3	2 1 0
0	0	1	1	Destination Register	Destination Mode	Source Mode	Source Register

Note register and mode locations

NEGX

15	14	13	12	11	10	9	8	7	6	5	4	3	2	1	0
0	1	0	0	0	0	0	0	Size		Effective Address					
										Mode			Register		

Size field: 00 = byte
01 = word
10 = long

MOVE from SR

15	14	13	12	11	10	9	8	7	6	5	4	3	2	1	0
0	1	0	0	0	0	0	0	1	1	Effective Address					
										Mode			Register		

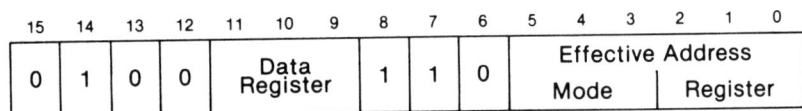

CHK

15	14	13	12	11	10	9	8	7	6	5	4	3	2	1	0
0	1	0	0	Data Register			1	1	0	Effective Address					
										Mode			Register		

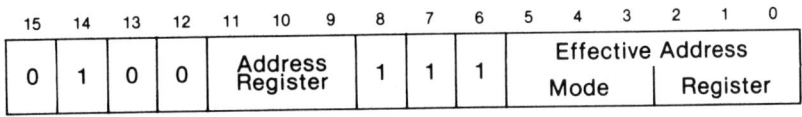

LEA

15	14	13	12	11	10	9	8	7	6	5	4	3	2	1	0
0	1	0	0	Address Register			1	1	1	Effective Address					
										Mode			Register		

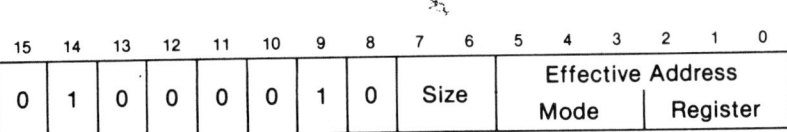

CLR

15	14	13	12	11	10	9	8	7	6	5	4	3	2	1	0
0	1	0	0	0	0	1	0	Size		Effective Address					
										Mode			Register		

Size field: 00 = byte
01 = word
10 = long

MOVE from CCR   MC68010

15	14	13	12	11	10	9	8	7	6	5	4	3	2	1	0
0	1	0	0	0	0	1	0	1	1	Effective Address Mode			Register		

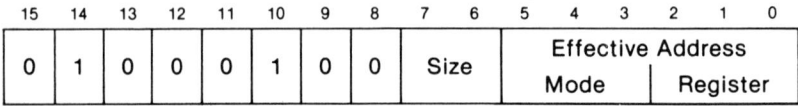

NEG

15	14	13	12	11	10	9	8	7	6	5	4	3	2	1	0
0	1	0	0	0	1	0	0	Size		Effective Address Mode			Register		

Size field: 00 = byte
01 = word
10 = long

MOVE to CCR

15	14	13	12	11	10	9	8	7	6	5	4	3	2	1	0
0	1	0	0	0	1	0	0	1	1	Effective Address Mode			Register		

NOT

15	14	13	12	11	10	9	8	7	6	5	4	3	2	1	0
0	1	0	0	0	1	1	0	Size		Effective Address Mode			Register		

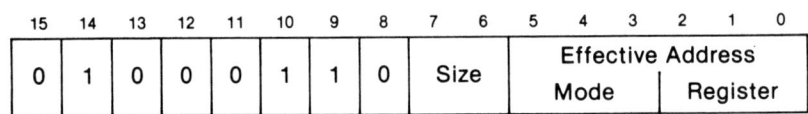

Size field: 00 = byte
01 = word
10 = long

MOVE to SR

15	14	13	12	11	10	9	8	7	6	5	4	3	2	1	0
0	1	0	0	0	1	1	0	1	1	Effective Address Mode			Register		

NBCD

15	14	13	12	11	10	9	8	7	6	5	4	3	2	1	0
0	1	0	0	1	0	0	0	0	0	Effective Address Mode			Register		

SWAP

15	14	13	12	11	10	9	8	7	6	5	4	3	2	1	0
0	1	0	0	1	0	0	0	0	1	0	0	0	Data Register		

PEA

15	14	13	12	11	10	9	8	7	6	5	4	3	2	1	0
0	1	0	0	1	0	0	0	0	1	Effective Address Mode			Register		

EXT Word

15	14	13	12	11	10	9	8	7	6	5	4	3	2	1	0
0	1	0	0	1	0	0	0	1	0	0	0	0	Data Register		

MOVEM Registers to EA

15	14	13	12	11	10	9	8	7	6	5	4	3	2	1	0
0	1	0	0	1	0	0	0	1	Sz	Effective Address Mode			Register		

Sz field: 0 = word transfer
1 = long transfer

EXT Long

15	14	13	12	11	10	9	8	7	6	5	4	3	2	1	0
0	1	0	0	1	0	0	0	1	1	0	0	0	Data Register		

TST

15	14	13	12	11	10	9	8	7	6	5	4	3	2	1	0
										Effective Address					
0	1	0	0	1	0	1	0	Size		Mode			Register		

Size field: 00 = byte
01 = word
10 = long

TAS

15	14	13	12	11	10	9	8	7	6	5	4	3	2	1	0
										Effective Address					
0	1	0	0	1	0	1	0	1	1	Mode			Register		

ILLEGAL

15	14	13	12	11	10	9	8	7	6	5	4	3	2	1	0
0	1	0	0	1	0	1	0	1	1	1	1	1	1	0	0

MOVEM EA to Registers

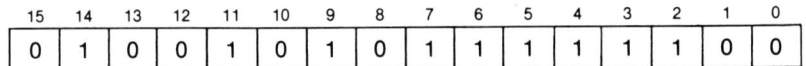
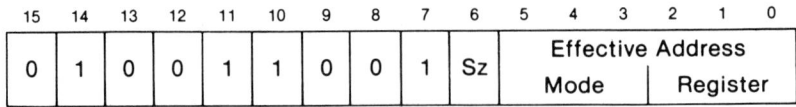

15	14	13	12	11	10	9	8	7	6	5	4	3	2	1	0
										Effective Address					
0	1	0	0	1	1	0	0	1	Sz	Mode			Register		

Sz field: 0 = word transfer
1 = long transfer

TRAP

15	14	13	12	11	10	9	8	7	6	5	4	3	2	1	0
0	1	0	0	1	1	1	0	0	1	0	0	Vector			

LINK

15	14	13	12	11	10	9	8	7	6	5	4	3	2	1	0
0	1	0	0	1	1	1	0	0	1	0	1	0	Address Register		

UNLK

15	14	13	12	11	10	9	8	7	6	5	4	3	2	1	0
0	1	0	0	1	1	1	0	0	1	0	1	1	Address Register		

MOVE to USP

15	14	13	12	11	10	9	8	7	6	5	4	3	2	1	0
0	1	0	0	1	1	1	0	0	1	1	0	0	Address Register		

MOVE from USP

15	14	13	12	11	10	9	8	7	6	5	4	3	2	1	0
0	1	0	0	1	1	1	0	0	1	1	0	1	Address Register		

RESET

15	14	13	12	11	10	9	8	7	6	5	4	3	2	1	0
0	1	0	0	1	1	1	0	0	1	1	1	0	0	0	0

NOP

15	14	13	12	11	10	9	8	7	6	5	4	3	2	1	0
0	1	0	0	1	1	1	0	0	1	1	1	0	0	0	1

STOP

15	14	13	12	11	10	9	8	7	6	5	4	3	2	1	0
0	1	0	0	1	1	1	0	0	1	1	1	0	0	1	0

RTE

15	14	13	12	11	10	9	8	7	6	5	4	3	2	1	0
0	1	0	0	1	1	1	0	0	1	1	1	0	0	1	1

RTD   MC68010

15	14	13	12	11	10	9	8	7	6	5	4	3	2	1	0
0	1	0	0	1	1	1	0	0	1	1	1	0	1	0	0

RTS

15	14	13	12	11	10	9	8	7	6	5	4	3	2	1	0
0	1	0	0	1	1	1	0	0	1	1	1	0	1	0	1

TRAPV

15	14	13	12	11	10	9	8	7	6	5	4	3	2	1	0
0	1	0	0	1	1	1	0	0	1	1	1	0	1	1	0

RTR

15	14	13	12	11	10	9	8	7	6	5	4	3	2	1	0
0	1	0	0	1	1	1	0	0	1	1	1	0	1	1	1

MOVEC   MC68010

15	14	13	12	11	10	9	8	7	6	5	4	3	2	1	0
0	1	0	0	1	1	1	0	0	1	1	1	1	0	1	dr

dr field: 0 = control register to general register
           1 = general register to control register

JSR

15	14	13	12	11	10	9	8	7	6	5	4	3	2	1	0
0	1	0	0	1	1	1	0	1	0	Effective Address					
										Mode			Register		

JMP

15	14	13	12	11	10	9	8	7	6	5	4	3	2	1	0
0	1	0	0	1	1	1	0	1	1	Effective Mode					
										Mode			Register		

ADDQ

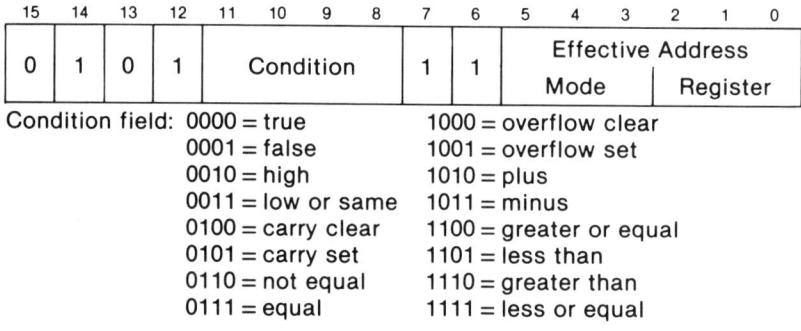

15	14	13	12	11	10	9	8	7	6	5	4	3	2	1	0
0	1	0	1	Data			0	Size		Effective Address					
										Mode			Register		

Data field: Three bits of immediate data, 0, 1-7 representing a range of 8, 1 to 7 respectively.

Size field: 00 = byte
01 = word
10 = long

Scc

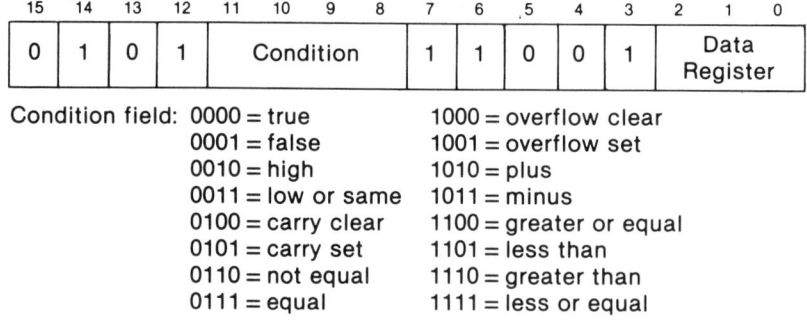

15	14	13	12	11	10	9	8	7	6	5	4	3	2	1	0
0	1	0	1	Condition				1	1	Effective Address					
										Mode			Register		

Condition field: 0000 = true   1000 = overflow clear
0001 = false   1001 = overflow set
0010 = high   1010 = plus
0011 = low or same   1011 = minus
0100 = carry clear   1100 = greater or equal
0101 = carry set   1101 = less than
0110 = not equal   1110 = greater than
0111 = equal   1111 = less or equal

DBcc

15	14	13	12	11	10	9	8	7	6	5	4	3	2	1	0
0	1	0	1	Condition				1	1	0	0	1	Data Register		

Condition field: 0000 = true   1000 = overflow clear
0001 = false   1001 = overflow set
0010 = high   1010 = plus
0011 = low or same   1011 = minus
0100 = carry clear   1100 = greater or equal
0101 = carry set   1101 = less than
0110 = not equal   1110 = greater than
0111 = equal   1111 = less or equal

SUBQ

15	14	13	12	11	10	9	8	7	6	5	4	3	2	1	0
0	1	0	1	Data			1	Size		Effective Address					
										Mode			Register		

Data field: Three bits of immediate data, 0, 1-7 representing a range of 8, 1 to 7 respectively.
Size field: 00 = byte
01 = word
10 = long

Bcc

15	14	13	12	11	10	9	8	7	6	5	4	3	2	1	0
0	1	1	0	Condition				8-Bit Displacement							

Condition field: 0010 = high   1001 = overflow set
0011 = low or same   1010 = plus
0100 = carry clear   1011 = minus
0101 = carry set   1100 = greater or equal
0110 = not equal   1101 = less than
0111 = equal   1110 = greater than
1000 = overflow clear 1111 = less or equal

BRA

15	14	13	12	11	10	9	8	7	6	5	4	3	2	1	0
0	1	1	0	0	0	0	0	8-Bit Displacement							

BSR

15	14	13	12	11	10	9	8	7	6	5	4	3	2	1	0
0	1	1	0	0	0	0	1	8-Bit Displacement							

MOVEQ

15	14	13	12	11	10	9	8	7	6	5	4	3	2	1	0
0	1	1	1	Data Register			0	Data							

Data field: Data is sign extended to a long operand and all 32 bits are transferred to the data register.

OR

15	14	13	12	11	10	9	8	7	6	5	4	3	2	1	0
1	0	0	0	Data Register			Op-Mode			Effective Address					
										Mode			Register		

Op-Mode field:

Byte	Word	Long	Operation
000	001	010	(<Dn>)∨(<ea>)→Dn
100	101	110	(<ea>)∨(<Dn>)→ea

DIVU

15	14	13	12	11	10	9	8	7	6	5	4	3	2	1	0
1	0	0	0	Data Register			0	1	1	Effective Address					
										Mode			Register		

SBCD

15	14	13	12	11	10	9	8	7	6	5	4	3	2	1	0
1	0	0	0	Destination Register*			1	0	0	0	0	R/M	Source Register*		

R/M field: 0 = data register to data register
           1 = memory to memory
*If R/M = 0, specifies a data register.
 If R/M = 1, specifies an address register for the predecrement addressing mode.

DIVS

15	14	13	12	11	10	9	8	7	6	5	4	3	2	1	0
1	0	0	0	Data Register			1	1	1	Effective Address — Mode			Register		

SUB

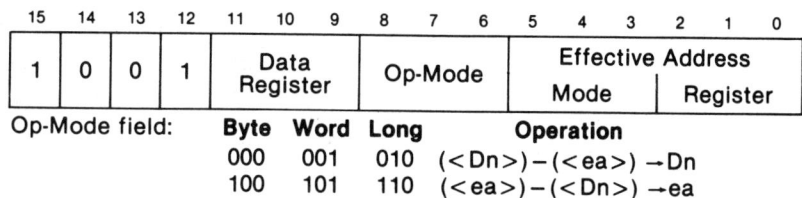

15	14	13	12	11	10	9	8	7	6	5	4	3	2	1	0
1	0	0	1	Data Register			Op-Mode			Effective Address — Mode			Register		

Op-Mode field:

Byte	Word	Long	Operation
000	001	010	(<Dn>)−(<ea>) →Dn
100	101	110	(<ea>)−(<Dn>) →ea

SUBA

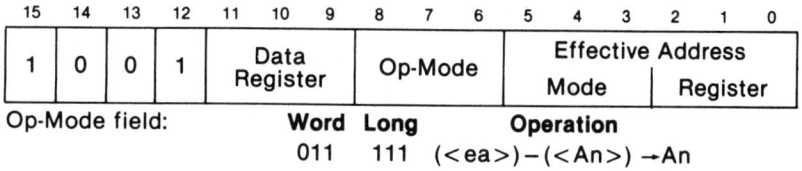

15	14	13	12	11	10	9	8	7	6	5	4	3	2	1	0
1	0	0	1	Data Register			Op-Mode			Effective Address — Mode			Register		

Op-Mode field:

Word	Long	Operation
011	111	(<ea>)−(<An>) →An

SUBX

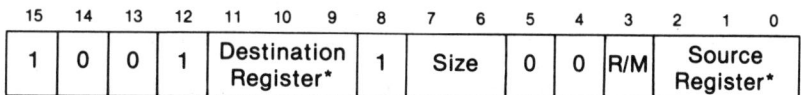

15	14	13	12	11	10	9	8	7	6	5	4	3	2	1	0
1	0	0	1	Destination Register*			1	Size		0	0	R/M	Source Register*		

Size field: 00 = byte
01 = word
10 = long
R/M field: 0 = data register to data register
1 = memory to memory
*If R/M = 0, specifies a data register.
If R/M = 1, specifies an address register for the predecrement addressing mode.

CMP

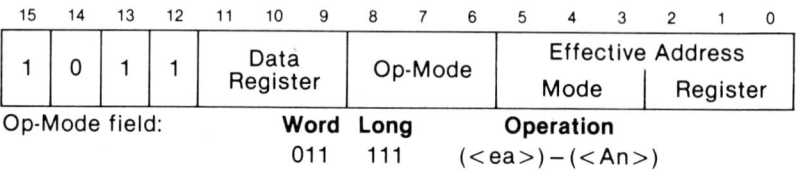

15	14	13	12	11 10 9	8 7 6	5 4 3	2 1 0
						Effective Address	
1	0	1	1	Data Register	Op-Mode	Mode	Register

Op-Mode field:

Byte	Word	Long	Operation
000	001	010	(<Dn>) – (<ea>)

CMPA

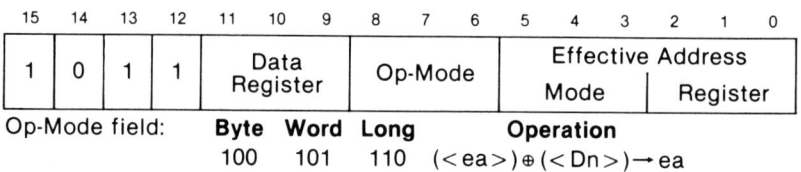

15	14	13	12	11 10 9	8 7 6	5 4 3	2 1 0
						Effective Address	
1	0	1	1	Data Register	Op-Mode	Mode	Register

Op-Mode field:

Word	Long	Operation
011	111	(<ea>) – (<An>)

EOR

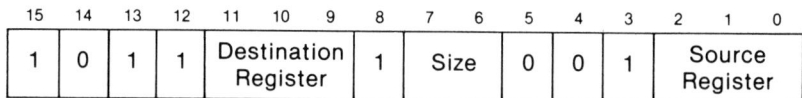

15	14	13	12	11 10 9	8 7 6	5 4 3	2 1 0
						Effective Address	
1	0	1	1	Data Register	Op-Mode	Mode	Register

Op-Mode field:

Byte	Word	Long	Operation
100	101	110	(<ea>) ⊕ (<Dn>) → ea

CMPM

15	14	13	12	11 10 9	8	7 6	5	4	3	2 1 0
1	0	1	1	Destination Register	1	Size	0	0	1	Source Register

Size field: 00 = byte
01 = word
10 = long

AND

15	14	13	12	11	10	9	8	7	6	5	4	3	2	1	0
1	1	0	0	Data Register			Op-Mode			Effective Address					
										Mode			Register		

Op-Mode field:

	Byte	Word	Long	Operation
	000	001	010	$(<Dn>)\Lambda(<ea>) \rightarrow Dn$
	100	101	110	$(<ea>)\Lambda(<Dn>) \rightarrow ea$

MULU

15	14	13	12	11	10	9	8	7	6	5	4	3	2	1	0
1	1	0	0	Data Register			0	1	1	Effective Address					
										Mode			Register		

ABCD

15	14	13	12	11	10	9	8	7	6	5	4	3	2	1	0
1	1	0	0	Destination Register*			1	0	0	0	0	R/M	Source Register*		

R/M field: 0 = data register to data register
1 = memory to memory
*If R/M = 0, specifies a data register.
If R/M = 1, specifies an address register for the predecrement addressing mode.

EXG Data Registers

15	14	13	12	11	10	9	8	7	6	5	4	3	2	1	0
1	1	0	0	Data Register			1	0	1	0	0	0	Data Register		

EXG Address Registers

15	14	13	12	11	10	9	8	7	6	5	4	3	2	1	0
1	1	0	0	Address Register			1	0	1	0	0	1	Address Register		

EXG Data Register and Address Register

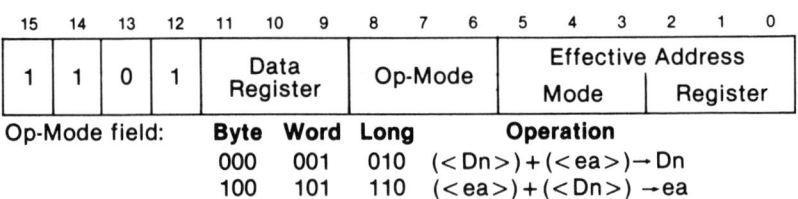

15	14	13	12	11 10 9	8	7	6	5	4	3	2 1 0
1	1	0	0	Data Register	1	1	0	0	0	1	Address Register

MULS

15	14	13	12	11 10 9	8	7	6	5 4 3	2 1 0
1	1	0	0	Data Register	1	1	1	Effective Address Mode	Register

ADD

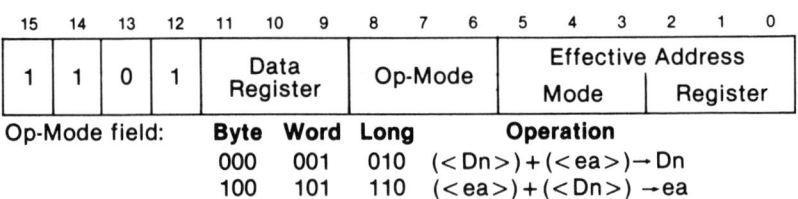

15	14	13	12	11 10 9	8 7 6	5 4 3	2 1 0
1	1	0	1	Data Register	Op-Mode	Effective Address Mode	Register

Op-Mode field:

Byte	Word	Long	Operation
000	001	010	$(<Dn>)+(<ea>) \rightarrow Dn$
100	101	110	$(<ea>)+(<Dn>) \rightarrow ea$

ADDA

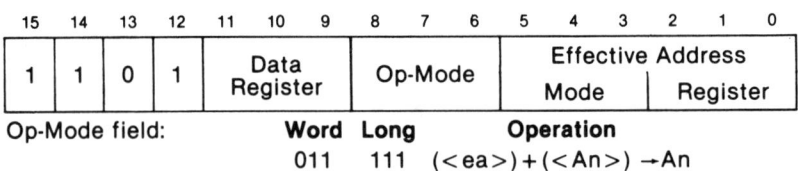

15	14	13	12	11 10 9	8 7 6	5 4 3	2 1 0
1	1	0	1	Data Register	Op-Mode	Effective Address Mode	Register

Op-Mode field:

Word	Long	Operation
011	111	$(<ea>)+(<An>) \rightarrow An$

ADDX

15	14	13	12	11	10	9	8	7	6	5	4	3	2	1	0
1	1	0	1	Destination Register*			1	Size		0	0	R/M	Source Register*		

Size field: 00 = byte
            01 = word
            10 = long
R/M field: 0 = data register to data register
            1 = memory to memory
*If R/M = 0, specifies a data register.
If R/M = 1, specifies an address register for the predecrement addressing
          mode.

SHIFT/ROTATE — Register

15	14	13	12	11	10	9	8	7	6	5	4	3	2	1	0
1	1	1	0	Count/ Register			dr	Size		i/r	Type		Data Register		

Count/Register field: If i/r field = 0, specifies shift count
                          If i/r field = 1, specifies a data register that contains the
                                   shift count
dr field: 0 = right
          1 = left
Size field: 00 = byte
            01 = word
            10 = long
i/r field: 0 = immediate shift count
          1 = register shift count
Type field: 00 = arithmetic shift
            01 = logical shift
            10 = rotate with extend
            11 = rotate

SHIFT/ROTATE · Memory

15	14	13	12	11	10	9	8	7	6	5	4	3	2	1	0
1	1	1	0	0	Type		dr	1	1	Effective Address					
										Mode			Register		

Type field: 00 = arithmetic shift
            01 = logical shift
            10 = rotate with extend
            11 = rotate
dr field: 0 = right
          1 = left

D

MC68000 Instruction Execution Times*

D.1 INTRODUCTION

This Appendix contains listings of the instruction execution times in terms of external clock (CLK) periods. In this data, it is assumed that both memory read and write cycle times are four clock periods. A longer memory cycle will cause the generation of wait states which must be added to the total instruction time.

The number of bus read and write cycles for each instruction is also included with the timing data. This data is enclosed in parenthesis following the number of clock periods and is shown as: (r/w) where r is the number of read cycles and w is the number of write cycles included in the clock period number. Recalling that either a read or write cycle requires four clock periods, a timing number given as 18(3/1) relates to 12 clock periods for the three read cycles, plus 4 clock periods for the one write cycle, plus 2 cycles required for some internal function of the processor.

NOTE

The number of periods includes instruction fetch and all applicable operand fetches and stores.

D.2 OPERAND EFFECTIVE ADDRESS CALCULATION TIMING

Table D-1 lists the number of clock periods required to compute an instruction's effective

Table D-1. Effective Address Calculation Times

Addressing Mode		Byte, Word	Long
Register			
Dn	Data Register Direct	0(0/0)	0(0/0)
An	Address Register Direct	0(0/0)	0(0/0)
Memory			
(An)	Address Register Indirect	4(1/0)	8(2/0)
(An)+	Address Register Indirect with Postincrement	4(1/0)	8(2/0)
−(An)	Address Register Indirect with Predecrement	6(1/0)	10(2/0)
d(An)	Address Register Indirect with Displacement	8(2/0)	12(3/0)
d(An, ix)*	Address Register Indirect with Index	10(2/0)	14(3/0)
xxx.W	Absolute Short	8(2/0)	12(3/0)
xxx.L	Absolute Long	12(3/0)	16(4/0)
d(PC)	Program Counter with Displacement	8(2/0)	12(3/0)
d(PC, ix)*	Program Counter with Index	10(2/0)	14(3/0)
#xxx	Immediate	4(1/0)	8(2/0)

*The size of the index register (ix) does not affect execution time.

*Courtesy of Motorola, Inc.

address. It includes fetching of any extension words, the address computation, and fetching of the memory operand. The number of bus read and write cycles is shown in parenthesis as (r/w). Note there are no write cycles involved in processing the effective address.

D.3 MOVE INSTRUCTION EXECUTION TIMES

Tables D-2 and D-3 indicate the number of clock periods for the move instruction. This data includes instruction fetch, operand reads, and operand writes. The number of bus read and write cycles is shown in parenthesis as (r/w).

Table D-2. Move Byte and Word Instruction Execution Times

Source	Destination								
	Dn	An	(An)	(An)+	−(An)	d(An)	d(An, ix)*	xxx.W	xxx.L
Dn	4(1/0)	4(1/0)	8(1/1)	8(1/1)	8(1/1)	12(2/1)	14(2/1)	12(2/1)	16(3/1)
An	4(1/0)	4(1/0)	8(1/1)	8(1/1)	8(1/1)	12(2/1)	14(2/1)	12(2/1)	16(3/1)
(An)	8(2/0)	8(2/0)	12(2/1)	12(2/1)	12(2/1)	16(3/1)	18(3/1)	16(3/1)	20(4/1)
(An)+	8(2/0)	8(2/0)	12(2/1)	12(2/1)	12(2/1)	16(3/1)	18(3/1)	16(3/1)	20(4/1)
−(An)	10(2/0)	10(2/0)	14(2/1)	14(2/1)	14(2/1)	18(3/1)	20(3/1)	18(3/1)	22(4/1)
d(An)	12(3/0)	12(3/0)	16(3/1)	16(3/1)	16(3/1)	20(4/1)	22(4/1)	20(4/1)	24(5/1)
d(An, ix)*	14(3/0)	14(3/0)	18(3/1)	18(3/1)	18(3/1)	22(4/1)	24(4/1)	22(4/1)	26(5/1)
xxx.W	12(3/0)	12(3/0)	16(3/1)	16(3/1)	16(3/1)	20(4/1)	22(4/1)	20(4/1)	24(5/1)
xxx.L	16(4/0)	16(4/0)	20(4/1)	20(4/1)	20(4/1)	24(5/1)	26(5/1)	24(5/1)	28(6/1)
d(PC)	12(3/0)	12(3/0)	16(3/1)	16(3/1)	16(3/1)	20(4/1)	22(4/1)	20(4/1)	24(5/1)
d(PC, ix)*	14(3/0)	14(3/0)	18(3/1)	18(3/1)	18(3/1)	22(4/1)	24(4/1)	22(4/1)	26(5/1)
#xxx	8(2/0)	8(2/0)	12(2/1)	12(2/1)	12(2/1)	16(3/1)	18(3/1)	16(3/1)	20(4/1)

*The size of the index register (ix) does not affect execution time.

Table D-3. Move Long Instruction Execution Times

Source	Destination								
	Dn	An	(An)	(An)+	−(An)	d(An)	d(An, ix)*	xxx.W	xxx.L
Dn	4(1/0)	4(1/0)	12(1/2)	12(1/2)	12(1/2)	16(2/2)	18(2/2)	16(2/2)	20(3/2)
An	4(1/0)	4(1/0)	12(1/2)	12(1/2)	12(1/2)	16(2/2)	18(2/2)	16(2/2)	20(3/2)
(An)	12(3/0)	12(3/0)	20(3/2)	20(3/2)	20(3/2)	24(4/2)	26(4/2)	24(4/2)	28(5/2)
(An)+	12(3/0)	12(3/0)	20(3/2)	20(3/2)	20(3/2)	24(4/2)	26(4/2)	24(4/2)	28(5/2)
−(An)	14(3/0)	14(3/0)	22(3/2)	22(3/2)	22(3/2)	26(4/2)	28(4/2)	26(4/2)	30(5/2)
d(An)	16(4/0)	16(4/0)	24(4/2)	24(4/2)	24(4/2)	28(5/2)	30(5/2)	28(5/2)	32(6/2)
d(An, ix)*	18(4/0)	18(4/0)	26(4/2)	26(4/2)	26(4/2)	30(5/2)	32(5/2)	30(5/2)	34(6/2)
xxx.W	16(4/0)	16(4/0)	24(4/2)	24(4/2)	24(4/2)	28(5/2)	30(5/2)	28(5/2)	32(6/2)
xxx.L	20(5/0)	20(5/0)	28(5/2)	28(5/2)	28(5/2)	32(6/2)	34(6/2)	32(6/2)	36(7/2)
d(PC)	16(4/0)	16(4/0)	24(4/2)	24(4/2)	24(4/2)	28(5/2)	30(5/2)	28(5/2)	32(6/2)
d(PC, ix)*	18(4/0)	18(4/0)	26(4/2)	26(4/2)	26(4/2)	30(5/2)	32(5/2)	30(5/2)	34(6/2)
#xxx	12(3/0)	12(3/0)	20(3/2)	20(3/2)	20(3/2)	24(4/2)	26(4/2)	24(4/2)	28(5/2)

*The size of the index register (ix) does not affect execution time.

D.4 STANDARD INSTRUCTION EXECUTION TIMES

The number of clock periods shown in Table D-4 indicates the time required to perform the operations, store the results, and read the next instruction. The number of bus read and write cycles is shown in parenthesis as (r/w). The number of clock periods and the number of read and write cycles must be added respectively to those of the effective address calculation where indicated.

In Table D-4 the headings have the following meanings: An = address register operand, Dn = data register operand, ea = an operand specified by an effective address, and M = memory effective address operand.

Table D-4. Standard Instruction Execution Times

Instruction	Size	op<ea>, An†	op<ea>, Dn	op Dn, <M>
ADD	Byte, Word	8(1/0) +	4(1/0) +	8(1/1) +
	Long	6(1/0) + * *	6(1/0) + * *	12(1/2) +
AND	Byte, Word	—	4(1/0) +	8(1/1) +
	Long	—	6(1/0) + * *	12(1/2) +
CMP	Byte, Word	6(1/0) +	4(1/0) +	—
	Long	6(1/0) +	6(1/0) +	—
DIVS	—	—	158(1/0) + *	—
DIVU	—	—	140(1/0) + *	—
EOR	Byte, Word	—	4(1/0) * * *	8(1/1) +
	Long	—	8(1/0) * * *	12(1/2) +
MULS	—	—	70(1/0) + *	—
MULU	—	—	70(1/0) + *	—
OR	Byte, Word	—	4(1/0) +	8(1/1) +
	Long	—	6(1/0) + * *	12(1/2) +
SUB	Byte, Word	8(1/0) +	4(1/0) +	8(1/1) +
	Long	6(1/0) + * *	6(1/0) + * *	12(1/2) +

NOTES:
+ add effective address calculation time
† word or long only
* indicates maximum value
* * The base time of six clock periods is increased to eight if the effective address mode is register direct or immediate (effective address time should also be added).
* * * Only available effective address mode is data register direct.
DIVS, DIVU — The divide algorithm used by the MC68000 provides less than 10% difference between the best and worst case timings.
MULS, MULU — The multiply algorithm requires 38 + 2n clocks where n is defined as:
MULU: n = the number of ones in the <ea>
MULS: n = concatanate the <ea> with a zero as the LSB; n is the resultant number of 10 or 01 patterns in the 17-bit source; i.e., worst case happens when the source is $5555.

D.5 IMMEDIATE INSTRUCTION EXECUTION TIMES

The number of clock periods shown in Table D-5 includes the time to fetch immediate operands, perform the operations, store the results, and read the next operation. The number of bus read and write cycles is shown in parenthesis as (r/w). The number of clock periods and the number of read and write cycles must be added respectively to those of the effective address calculation where indicated.

In Table D-5, the headings have the following meanings: # = immediate operand, Dn = data register operand, An = address register operand, and M = memory operand. SR = status register.

Table D-5. Immediate Instruction Execution Times

Instruction	Size	op #, Dn	op #, An	op #, M
ADDI	Byte, Word	8(2/0)	—	12(2/1) +
	Long	16(3/0)	—	20(3/2) +
ADDQ	Byte, Word	4(1/0)	8(1/0) *	8(1/1) +
	Long	8(1/0)	8(1/0)	12(1/2) +
ANDI	Byte, Word	8(2/0)	—	12(2/1) +
	Long	16(3/0)	—	20(3/1) +
CMPI	Byte, Word	8(2/0)	—	8(2/0) +
	Long	14(3/0)	—	12(3/0) +
EORI	Byte, Word	8(2/0)	—	12(2/1) +
	Long	16(3/0)	—	20(3/2) +
MOVEQ	Long	4(1/0)	—	—
ORI	Byte, Word	8(2/0)	—	12(2/1) +
	Long	16(3/0)	—	20(3/2) +
SUBI	Byte, Word	8(2/0)	—	12(2/1) +
	Long	16(3/0)	—	20(3/2) +
SUBQ	Byte, Word	4(1/0)	8(1/0) *	8(1/1) +
	Long	8(1/0)	8(1/0)	12(1/2) +

+ add effective address calculation time
* word only

D.6 SINGLE OPERAND INSTRUCTION EXECUTION TIMES

Table D-6 indicates the number of clock periods for the single operand instructions. The number of bus read and write cycles is shown in parenthesis as (r/w). The number of clock periods and the number of read and write cycles must be added respectively to those of the effective address calculation where indicated.

Table D-6. Single Operand Instruction Execution Times

Instruction	Size	Register	Memory
CLR	Byte, Word	4(1/0)	8(1/1) +
	Long	6(1/0)	12(1/2) +
NBCD	Byte	6(1/0)	8(1/1) +
NEG	Byte, Word	4(1/0)	8(1/1) +
	Long	6(1/0)	12(1/2) +
NEGX	Byte, Word	4(1/0)	8(1/1) +
	Long	6(1/0)	12(1/2) +
NOT	Byte, Word	4(1/0)	8(1/1) +
	Long	6(1/0)	12(1/2) +
S$_{CC}$	Byte, False	4(1/0)	8(1/1) +
	Byte, True	6(1/0)	8(1/1) +
TAS	Byte	4(1/0)	10(1/1) +
TST	Byte, Word	4(1/0)	4(1/0) +
	Long	4(1/0)	4(1/0) +

+ add effective address calculation time

D.7 SHIFT/ROTATE INSTRUCTION EXECUTION TIMES

Table D-7 indicates the number of clock periods for the shift and rotate instructions. The number of bus read and write cycles is shown in parenthesis as (r/w). The number of clock periods and the number of read and write cycles must be added respectively to those of the effective address calculation where indicated.

Table D-7. Shift/Rotate Instruction Execution Times

Instruction	Size	Register	Memory
ASR, ASL	Byte, Word	6 + 2n(1/0)	8(1/1) +
	Long	8 + 2n(1/0)	—
LSR, LSL	Byte, Word	6 + 2n(1/0)	8(1/1) +
	Long	8 + 2n(1/0)	—
ROR, ROL	Byte, Word	6 + 2n(1/0)	8(1/1) +
	Long	8 + 2n(1/0)	—
ROXR, ROXL	Byte, Word	6 + 2n(1/0)	8(1/1) +
	Long	8 + 2n(1/0)	—

+ add effective address calculation time
n is the shift count

D.8 BIT MANIPULATION INSTRUCTION EXECUTION TIMES

Table D-8 indicates the number of clock periods required for the bit manipulation instructions. The number of bus read and write cycles is shown in parenthesis as (r/w). The number of clock periods and the number of read and write cycles must be added respectively to those of the effective address calculation where indicated.

Table D-8. Bit Manipulation Instruction Execution Times

Instruction	Size	Dynamic		Static	
		Register	Memory	Register	Memory
BCHG	Byte	—	8(1/1) +	—	12(2/1) +
	Long	8(1/0) *	—	12(2/0) *	—
BCLR	Byte	—	8(1/1) +	—	12(2/1) +
	Long	10(1/0) *	—	14(2/0) *	—
BSET	Byte	—	8(1/1) +	—	12(2/1) +
	Long	8(1/0) *	—	12(2/0) *	—
BTST	Byte	—	4(1/0) +	—	8(2/0) +
	Long	6(1/0)	—	10(2/0)	—

+ add effective address calculation time
* indicates maximum value

D.9 CONDITIONAL INSTRUCTION EXECUTION TIMES

Table D-9 indicates the number of clock periods required for the conditional instructions. The number of bus read and write cycles is indicated in parenthesis as (r/w). The number of clock periods and the number of read and write cycles must be added respectively to those of the effective address calculation where indicated.

Table D-9. Conditional Instruction Execution Times

Instruction	Displacement	Branch Taken	Branch Not Taken
BCC	Byte	10(2/0)	8(1/0)
	Word	10(2/0)	12(2/0)
BRA	Byte	10(2/0)	—
	Word	10(2/0)	—
BSR	Byte	18(2/2)	—
	Word	18(2/2)	—
DBCC	CC true	—	12(2/0)
	CC false	10(2/0)	14(3/0)

+ add effective address calculation time
* indicates maximum value

D.10 JMP, JSR, LEA, PEA, AND MOVEM INSTRUCTION EXECUTION TIMES

Table D-10 indicates the number of clock periods required for the jump, jump-to-subroutine, load effective address, push effective address, and move multiple registers instructions. The number of bus read and write cycles is shown in parenthesis as (r/w).

Table D-10. JMP, JSR, LEA, PEA, and MOVEM Instruction Execution Times

Instr	Size	(An)	(An) +	– (An)	d(An)	d(An, ix) +	xxx.W	xxx.L	d(PC)	d(PC, ix) *
JMP	–	8(2/0)	–	–	10(2/0)	14(3/0)	10(2/0)	12(3/0)	10(2/0)	14(3/0)
JSR	–	16(2/2)	–	–	18(2/2)	22(2/2)	18(2/2)	20(3/2)	18(2/2)	22(2/2)
LEA	–	4(1/0)	–	–	8(2/0)	12(2/0)	8(2/0)	12(3/0)	8(2/0)	12(2/0)
PEA	–	12(1/2)	–	–	16(2/2)	20(2/2)	16(2/2)	20(3/2)	16(2/2)	20(2/2)
MOVEM M → R	Word	12 + 4n (3 + n/0)	12 + 4n (3 + n/0)	–	16 + 4n (4 + n/0)	18 + 4n (4 + n/0)	16 + 4n (4 + n/0)	20 + 4n (5 + n/0)	16 + 4n (4 + n/0)	18 + 4n (4 + n/0)
	Long	12 + 8n (3 + 2n/0)	12 + 8n (3 + 2n/0)	–	16 + 8n (4 + 2n/0)	18 + 8n (4 + 2n/0)	16 + 8n (4 + 2n/0)	20 + 8n (5 + 2n/0)	16 + 8n (4 + 2n/0)	18 + 8n (4 + 2n/0)
MOVEM R → M	Word	8 + 4n (2/n)	–	8 + 4n (2/n)	12 + 4n (3/n)	14 + 4n (3/n)	12 + 4n (3/n)	16 + 4n (4/n)	–	–
	Long	8 + 8n (2/2n)	–	8 + 8n (2/2n)	12 + 8n (3/2n)	14 + 8n (3/2n)	12 + 8n (3/2n)	16 + 8n (4/2n)	–	

n is the number of registers to move
* is the size of the index register (ix) does not affect the instruction's execution time

D 11 MULTI-PRECISION INSTRUCTION EXECUTION TIMES

Table D-11 indicates the number of clock periods for the multi-precision instructions. The number of clock periods includes the time to fetch both operands, peform the operations, store the results, and read the next instructions. The number of read and write cycles is shown in parenthesis as (r/w).

In Table D-11, the headings have the following meanings: Dn = data register operand and M = memory operand.

Table D-11. Multi-Precision Instruction Execution Times

Instruction	Size	op Dn, Dn	op M, M
ADDX	Byte, Word	4(1/0)	18(3/1)
	Long	8(1/0)	30(5/2)
CMPM	Byte, Word	–	12(3/0)
	Long	–	20(5/0)
SUBX	Byte, Word	4(1/0)	18(3/1)
	Long	8(1/0)	30(5/2)
ABCD	Byte	6(1/0)	18(3/1)
SBCD	Byte	6(1/0)	18(3/1)

D.12 MISCELLANEOUS INSTRUCTION EXECUTION TIMES

Tables D-12 and D-13 indicate the number of clock periods for the following miscellaneous instructions. The number of bus read and write cycles is shown in parenthesis as (r/w). The number of clock periods plus the number of read and write cycles must be added to those of the effective address calculation where indicated.

Table D-12. Miscellaneous Instruction Execution Times

Instruction	Size	Register	Memory
ANDI to CCR	Byte	20(3/0)	—
ANDI to SR	Word	20(3/0)	—
CHK	—	10(1/0) +	—
EORI to CCR	Byte	20(3/0)	—
EORI to SR	Word	20(3/0)	—
ORI to CCR	Byte	20(3/0)	—
ORI to SR	Word	20(3/0)	—
MOVE from SR	—	6(1/0)	8(1/1) +
MOVE to CCR	—	12(2/0)	12(2/0) +
MOVE to SR	—	12(2/0)	12(2/0) +
EXG	—	6(1/0)	—
EXT	Word	4(1/0)	—
EXT	Long	4(1/0)	—
LINK	—	16(2/2)	—
MOVE from USP	—	4(1/0)	—
MOVE to USP	—	4(1/0)	—
NOP	—	4(1/0)	—
RESET	—	132(1/0)	—
RTE	—	20(5/0)	—
RTR	—	20(5/0)	—
RTS	—	16(4/0)	—
STOP	—	4(0/0)	—
SWAP	—	4(1/0)	—
TRAPV	—	4(1/0)	—
UNLK	—	12(3/0)	—

+ add effective address calculation time

Table D-13. Move Peripheral Instruction Execution Times

Instruction	Size	Register → Memory	Memory → Register
MOVEP	Word	16(2/2)	16(4/0)
MOVEP	Long	24(2/4)	24(6/0)

D.13 EXCEPTION PROCESSING EXECUTION TIMES

Table D-14 indicates the number of clock periods for exception processing. The number of clock periods includes the time for all stacking, the vector fetch, and the fetch of the first two instruction words of the handler routine. The number of bus read and write cycles is shown in parenthesis as (r/w).

Table D-14. Exception Processing Execution Times

Exception	Periods
Address Error	**50**(4/7)
Bus Error	**50**(4/7)
CHK Instruction	**44**(5/4) +
Divide by Zero	**42**(5/4)
Illegal Instruction	**34**(4/3)
Interrupt	**44**(5/3) *
Privilege Violation	**34**(4/3)
RESET**	**40**(6/0)
Trace	**34**(4/3)
TRAP Instruction	**38**(4/4)
TRAPV Instruction	**34**(4/3)

+ add effective address calculation time

*The interrupt acknowledge cycle is assumed to take four clock periods.

**Indicates the time from when RESET and HALT are first sampled as negated to when instruction execution starts.

E

ASCII Table

dec	hex	ASCII		dec	hex	ASCII		dec	hex	ASCII		dec	hex	ASCII
0	0	NUL		32	20			64	40	@		96	60	`
1	1	SOH		33	21	!		65	41	A		97	61	a
2	2	STX		34	22	"		66	42	B		98	62	b
3	3	ETX		35	23	#		67	43	C		99	63	c
4	4	EOT		36	24	$		68	44	D		100	64	d
5	5	ENQ		37	25	%		69	45	E		101	65	e
6	6	ACK		38	26	&		70	46	F		102	66	f
7	7	BEL		39	27	'		71	47	G		103	67	g
8	8	BS		40	28	(		72	48	H		104	68	h
9	9	HT		41	29	)		73	49	I		105	69	i
10	A	LF		42	2A	*		74	4A	J		106	6A	j
11	B	VT		43	2B	+		75	4B	K		107	6B	k
12	C	FF		44	2C	,		76	4C	L		108	6C	l
13	D	CR		45	2D	-		77	4D	M		109	6D	m
14	E	SO		46	2E	.		78	4E	N		110	6E	n
15	F	SI		47	2F	/		79	4F	O		111	6F	o
16	10	DLE		48	30	0		80	50	P		112	70	p
17	11	DC1		49	31	1		81	51	Q		113	71	q
18	12	DC2		50	32	2		82	52	R		114	72	r
19	13	DC3		51	33	3		83	53	S		115	73	s
20	14	DC4		52	34	4		84	54	T		116	74	t
21	15	NAK		53	35	5		85	55	U		117	75	u
22	16	SYN		54	36	6		86	56	V		118	76	v
23	17	ETB		55	37	7		87	57	W		119	77	w
24	18	CAN		56	38	8		88	58	X		120	78	x
25	19	EM		57	39	9		89	59	Y		121	79	y
26	1A	SUB		58	3A	:		90	5A	Z		122	7A	z
27	1B	ESC		59	3B	;		91	5B	[		123	7B	{
28	1C	FS		60	3C	<		92	5C	\		124	7C	|
29	1D	GS		61	3D	=		93	5D	]		125	7D	}
30	1E	RS		62	3E	>		94	5E	^		126	7E	~
31	1F	US		63	3F	?		95	5F	_		127	7F	DEL

Index

ABCD (Add BCD) instruction, 35–36, 52, 55, 117–118
absolute long address, 15
absolute short address, 14–15
activation record, 121
actual column, 216
Ada, 120, 121, 138, 226, 311
ADD instruction, 36–37, 38–39, 113, 118
ADDA instruction, 38, 118
ADDI (ADD Immediate) instruction, 38–39
ADDQ (Add Quick) instruction, 39, 40–41, 116
address/data bus (68020), 305
ADDRESS ERROR exception, 130, 133, 300
address register direct, 10–11
address register indirect, 11–12
  with displacement, 13
  with index, 14
  with postincrement, 12–13
  with predecrement, 13
address registers, 2
addressing modes, 305, 307
  See also memory addressing modes; register direct address modes; special address modes
ADDX (ADD Extended) instruction, 41, 118
Advanced User Guide, 155
allocation, algorithm for, 181–182
AND (AND Logical) instruction, 65–66, 67, 113, 117–118
ANDI (AND Immediate) instruction, 17, 65, 67
ANDI to CCR (AND Immediate to Condition Code Register) instruction, 67–68
ANDI to SR (AND Immediate to Status Register) instruction, 68–69, 131, 132
ANSI standard, 149
arithmetic instructions, 35–63
arrays, 187–188
ASCII, 160, 199, 307
  table, 395
ASL (Arithmetic Shift Left) instruction, 69–70
ASR (Arithmetic Shift Right) instruction, 69–70
autovectors, 276
auxiliary stacks, 182–183

backwards compare, 310
backwards operand, 310
Bcc (Branch Conditionally) instruction, 85–86, 116, 306, 307
BCD (binary-coded-decimal), 2, 5, 35, 52, 232, 285, 307
BCHG (Test Bit and Change) instruction, 95–96
BCLR (Test Bit and Clear) instruction, 96–97
BCS (Branch Carry Set), 85
BEQ instruction, 202
best fit algorithm, 180–181
BF (Branch False) instruction, 116
binary conversions, string to, 229–233
bit-field instructions, 307–308
bit instructions, 95–99
block, 120
block storage segment (BSS), 177, 178, 183
BRA (Branch Always) instruction, 86, 89, 116, 202, 306
break change, 284
BSET (Test Bit and Set) instruction, 97–98
BSR (Branch to Subroutine) instruction, 86–87, 90, 116, 125, 202, 306
BT (Branch True) mnemonic, 86, 116
BTST (Test Bit) instruction, 99
BUS ERROR exception, 129–130, 133, 300
byte data type, 5
byte operations, 2

C (programming language), 120, 138, 149–150, 178, 187, 188–189, 205
  parameter passing techniques, general, 124–126
carry flag, 5
CAS instruction, 307
case structure, 201–202
CAS2 instruction, 307
cheap screw heap manager, 179
CHK exception, 133, 307
CHK (Check register against bounds) instruction, 87–88, 114–115, 133, 307
CHK2 instruction, 307
Christensen, Ward, 118

circular buffer, 190
clear mode, 244
CLR (Clear) instruction, 42, 61
CMP (Compare) instruction, 43–44, 45, 46, 117
CMPA (Compare Address) instruction, 44–45, 117
CMPI (Compare Immediate) instruction, 45–46, 307
CMPM (Compare Memory) instruction, 46–47, 117
CMP2 instruction, 307
compiler, 225–226
complement mode, 243
condition code register (CCR), 3–5
    addressing, 17
conditional, branch, and trap instructions, 85–94
control string, 226–229
conversion characters, 227
coprocessor support (68020), 306
CP/M, 118, 123, 135, 149, 150, 154–162 passim, 277, 282
CPU, 123, 128, 129, 130, 131, 134, 189
CRTs, 149, 151, 154, 162, 199, 201

data management, see data structures
data register direct, 10
data registers, 2
data segment (DATA), 177, 178
data structures, 177, 178, 190
    arrays, 187–188
    auxiliary stacks, 182–183
    heaps, 178–182
    linked lists, 183–185
    Modules, 191–198
    queues, 189, 190
    records, 185–187
    strings, 188–189
data transfer instructions, 19–33
DBcc (Test, Decrement, and Branch) instruction, 88–89, 116, 138, 302
DBF (decrement-and-branch), 88
DDT disassembler, 118
debugging, 309
    backwards compare, 310
    backwards operand, 310
    inconsistent definition, 311–312
    loop-off-by-one syndrome, 311
    misaligned instruction, 310–311
    tools, 312–316
    unbalanced stack, 309
    unsized instruction, 309–310
DEC and DEC clones, 149
define space (DS) directive, 178, 183
definition, inconsistent, 311–312

Destination Function Code (DFC) register, 298–300, 303
device-supplied vectors, 276
displacement(s)
    address register indirect with, 13
    program counter with, 15
    68020, 306
division and multiplication (68020), 307
DIVS (Signed Divide) instruction, 47–48, 116–117, 133
DIVU (Unsigned Divide) instruction, 48–49, 116–117, 133
DMA controllers, 61, 118, 276–277
DOS-EDIT, 199
double bus error, 130
Dual Universal Asyncronous Receiver Transmitter (DUART), 275, 276, 277

EBCDIC, 307
edit buffers, 141–144, 184, 185, 186
effective address, 9–10
EOF characters, 161, 162
EOR (Exclusive OR) instruction, 71, 72, 117
EORI (Exclusive OR Immediate) instruction, 17, 71, 72
EORI to CCR (Exclusive OR Immediate to Condition Code Register) instruction, 72–73
EORI to SR (Exclusive OR Immediate to Status Register) instruction, 73, 131, 132
equates, 186, 200
error walkback, 183
errors, see debugging
EVEN pseudo-op, 161
exception(s), 120, 127
    handlers, 120, 134–135
    overview, 127
    processing, 128
    stack formates, 129, 131, 133, 300–302
    types of, 128–133
    vector table, 6–7, 127
EXG (Exchange) instruction, 30–31, 117–118
EXT (Extend) instruction, 49, 114, 115
extend flag, 5

fast circle procedure, 248
FIFO (First In, First Out), 189, 190, 207, 286
File Control Block (FCB), 155–159
first fit algorithm, 178–180, 181
fixed-size block (FSB), 181
floating-point hardware, 246
frame pointer, 120, 122

gap system, 139
graphics, bit mapped, 241–255

Hallock Systems (HSC) PRO-68 card, 149
HALT state, 130
hardware debugger, 316
header file, 242–243, 277–281
heaps, 178–182

icon procedure, 253–254, 255
ILLEGAL exception, 130, 132
immediate data, 16
inconsistent definition, 311–312
index
    address register indirect with, 14
    program counter with, 16
initialization, 281–282, 284
input/output (I/O) interfaces, 149–151
    Modules, 163–176
    rewriting display, 151–153
    words of caution, 153–162
input port change, 284
instruction(s)
    cache (68020), 305
    execution times, 385–393
    format summary, 363–383
    misaligned, 310–311
    miscellaneous, 101–103
    unsized, 309–310
    See also names of individual instructions
Intel 8251 UART, 277
interrupt controller, 276
interrupt driven I/O system, 275–287
INTERRUPT exception, 128, 131–132, 282–283
interrupt handler, 276, 277, 281, 282, 283–286
interrupt mask, 4
interrupt mask register (IMR), 284
interrupt service routines (ISRs), 315, 316
interrupt status register (ISR), 284, 285

jam mode, 243, 244, 254
JMP (Jump) instruction, 89–90, 116, 202
JSR (Jump to Subroutine) instruction, 90–91, 116, 125

LEA (Load Effective Address) instruction, 5, 16, 29, 114–115
LED latch, 23
line editor, 199, 201, 202, 203, 204
LINK instruction, 32, 116, 119–121, 122, 123, 306
linked lists, 183–185
local storage, 123

logical, shift, and rotate instructions, 65–83
logical column, 207
longword data type, 5
longword operations, 2
loop-off-by-one syndrome, 311
loop setup (68010), 302
LSL (Logic Shift Left) instruction, 74–75
LSR (Logic Shift Right) instruction, 74–75

Macintosh, 139
masks, 249–250
master bit (68020), 306
members, of records, 185, 187
memory addressing modes, 11
    address register indirect, 11–12
        with displacement, 13
        with index, 14
        with postincrement, 12–13
        with predecrement, 13
memory data formats, 5–6
memory management unit, see MMU
memory map, 6–7
memory passing, common, 124
MMU (memory management unit), 8, 129, 177, 298, 302
mode truth tables, 243–244
Module BCD.PRN, 356–358
Module BIT.H, 242
Module BITPRIM.PRN, 256–263
Module CASE.PRN, 201–202, 216
Module CREEP.PRN, 251–253, 267–268
Module CRT.PRN, 154, 163–164
Module CURSOR.H, 200
Module DEMO.PRN, 254–255, 273–274
Module ECH.PRN, 285, 293–295
Module EDIT.H, 142
Module EDIT0.PRN, 323–325
Module EDIT1.PRN, 162, 174–176
Module EDIT2.PRN, 221–224, 207
Module EDIT3.PRN, 326–336
Module EDIT4.PRN, 337–340
Module ERRORS.PRN, 341–342
Module EXEC.PRN, 140–147, 184
Module FCB.H, 156
Module FILEPRIM.PRN, 155–162, 168–173
Module GROUP1.PRN, 343–347
Module GROUP2.PRN, 348–353
Module GROUP3.PRN, 184, 185, 191–195
Module GROUP4.PRN, 354
Module LINEED.PRN, 199, 211–215, 201
Module MC68681.H, 278–281

Module OKI.PRN, 251, 264–266
Module OLAY.PRN, 253, 269–272
Module PRINTF.PRN, 226–239
Module QUEUE.PRN, 189, 196–198
Module SERINT.PRN, 282, 284, 290–292
Module SINIT.PRN, 281, 288–289
Module SQRT.PRN, 359
Module SQRT2.PRN, 360
Module SQRT3.PRN, 361
Module VSCREEN.PRN, 154, 165–167
Module WINDOW.PRN, 205, 217–220
MOVE from CCR (Move from Condition Code
    Register) instruction, 303
MOVE from SR (Move from Status Register)
    instruction, 23, 114, 302
MOVE instruction, 3, 8, 19–20, 61, 105, 112
 and addressing modes, 9–10, 11, 15, 17
MOVE to CCR (Move to Condition Code Register)
    instruction, 21–22, 114
MOVE from SR (Move from Status Register), 23,
    297
MOVE to SR (Move to Status Register) instruction,
    22, 114, 131, 132, 297
MOVE USP (Move to/from User Stack Pointer)
    instruction, 24, 116, 132
MOVEA (Move Address) instruction, 19, 24–25
MOVEC (Move Control Register) instruction, 298,
    303
MOVEM (Move Multiple) instruction, 25–27,
    114–115, 157
MOVEP (Move to/from Peripheral) instruction,
    27–28, 113–114
MOVEQ (Move Quick) instruction, 28–29
MOVES (Move Address Space) instruction, 299,
    303–304
MS-DOS, 199
MULS (Signed Multiply) instruction, 50, 51,
    117–118
MULU (Unsigned Multiply) instruction, 51, 117–118

NBCD (Negate BCD with Extend) instruction, 52,
    115
NEC 7220 Graphics Display Controller, 241, 243
NEG (Negate) instruction, 53, 54, 75
negative flag, 4
NEGX (Negate with Extend) instruction, 54, 75,
    114
NMI (Non-Maskable-Interrupt) line, 134
node, 184
NOP (No Operation) instruction, 116
NOT (Logical NOT) instruction, 75–76, 114

op code(s), 105, 113, 132
  0000, 113–114
  0001, 0010, 0011, 114
  0100, 114–116
  0101, 116
  0110, 116
  0111, 116
  1000, 116–117
  1001, 117
  1011, 117
  1100, 117–118
  1101, 118
  1110, 118
OR instruction, 76–77, 78, 113, 116–117
ORI (OR Immediate) instruction, 17, 76, 78
ORI to CCR (OR Immediate to Condition Code
    Register) instruction, 78–79
ORI to SR (OR Immediate to Status Register)
    instruction, 79, 131, 132
output routine, 226–229
overflow flag, 4, 94

paint program, 251–253
parameter passing techniques, 119, 126
  common memory passing, 124
  general C, 124–126
  LINK and UNLK, 119–121
  local and variable storage, 123
  register passing, 123
  standard stack-based, 122
Pascal, 120, 135, 138, 178, 187, 188–189, 233
PEA (Push Effective Address) instruction, 30, 114,
    115
pixels, 243–248, 251–254
polled I/O system, 275, 276
POP operations, 3
postincrement, address register indirect with, 12–13
predecrement, address register indirect with, 13
PRIVILEGE exception, 130, 132
privilege states, 8
program counter (PC), 5, 128
  with displacement, 15
  with index, 16
PUSH operations, 3, 17

queues, 189, 190, 286–287

random logic approach, 202
raster line, 241, 242
records, 185–187
recursion, 230–231

recursive-descent parser, 183
register direct address modes, 10
   address register direct, 10–11
   data register direct, 10
register passing, 123
register set, 2–5
RESET exception, 128, 129, 130
RESET instruction, 8, 101, 116, 129, 132
RESOURCE disassembler, 118
RMW (read-modify-write) memory cycle, 61, 91, 302
ROL (Rotate Left) instruction, 80–81
ROM, 177, 178
root, 184
ROR (Rotate Right) instruction, 80–81
ROXL (Rotate Left with extend) instruction, 81–83
ROXR (Rotate Right with extend) instruction, 81–83
RTD (Return and Deallocate) instruction, 300, 304
RTE (Return from Exception) instruction, 102, 116, 128, 131, 132, 283, 284, 300, 302
RTR (Return and Restore CCR) instruction, 91, 116
RTS (Return from Subroutine) instruction, 93, 116, 202, 203
Runtime Support Library (RSL), 225

SBCE (Subtract BCD with extend) instruction, 55, 116–117
Scc (Set According to Condition) instruction, 91–93, 116
scrolling ASCII model, 199
SDLC mode, 275
set mode, 244, 254
68010 processor, 297–298
   additions to, 298–304
68020 processor, 297, 304–307
   miscellaneous new instructions and enhancements for, 307–308
software debug process (software probes), 314
software debuggers, 314–316
source count, 95, 96, 98, 99
Source Function Code (SFC) register, 298–300, 303
special address modes, 14
   absolute long address, 15
   absolute short address, 14–15
   immediate data, 16
   program counter with displacement, 15
   program counter with index, 16
   status register and condition code register addressing, 17
spurious interrupt exception, 276
SPURIOUS INTERRUPT vector, 130

SSP (supervisor stack pointer), 3
Stachour, Paul, 225
stack(s), 3, 119–120
   auxiliary, 182–183
   supervisor, 128, 133, 135
   unbalanced, 309
stack-based parameter passing, standard, 122
stack formats, exception
   extended, 131, 133
   long form, 300–302
   short form, 300, 301
   standard, 129, 133
stack frames, 119–121, 122
stack pointer, 3, 119–120
stats routine, 209–210, 233
status register (SR), 3–5
   addressing, 17
STOP instruction, 8, 102–103, 115–116, 132
storage, local and variable, 123
string to binary conversions, 229–233
strings, 188–189
SUB (Subtract) instruction, 55–57, 59, 60, 113, 117
SUBA (Subtract Address) instruction, 56, 57–58, 117
SUBI (Subtract Immediate) instruction, 56, 58–59
SUBQ (Subtract Quick) instruction, 56, 59–60, 116
SUBX (Subtract Extend) instruction, 60–61, 117
supervisor
   bit, 5
   mode, 5
   stack, 128, 133, 135
SWAP instruction, 31, 114, 115

TAS (Test and Set) instruction, 61–62, 114, 116, 286, 302, 307
teletype model, 199
termcap, 149–150
text editor overview, 137–147
text segment (TEXT), 177
trace bits, 5, 306
TRACE exception, 5, 130–131
TRAP exception, 131, 132
TRAP instruction, 93–94, 116, 123, 283, 307
TRAPcc instruction, 307
TRAPV exception, 133
TRAPV instruction, 94, 116, 133
TST (Test) instruction, 62–63, 114, 116, 307

unbalanced stack, 309
uninitialized exception, 133
UNIX, 124, 139, 149–150
UNLK (unlink) instruction, 32–33, 116, 119–121

unsized instruction, 309–310
update, 202
user interface, 199–210
   Modules, 211–215, 216–220, 221–224
USP (user stack pointer), 3, 8, 24, 298

variable storage, 123
Vector Base Register (VBR), 298
vectors, 6–7, 93, 127, 134
   device-supplied, 276
   See also autovectors

walkback, 120, 121
window commands, 141–144
windowing, 204–206
word data type, 5

word operations, 2
WordStar, 199
YASE (Yet Another Screen Editor), 140–142, 199, 202, 207, 210, 225
   and data management, 177
   and editing buffer, 186
   input/output for, 149, 150, 154, 162
   and linked lists, 184
   operation of, 318–322
   pieces necessary for, 317–318
   and windowing, 204

zero divide exception, 133, 134
zero flag, 4, 95, 96, 97, 99
Zilog 8230 Serial Communications Controller, 275, 277